Contemporary Tourism:

An International Approach

Chris Cooper and C. Michael Hall

(G) **Goodfellow Publishers Ltd**

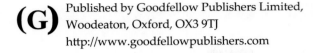 Published by Goodfellow Publishers Limited,
Woodeaton, Oxford, OX3 9TJ
http://www.goodfellowpublishers.com

British Library Cataloguing in Publication Data: a catalogue record for this title is available from the British Library.

Library of Congress Catalog Card Number: on file.

ISBN: 978-1-906884-25-3

 Design and typesetting by P.K. McBride, www.macbride.org.uk

Printed by Marston Book Services, www.marston.co.uk

Cover design by Cylinder, www.cylindermedia.com

Contents

List of figures

List of tables

List of case studies

Acknowledgements

We have a number of people to thank for their witting – or unwitting – help in our ideas and writing for this book. As commissioning editor, Sally North at Goodfellow Publishers and previously at Elsevier Butterworth Heinemann has, as always, been a constant source of encouragement, and when necessary, gentle pressure. Both Sally and Tim Goodfellow have been enthusiastic about a new edition of the book and have greatly assisted us in completing it without undue stress. We would also like to thank David Solnet again for undertaking the services chapter in the first edition of this book and which has served as the base for the current edition. Chris would also like to say a big thank you for Amy Cooper's Internet search skills and robust editing of his chapters.

Michael would like to pay particular thanks to the support of University of Canterbury administrative staff Donna Heslop-Williams and Irene Edgar and especially Angela Zhang for managing the accounts and Irene Joseph for managing Michael. The support of the ever-capable Paul Ballantine for encouraging research and scholarship is also gratefully acknowledged. In addition, Michael would also like to note the support of the various other institutions with which he is engaged for the support they provide for research, travel, accommodation and the time to work on other projects such as this text. These include Lund and Linneaus Universities in Sweden; the Universities of Oulu and Eastern Finland in, quite obviously, Finland; and the Frieburg Institute of Advanced Studies in Germany.

Although Michael did not need the assistance of the Cooper household he would still like to thank them for their continued assistance of Chris. In addition he would like to thank Tim Baird, Tim Coles, David Duval, Stefan Gössling, Johan Hultman, Michael James, John Jenkins, Alan Lew, Dieter Müller, Stephen Page, Jarkko Saarinen, Daniel Scott, and Allan Williams, as well as colleagues and students in marketing at the University of Canterbury's Department of Management and Lund University's Department of Service Management, who have all contributed in various ways to help develop some of the ideas within. Beirut, Fiona Apple, Nick Cave, Bruce Cockburn, First Aid Kit, and Indigo Girls also helped ensure that the book was completed, while Chris Difford, Glen Tilbrook and David Sylvian also helped with the indexing. Finally, he would like to especially thank Jody, Cooper and JC for the morning coffees while completing the book.

Hyperlinks: This QR code will take you to a webpage with links to the URLs given in this book.

Section 1: Contemporary Tourism Systems

1 Contemporary Tourism Systems

Chapter objectives

After reading this chapter you will:

- Understand the core elements in the service dimension of tourism.

- Understand that the tourism experience does not exist independently of the interaction of tourism consumers and producers.

- Recognise the different stages in the tourism system and their implication for the tourist experience.

- Appreciate the importance of scale of analysis in studying tourism.

- Identify some of the key constraints on tourism related travel.

- Understand the characteristics that are used to define concepts of tourism, tourist and mobility.

Introduction

Contemporary tourism is at the same time one of the most significant yet misunderstood phenomenon in the world today. It is something that is engaged in by many people in the developed world, and increasingly in developing countries, and is regarded as an important mechanism for economic development. The extent of tourism activities across the globe and the sheer number of people who travel mean that tourism is often described as one of the world's largest industries. Yet tourism is simultaneously an agent of socio-cultural, environmental and economic change at both a local and global scale. Given the popular image of tourism as being connected to leisure and fun, the scope of the study of tourism is serious indeed.

This first chapter examines some of the key concepts by which we analyse and describe contemporary tourism. These concepts lie at the core of the field of tourism studies and set out the domain of tourism research. Because tourism is essentially an experiential industry, that is people are consciously seeking to purchase particular ephemeral or intangible experiences, even if the tourist does not necessarily think of it that way, tourism is regarded as a service industry. Therefore, the chapter first discusses the service dimension of tourism, a theme that runs throughout this book. The chapter then goes on to outline the concept of the tourism system and its implications with respect to understanding how tourism is consumed and produced, and approaches to defining tourism, tourist and mobility including some of the constraints on mobility.

The service dimension of tourism

The essential characteristics of services are that they cannot be produced without the agreement and cooperation of the consumer and that the outputs produced are not separate entities that exist independently of the producers or consumers (Hill 1999). One of the key service characteristics of tourism is that the main location at which the consumption of experiences occurs is outside of the normal home environment of the purchaser. Although tourism is a service industry this does not mean that it is completely intangible - far from it. Tourism is based on a complex set of infrastructure and physical resources that have a significant impact on the places in which they are situated and, in the case of greenhouse gas emissions from transport for example, at a far wider scale. However, the tourist is purchasing the experiences provided by this infrastructure and set of resources, and not the infrastructure itself. Because tourism is an experience-based product it means that in order to be able to understand tourism phenomenon we need to be able to understand both its consumption and production. This is an almost deceptively simple statement but its implications are enormous: tourism cannot be understood by looking at one aspect in isolation; consumption cannot occur without production and vice versa. The inseparability of production and consumption is therefore one of the hallmarks of tourism, with the value of the tourism experience therefore being determined by both the consumer and the producer of the experience and the tourism product (Figure 1.1).

Figure 1.1: Locating the tourism experience and tourism product

This inseparability also means that the factors that make up consumption and production are constantly feeding back into one another, thereby influencing the development of tourism products and their appeal to consumers.

In seeking to understand contemporary tourism we are therefore seeking to understand the interrelationships between consumers and producers and the variety of experiences that are created. Yet one of the distinguishing aspects of tourism from other service and experience-based products is that it refers to the experience of people voluntarily traveling outside of their place of permanent residence. This therefore means that the primary focus of much of tourism is on the places or destinations that people travel to in order to satisfy their motivations for particular experiences. The mobile nature of tourism provides another really important dimension in its understanding in that, because the service and tourist experience does not exist independently of the direct interaction between consumers and producers, it therefore cannot be stocked or have its ownership transferred. In order to understand the tourist experience we therefore have to be able to chart how it changes over time to see how the different elements of consumption and production come together to produce different experiences and therefore different outcomes for the consumer and the producer.

The tourism system and industry value chain

In order to be able to understand the complex and dynamic nature of the contemporary tourism experience many researchers utilize the concept of a tourism system. A system is an assemblage or interrelated combination of things or elements forming a unitary whole (Hall 2008). At its most basic, the tourism system consists of consumption and production and the experiences that are generated. To increase our understanding of tourism we are also interested in identifying those elements and factors that contribute to tourism consumption and production.

Given that movement is integral to tourism, one way in which the tourism system can be understood is through the travel paths taken by individual consumers. This approach is usually termed a geographical system of tourism and consists of four basic elements:

- a *generating* or *source region* – the permanent residence of the tourist and the place where the journey begins and ends;
- a *transit route* – the path through the region across which the tourist must travel to reach his or her destination;
- a *destination region* – the region which the tourist chooses to visit and which is a core element of tourism; and
- the *environment* – that surrounds the other three regions.

The geographical tourism system model is useful for identifying the flow of tourists from one location to another and the importance of connectivity between the generating region and the destination (Figure 1.2). Of course there might be more than one destination and therefore a whole system of destination regions and transit route regions can exist for some tourists. Nevertheless, the basic form of the geographical tourism system is sufficient to illustrate a range of important dimensions of tourism.

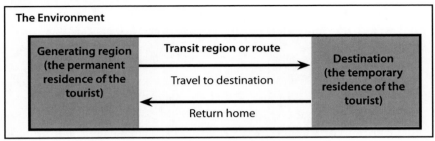

Figure 1.2: The geographical tourism system

1   While the destination is the focal point of tourism activity, tourism will have affects over all elements of the tourism system. For example, while assessment of the economic and environmental effects of tourism can clearly be undertaken at the destination, a full assessment of impacts as a result of a tourist trip will need to include not only what happens at the destination but also in getting to and from that destination.

2   Destinations are accessible to tourism source regions. Such a statement may seem to be obvious yet its implications are profound. Different destinations will be variably accessible to source regions and vice versa. This means that some destinations will have natural advantages over others in relation to their accessibility and therefore potential market area. This is a factor that destinations will seek to exploit in competition with other destinations (Hall & Page 2006; Coles & Hall 2008).

3   In relation to travel to the destination, different elements of the system will have different productive components even though they are used by the same consumer. The different elements that enable the production of tourism are identified in Table 1.1. In examining Table 1.1 it is important to realize that it does not suggest that the elements that have been identified only occur in specific regions, rather it highlights the relative importance of various aspects of the tourism industry from the perspective of the consumer as they go from one stage of their trip to another, and hence from one part of the tourism system to another.

The different production components of the tourism system also make up the tourism industry value system or value chain (Figure 1.3). At an industry level, the economic value of tourism over the longer term is dependent on the capacity of the tourism businesses within the system to maximize service qualities and experiences for tourists. The value chain is also consumption driven as the tourist travels through the tourism system and usually commences via contact with the distribution system that includes tourism intermediaries, such as travel agents and online travel brokers, e.g. Expedia.

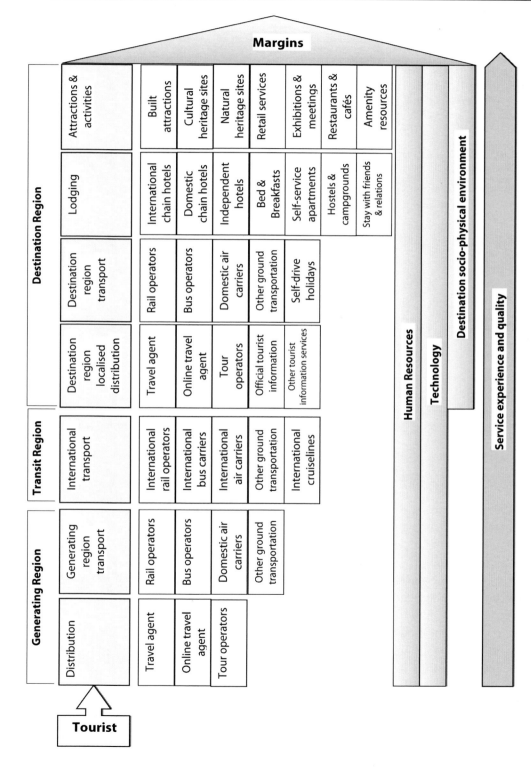

Figure 1.3: The tourism Value Chain: Simplified International Value System

Initial selection of tourism products via the distribution system, i.e. destination selection, will then have flow-on effects for the selection of other products as firms seek to capture value generated along the chain by utilizing the services of some businesses in the delivery of tourism products and not others. This is unlike production-driven systems in which distribution is usually one of the last elements of the value chain.

Table 1.1: Main elements of tourism production at different components of the tourism geographical system.

Generating region	Transit region	Destination
Distribution and promotion channels for the destination in the source region - travel agents - tour operators - online retailers and distributors	Transport links between the source region and the destination - aviation services - bus and train services - cruise and ferry services - private and hire cars	Facilities and attractions - accommodation - meetings and exhibitions - theme parks - casinos - retail - visitor centres - national parks
Transport infrastructure	Transit facilities, i.e food, accommodation, toilets where tourists have to stop prior to final destination	- restaurants - activities - amenity resources
		Transport infrastructure - local transport

Case study 1.1: Using a tourism systems approach to understand the environmental impact of tourism

There is growing concern about the contribution of tourism to environmental change, especially climate change (Scott et al. 2012). Historically, many studies of the environmental impacts of tourism have only occurred at the destination level. However, taking into consideration the entire trip, from the generating region to the destination and return, can provide a substantially different perspective on impacts. For example, Gossling et al. (2002) undertook an ecological footprint analysis of the approximate 118,000 international leisure tourists who visited the Seychelles in 2000. Ecological footprint analysis estimates how much of the biophysical output of the earth is required to meet the resource consumption and waste absorption needs of an individual or a given community, region, state or continent (Rees 1992). Unlike other impact studies which occur just at the destination, studies of the ecological footprint of tourism incorporates the travel of consumers to and from the destination, thereby including all elements of the tourism system. Gössling et al. (2002) reported that long-distance travel was the biggest contributor to the ecological footprint of tourism on the island with more than 97% of the energy footprint being a result of air travel to and from the destination. Just as tellingly the authors extrapolated the footprint of a typical journey to the Seychelles (10.4 days) to one year and found that a single journey to the Seychelles required almost the same area as available per human being on a global scale.

Ocean Frontiers, in the Cayman Islands, one of the first scuba diving companies to offer carbon offsets for scuba holidays, stated that the amount of carbon emitted by a couple on a round-trip flight from London (UK), to Grand Cayman island was 5.76 tons of CO_2, while 14 dives during a one-week-trip only generates an additional 0.26 tons of CO_2 (Sustainable Travel International 2007). Such trips would be more than double the amount of greenhouse gas generated on an average domestic or international tourist trip (Scott et al. 2012).

Research indicates that although long-haul flights and extended cruise ship journeys account for only a minor share of trips, they are responsible for the majority of emissions from tourism (Scott et al. 2012). For instance, in the EU, 6% of trips cause 47% of CO_2-eq emissions (Peeters et al. 2004). In France, 2% of the longest flights account for 43% of aviation emissions (Dubois & Ceron 2009). In the Netherlands, 4.5% of long-haul trips cause 26.4% of all tourism emissions (de Bruijn et al. 2008). Such findings have significant implications for many destinations, because although such long-distance 'high-value tourists might generate the largest foreign exchange earnings per capita… they also seem to be characterised by the highest resource use per capita' (Gössling et al. 2002: 209). Such a finding presents a significant challenge to not only our understanding of how to evaluate the environmental impacts of tourism, but also how to manage such impacts. Gossling et al. (2002) suggest that to reduce the environmental impacts of tourism there is a need to attract visitors from closer generating areas, but the reality is that for many destinations, including the Seychelles, only a small market is locally accessible. Furthermore, carbon-offsets may not provide a solution. In a study of carbon emission offsets for aviation-generated emissions due to international travel to and from New Zealand, Smith and Rodger (2009) found that the sheer size of the CO_2-e emissions produced by the air travel of visitors to New Zealand, and of New Zealand residents travelling overseas (7893 and 3948 Gg, respectively in 2005) meant that that no single offsetting scheme targeted inside the country appeared physically and/or politically achievable.

Key sources

Gössling, S., Hansson, C.B., Hörstmeier, O. & Saggel, S. (2002). Ecological footprint analysis as a tool to assess tourism sustainability. *Ecological Economics* 43, 199-211.

Scott, D., Gössling, S. & Hall, C.M. (2012). *Tourism and Climate Change: Impacts, Adaptation and Mitigation*, London: Routledge.

Discussion questions

1   If the greatest environmental impacts of tourism occur in travelling to and from destinations how might the overall environmental impact best be reduced?

> **2**   As a tourism manager, what initiatives could you undertake at the destination to reduce the environmental impact of tourism?
>
> **3**   What affect might the imposition of a 'green tax' have on A) travel to destinations such as the Seychelles? B) travel to your country?

The tourism experience

Because contemporary tourism experiences are simultaneously produced between the consumer and the producer, another interesting dimension of the geographical tourism system model is that at each stage consumer will be encountering different elements of the tourism industry. This therefore means that the tourist experience will be different not only from one region to another but even within regions as different service encounters occur and different environments, sites and people are encountered. Importantly, each new experience of the tourist will be added to the previous sum of experiences, leading to new sets of understandings and expectations. The travelers are therefore constantly gaining new information as they travel through the tourism system which will not only influence the nature of the experience and decision-making processes in this trip, but significantly, in later trips as well. Tourist travel within the basic geographical tourist system can therefore be regarded as consisting of five stages in which different psychological elements regarding the consumption of tourism exist (Figure 1.4).

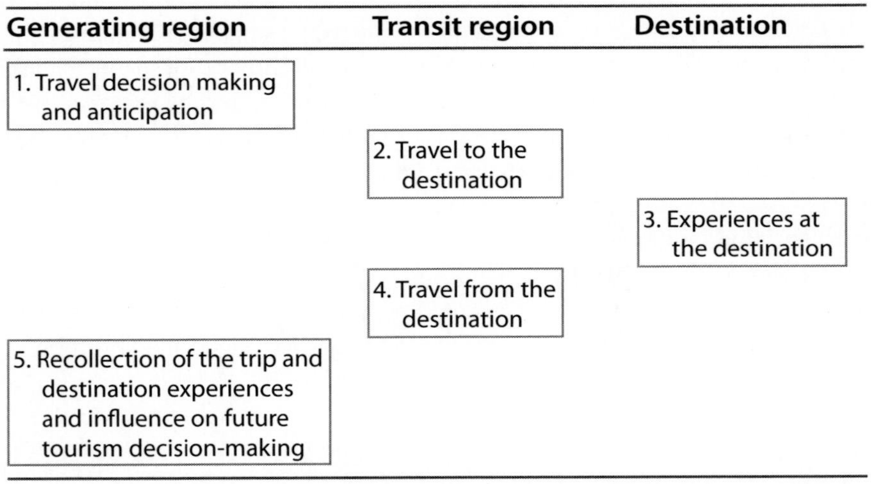

Generating region	Transit region	Destination
1. Travel decision making and anticipation		
	2. Travel to the destination	
		3. Experiences at the destination
	4. Travel from the destination	
5. Recollection of the trip and destination experiences and influence on future tourism decision-making		

Figure 1.4: Key elements of consumer psychology at different components of the tourism geographical system

The different stages of the travel experience create a major issue for studying the behaviour and motivations of tourism consumers. This is because where a consumer is at different stages of their trip may lead to different responses with respect to the nature and quality of the tourism experience. Just as significantly, it highlights the importance of understanding the prior tourism experiences of a consumer when seeking to explain or predict future preferences, decisions and activities. An important concept here is to think of consumers having tourism careers in the same way that we think of personal careers in employment and education. Our prior employment experiences and what we have learned in those positions influences future choice of employment. Similarly, our previous travel experiences when combined with new information sources assist us in determining where we may chose to travel to next. In fact, in cases such as working holidays, our travel and employment careers may even be closely entwined especially as international experiences come to be valued in an increasingly globalised economy and labour market. This perspective therefore means that in some cases, when studying the consumption of tourism within the tourism system, we may increase the focus of analysis from a very specific part of one trip to a lifecourse or life-stage perspective covering several years or even decades of tourism consumption in order to understand tourism phenomenon. Of course, while such studies are possible they are actually very difficult to do. Nevertheless, the concept that prior tourism experiences influences future ones over the course of a lifetime is a very important element in seeking to understand tourism consumer behaviour.

The tourism product

If the nature of the tourism experience changes at different stages of the tourism system what does this mean for how we understand the tourism product. Can there even be such a thing? The answer is yes, but the complexity of the tourism experience, given its constant co-creation, means that it is extremely difficult for producers to be able to control the experiences that the consumer has or to be certain that it will meet the consumer's expectations including perceptions of value. A tourism product is a particular set of commodified tourism experiences. However, it is important to recognize that there is more than one form of tourism product and that these different forms are often consumed simultaneously as we discuss in Chapter 4. The different forms of product include:

- *The trip product* This is the overall trip that a tourism consumer experiences including all firms, organizations, and service moments from the initial decision to purchase to the return home. In some cases such products are the result of packages put together by travel agents. One way of reducing uncertainty for consumers and producers with respect to the quality of such trip products is to provide all-inclusive packages in which many elements of the trip are included. Where consumers have assembled their own itineraries, the trip product is one they have produced rather than one packaged by a retailer or agency. Such products and consequent arrangements of the tourism system are therefore more individualized than those provided by agencies and consequently more open to chance and surprise.

- *The destination product* This is the sum of all experiences the tourist has at the destination as a result of encounters with firms, people, communities and the destination environment. The destination product is usually best identified through the marketing and promotion campaigns of Destination Marketing Organisations (DMOs) which seek to commodify what the DMO identifies as being the key experiences that a destination can provide the consumer. A characteristic of the destination product that distinguishes it from the products of many other industries is that the DMO does not actually own the product that it is promoting. To a limited extent this also occurs with the offerings of some tourism firms, such as those that provide sightseeing opportunities for example, nevertheless, it is most pronounced at the destination level. We discuss the destination product in detail in Chapter 9.

- *The tourism business product* This is the set of experiences provided by an individual firm or agency over different stages of the trip. In some cases, for example with respect to all inclusive package holidays where the same firm owns or controls the core elements of the tourism system at each stage, the tourism business product may be virtually synonymous with the trip product. However, in the majority of cases the consumer is actually encountering a series of different business products one after the other. In order to provide quality assurance to consumers within destinations, many tourism firms will cooperate with each other so as to provide a more consistent standard of service and visitor experience.

- *The service product* These are the various sets of service encounters that the tourism consumer experiences through their trip and at the destination. The service product can be formal or informal in nature. The service product can be described as 'formal' when it is related to the experience production of tourism businesses and 'informal' when it is the experience provided by meeting local people for example. Each tourism business product actually consists of a series of formal service products, each of which is a service 'moment of truth' for the consumer and the producer. Informal service products exist through the interaction of the consumer with people, communities and the environment at the destination outside of those provided by tourism businesses. Although such experiences are not the result of a formal tourism business they are nevertheless experiential products that exist within the product that is marketed and promoted by DMOs. In order to improve the service experience for tourists, DMOs will sometimes engage in promotional campaigns to encourage businesses and people within the destination to be friendly to tourists. We discuss the service product in more detail in Chapters 4 and 12.

The consumption of the various combinations of the different types of tourism product helps create the wide variety of tourist experiences that characterize destination, travel and operation offerings. The potential range of product combinations can help ensure that consumers find a variety of experiences that match their expectations and motivations. The challenge for the tourism industry of course is to find the right series of combinations for different sets of consumers, and this provides the foundation for much of what is contained in this book.

Another implication of our understanding of the tourism system is that it is constantly subject to change. Changes in one element in either the production or consumption of tourism will affect other elements in the system. For example, changes in transport in the transit component will affect the relative connectivity between destinations and generating areas. Changes at a destination, such as the imposition of new visa requirements, may affect the relative attractiveness of a destination with respect to other potential destinations. Similarly, alterations in the perception of the relative safety of destinations for travelers will also affect tourist flows. In the case of an example of change at the generating area, changes in foreign exchange rates will affect the flow of tourists to destinations on the basis of the relative favorability of exchange rates. In fact the relative exchange rate between countries is a major determinant in international and consequently domestic travel flows of leisure tourists, as well as the relative attractiveness of holiday destinations. Such a situation reinforces Mill and Morrison's observation that the tourism system 'is like a spider's web – touch one part of it and reverberations will be felt throughout' (1985: xix).

Who are the tourists?

Given the potential extent for change in the tourism system it becomes important that we can chart the patterns of consumption of tourism consumers. In order to do this we need a clear set of terminology. The term 'tourist' is the concept we use to describe those consumers who are engaged in voluntary temporary mobility in relation to their home environment. Key concepts here are 'voluntary', 'temporary' and mobility. If an individual is temporarily away from their home environment on an involuntary basis, for example as the result of a war, natural disaster, or other crisis, they are usually termed 'refugees' or if they have been forced into cross-border labour or sexual slavery, then they may be referred to as 'trafficked persons'. If someone has moved from one location to another on a permanent basis then they are usually referred to as an 'emigrant' by the country of departure and 'immigrant' by the country of arrival.

The concept of mobility in the context of tourism studies refers to the capacity of individuals to move from one location to another. In order to be able to do this, individuals need to be able to overcome various factors that act as constraints on tourism-related mobility including:

- ■ *Income* – People need sufficient disposable income to be able to engage in tourism once they have satisfied other basic needs. Poverty is a major determinant of travel behaviour as it affects the capacity to travel by different transport modes as well as the capacity to own personal transport such as a car. In countries such as the United Kingdom, the car is the dominant form of transport for tourism (Hall, 2010).

- *Time* – There needs to be time available for travel. Just as importantly the amount of time available will be a major determinant on how far people can travel and therefore influence their destination choice.

- *Political rights* – In order to be able to travel, particularly internationally, people need to have the political right to travel to destinations. Such rights are given by the nation state of both the generating region and the destination and are enabled through international law as well as systems of passports, visas and travel regulations.

- *Health* – Poor health, frailty or disability may constrain travel options.

- *Information and education* – Potential travelers need to have information in order to be able to access the tourism system and select and reach destinations.

- *Safety and security* – Concerns over the perceived level of safety and security will affect the selection of destinations and transport medium and may even influence the decision as to whether to travel at all. Safety factors include perceived threat of crime, political instability, and health risks.

- *Family* – The requirement of looking after family members will influence travel decision-making, particularly for care-givers.

- *Legislated holidays* – The availability of officially legislated holidays will affect travel patterns. In the United States, Thanksgiving and Christmas holidays are the two most significant in terms of the number of people who travel away from their home. Nevertheless, there are substantial variations between countries with respect to statutory leave requirements and public holidays. For example, Australia, Netherlands and the UK have 20 days statutory leave days per year whereas France has 25 and China 10 (World Tourism Organization 1999; Hall 2005).

- *Work* – Even if there are legislated holidays, individuals still need to feel that they are able to take holidays. This is especially important during periods of economic uncertainty when there may be concerns over job security or when there is a corporate culture that makes employees feel that reducing their working hours in order to engage in leisure and tourism was perceived to have a negative or very negative effect on their careers. In Japan there is even a term, *karashi*, that refers to death from overwork (Hall & Brown 2006).

- *Location* – The relative location of where someone lives on a permanent basis in relation to transport will be a constraining factor on his or her travel behavior because of their relative degree of accessibility. Furthermore, transport infrastructure location relative to consumers will also affect both the costs and pattern of travel. In a study of airports in the United States, Grubesic and Zook (2007) found that the largest hub locations have the most non-stop flights available to consumers. In airports where airline competition is strong (e.g., Chicago O'Hare), fare prices are relatively low. Conversely, in locations where competition is low, fare prices appear inflated. Passengers also pay higher fares in locations where flight departures are limited or in locations that are geographically remote because economies of scale and scope do not exist (Grubesic & Zook 2007).

- *Gender* – Gender may act as a constraint on travel because of fears over personal security or cultural issues regarding the appropriateness of travel for members of certain genders.

- *Culture* – The situation of individuals in different cultures creates variations with respects to attitudes towards tourism, particularly when temporary movement away from home is associated with what are regarded as non-essential behaviours. The development of a consumer culture that values travel for reasons of leisure as opposed to business or visiting family is therefore arguably one of the essential factors in influencing the growth of tourism.

Given the range of constraints noted above it should therefore come as little surprise that the majority of the world's population do not go on the international or long-distance holidays that are typically associated with tourism in the developed world. The vast majority of air travellers, for example, currently originate from industrialized countries, even though there are some rapidly developing countries, such as Brazil, China, India, Malaysia and Indonesia showing rapid growth in air travel. Peeters et al. (2006) estimated that the percentage of the world's population participating in international air travel is in the order of just 2–3%. Air travel is also unevenly distributed within nations, particularly those with already high levels of individual mobility. In industrialized countries there is evidence of a minority of highly mobile individuals, described as 'hypermobile' in terms of participation in frequent trips, often over great distances, who account for a large share of the overall kilometres travelled, especially by air, although a large share of mobility may be work-related. For example, in a study of air travellers at Gothenburg Airport, Sweden the 3.8% of hypermobile air travellers (>50 return flights per year) accounted for about 28% of all trips made by the sample (Gössling et al. 2009). Such mobility may have substantial implications for greenhouse gas emissions. Half the emissions caused by the mobility of French citizens are estimated to be caused by just 5% of the population, indicating the major importance of hypermobile travellers in addressing transport-related emissions (Gossling et al. 2009).

Yet even in developed countries there are significant proportions of the population that do not engage in long-distance holiday travel. In the United Kingdom this has been estimated at around 20% - 30% of the population (Hall & Brown 2006). Within the EU-27, almost two-thirds of those at risk of poverty were unable to afford a one week annual holiday (65%). By type of household, single parents with dependent children had the highest relative incapacity to afford a one week holiday (76%) (Hall 2010). In the case of the United States, Hall (2005) used US national transportation survey data to illustrate the increase in long-distance trip generation associated with a rise in income. In the US the trip generation rate almost triples when one transitions from the very low-income group to a very high-income group. Whereas 46% of the lowest income group households made zero long-distance trips, just 17% of the highest income group did so. Furthermore, income also influences the mode of travel. Lower income groups were much more likely to travel by road (either by car or bus) when compared to other income groups. The share of air travel also steadily increased in relation to rising income levels as does the distance of the average one-way trip, although no substantial differences were noticeable with respect to overall trip duration.

Despite the fact that many people do not travel, there are also many who do. These are the people we usually refer to as tourists. However, there are substantial challenges with respect to the statistical analysis of tourists. Most importantly the need to define 'tourist' and 'tourism'. Principle features that need to be defined in a statistical or 'technical' approach to tourism include:

- *The purpose of travel*, e.g. the type of travel, such as visiting friends and relations (VFR).
- *The time dimension* involved in the tourism visit, which may set minimum and maximum periods of time spent away from permanent residence and time spent at the destination.
- *Situations in which travellers may not be defined as tourists*, e.g. the voluntary nature of their travel, whether they are military or whether people are in transit from one location to another.

At the World Tourism Organization's (WTO) conference on tourism statistics held in 1991, tourism was defined as comprising:

> *'the activities of a person travelling outside his or her usual environment for less than a specified period of time and whose main purpose of travel is other than exercise of an activity remunerated from the place visited'*

where 'usual environment' is intended to exclude trips within the areas of usual residence and also frequent and regular trips between the domicile and the workplace and other community trips of a routine character, where 'less than a specified period of time' is intended to exclude long-term migration, and 'exercise of an activity remunerated from the place visited' is intended to exclude only migration for temporary work (Cited in Chadwick 1994: 66).

With respect to the definition of a tourist the WTO recommended that an international tourist be defined as:

> *'a visitor who travels to a country other than that in which he/she has his/her usual residence for at least one night but not more than one year, and whose main purpose of visit is other than the exercise of an activity remunerated from within the country visited'*

and that an international excursionist (for example, a cruise-ship visitor) or day-tripper should be defined as

> *'[a] visitor residing in a country who travels the same day to a country other than which he/she has his/her usual environment for less than 24 hours without spending the night in the country visited and whose main purpose of visit is other than the exercise of an activity remunerated from within the country visited'.*

1

In the case of a domestic tourist the travel time limit away from the home environment should be 'not more than six months' (WTO 1991; United Nations 1994).

Although the above guidelines are useful in thinking about tourism and measuring it statistically, there are significant variations between countries with respect to defining tourist activity as well as in collecting tourism data. Nevertheless, approaches to defining tourist and tourism rely on four different characteristics to define and hence measure activity (Figure 1.5):

■ *Time*, i.e. as discussed above how long someone is away from their place of permanent residence will affect their statistical and general description. For example, if undertaking a trip that does not require an overnight stay before returning the person would be classified as a day-tripper or excursionist. If undertaking an extended trip, e.g. of over 12 months in some jurisdictions, a person may be classified as a migrant.

■ *Space* (distance), i.e. how far does a person travel before being classified as a tourist? In some jurisdictions a minimum travel distance is required before being classified as a tourist. Such an approach can differentiate tourism from localized leisure or other travel behaviour such as commuting.

■ *Boundary crossing*, i.e. crossing a national border can enable a person to be classified as an international tourist arrival and/or departure depending on where a person is in the tourism system. Boundaries are also significant for the development of domestic and regional tourism figures.

■ *Purpose of travel*, i.e. as noted above some purposes are deemed suitable for definition of a tourist while others are not, e.g. military and diplomatic travel is not classified for tourism purposes, although a wide range of other travel purposes, such as health and education can be. The identification of the range of purposes for travel and application to tourism is extremely important for the management of international travel flows through the provision of different visa requirements within national jurisdictions. However, the range of purposes are also significant as they reflect the development of new forms of tourism products such as medical tourism, health tourism, sport tourism, educational tourism, business and meetings tourism, and visiting friends and relations as well as more 'traditional' leisure tourism. Indeed, for many destinations leisure tourism may only be a minor purpose of travel. In addition, some trips will be characterized by multiple purposes of travel.

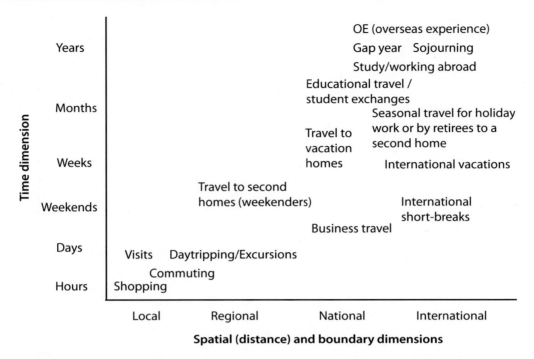

Figure 1.5: The characteristics of tourism in relation to time, distance, boundaries and description of purpose of travel (after Hall 2003)

Contemporary perspectives

Although important for determining tourism and tourists from a technical perspective, the elements identified in Figure 1.5 have also been argued as providing the basis for rethinking tourism as a form of temporary mobility. Coles et al. (2004, 2005) argued that in order to understand voluntary temporary human movement or mobility, we need to develop an appropriate framework for tourism, or a theoretically-oriented concept of tourism, i.e. one that seeks to incorporate all dimensions of tourism phenomenon. This framework involves the relationships between tourism, leisure and other social practices and behaviours related to human mobility, e.g. retirement and amenity migration, second homes, sojourning, 'gap years', and working holidays. Many of these forms of mobility go beyond the more traditional divide between tourism (temporary movement) and migration (permanent movement) and have only recently become apparent, yet they are an increasingly important part of what is studied in tourism and personal mobility and, just as importantly, what destinations and firms try and achieve with respect to promoting tourism.

One of the reasons why old barriers between different forms of human mobility, such as tourism and migration, have been severely eroded is that improvements in transport technology has made it easier for those with sufficient time and money to travel further and faster than ever before. Travel which once took two or three days to accomplish may now be completed as a daytrip. In addition, advances in travel technology have been matched by developments in communications and information technology allowing people greater access to the world as actual or potential destinations than ever before. Importantly, for many people in the developed world this means that tourism is now a routine, everyday part of life and travel is something that they readily engage in and indeed, expect to engage in (Hall 2005). Simultaneously, and as one would expect from our knowledge that tourism consumption and production are inseparable, we have also witnessed an explosion in the number of places and firms that are seeking to attract the mobile, and an absolute expansion in the number of people who are mobile and the different types of tourism product they consume.

Approach of this book

A contemporary understanding of tourism requires the utilization of contemporary approaches. We have therefore drawn heavily upon a range of relevant subject areas and disciplines to inform our chapters and understanding of contemporary tourism. In addition to studies of tourism, we particularly encourage readers to explore the literature on consumer studies, marketing, services and sustainability and we point to a number of key references in our annotated reading lists. As a result of this wider perspective, this book utilizes an approach to managing, marketing and developing tourism that goes well beyond the popular conception of tourism as holiday travel, as important as this form of tourism activity is, and instead embraces a broader understanding that sees such leisure-oriented holiday travel as part of a realm of voluntary temporary mobility (Figure 1.6) (Hall 2005).

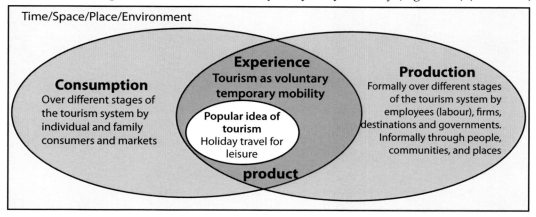

Figure 1.6: Understanding the nature of contemporary tourism

Such temporary movements of people for the consumption of tourism products and experiences are the focal point of this book. Importantly, the book takes a product-oriented approach that seeks to convey how products and experiences of tourists should be understood from the perspective of tourism firms and organizations in order that they can be best managed in order to reach satisfying outcomes for consumers, firms and destinations.

The book is divided into five sections so as to reflect a contemporary approach to understanding the tourism system. This first section of the book outlines our approach to a contemporary tourism system and in Chapter 2 goes onto to examine tourism products and markets. Chapter 2 shows how contemporary tourism products and markets are inextricably linked and draws upon consumer and marketing theory to help understand tourism products and market evolution.

The second section examines the contemporary tourist with respect to tourist behaviours and flows (Chapter 3) and contemporary tourism marketing (Chapter 4) where we draw heavily upon contemporary marketing theory to help understand contemporary tourism marketing.

The third section examines some of the key dimensions for understanding tourism destinations. Chapter 5 describes the various ways in which destinations are perceived by consumers and the consequences this has for tourism destinations. Most significantly, the chapter emphasises that the destination is the sum of its component parts: attractions, resources, people and individual businesses – the majority of which are not under the direct control of any DMO. Chapter 6 discusses the key role of government in tourism destinations and the emerging role of governance strategies and tourism policy. Chapter 7 examines the consequences of visitation to destinations while Chapter 8 looks at some of the responses to the implications of visitation via planning and management mechanisms that seek to achieve sustainable development objectives. Chapter 9 discusses the marketing of the contemporary tourism destination and identifies a range of contemporary issues facing destination marketers.

The fourth section, on the contemporary tourism industry, deals with various scales of analysis. It takes a contemporary approach that examines first, how we measure and assess the size of the industry and debates surrounding its component parts (Chapter 10). We then go on to identify a range of key issues facing the industry (Chapter 11). These issues include human resources, technology, globalisation, networking, knowledge management and entrepreneurship. Chapter 12 looks at the importance of taking a service management approach to delivering and managing the tourist experience and draws heavily upon the services management literature as it applies to tourism.

The final chapter discusses key emerging issues in tourism and how these are affecting tourism futures. Such concerns include not only security issues but also the role of pro-poor tourism, environmental change, and virtual tourism.

Summary

This chapter has provided an account of some of the key conceptual issues by which we come to understand contemporary tourism. It first identified tourism as a form of service industry. This was very important as it not only highlighted several of the characteristics of services but it also emphasized the key point that the consumption and production of tourism experiences and hence tourism product are inseparable. The one affects and informs the other. Some of the implications of this are then played out through the concept of the tourism system. The tourism system approach initially starts as a geographical approach but, as we have seen, then starts to have effects on how we understand the psychology of tourism and mobility, the different dimensions of tourism product and how they are simultaneously consumed by the tourist, as well as how the interaction of consumption and production are different over different stages of the system. The chapter then went on to consider how we define key concepts in tourism and how these then tie back into our understandings of consumption and production and the importance of the product and the experience. Most significantly, the chapter emphasized that a contemporary approach to tourism must look at all aspects of voluntary temporary mobility in order to be able to identify the potential full range of products and experiences that exist in contemporary tourism. We argue that such an approach will not only help us better understand contemporary tourism but also, by using the concepts, findings and strategies in this book, help increase returns to firms, destinations and the tourist.

Self-review questions

1 What are the distinguishing features of *services* as they apply to tourism?

2 Why is it difficult to discuss tourism *consumption* in isolation from *production*?

3 What are the five stages of a trip in relation to the *tourism system*? Discuss how the different stages of a trip might lead to different psychological dimensions of tourism.

4 What are the *constraints* that affect tourism? Discuss how such constraints affect your own travel decision-making and behaviours.

5 In seeking to understand tourism should more attention be given to the *immobility* of people?

6 Recall the four different *characteristics* that help define and hence study tourism activity.

7 Why have the concepts that describe *human mobility*, such as tourism and migration, become more closely connected in recent years?

8 How important are *time* and *space* in understanding tourism?

9   Are there differences in *popular* or public understandings of tourism and those of tourism researchers and managers?

10   Identify a particular environmental impact of tourism and review its relative importance in each component of the tourism system.

Recommended reading

Coles, T. & Hall, C.M. (eds) (2008). *International Business and Tourism: Global Issues, Contemporary Interactions*, London: Routledge.

Provides a detailed collection of chapters on key aspects of international tourism, including issues associated trade in services as well as the promotion of tourism.

Lennon, J. (ed.) (2003) *Tourism Statistics: International Perspectives and Current Issues*, London: Continuum.

An excellent overview of various issues associated with tourism statistics in a range of different national jurisdictions.

Hall, C.M. & Page, S. (2006). *The Geography of Tourism and Recreation: Space, Place and Environment*, 3rd ed. Routledge, London.

Chapter 2 provides a detailed account of issues associated with defining tourism demand and research on international and domestic tourism statistics.

Lovelock, C. & Gummesson, E. (2004). 'In search of a new paradigm and fresh perspectives', *Journal of Service Research*, 7(1), 20-41.

A seminal paper with respect to understanding services and service marketing.

Coles, T., Hall, C.M. & Duval, D. (2005). 'Mobilising tourism: A post-disciplinary critique', *Tourism Recreation Research*, 30(2), 31-41.

Discusses the significance of a mobilities based approach to tourism and its implications for key concepts.

Hall, C.M. (2005). *Tourism: Rethinking the Social Science of Mobility*, Harlow: Prentice-Hall.

Provides a more detailed extension of the mobilities approach and provides links into contemporary sociology, geography and regional development thinking in relation to tourism in both quantitative and qualitative terms.

Tribe, J. (2009) *Philosophical Issues in Tourism*, Bristol: Channel View.

Provides an introduction to some of the key research frameworks and issues in tourism.

Hall, D. & Brown, F. (2006). *Tourism and Welfare: Ethics, Responsibility and Sustained Well-Being*, Wallingford: CABI.

Provides an excellent account of the issues of participation and non-participation in tourism and how this relates to ethical and quality of life concerns

Singh, T.V. (ed.) (2012). *Critical Debates in Tourism*, Bristol: Channelview.

The various chapters in the book provide discussions on some of the major issues in the study of tourism and how they may affect our understanding of what constitutes tourism.

Gössling, S. & Hall, C.M. (2006). *Tourism and Global Environmental Change*, London: Routledge.
  Provides a challenging account of the implications of thinking about the impacts of tourism over all the stages of the tourism system and beyond.

Recommended websites

United Nations World Tourism Organization (UN body responsible for tourism): www.unwto.org/
World Travel & Tourism Council (an international organization of travel industry executives promoting travel and tourism worldwide): www.wttc.org/

References cited

Chadwick, R. (1994). Concepts, definitions and measures used in travel and tourism research. In J.R.B. Ritchie & C. Goeldner (eds), *Travel, Tourism and Hospitality Research: A Handbook for Managers and Researchers*, 2nd ed., pp. 65–80. New York: Wiley.

Coles, T., Duval, D. & Hall, C.M. (2004). Tourism, mobility and global communities: New approaches to theorising tourism and tourist spaces. In W. Theobold (ed.), *Global Tourism*, 3rd ed., pp. 463-481. Oxford: Heinemann.

Coles, T., Hall, C.M. & Duval, D. (2005). Mobilising tourism: A post-disciplinary critique. *Tourism Recreation Research* 30(2), 31-41.

de Bruijn, K., Dirven, R., Eijgelaar, E. & Peeters, P. (2008). *Reizen op grote voet 2005. De milieube-lasting van vakanties van Nederlanders. Een pilot-project in samenwerking met NBTC–NIPO Research*. Breda: NHTV Breda University of Applied Sciences.

Dubois, G. & Ceron, J.P. (2009). Carbon labelling and restructuring travel systems: involving travel agencies in climate change mitigation. In S. Gössling, C.M. Hall and D. Weaver (eds), *Sustainable Tourism Futures. Perspectives on Systems, Restructuring and Innovations*, pp. 84-101. London: Routledge.

Gössling, S., Ceron, J-P., Dubios, G. & Hall, C.M. (2009). Hypermobile travelers. In S. Gössling and P. Upham (eds), *Climate Change and Aviation*, pp. 131-149. London: Earthscan.

Gössling, S., Hansson, C.B., Hörstmeier, O. & Saggel, S. (2002). Ecological footprint analysis as a tool to assess tourism sustainability. *Ecological Economics* 43, 199-211.

Gössling, S. & Hall, C.M. (eds) (2006). *Tourism and Global Environmental Change*, London: Routledge.

Grubesic, T. & Zook, M. (2007). A ticket to ride: Evolving landscapes of air travel accessibility in the United States. *Journal of Transport Geography* 15, 417–430.

Hall, C.M. (2003). 'Tourism and Temporary Mobility: Circulation, Diaspora, Migration, Nomadism, Sojourning, Travel, Transport and Home', International Academy for the Study of Tourism (IAST) Conference, 30 June – 5 July 2003, Savonlinna, Finland.

Hall, C.M. (2005). *Tourism: Rethinking the Social Science of Mobility*. Harlow: Prentice-Hall.

Hall, C.M. (2007). *Introduction to Tourism in Australia*, Melbourne: Pearson Australia.

Hall, C.M. (2008). *Tourism Planning, 2ⁿᵈ ed.*, Harlow: Prentice-Hall.

Hall, C.M. (2010). Equal access for all? Regulative mechanisms, inequality and tourism mobility. In S. Cole and N. Morgan (eds), *Tourism and Inequality: Problems and Prospects*, pp. 34-48. Wallingford: CABI.

Hall, C.M. & Page, S. (2006). *The Geography of Tourism and Recreation: Space, Place and Environment*, 3ʳᵈ ed. Routledge, London.

Hall, D. & Brown, F. (2006). *Tourism and Welfare: Ethics, Responsibility and Sustained Well-Being*. Wallingford: CABI.

Hill, P. (1999). Tangibles, intangibles and services: A new taxonomy for the classification of output, *Canadian Journal of Economics* 32, 426-446.

Lovelock, C. & Gummesson, E. (2004). In search of a new paradigm and fresh perspectives, *Journal of Service Research* 7(1), 20-41.

Mill, R.C. & Morrison, A.M. (1985). *The Tourism System: An Introductory Text*, Englewood Cliffs: Prentice-Hall International.

Peeters, P., Gössling, S. & Becken, S. (2006). Innovation towards tourism sustainability: climate change and aviation. *International Journal of Innovation and Sustainable Development* 1, 184–200.

Peeters, P.M., van Egmond, T. & Visser, N. (2004) *European Tourism, Transport and Environment*. Breda: NHTV Breda University of Applied Sciences, Centre for Sustainable Tourism and Transport.

Rees, W.E. (1992). Ecological footprints and appropriated carrying capacity: What urban economics leaves out. *Environment and Urbanisation* 4(2), 121-130.

Scott, D., Gössling, S. and Hall, C.M. (2012). *Tourism and Climate Change: Impacts, Adaptation and Mitigation*, London: Routledge.

Smith, I.J. & Roger, C.J. (2009). Carbon emission offsets for aviation-generated emissions due to international travel to and from New Zealand. *Energy Policy* 37, 3438–3447.

Sustainable Travel International (2007). Scuba dive industry addresses global warming and climate friendly diving: world's first scuba diving carbon 'finprint' and custom carbon dive calculator developed, *Responsible Travel Report*, April. Available at http://www.responsibletravelreport.com/sti-news/news/2241-scuba-dive-industry-addresses-global-warming-and-climate-friendly-diving (accessed 1 April 2012).

United Nations (1994). *Recommendations on Tourism Statistics*, New York: United Nations.

World Tourism Organization (WTO) (1991). *Resolutions of International Conference on Travel and Tourism, Ottawa, Canada*, Madrid: World Tourism Organization.

2 Contemporary Tourism Product Markets

Chapter objectives

After reading this chapter you will:

- Understand the various approaches to tourism products.

- Appreciate the concept of experiences as tourism products.

- Recognise the various approaches to tourism markets.

- Be aware of the changing nature of tourism markets and the 'post tourist'.

- Understand the significance of tourism market segmentation.

- Recognise the importance of the tourism product market.

- Recognise the importance of market stories in market shaping.

- Understand the nature of exchanges and interactions in tourism product markets.

Introduction

This chapter introduces the pivotal concept of tourism product markets as a key to understanding contemporary tourism marketing. We begin with a discussion of tourism products, stressing that a contemporary approach to tourism products recognises that the tourism consumer is a co-creator of products, delivering a marketing approach that allows interaction with the tourist in a continuous process. A contemporary approach is to engineer experiences as tourism products, appealing to the 'post tourist' market and delivering memorable, engaging tourism experiences that 'transform' the visitor. We then consider tourism markets and how consumer behaviour is changing. It is clear that to reach and understand these new markets demands deep and meaningful research and contemporary approaches to market segmentation. We introduce the concept of tourism product markets to provide a framework for the interaction of buyers and sellers in tourism. The main message of the chapter is that tourism products and markets are inextricably linked; it will be seen that tourism product markets allow the clear definition of tourism products and the boundaries between them. Finally we examine the nature of the continuous exchanges and interactions in tourism product markets and the response of marketers to the challenges that these present.

■ Tourism products

As we noted in Chapter 1, tourism products are complex and multifaceted. As a result they have generated a considerable debate as to their nature and definition, including whether they are sufficiently different to merit a separate approach to marketing. The traditional view of a tourism product has been inherited from economics and is based upon the framework of exchange. Tourism products package together utilities and benefits for the consumer and, in tourism, exchange takes place at a destination and within a particular socio-political, environmental, technological and economic setting. There are two elements to this approach:

1 The nature of the social exchange when a purchase takes place; and

2 The functional nature of the tourism product included in the transaction.

More recently, new perspectives have been introduced including those based upon relationships, the co-creation of value and the recognition of intangible products. These new perspectives are based upon the concept of marketing services rather than physical goods; they allow consideration of all market actors and recognise that these actors will have a continuous relationship with each other. This provides a more realistic approach to the tourism product as it integrates both goods and services and recognises that tourists will purchase both when they construct a trip. This approach recognises the tourism consumer as a co-creator of goods and delivers a marketing approach that allows interaction with the customer in a continuous process, facilitated by the use of technology. This can then be taken a step further by viewing the tourism product as a bundle of tangible and intangible product attributes, with all products lying on a continuum between these types of attributes. The tourism product can also be viewed along a second continuum: from a single component; through a composite of components that are packaged or bundled together; to the total destination product itself. Gilbert (1990) extends these ideas, arguing that the tourism product is in fact the total experience. He defines the tourism product as:

> *'An amalgam of different goods and services offered as an activity experience to the tourist' (Gilbert 1990: 20).*

Clearly then, there are a number of approaches to the tourism product. For example, building on Gilbert's notion of the tourism product as the total experience, the product can be disaggregated into stages of the vacation from anticipation and planning, to booking, travel and evaluation. The merit of this approach is that it takes into account the important pre- and post-product purchase stages that influence future buying behaviour, as noted in Chapter 1. A second approach is to view the product as synonymous with the destination, such that the tourism product is an 'amalgam' of destination elements including attractions, supporting services such as accommodation, food & beverage, and transportation (Figure 2.1). There are significant implications of this 'amalgam' for tourism marketing, particularly the challenge of managing quality across the various elements, each of which is often supplied by a different organisation.

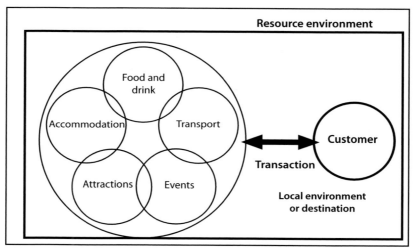

Figure 2.1: The Tourism product market. Source: Cooper, Scott and Kester (2005)

This approach is perhaps mirrored in the more traditional approach to understanding tourism products that is drawn from the physical goods marketing literature (Kotler et al. 2010). This approach argues that products have three key dimensions:

1 The core product delivers the product's benefits and features and provides a reason for purchase. An example here would be the offer of a vacation in Hawaii.

2 The facilitating product must be present for the tourists to use the services. For a vacation these include transportation and accommodation. It is interesting that it is this part of the product that is cut to a bare minimum in the business model of low cost carriers. They replace paper tickets with e-tickets and bookings are made on the Internet to avoid interaction with an expensive sales person. The low cost carrier business model delivers the facilitating elements of the product in a different way.

3 The augmented product delivers added extras that allow the product to compete. For a vacation in Hawaii, it may include a free night, free transfer or complimentary drinks on arrival. For low cost carriers, in the early days of

their operation, free seating was common, but some carriers now augment their service by providing allocated seating.

Finally, tourism products can be viewed as evolutionary, beginning with the development and formulation of new products, then building sales along a cycle of evolution. Development of new products is the main form of innovation in tourism and is essential for sector growth. They are important to diversification, increasing sales and profits and competitive advantage. As the product becomes established it may then move through the various stages of the life cycle, an approach adapted by Butler (1980) for destinations in the 'tourism area life cycle'.

Experiences as tourism products

An example of the development of a new product in tourism, and a core concept of this book, is the idea of the product as an experience. This is different to Gilbert's (1990) idea of the tourism product as the total vacation experience; rather in this case we are looking at specific tourism products developed and engineered as 'experiences'.

In 1982, Holbrook and Hirschman's pioneering paper came up with the idea of seeing consumer behaviour as seeking hedonic and aesthetic experiences to add to the notion of consumer behaviour being purely about information processing. This approach works well for tourism because, as tourism markets mature, they seek authentic tourism products. Effectively, tourism sells a staged experience, and suppliers and destinations are responding to this challenge by delivering experience-based products. In 1999, the experiences concept saw two important publications. Pine and Gilmore (1999) came up with the term 'experience economy', whilst Schmitt (1999) published an influential paper on the idea of experiential marketing with the focus upon consumers achieving pleasurable experiences.

In the experience economy, changing values from older to younger generations mean that consumers are seeking new meaning and self-actualisation in their tourism consumption patterns as they move beyond material possessions and services to experiences. Arnould et al. (2002) show that this consumption of the tourism experience takes place over a stretched period of time and can be thought of as taking place in four distinct stages:

1 *The pre-consumption experience.* This involves searching for information about the experience, planning it, daydreaming about it and imagining the experience.

2 *The purchase experience.* This derives from choosing the experience, paying for it and packaging the encounter with the service delivered and the environment where the experience takes place.

3 *Core consumption experience.* This takes place whilst the experience is performed or delivered and includes the sensation of the experience, satisfaction or dissatisfaction with it and the way that the experience transforms the consumer.

4 *The remembered consumption experience and the nostalgia experience.* Here photographs can help relive a past experience, as can accounts, stories and posts on social networking sites about a past experience.

Tourism products are increasingly being formulated to serve demand and experiences are engineered to match the expectations of the market place, not only in tourism but also across the services sector (Sharpley & Stone 2012). Here, Pine and Gilmore (1999) see experiences along two dimensions: passive to active; and absorption to immersion, with the ability of a good experience to 'transform' the visitor. Experiences are therefore personal and memorable; they evoke an emotional response as the tourist enters into a multi-facetted relationship with both the actors and destination setting of the experience. Research has focussed on evaluating the experience and in particular developing approaches to a scale for 'memorable tourism experiences'. Here research shows that positive memories are a good predictor of wanting to consume a future experience, and that memory is enhanced when the experience appeals to the five senses (Kim et al. 2012).

At the destination, 'experience providers' sequence and stage carefully choreographed activities, personal encounters, and authentic experiences, designed to create long-lasting memories, engaging travel, and increased customer loyalty (Morgan et al. 2010). Pine and Gilmore (1999) developed five principles of experience design:

1 Theme the experience

2 Harmonise impressions with positive cues

3 Eliminate negative cues

4 Mix in memorabilia

5 Engage the five senses

O'Sullivan and Spangler (1998: 5) classify experience providers into three types:

1 Infusers – manufacturers who 'infuse' their products with experiences;

2 Enhancers – service providers who use experiences to heighten satisfaction or differentiate from competitors; and

3 Makers – service providers who create experiences as the core of their service. For example, the 2012 London Olympics called the employees and volunteers who delivered the games 'game makers'.

For the destination, delivering and engineering the experience involves infrastructure, narrative content and a context, each of which are heightened by technology. In effect, engineering these experiences demands that destinations and operators migrate to experience-oriented tourism strategies, where the common thread is authenticity, delivering experiences that are perceived to be real, unsullied and rooted in the destination. Here, the notion of 'endemic resources' such as food and culture deepen the experience and link to sustainability strategies at the destination by building on the core appeal and adding value at each stage of the experience. It is the dimensions of authenticity and its delivery that will influence the buying decision and be central to the maturation of the experience economy at the destination level (Scott et al. 2012). Alongside the success of those who deliver experiences to create 'memorable' and unique experiences is research into successful experience consumption environments, such as Starbucks or Disney, which will determine whether their service experience can be 'stretched' to other sectors of tourism (Marketing Science Institute 2012). Each of these elements has been factored into Tourism Tasmania's 'experience product strategy' which is detailed here as a case study.

Case Study 2.1: Tourism Tasmania's 'experience product' strategy

Introduction

Engineering tourism experiences is at the cutting edge of contemporary tourism product development, recognising the expectations of a marketplace that is used to high quality entertainment, visual images and sound in their own homes. Australia recognises the importance of this approach and has a set of 'Experience Development Strategies' (Tourism Australia 2012). These were developed as part of Australia's National Landscapes Programme, designed to provide new and engaging experiences to enhance visitor length of stay and sustainability of the landscapes.

Tourism Australia (2012:3) sees an experience development strategy (EDS) as:

> a planning tool to facilitat e focussed destination development and marketing, based on the national landscapes destination positioning. The EDS aims to improve the stock of world class visitor experiences! to the experience seeker market, providing pathways to increase tourism's contribution to conservation within the national landscape.

The programme targets the 'experience seeker' – 'a global target market, existing in both the domestic and international markets that is identified by Tourism Australia as being the most responsive to Australia's tourism offering' (Tourism Australia 2012:3). This group seeks unique and personal experiences and are an important segment for Australia as they are more likely to deliver economic benefits to parts of regional Australia. This segment is well educated, media and marketing savvy and worldly; they differ by demographics and spending power but are linked by their values, attitudes and motivations. They form a high yielding market segment, and are leaders of their peer groups influencing others' purchasing habits. They are early adopters and travel is an important part of their lifestyle (Australian Government 2011).

'The Australian island of Tasmania is designated as one of Australia's national landscapes and has a visionary EDS which is an integral part of its tourism strategy. The island's overarching tourism strategy – Tourism 21 – aims to increase jobs and tourism expenditure through a number of strategies, one of which is linked closely to the experience economy

(Pine & Gilmore 1999). The Tasmanian Experience Strategy (TES) contributes to the goal of Tourism 21 by enhancing engagement with the visitor through the development of holiday experiences on the island (Tourism Tasmania 2002). The strategy builds in the key elements of narrative and engagement (in this case through the local community and interpretation), high quality memorable experiences and endemic tourism through food and wine – all designed to 'transform' the visitor.

2

Understanding the market

The strategy recognises that tourists' needs and desires are changing and that the island may not have kept up with these developments. Tourism Tasmania has therefore underpinned the strategy with research designed to understand the triggers that lead consumers to purchase a Tasmanian vacation. The research identified five key tourism market segments for the island:

1   International visitors
2   Touring visitors
3   Short break visitors
4   Special interest tourists
5   Niche visitors

Understanding the product

Tasmania has identified three core attributes of its product, which form the basis of the experiences:

■   Nature;
■   Cultural heritage; and
■   Fine wine and food.

However, the strategy recognises that on their own, these attributes are not a sufficient reason to visit; after all, many other destinations have similar attributes. In addition Tourism Tasmania has recognised that in the past it has placed too much emphasis on the 'supporting elements' of the product (infrastructure, accommodation, transport and service) and not enough on the holiday experience. Whilst visitors do expect high quality support for their visit in terms of service and accommodation, this is expected in all destinations and does not give Tasmania a competitive edge.

As a result of this thinking, the TES develops a new approach to combining these elements of the Tasmanian product by 'augmenting' it with experiences tailored to market needs. The mission of the strategy is to create:

'extraordinary and unforgettable holiday experiences by focussing on presentation, interpretation and customer engagement' (Tourism Tasmania 2002: 1).

Engineering the experience

Tourism Tasmania defines an experience as:

'Memorable events or interactions that engage people in a personal way and connect them within a place – Tasmania, its people and their ideas' (Tourism Tasmania 2002: 4).

The key here is the notion of the experience-based product as 'memorable and personalised' – in other words augmenting experiences are wrapped around the core elements of the island's product (Pine & Gilmore 1999). The strategy is based upon engineering experiences through developing means of connecting visitors to place, delivering quality infrastructure and personalised service underpinned by interpretation and engagement (Figure 2.2).

Figure 2.2: The Tasmanian experience concept. Source Tourism Tasmania (2002)

The context of the experience is a visit to the island. Engineering the experience builds upon combining the island's three core attributes of nature, cultural heritage, wine and food with 'community enthusiasm and involvement, highly developed interpretative skills, local knowledge and a passion for place' (Tourism Tasmania 2002: 7). The strategy views communities as critical stakeholders and as such the strategy is dependent upon community support. Communities are viewed as keepers of the stories of their areas and the strategy is therefore seeking community engagement and looking to them for interpretation of local places. The strategy also has the notion of 'endemic tourism' as a core element by encouraging interaction with communities and the island's food and wine.

The strategy envisages that experiences will be designed in clusters focussed on key precincts around the island and linked by tourism routes. These distinctive combinations of experiences allow spatial differentiation across the island and, for each cluster, the development of brand appeals to be pinned back to the overall Tasmanian brand. For each cluster the strategy engages the tourism industry to package vacation experiences to attract key market categories. For some clusters there are gaps in provision and Tourism Tasmania has developed a portfolio of development opportunities to fill these.

Linking the Tasmanian brand to experiences

It is important that the experiences are linked to the Tasmanian brand, which communicates the island as an experience-rich destination. In effect, the experiences become the delivery of the brand on the ground for the visitor. The brand and the experience support each other so that the Tasmanian brand promise is that of a host of unforgettable experiences based upon the three core attributes of the island. To support this approach, a brand management system has been developed to communicate and integrate the delivery of the experience. For intermediaries, sales tools have been developed to help them package products for targeted consumers based on the experience clusters.

Benefits of the approach

The goal of the TES is to deliver the following benefits:

- Boost the island's economy through tourism spending and job creation;
- Boost yield for tourism businesses; and
- Enhance the sustainability of Tasmania's natural and cultural assets.

These benefits will be achieved by deepening visitor and community appreciation of the cultural and natural environment. In addition, heightened awareness and appreciation of local food and wine will sustain and enhance the profitability of local suppliers and businesses. In terms of boosting the tourism economy, the strategy will encourage new markets, repeat visits and facilitate memories and market stories.

The strategy represents a significant shift in thinking for the Tasmanian tourism sector. It will therefore require the sector to share research and knowledge, and will involve a major education and communication exercise to achieve the change in focus and branding of the island.

Key sources

Australian Government (2011). *Flinders Ranges. Experience Development Strategy Pilot*, Canberra: Australian Government.

Pine, J.B. & Gilmore J.H. (1999). *The Experience Economy*, Harvard: Harvard Business School Press.

Tourism Australia (2012). *Experience Development Strategies. Guidelines for Australia's Landscape Steering Committees*, Sydney: Tourism Australia.

Tourism Tasmania (2002). *The Tasmanian Experience. Creating Unforgettable Natural Experiences*, Hobart: Tourism Tasmania.

Discussion questions

1   Discuss the pros and cons of engagement with the experience strategy from the Tasmanian community's point of view.

2   The TES is very dependent upon the technique of interpretation to transform the visitor experience. What are some of the problems that accompany this technique?

3   What should be the shape of the education and communication exercise undertaken to make the Tasmanian tourism sector aware of their role in the experience strategy?

Tourism markets

Tourism markets are comprised of actual and potential consumers. White (1981) defines markets as:

> 'self-reproducing social structures among cliques of firms and other actors who evolve roles from observations of each other's behaviour (White 1981: 518).

This definition works well for tourism and supports the approaches to products and markets outlined in this chapter. These approaches can be summarised as:

1 Products and markets evolve together with the tourist as a co-creator of goods; and

2 They deliver a marketing approach that allows interaction with the customer in a continuous process.

This approach recognises that the environment is volatile and that markets and emerging product structures are dynamic. For example, the tourism market has changed as a result of increased travel, shifting values and perceptions, technology and demographics. Feifer (1985) has termed these new consumers 'post-tourists'. They are experienced, discerning and caring of the places that they visit, demonstrating ethical consumption and behaviour at the destination. Post-tourists demonstrate changing values and preferences, increasingly seeking authenticity and well-managed, tailored individual experiences that allow them to both get closer to and also participate in the intimacy of the destination – in other words they seek the type of experience products that are being developed in Tasmania as we showed in the case study above. They also use technology to create networks and on-line communities of like-minded tourists.

This new consumer behaviour is resistant to traditional forms of marketing and, for marketers, is more difficult to understand and analyse as market segments are less stable, constantly fragmenting and reforming. Addressing this challenge of the 'post- tourist' demands a contemporary approach to segmenting and analysing tourism markets, one which must be based upon deep and meaningful research that delivers specialised and tailored solutions to destinations and operators.

Traditionally, tourism market research has been locked in the 1960s – with large-scale omnibus and national-level holiday taking surveys – and has been unable to deliver support to contemporary market segmentation approaches. Contemporary approaches to research, particularly using qualitative and multivariate analysis approaches as well as approaches to research on line behaviour, are needed to understand the 'post-tourist' market and to support the development of new segmentation techniques. Deep and meaningful research, that can deliver detailed customer profiles and identify elements of consumer behaviour, underpins new approaches to market segmentation which is central to understanding the relationship between tourism products and markets. Market segmentation involves dividing a tourism market into distinctive sub-sets each with common characteristics, such that the formulation and positioning of tourism products and experiences, designed to attract pre-identified segments. This approach can deliver a full understanding of the needs of the segment, which itself becomes the focus for the marketing effort. To be effective, market segments must be:

- Measurable – marketers must be able to 'calibrate' the segment in order to access it;

- Accessible – the segment must be 'reachable' through promotion;

- Substantial – the segment must be large enough to support the design of particular tourism products;

- Sustainable – the segment must be durable in time if it is to justify the design of products; and

- Actionable – an organization must be able to develop products that will compete effectively for the segment's purchases.

Traditionally, tourism marketing has not utilised sophisticated segmentation techniques, preferring instead to use single variable segments based upon say, demographics (e.g. the youth market), geography (e.g. the German market), or buyer behaviour (e.g. the business market). However, as the tourism market has matured it has also fragmented and the old techniques of segmentation are no longer adequate. Increasingly, tourism is seen as a way to express lifestyle by purchasing products such as adventure tourism, eco-tourism or cultural tourism. Examples of new segmentation approaches include psychographics, where the underlying psychology of the tourist is analysed; attitudinal and ethical segmentation where travel behaviour is the basis for segmentation; and technographics which analyses the ability to use technology for searching and purchasing tourism products as well as social media behaviour. There is a danger though that as information about consumers expands, our insights into segments and behaviours is getting 'cloudier' rather than more precise (Marketing Science Institute 2012).

Tourism product markets

It is clear from this chapter so far that tourism products and tourism markets are inextricably linked. The 'product market' concept recognises this interdependence and exists within a framework of the interaction of buyers and sellers in a marketplace (Figure 2.3). The concept of product markets is intuitively appealing and fundamental to marketing theory. This is because they help explain how markets function and evolve, how new products are accepted and whether market boundaries are distinct or shifting. In other words, because product markets are formed by the interaction of tourists and suppliers, their boundaries are flexible as they represent the aggregate of many exchanges. This is outlined in Rosa et al's pioneering paper on the subject (Rosa et al. 1999) in which they see product markets as 'meeting grounds for buyers and sellers' (Rosa et al. 1999: 64). Two further definitions of 'product markets' are helpful in describing the concept:

> *'[the] set of products, judged to be substitutes within those usage situations in which similar patterns of benefits are sought and the customers for whom such usages are relevant... they are bounded arenas in which prices and quantities for substitutable goods and services are negotiated by consumers and producers and are separated from other bounded arenas by gaps in demand between the product groupings' (Day et al. 1979: 10).*

> *'The area of actual and potential exchanges, between consumers and producers, involving the offerings of producers and the wants of customers, and with respect to a particular situation' (Bourgeois et al. 1987: 370).*

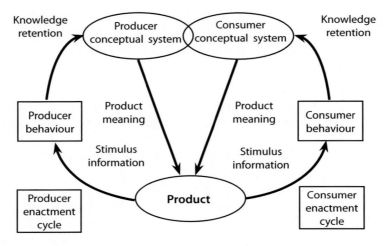

Figure 2.3: A sociocognitive market system (Source: Rosa et al 1999)

Product markets are very helpful in understanding different types of tourism and how they can be classified. In tourism, each exchange between a tourist and a supplier is unique, simply because of the nature of tourism supply is highly heterogeneous - many different levels of involvement by the tourist exist. There are two processes at work here:

1 Exchanges can be grouped and aggregated into a product market; and

2 The product market concept shows that both the supplier and the tourist can influence these exchanges.

In other words, different tourism product markets are defined by the interaction between suppliers and tourists and examples include eco-tourism, dark tourism, adventure tourism, heritage tourism and cultural tourism. In each product market, tourists can be classified by their behaviour and involvement, as their 'wants' will tend to cluster, whilst suppliers will tend to specialise in particular product markets.

It must, however, be remembered that product markets are *not* destinations. Destinations are bounded geographical entities which act as the setting for product markets. Destinations can therefore be the setting for many product markets – each with its own group of customers and suppliers; indeed we can think of the destination as the stage for the enactment of the 'experience'.

The concept of product markets is useful for tourism because it allows:

- The definition of tourism product markets based on particular groups of attributes; and
- Identification of differences and delimitation of boundaries between tourism product markets.

■ Creating product markets: Market stories

One way that product markets are created is through market stories and narratives. Here, both consumers and producers achieve shared understanding of a product market – and its boundaries – through conversations built around product offerings. In this way, the various actors that create a product market make sense of the environment from market-shaping knowledge (Shankar et al. 2001). This knowledge comes from, and is observable in, the narratives surrounding both the physical products and the tourism experiences of market actors. In a tourism product market, these actors will include consumers, producers, operators, media, retailers, intermediaries, government agencies and destination marketing organizations.

For the consumer, these stories are important, particularly when they are not familiar with the product. Social media now plays an increasingly important role in consumer decision-making and in the creation of market stories and narratives. Social media allows vast scalability for a credible and authentic view of a product or destination to develop in a way that was simply not possible before the emergence of social media. This means that the tourist connects with both destinations and brands in a fundamentally different way – and in ways beyond the control of either the company or the destination (Edelman 2010). This disturbs the traditional relationship between the product or destination and the tourist and means that marketing strategy has to be re-thought to include the influence of advocacy by other social media users. As product markets evolve, so these market stories change. In newly emerging product markets, consumers face new product ideas that do not readily fit into existing categories and the stories are highly variable. As tourism products mature, the stories align more closely with each other as agreement over the product market is reached (Table 2.1).

These stories contribute to our understanding of how tourists make sense of their consumption experiences as we see in the following case study. Skydiving is a classic product market and the case study demonstrates how both the activity of the skydiving and its participants interact to shape and bound the skydiving product market.

Table 2.1: The changing nature of market stories with product maturity. Source: Rosa et al. (2005)

Characteristics of stories about emerging product markets	Characteristics of stories about mature product markets
Highly complex	Less complex
Less accurate	More accurate
Judgements disagree	Judgements agree
Disagree on product image	Agree on product image

Case study 2.2: Market-shaping behaviour in adventure tourism product markets: skydiving

Introduction

Adventure tourism is a growing but still minority product market, nesting within sports tourism (Klaus & Maklan 2011). The unique characteristics of adventure tourism have generated a considerable literature (Hudson 2003; Swarbrooke et al. 2003; Buckley 2010). However, the literature focuses more on the destination and the activity than upon how the sports product market is experienced by the tourist. In terms of considering experiences, Klaus and Maklan (2011) state that it is the extraordinary experience that has a profound, life changing effect on the participant - the transformational element that Pine and Gilmore (1999) speak of. Clearly, extreme sports such skydiving fall into this category, providing participants with an extraordinary peak experience, a peak experience that also leaves the participant feeling more 'authentic'.

Sky diving

At first glance skydiving does not appear to be an activity that human beings were designed to perform – to step out of an aircraft at thousands of feet above sea level is nonsensical. Celsi et al's pioneering 1993 paper examines how this product market is structured and provides insights into how market stories and activities have developed both the structure of the skydiving product market and the experience itself.

Skydiving is part of the growing adventure tourism product movement that includes activities such as bungee jumping and white water rafting. Whilst there is no agreed definition of adventure tourism, Swarbrooke et al. (2003) characterise it as a niche area with descriptors such as uncertainty, risk, danger, challenge, stimulation, excitement and focus. Indeed, adventure tourism involves considerable risk to participants as Bentley et al's (2001) analysis of injuries and fatalities in New Zealand hospitals shows. They found that 22% of visitor fatalities were due to participating in adventure tourism.

As this case study shows, adventure tourism is characterised as much by the process of engagement and the tourists' state of mind as the activity itself. A common distinction is between hard and soft adventure, and in this case study, skydiving is definitely in the 'hard' category, defined as 'activities with high levels of risk, requiring intense commitment and advanced skills' (Swarbrooke et al. 2003: 33).

The skydiving market

Adventure tourism shows how tourism products have differentiated and specialised to cater for a small part of the tourism market with special needs. For the 'post tourist', consumption of tourism represents a lifestyle choice – a search for fulfilment and happiness, and for transforming and individual experiences. Here, adventure tourism delivers a high involvement and extraordinary experience that is intense, positive and intrinsically enjoyable. However, until the 1980s, the 'experience' of consumption was not recognised in consumer behaviour models. Yet, feelings, fun and leisure all play a part in understanding the use and consumption of products and are closely linked to the consumer's level of involvement with the product.

Skydiving, along with underwater diving, hang-gliding or mountain climbing is a dangerous and potentially lethal activity. Yet, skydivers are drawn from a population who have mortgages, insurance, wear car seat belts and recycle. Despite this they engage in an activity with high physical risk, and indeed some do die. In Figure 2.4 Celsi et al. (1993) suggest that three factors conspire to make people want to skydive:

1   The external environment which increasingly encourages risky, dramatic behaviour;

2   The availability of outlets for skydiving and through technology, the theatrical 'props and equipment for play'; and

3   The individual's own psychological makeup and their pre-disposition to risk and thrill-seeking behaviour. Often they seek to live their lives through leisure experiences as a foil to their working life.

Given these factors, skydiving exemplifies the phenomena of the 'post-tourist' as it is very difficult to identify measurable characteristics of the group and to reach them for marketing purposes.

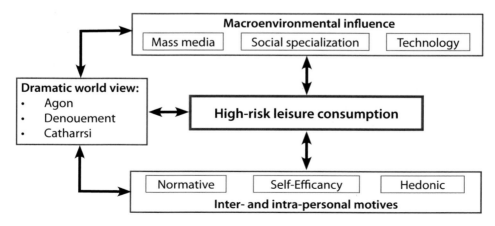

Figure 2.4: An extended model of high-risk leisure consumption. Source: Celsi Et Al (1993)

The skydiving product

Celsi et al. (1993) describe sky diving as:

> 'A dramatic, self-fulfilling behaviour that occurs on a specific stage with carefully cast actors and co-actors. The act is clearly defined, with the skydive planned and rehearsed' (Celsi et al. 1993: 21).

Although the pre- and post-dive activities are important, the actual activity itself is of relatively short duration; for example, Celsi et al. (1993) suggest that active skydivers will only be exposed to risk for around eight hours in any year.

The growth of skydiving has created its own clubs, suppliers and folklore. Like many adventure pursuits, in the early years of amateur skydiving, professional equipment was not available and the participants relied on army surplus materials. This has changed however with the growth of the activity, and specialist suppliers produce parachute equipment for the sport.

Market stories and theatre

There are two strong characteristics that shape the product market of skydiving. The first is the very strong sense of group identity that characterises the skydivers; whilst the second is the choreographed nature of the skydiving activity.

Skydivers

There is no doubt that extreme activities such as skydiving create a very strong bond between participants. For example in Celsi et al's (1993) research on skydiving, based on a club in the USA, skydivers view themselves as a family. As part of the experience, skydivers see themselves as creating a new self-identity and camaraderie, perhaps transcending that of normal group belonging. This is because not only is the activity so extreme, but also because the experience is a shared one with its own technical language. In skydiving, the market actors play various roles based either upon:

1   Their level of experience – students, novices, intermediates and experts. Here progression though the various stages of initiation (for example, the first jump) is seen as a rite of passage; or

2   Their part in the overall drama – owners, instructors, dive organisers and pilots.

Skydiving

The theatrical experience of skydiving is supported by its own technical language and props including parachutes, jumpsuits, helmets, goggles, logbooks, wrist altimeters, cameras, airplanes and landing markers. It is interesting that the equipment and language of adventure sports has permeated everyday life; clothing styles, fabrics and colours, as well as slogans such as 'just do it' owe their origins to extreme adventure sports.

The activity of skydiving is highly structured with an identifiable beginning, middle and end. This is very much along theatrical lines equating to an opening, performance and finale, rather as described by Pine and Gilmore (1999) as the basis for the experience economy. O'Sullivan and Spangler (1998) break experiences into three key stages and these are clear in Celsi et al's (1993) description of the choreographed nature of skydiving:

- **Pre-experience**
  - ☐ On the ground – coordinating and rehearsal;
  - ☐ The ascent – anticipation as the airplane ascends to the dive point;
- **The experience**
  - ☐ The exit – total commitment to the activity by stepping out of the aircraft;
  - ☐ Free fall - the main reason for skydiving, bringing a sense of freedom;
  - ☐ Under canopy – once the parachute has opened bringing a sense of relief, but also disappointment; and
- **Post-experience**
  - ☐ Post-performance rituals – feedback and congratulations to participants.

Each stage has its own rituals and stories, as do the interruptions to this highly choreographed activity when accidents occur. Indeed, as well as physical risk, stories surround the fact that if participants fail to deal with the failures in the activity then there is also an element of psychological risk. Above all, the activity is characterised by the intensity of emotion and the rituals surrounding it.

It is this combination of a close-knit group of participants, with a highly choreographed activity that interacts to create market-shaping activity and so defines the skydiving product market.

Key sources

Bentley, T., Page, S., Meyer, D., Chalmers, D. & Laird, I. (2001). How safe is adventure tourism in New Zealand? An exploratory analysis. *Applied Ergonomics* 32(4), 327-338.

Buckley, R. (2010). *Adventure Tourism Management*. Oxford: Butterworth Heinemann.

Celsi, R.L., Rose, R.L. & Leigh, T.W. (1993). An exploration of high-risk leisure consumption through skydiving. *Journal of Consumer Research* 20, 1-23.

Hudson, S. (2003). *Sport and Adventure Tourism*, Binghampton, NY: Haworth.

Klaus, P. & Maklan, S. (2011). Bridging the gap for extreme sports: a model of sports tourism customer experience. *Journal of Marketing Management* 27(13-14), 1341-1365.

O'Sullivan, E.L. & Spangler K.J. (1998). *Experience Marketing: Strategies for the New Millennium*, Pennsylvania: Venture.

Pine, J.B. & Gilmore J.H. (1999). *The Experience Economy*, Harvard: Harvard Business School Press.

Swarbrooke, J., Beard, C., Leckie, S. & Pomfret, G. (2003). *Adventure Tourism: The New Frontier*, Oxford: Butterworth Heinemann.

Discussion questions

1   List as many adventure tourism activities as you can. Place these in a continuum from 'hard' to 'soft' adventure noting the criteria that you use to classify each activity.

2   What characteristics of tourists might be used to produce a market segmentation based upon 'adventureness'?

3   As a market researcher, how might you begin to research and measure market stories?

Interactions and exchanges in product markets

The concept of exchange and interaction permeates the discussion on tourism product markets. The continuous interaction between market actors takes place within the context of a tourism destination. Each exchange or interaction has all the classic features of a service encounter. As such it is possible to benchmark the exchanges and interactions against a quality level. The challenges of the interactions that take place in tourism product markets are found in Figure 2.5. It is clear that whilst these interactions display the classic characteristics of services, they are exacerbated by the nature of tourism not only as an activity, but also as a product.

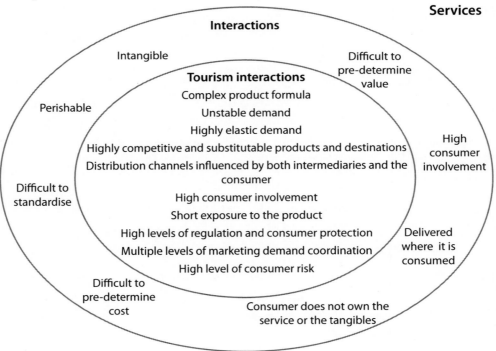

Figure 2.5: The environment of product market interactions.

Both tourists and suppliers are now designing strategies to deal with these challenges. Tourists, for example, are seasoned travellers and fully understand the tourism market place – they will purchase late, look at on-line reviews, travel flexibly and understand their rights if the product or service is not as described. For the supplier these strategies include relationship marketing, e-marketing and service quality management:

1   Relationship marketing is designed to secure a loyal customer base, creating, maintaining and enhancing strong relationships with consumers.

2   E-marketing will ensure that the producer connects with the tourist through social media and other on-line features such as web sites.

3   Service quality management is designed to 'industrialise' service delivery by guaranteeing standardised and consistent services.

These three strategies combined will help retain customers, avoid price competition, retain employees and reduce costs. The strategies are augmented by other techniques such as yield management to adjust pricing to demand and so smooth out the demand curve; strong branding to communicate product attributes and reduce any perceived risk of purchase; managing the evidence of the interaction through investment in the physical environment or 'servicescape'; and staff training as the tourist's short exposure to the product means that staff are part of the interaction.

Summary

This chapter has outlined the concept of contemporary tourism product markets as a key to understanding tourism marketing. Product markets assist in the understanding of tourism products, particularly in tourism where there is much debate as to the nature of the product. An important point here is to recognise that the tourism consumer is a co-creator of products. This allows for the development of a marketing approach that emphasises the importance of continuous interaction with the tourist. Here the chapter introduced the contemporary approach of experiences as tourism products and outlined Tasmania's tourism experience product strategy as a case study. The experience product appeals directly to the 'post-tourist' market; a market that is used to high-quality visual and experiential products from entertainment and the media and also looks for authenticity. The chapter considered the changing nature of the tourism market and in particular the need for tourism to engage in deep and meaningful market research and innovative market segmentation. The message from this chapter is that tourism products and markets are inextricably linked, hence the strong endorsement of the concept of tourism product markets. They provide a framework for understanding the interaction of buyers and sellers in tourism and allow the clear definition of tourism products and the boundaries between them. The pivotal position of the various actors in a market have led to the study of 'market shaping' stories where consensus emerges amongst market actors as to what constitutes a particular product market. This is clearly demonstrated by the case study on skydiving. Finally, the chapter examined the nature of the continuous exchanges and interactions in tourism product markets and the response of marketers using relationship marketing, e-marketing and service quality management

Self review questions

1   Outline the main approaches to conceptualising tourism products and devise your definition of a tourism product.

2   Why is the tourism experience product well suited to the 'post-tourist'?

3   What might be the key elements of a market research project to underpin a market segmentation approach based upon use of social media?

4   How does the behaviour of the post-tourist differ from that of a typical inclusive tour client?

5   What do you understand by the term 'tourism product market'?

6   Choose a tourism product market (for example adventure tourism, or eco-tourism) and define the market and product characteristics of that market. How distinct are the product market boundaries?

7   Using the media and the Internet, find examples of market stories shaping tourism product markets.

8   How do the interactions and exchanges in a tourism product market differ from those in a product market based on physical goods?

9   What strategies can a tourism organization devise to overcome the challenging nature of product market exchanges and interactions in tourism?

10 What are the key advantages of taking a product market approach to tourism marketing?

Recommended reading

There are an increasing number of excellent marketing texts with a tourism and hospitality flavour. These include:

Hudson, S. (2012). *Tourism and Hospitality Marketing. A Global Perspective*. London: Sage.

Morgan, M. & Ranchhod, A. (2012). *Marketing in Travel and Tourism*. London: Routledge.

Kotler, P., Bowen, J. & Makens, J. (2010). *Marketing for Hospitality and Tourism*, 5th ed., New Jersey: Prentice Hall.

McCabe, S. (2008). *Marketing Communications in Tourism and Hospitality*, London: Routledge.

Tressider and Hirst (2012). *Marketing in Food, Hospitality, Tourism and Events*. Oxford: Goodfellow.

Celsi, R.L., Rose, R.L. & Leigh, T.W. (1993). An exploration of high-risk leisure consumption through skydiving. *Journal of Consumer Research* 20, 1-23
An innovative paper exploring the product market dynamics of the skydiving product market

Cooper, C., Scott, N. & Kester, J. (2005). New and emerging markets. In D. Buhalis and C. Costa (eds.), *Tourism Business Frontiers*, pp. 19-29. Oxford: Elsevier Butterworth Heinemann.
Chapter exploring the nature of product markets and in particular how new markets emerge.

Kandampully, J. (2002). *Services Management. The New Paradigm in Hospitality*. Melbourne: Hospitality Press.
A clear exposition of services theory and its application to tourism and hospitality.

Kotler, P., Bowen, J. & Makens, J. (2010). *Marketing for Hospitality and Tourism*, 5th ed. New Jersey: Prentice Hall.
Thorough text covering all the mainstream approaches to both products and markets.

Kotler, P., Brown, L., Adam, S. & Armstrong, G. (2004). *Marketing*, 6th ed. New Jersey: Prentice Hall.
A classic text covering the generic marketing theory of products and markets.

Pine, J.B. & Gilmore, J.H. (1999). *The Experience Economy*, Harvard: Harvard Business School Press.
A ground-breaking book reconceptualising the way we think about experiences as products.

Rosa, J.A. & Spanjol, J.R. (2005). Micro-level product market dynamics: shared knowledge and its relationship to market development. *Journal of the Academy of Marketing Science* 33(2), 197-216
A thorough discussion of the approaches to, and the literature of, product markets including the role of market stories.

Recommended web sites

Tourism Australia: http://www.tourism.australia.com

Tasmania online (government website): http://www.tas.gov.au/

Tourism Tasmania corporate website: http://www.tourismtasmania.com.au/

Discover Tasmania (promotional website): http://www.discovertasmania.com/

References cited

Arnould, E., Price, L. & Zinkhan, G. (2002). *Consumers*. Columbus: McGraw Hill.

Australian Government (2011). *Flinders Ranges. Experience Development Strategy Pilot*, Canberra: Australian Government.

Bentley, T., Page, S., Meyer, D., Chalmers, D. & Laird, I. (2001). How safe is adventure tourism in New Zealand? An exploratory analysis. *Applied Ergonomics* 32(4), 327-338.

Bourgeois, J.C., Haines, G.H. & Sommers, M.S. (1987). Product market structure: problem, definition and issues. In M. Houston (ed.), *Review of Marketing*, pp. 327-384. Chicago: American Marketing Association.

Buckley, R. (2010). *Adventure Tourism Management*. Oxford: Butterworth Heinemann.

Butler, R. (1980). The concept of a tourist area cycle of evolution: implications for management of resources, *Canadian Geographer* 24(1), 5-12.

Celsi, R.L., Rose, R.L. & Leigh, T.W. (1993). An exploration of high-risk leisure consumption through skydiving. *Journal of Consumer Research* 20, 1-23.

Day, G.S., Shocker, A.D. & Srivastava, R.K. (1979). Customer-oriented approaches to identifying product markets. *Journal of Marketing* 43, 8-19.

Edelman D.C. (2010). Branding in the digital age. *Harvard Business Review* 88, 62-69

Feifer, M. (1985). *Going Places*. London: Macmillan.

Gilbert, D.C. (1990). Conceptual issues in the meaning of tourism. In C.P. Cooper (ed.), *Progress in Tourism, Recreation and Hospitality Management*, Vol. 2, pp. 4-27. London: Belhaven.

Holbrook, M. & Hirschman, E. (1982). The experiential aspects of consumption: consumer fantasies, feelings and fun. *Journal of Consumer Research* 9, 132-140.

Hudson, S. (2003). *Sport and Adventure Tourism*, Binghampton, NY: Haworth.

Kim, J.H., Ritchie, J.R.B. & McCormick, B. (2012). Development of a scale to measure memorable tourism experiences. *Journal of Travel Research* 51, 12–25.

Klaus, P. & Maklan, S. (2011). Bridging the gap for extreme sports: a model of sports tourism customer experience. *Journal of Marketing Management* 27(13-14), 1341-1365.

Kotler, P., Brown, L., Adam, S. & Armstrong, G. (2004). *Marketing*, 6th ed. New Jersey: Prentice Hall.

Kotler, P., Bowen, J. & Makens, J. (2010). *Marketing for Hospitality and Tourism*, 5th ed. New Jersey: Prentice Hall.

Marketing Science Institute (2012). *2012-2014 Research Priorities*, Cambridge, MA: MSI.

Morgan, M., Lugosi, P. & Ritchie, J.R.B. (2010). *The Tourism and Leisure Experience*. Bristol: Channel View.

O'Sullivan, E.L. & Spangler K J (1998). *Experience Marketing: Strategies for the New Millennium*, Pennsylvania: Venture.

2

Pine, J.B. & Gilmore, J.H. (1999). *The Experience Economy*, Harvard: Harvard Business School Press.

Rosa, J.A., Porac, J.F., Spanjol, J.R. & Saxon, M.S. (1999). Sociocognitive dynamics in a product market. *Journal of Marketing* 63(4), 64-77.

Rosa, J.A. & Spanjol, J.R. (2005). Micro-level product market dynamics: shared knowledge and its relationship to market development. *Journal of the Academy of Marketing Science* 33(2), 197-216.

Schmitt, B. (1999). Experiential marketing. *Journal of Marketing Management* 15, 53-67.

Scott, N., Laws, E. & Boksberger, P. (2012). *Marketing of Tourism Experiences*, London: Routledge.

Shankar, A., Elliott, R. & Goulding, C. (2001). Understanding consumption: Contributions from a narrative perspective. *Journal of Marketing Management* 17, 429-453.

Sharpley, R. & Stone, P. (eds) (2012). *Contemporary Tourist Experience*, London: Routledge.

Swarbrooke, J., Beard, C., Leckie, S. & Pomfret, G. (2003). *Adventure Tourism: The New Frontier*, Oxford: Butterworth Heinemann.

Tourism Australia (2012). *Experience Development Strategies. Guidelines for Australia's Landscape Steering Committees*, Sydney: Tourism Australia.

Tourism Tasmania (2002). *The Tasmanian Experience. Creating Unforgettable Natural Experiences*, Hobart: Tourism Tasmania.

White, H. (1981). Where do markets come from? *The American Journal of Sociology* 87(3), 517-547.

Section 2: The Contemporary Tourist

3 Contemporary Tourists, Tourist Behaviour and Flows

Chapter objectives

After reading this chapter you will:

- Understand different approaches to categorising types of tourism .

- Appreciate factors that have contributed to the growth of international tourism

- Understand the significance of wildcard events that may slow or reduce tourism growth.

- Identify factors that may explain the short-term stability of tourist flows and patterns.

- Understand the roles of distance and accessibility as key factors in determining tourism flows.

- Understand the characteristics of mass and alternative tourism.

- Understand the nature of special interest tourism.

- Appreciate psychographic and motivational approaches to explaining tourist behaviour.

- Appreciate the significance of lifecourse approaches to explaining changes in tourism behaviour over the life of an individual as well as cohort value shift with respect to tourism.

Introduction

The movement of tourists with respect to both the number of people traveling and the geographic spread of where people travel has continued almost unabated at the global scale since the end of World War Two. Multiple reasons exist for the growth in international and domestic travel. However, critical are increasing disposal incomes and available time for travel. Yet there are also a number of other factors that determine both the generation of tourists from countries and their reception at destinations. This chapter examines a range of factors that determine the patterns, flows and behaviours of contemporary tourists. These will be examined at various scales of analysis and detail.

Macro-level analyses of tourism examine the movement of people in aggregate form (Table 3.1). Descriptions of tourism at this level focus on the spatial aspects of tourism, i.e. tourist patterns and flows, and on different forms of tourism, i.e. broad accounts of tourism that have been defined on the basis of activity or motivation. Micro-level analyses of tourism often seek to explain individual tourist behaviours on the basis of theories of tourist psychology and motivation. Nevertheless, there is clearly a link between individual and aggregate accounts of tourism as aggregate descriptions of tourism are the sum of behaviours of large number of individuals. There is then a third group of analyses of tourism that may be described as mid- or meso-level accounts that seek to integrate aggregate and individual accounts of tourist behavior; examples here include the use of time-geography techniques (Hall 2005b; Coles et al. 2006; Frändberg 2006, 2010).

Table 3.1: Scales of analysis of tourism

Scale of analysis and description of tourism	Focus	Key concepts
Macro	Aggregate	• Distribution, patterns, flow • Activity
Meso	Combines aggregate and individual analysis	• Mobility, trip stage, life course, travel career
Micro	Individual	• Personality, psychographics/lifestyle • Motivation, expectation, satisfaction

The first part of the chapter describes travel movements at a global scale. The second section then explains changes in tourism at a macro-level with reference to structural factors that influence tourism as well as other descriptions of different types of tourism. The third section describes tourist behaviors and demands at a micro-level by examining how individual travel preferences may be explained in terms of psychographics or personal motivations. The final section outlines a meso approach that examines how travel motivations and constraints change over an individual's life.

Global travel movement

The movement of tourists is not evenly spread around the globe. Tourism is subject to a range of influences and factors that determine its relative distribution. Flows are not random but are patterned. Tables 3.2 and 3.3 provide figures on the number of international visitor arrivals for different regions of the world and the relative growth in tourism for those regions since 1950. One of the immediate results of an analysis of international tourism in terms of patterns of movement is that it shows that international tourism has historically been concentrated in the more advanced economies of North America and Europe. However, over time the Asia-Pacific region has experienced significant growth relative to Europe and the Americas because of its own substantial rate of economic development, especially with respect to the emerging economies of China and India, and the development of large middle classes. This has also meant that over time the relative global market share of international arrivals has been declining for the Americas and Europe but increasing for the Asia-Pacific and, to a lesser extent, for other regions as well. The UNWTO (2012) estimate that by 2030 Asia and the Pacific will receive just under 30% of international arrivals while the Americas will receive only 13.7%, with more than half of this derived from North American arrivals. By 2030 it is expected that Europe will still receive just over 41% of world arrivals. Differences in inbound travel arrival rates (Table 3.4) are also reflected and outbound participation rates with both metrics influenced by personal levels of disposable income (Table 3.5).

Table 3.2: International tourism arrivals and forecasts 1950-2030 (millions)

Year	World	Africa	Americas	Asia & Pacific	Europe	Middle East
1950	25.3	0.5	7.5	0.2	16.8	0.2
1960	69.3	0.8	16.7	0.9	50.4	0.6
1965	112.9	1.4	23.2	2.1	83.7	2.4
1970	165.8	2.4	42.3	6.2	113.0	1.9
1975	222.3	4.7	50.0	10.2	153.9	3.5
1980	278.1	7.2	62.3	23.0	178.5	7.1
1985	320.1	9.7	65.1	32.9	204.3	8.1
1990	439.5	15.2	92.8	56.2	265.8	9.6
1995	540.6	20.4	109.0	82.4	315.0	13.7
2000	687.0	28.3	128.1	110.5	395.9	24.2
2005	799.0	34.8	133.3	153.6	440.7	36.3
2010 forecast	940.0	50.2	150.7	204.4	474.8	60.3
2020	1360	85	199	355	620	101
2030	1809	134	248	535	744	149

Source: WTO 1997; UNWTO 2006, 2012

Table 3.3: Average annual growth in international tourism arrivals and forecasts 1980-2030 (%)

Year	World	Africa	Americas	Asia & Pacific	Europe	Middle East
1950-2000	6.8	8.3	5.8	13.1	6.5	10.1
1950-2005	6.5	8.1	5.4	12.5	6.1	10.1
1950-60	10.6	3.7	8.4	14.1	11.6	12.3
1960-70	9.1	12.4	9.7	21.6	8.4	11.5
1970-80	5.3	11.6	4.0	13.9	4.7	14.3
1980-90	4.7	7.8	4.1	9.3	4.1	3.1
1980-1985	2.9	6.1	0.9	7.4	2.7	2.7
1985-1990	6.5	9.5	7.3	11.3	5.4	3.5
1980-1995	4.4	6.7	3.8	8.9	3.7	4.5
1990-2000	4.6	6.4	3.3	7.0	4.1	9.6
1990-1995	4.2	6.1	3.3	8.0	3.5	7.3
1995-2000	4.9	6.7	3.3	6.0	4.7	12.0
2000-2005	3.3	5.7	0.8	7.1	2.2	10.0
1995-2010	3.9	6.7	2.1	6.3	3.0	10.5
forecast						
2010-2030	3.3	5.0	2.6	4.9	2.3	4.6
2010-2020	3.8	5.4	2.9	5.7	2.7	5.2
2020-2030	2.9	4.6	2.2	4.2	1.8	4.0

Source: UNWTO 2006, 2012

Table 3.4: International tourist arrivals by region per 100 population 1995-2030

(sub)region	1995	2010	2030
Western Europe	62	81	114
Southern / Mediterranean Europe	47	71	103
Northern Europe	42	63	80
Caribbean	38	48	65
Central / Eastern Europe	15	25	47
Middle East	9	27	47
Southern Africa	9	22	46
Oceania	28	32	40
Central America	8	19	38
North Africa	6	15	28
South-East Asia	6	12	27
North America	21	21	26
North-East Asia	3	7	18
South America	4	6	13
East Africa	2	4	7
West and Central Africa	1	2	3
South Asia	0	1	2

Note: figures are rounded off. Source: After UNWTO 2011

Table 3.5: Generation of outbound tourism by region per 100 population 1980-2030

Year	World	Africa	Americas	Asia & Pacific	Europe	Middle East
1980	6	1	12	1	21	6
1995	9	2	14	3	36	6
2010	14	3	17	5	57	17
forecast						
2030	22	6	24	12	89	25

Source: After UNWTO 2011

In 2011 the UNWTO revised its long-term forecasts for international tourism. According to the UNWTO (2011, 2012), the number of international tourist arrivals worldwide is expected to increase by an average 3.3% a year from 2010 to 2030. Over time, the rate of growth is forecast to gradually slow down, from 3.8% between 2010 and 2020 to 2.9% from 2020 to 2030. In absolute numbers, international tourist arrivals are forecast to increase by some 43 million a year, compared to an average increase of 28 million a year during the period 1995 to 2010. At the projected rate of growth, international tourist arrivals worldwide will reach 1.36 billion by 2020 and 1.8 billion by the year 2030, after exceeding one billion for the first time in 2012. The forecast figure for 2020 is a lower estimate that the World Tourism Organization's (1997, 2001) previous estimate that by 2020 international arrivals were predicted to reach nearly 1.6 billion. According to the UNWTO (2011) four reasons can be identified for the more moderate pace of growth in international arrivals:

- The base volumes are higher, so smaller increases still add substantial numbers
- Lower GDP growth, as economies mature
- A lower elasticity of travel to GDP
- A shift from falling transport costs to increasing ones

On a regional basis, the UNWTO (2012) predict that international tourist arrivals in the emerging economy destinations of Asia, Latin America, Central and Eastern Europe, Eastern Mediterranean Europe, the Middle East and Africa will grow at double the rate (4.4% a year) of advanced economy destinations (2.2% a year). As a consequence, the UNWTO estimate that international arrivals to emerging economies will surpass those to advanced economies by 2015. By 2030, the UNWTO (2012) suggest that 57% of international arrivals will be in emerging economy destinations (versus 30% in 1980) and 43% in advanced economy destinations (versus 70% in 1980). In regional terms the biggest growth is expected to be in the Asia-Pacific, where arrivals are forecast to increase by 331 million to reach 535 million in 2030 (an average growth rate of 4.9% per year). The Middle East and Africa are also expected to more than double their arrivals in this period, although from a much lower base than that of other regions, from 61 million to 149 million in the Middle East and from 50 million to 134 million in Africa. In the same period Europe is forecast to grow from 475 million to 744 million international arrivals and the Americas from 150 million to 248 million international arrivals. As noted above, the different rates of growth in arrivals between regions will also alter their relative market shares of global international arrivals.

As Tables 3.4 and 3.5 illustrate, despite the substantial actual and forecast growth in international tourism arrivals there is substantial regional variability in rates of inbound and outbound international tourism. The international tourism figures also do not account for the enormous amount of domestic tourism activity that exists. Although there is no internationally consistent and comprehensive set of data for domestic tourism the UNWTO estimated that in 2005 five billion arrivals were by same-day visitors (four billion domestic and one billion international) and 4.8 billion from arrivals of tourists staying overnight (four billion domestic and 800 million international). Taking into account that an international trip can generate arrivals in more than one destination country, the number of trips is regarded as somewhat lower than the number of arrivals. Therefore for 2005, the global number of international tourist trips (i.e., trips by overnight visitors) was estimated at 750 million corresponding to 16% of the total number of tourist trips, with domestic trips representing 84% or four billion tourist trips (Scott et al. 2008). The figures for international and domestic overnight tourist arrivals are illustrated in Table 3.6 together with extrapolations for 2010, 2020 and 2030. We can see from the table that sometime between 2013 and 2015 that the total number of visitor arrivals by international and domestic overnight visitors will exceed the world's population for the first time. As discussed above and in Chapter 1 this does not mean that everyone is a tourist but it does highlight the extent to which the world has become mobile.

Table 3.6: Global international and domestic tourist arrivals 2005-2030

	Year/billions			
	2005	2010	2020	2030
Actual/estimated number of international visitor arrivals	0.80	0.94	1.36	1.81
Approximate/estimated number of domestic tourist arrivals	4.00	4.70	6.80	9.05
Approximate/estimated number of total tourist arrivals	4.80	5.64	8.16	10.86
Approximate/estimated global population	6.48	6.91	7.67	8.31

Note: Actual and estimated forecasts of international visitor arrivals based on UNWTO (2012); 2005 approximate figures based on Scott et al. (2008); Approximate and estimated global population figures are based on United Nations Department of Economic and Social Affairs Population Division 2010 revisions.

Of course it is important to bear in mind that these are global aggregate figures. The more localized an examination of tourism patterns and flows is, the more likely it is to find variation in tourism numbers, particularly in terms of the impact of 'wildcard' – high magnitude, low frequency – events such as hallmark events which may increase arrivals, or political conflicts or natural disasters which may reduce arrivals at a destination or even reduce the overall amount of travel within, to and from the affected region (Hall 2005a, 2010) (See also Chapter 13). In fact, the only events which have had aeffects on the entire global tourism system since modern tourism began in the 1850s are:

- World wars or major international conflicts
- Economic depression or periods of severe recession over a large number of countries
- Rapid increase in the price of a major energy source that is used for transportation, particularly oil
- Outbreaks of contagious disease.

Case study 3.1: Icelandic tourism and crisis

International tourism to Iceland has grown from being practically nonexistent in the mid-20th century to being one of the three main sectors of the Icelandic economy (along with fisheries and aluminium production). However, its role has arguably become even more important following the international economic and financial crisis that has affected Europe in particular from 2007 on. Following the privatization of the banking sector Iceland positioned itself as a significant financial centre with the country's major commercial banks becoming increasingly involved in international investment banking. However, in September and October 2008 the countries three major banks, Landsbanki, Glitnir and Kaupthing, were placed into receivership with their domestic operations being nationalized. This precipitated Iceland's worse economic crisis and recession and resulted in substantial increases in unemployment and inflation and a significant drop in the country's GDP by 5.5% in real terms in the first six months of 2010. The national currency, the Icelandic krona, fell sharply in value, foreign currency transactions were virtually suspended for weeks, and the market capitalisation of the Icelandic stock exchange dropped by more than 90%.

However, the economic downturn and financial crisis of 2008 and 2009 has only served to increase the perceived importance of tourism to the Icelandic economy (Hall et al. 2009; Jóhannesson 2010), particularly as the value of the Icelandic krona dropped considerably against the Euro and the currencies of Iceland's main Nordic markets. Table 3.7 illustrates that the number of overnight stays in Iceland has continued to increase as well as outlining other parameters of tourism's contribution to the country's economy, including its contribution to GDP and as a source of foreign exchange. Cruise tourism is also continuing to grow with Iceland being part of itineraries that include Norway, the Faroe Islands and the Shetland Islands by some operators (e.g. P&O), and Greenland and Labrador by others (e.g. Hurtigruten) (Hall & Saarinen 2010). The role of tourism in the revitalization of Iceland's economy is all the more impressive given that the World Tourism Organization (UNWTO) (2010) estimated that international tourist arrivals fell by 4% in 2009. However, the role of tourism in Iceland's economic recovery reinforces the need to understanding tourism and crisis at multiple scales while, figures also point to the importance of changes in exchange rates in influencing tourist flows.

A further crisis for Iceland and much of Europe were the 2010 eruptions of Eyjafjallajökull, which although relatively small, generated volcanic ash clouds that had an enormous impact on trans-Atlantic and European aviation from 14-20 April when large amounts of airspace were closed. Limited further disruptions continued until late May 2010. According to the International Air Transport Association (IATA), costs of the disruption to the global airline industry caused by the volcanic ash cloud were estimated at US$1.7 billion (£1.1 billion) after just a week of flight restrictions in European airspace (Wearden 2010). The EU transport commissioner also stated that the disruption caused by the ash cloud could have cost firms across Europe up to €2.5 billion (£2.15 billion) (Gabbatt 2010). However, while the volcanic eruptions undoubtedly had significant short-term impacts on Icelandic and European tourism, in the longer term they have potentially reinforced Iceland's wilderness image that it uses to promote nature-based tourism (Hall et al. 2009). As Sæþórsdóttir et al. (2011: 269) noted, 'even the well-reported impacts of ash cloud from volcanic eruptions may only further add to the wilderness mythologies of Iceland' as they reinforce long-standing images of Iceland. Indeed, walking tours to, on and even in, volcanoes are now a part of Iceland's nature-based tourism products.

Table 3.7: Tourism in Iceland

| Year | Employment in tourism | Tourism industry share of GDP (%) | Total tourism export of goods & services (million ISK) | Number of overnight stays all accommodation | | | Passengers through Keflavik airport |
				Total	Domestic	Inter-national	
2000	8 009	5.1	30 459	1 736 919	594 700	1 142 219	
2001	8 190	5.4	37 720	1 744 488	560 274	1 184 214	
2002	7 867	5.6	37 137	1 860 685	604 167	1 256 518	
2003	7 904	5.1	37 305	1 984 448	607 660	1 376 788	600 369
2004	8 158	5.0	39 335	2 130 230	651 382	1 478 848	693 883
2005	8 566	4.5	40 049	2 232 911	682 728	1 550 183	747 534
2006	8 897	4.8	49 670	2 457 068	737 928	1 719 140	830 158
2007	9 113	4.6	53 853	2 644 745	776 572	1 868 173	927 689
2008	9 241	5.9	75 502	2 735 989	793 291	1 942 698	879 122
2009	9 241		153 929	2 999 959	870 384	2 129 575	719 073
2010			160 838	2 991 015	854 707	2 136 308	753 022
2011				3 238 616	803 055	2 435 561	881 915

Source: Statistics Iceland (2006, 2009, 2012).

Key sources

Hall, C.M., Müller, D. & Saarinen, J. (2009). *Nordic Tourism*. Bristol: Channelview Press.

Jóhannesson, G.T. (2010). Tourism in times of crisis: Exploring the discourse of tourism development in Iceland. *Current Issues in Tourism* 13, 419-434.

Sæþórsdóttir, A.D., Hall, C.M. & Saarinen, J. (2011). Making wilderness: Tourism and the history of the wilderness idea in Iceland. *Polar Geography* 34(4), 249-273

Statistics Iceland Tourism Statistics: http://www.statice.is/Statistics/Tourism,-transport-and-informati

Visit Iceland (official tourism information site): http://www.visiticeland.com/

Discussion questions

1   Are there any lessons that other countries or tourism destinations facing economic crisis or natural hazards could learn from the Icelandic case?

2   To what extent is it true to sat that travelers react more to perceived risk as opposed to real risk in undertaking travel and decision-making?

3   What information does Visit Iceland provide to a) tourists and b) the media with respect to the information on volcanoes or other types of risks that tourist may perceive in wilderness areas.

The stability of tourism: tourism inertia

One of the most significant observations of flows of international tourists is that, barring major crises, there is a great deal of year-to-year stability in aggregate travel patterns. This situation has long been recognized, as Williams and Zelinsky (1970: 563) in one of the seminal works on international tourism observed: 'once established, a stream of tourists has its own inertia, and one can predict future flows with considerable confidence without being able to explain the causes of past or present patterns'. Nevertheless, identifying causal factors remains useful. For example, the hypothesis of reciprocity, that is a flow of tourist in one direction should generate a counterflow in the other direction, is not generally supported when examining international tourism data. Nevertheless, Williams and Zelinsky (1970) suggested several reasons as to the factors that may explain the short-term stability of tourist flow patterns. These remain relevant to contemporary travel patterns and are noted below:

- Information fed back to people in the generating country from tourists who have made previous visits to the destination country (see also Chapters 2, 4 and 9 on different aspects on the marketing of the tourism product).

- Distance as a factor influencing travel patterns (including route, time and cost distance rather than just absolute distance). This is discussed further in the next section.

- The presence or absence of other types of international connectivity, past or present, will tend to stimulate or inhibit international tourist patterns. Examples of connectivity include international trade, labour migration, political allegiances, colonial ties and shared culture (McKercher & Decosta 2007). It was also noted that political-cultural barriers would inhibit tourist flows.

- Some factors of attractiveness, such as climate, have a strong influence on travel flows (Scott et al. 2012). For example, the existence of a heliotropic or sun-seeking factor in international tourism is borne out in the north-south flows that can be identified in terms of the substantial northern European international travel to the Mediterranean countries and similar flows from Canada and the northern United States to the southern United States, Mexico and the Caribbean.

- The relative cost of different potential destinations (Dwyer and Kim 2003).

- The existence of intervening opportunities, i.e. the potential for a stopover while undertaking long-haul travel between other countries, some of the best known examples include Hong Kong and Singapore with others such as Malaysia, Thailand and Vietnam also competing for hub status and therefore a potential stopover location for travel flows between Europe and Australasia.

- Events have only a short-term effect on travel flows.

- The stability of destination image in generating areas.

- National cultural traits in generating areas with respect to factors such as risk.

Distance as a determinant of the flows and patterns of contemporary tourism

Many of the factors identified by Williams and Zelinsky have been picked up in more contemporary tourism literature (e.g. Lew et al. 2004; Shaw & Williams 2004; Romão et al. 2012). For example, Hall (2005a) focused on the importance of distance as an explanatory variable for the distribution of tourists and tourism production, as the distribution of travel behaviour in space and time reflects an ordered adjustment to the factor of distance, whether it be in the form of space-time, economic, network, cognitive, social, or cultural distance. According to Tobler (1970, 2004) the first law of geography is that everything is related to everything else, but near things are more related than distant things. This statement provides an accurate assessment of observed regularity in human behaviour and the role of distance as a fundamental concept with respect to notions of the relations between places, such as tourism destinations and generating regions. For example, travel and locational decisions are generally taken in order to minimise the frictional effects of distance, with some destinations being more accessible than others (McKercher et al. 2008). Hall (2005a, 2008a) has even gone so far as to suggest that there are six laws of tourism although they are related to mobility overall:

1 *The distribution of travel behaviour in space and time reflects an ordered adjustment to the factor of distance.* Types of distance that influence tourism include

   - *Euclidean distance* which is the direct physical distance between locations.

   - *Time-distance* which is the time taken to travel between locations;

- *Economic-distance* (*cost distance*) which is the monetary cost incurred in overcoming physical distance between two locations.

- *Gravity distance*, a subset of time/economic distance but reinforces notion that closer means less effort and is important for a range of behaviours including estimated size of markets for locations and attractions.

- *Network distance*, which is the distance between locations via intermediate points, as in a transport network or telecommunication network. This can also sometimes be referred to as *route* or *'Manhattan'* distance.

- *Cognitive distance* (*perceived distance*) which are judgments regarding the spatial separation of locations. Cognitive distance is particularly important, for example, to the ways that actual or potential travellers collect, structure and recall information with respect to locations in physical space and establish mental maps.

- *Social distance* which is a distance component associated with differences between social classes (which possess different socio-economic characteristics) which may be expressed in terms of the locational characteristics of class or status.

- *Cultural distance*, related to the above but refers more specifically to differences between cultures and how that is expressed in perceptions of distance.

2 *Travel and locational decisions are generally taken in order to minimise the frictional effects of distance.* This concept is also often referred to as the 'law of minimum effort' or 'least effort'. In tourism, exceptions to this rule arguably apply when the trip itself is part of the attraction or is the 'destination', e.g. travel on a cruiseship.

3 *Destinations and locations are variably accessible with some destinations more accessible than others.* Accessibility is a variable quality of any location but basically refers to the ease of getting to a place and is closely related to the concept of movement-minimization, especially when this is measured by the costs involved in overcoming distance.

4 *There is a tendency for human activities to agglomerate to take advantage of scale economies.* Scale economies refers to how activities, such as firm operations, may be concentrated in certain locations in order to make savings with respect to economic and time/distance costs. This can apply to industrial agglomerations and business clustering, including with respect to tourism related businesses, as well as to interdependent businesses within a tourism system at a destination level (Michael et al. 2007). However, it can also apply to social relationships as well, for example, with respect to meetings and conventions.

5 *The organization of spatial and non-spatial aspects of human activity is essentially hierarchical in nature.* In part this occurs as a result of interrelationships between agglomeration tendencies and accessibility. More accessible locations appear to be the sites of larger agglomerations and vice versa. One of the implica-

tions from this is that for a given geographical area, e.g. a country, there is a hierarchy of locations in terms of accessibility. This is something that becomes readily apparent when considering relationships between airport traffic or that of other transport nodes and the areas they serve.

6   *Human activities and occupancy are focal in character.* The nodes about which human activity is organized are agglomerations of varying size. Since these are hierarchically arranged it follows that there is a hierarchy of different sized focal regions. Again, this becomes evident when considering the order ranking of airports in any given country and the relative size of the regions that they service.

3

Of these six 'laws' Hall (2005a) argues that the first four are the most significant for describing tourism patterns, especially at a local level. Especially important is the concept of *distance decay*, which refers to the notion that the degree of spatial interaction (flows between regions, e.g. travellers) is inversely related to distance. The empirical regularity of this relationship is such that it is open to mathematical analysis through what are described as gravity models in a wide variety of fields such as transport and retailing. It is a deceptively simple but critical idea which in layperson's terms can be crudely restated as a tourist attraction or destination tends to attract more people from near locations than far ones (McKercher & Lew 2003). For example, Lee et al. (2011) studies the relationship between distance and destination choice of Hong Kong international pleasure travellers' activity over a decade and identified a constant pattern of distance decay with two secondary peaks. Their study suggested a threshold of a three-hour flight to Hong Kong for a five-day trip existed before demand declined exponentially. The concept is therefore very important as it highlights the way in which changed accessibility of a destination or attraction relative to that of other potential destinations and attractions available to the consumer becomes a critical variable in the success of the destination in the market (Albayrak & Caber 2012).

Describing tourism

Although mathematical modeling of human mobility, including leisure travel, is one way of analyzing and describing tourism patterns and flows, a more common descriptive approach in tourism studies is to describe tourism according to the motivations, behaviours and activities of tourists or by other characteristics. For example, an extremely widely term that combines aspects of both the characteristics of the tourist as well as the production of tourism experiences which is used by both academics and in the media is 'mass tourism' but what exactly is it?

■   Mass and alternative tourism

At its simplest interpretation, mass tourism refers to the production of industrially organised tourism that supports the movement of large numbers of people. The primary quantitative element of mass tourism is the large numbers of people undertaking leisure travel that requires overnight stays away from home (e.g. Bramwell 2004). A secondary quantitative element of mass tourism is the relatively high proportion of visitors to a destination who have purchased a package tour (e.g. Burns 1999). However, many of the elements of mass tourism are more qualitative in scope, with mass tourists often being stereotyped in terms of 'herd-like, lacking internal social distinctions, doggedly seeking amusement, and guided by mass produced tour books' (Furlough 1998: 248).

The beginning of mass tourism is usually identified with the development of the first packaged tours utilizing railway and/or steamship based travel in the mid-nineteenth century (Walton 1983, 2000). However, its contemporary form is usually associated with jet-based package tours. The expression 'mass tourism' also arguably has an elitist connotation to it, as it often implies travel by poorer, less well-educated people to destinations that the wealthier and 'more discerning' do not travel to, or have ceased traveling to (Hall 2011). For example, Burns (1999: 46) described mass tourists as 'a continuous flux of visitors of middle class income and values expecting trained multilingual hotel and tourists' staff to fulfill their needs as wanted. They obviously expect western amenities'. As such the mass tourist is sometimes described as being dependent on their 'environmental bubble'. This bubble serves 'both to preserve some familiarity within a strange environment and to familiarise the traveller with strangers' (Mittleberg 1998: 28).

A number of elements of mass tourism have been described (Burns 1999; Bramwell 2004; Duval 2004):

- Highly seasonal tourism demand
- Middle and low class tourists from urban-industry areas
- Large numbers of tourists in ratio with locals
- Spatial focus on a few areas within the destination, associated with spatial concentration of facilities
- Exploitation of local values, behaviours and languages
- Organisation by international tourism operators
- Exploitation of natural resources
- Undifferentiated products
- Origin-packaged holidays
- Reliance upon developed generating markets

Because of these characteristics, mass tourism is also usually regarded as being harmful to the destination. For example, Bramwell (2004: 19) stated that 'concentrated mass tourism resorts have been criticised as they can overwhelm local environmental systems'. Bramwell argues that in many cases tourist may surpass the capacity that the host community can adequately handle and can discourage local economic and employment linkages. Stamboulis and Skayannis (2003) comment on the environmental degradation associated with mass tourism, and also the stress on the existing infrastructure and services within the destination. Similarly,

Conway (2004: 190) notes 'a very important *direct* environmental impact of mass tourism concerns the industry's increasing demand for receptor services that will take care of unwanted by-products'. However, the negative impacts of mass tourism are seen as extending beyond the physical environment. For example, Khan (1997: 989) states 'mass tourism development also creates an economic demand for the trappings of local culture' which indicates the possible commoditisation of local cultures within the destination where mass tourism is occurring. Mowforth and Munt (1998) also argue that mass tourism, aided by large corporations, results in the mass displacement of communities.

3

However, while mass tourism undoubtedly has impacts on destinations, the nature of those impacts are increasingly being questioned. In particular, there is a realization that the impacts of tourism in terms of urbanization (Hall 2006) and even cultural change are arguably little different from other forms of economic development. This may mean that although tourism is not necessarily as clean and green as sometimes made out, it is not necessarily any worse (Butcher 2003). And, in the case of cultural change, the role of international media and the activities of proselytizing church groups and missionaries may be much more substantial than international tourism, but are all part of processes of cultural globalization and human mobility (Salazar 2010).

Furthermore, detailed analysis of the environmental dimensions of mass tourism from a tourism system approach (see Chapter 1) also raises questions about its relative environmental impact. In a study comparing the environmental footprint of Tunisia as a mass tourism destination and the Seychelles as an ecotourism destination, Marzouki et al. (2012) found that tourists to Tunisia had a footprint of the order of 0.53 gha per tourist for a length of stay of 5.1 days and those to the Seychelles a footprint of the order of 1.85 gha per tourist for a length of stay of 10.4 days. The distance travelled to such an ecotourism destination had a substantial impact on the footprint (see also case study 1.1). 'The shorter the distance tourists travel, the less pressure is brought to bear on the environment at the global level' (Marzouki et al. 2012: 131). However, the study also highlights the difference between understanding the environmental effects of tourism in relative or absolute terms. On a relative per visitor basis, tourism in mass tourism destinations may be extremely efficient and have smaller environmental impacts than an ecotourism destination. However, in absolute terms the impacts are larger at the destination scale. The volume of tourists going to Tunisia was at least 30 times greater than that visiting the Seychelles (for the baseline years chosen by Marzouki et al. (2012) for the two countries). In this way, the aggregated environmental footprint of tourism for the Seychelles corresponds to 12% of the total aggregated footprint for Tunisia, although the arrivals in the Seychelles represent only 3% of the total tourism arrivals in Tunisia.

Because of the perceived negative impacts of mass tourism and changes in tourism consumption, some people have argued that there is a move away from mass tourism towards 'alternative' or more 'special interest' forms of tourism.

Eadington and Smith (1992: 3) defined alternative tourism as 'forms of tourism that are consistent with natural, social and community values and which allow both hosts and guests to enjoy a positive and worthwhile interaction and shared experiences'. Pearce (1992) developed the notion of *polar opposites* whereby alternative tourism and mass tourism were complete opposites, moving in different directions. Hunter (2002) described the differences between these two forms of tourism. Mass tourism involves large-scale businesses, large numbers of tourists being transported *en masse*, and experiences for the tourists which are much like their own home lifestyle (Hunter 2002). Alternative tourism, on the other hand, is described by Hunter (2002) as being small in scale, has minimal impacts on local culture and the environment, and the tourists wish to have a genuine experience of the local lifestyle with 'ecotourism', 'soft tourism' and 'sustainable tourism' being identified as some of these forms of alternative tourism. However, this dualistic approach to mass and alternative tourism has come to be substantially criticized (Weaver 2011).

Clarke (1997) argued that constructing sustainable tourism and mass tourism as polar opposites that represented the 'good' and the 'bad' respectively was a conceptual barrier between both types of tourism (Clarke 1997). Instead, mass and sustainable tourism formed more of a continuum (Hall 1998, 2008b) (Figure 3.1). Indeed, Bramwell in his review of mass coastal tourism in the Mediterranean noted the 'appropriateness of mass tourism depends on the precise context of each destination' (Bramwell 2004: 18). Similarly, Butcher (2003: 26) argued that 'mass tourism can be sustainable' and that when researchers focus only on the new aspects of tourism (such as alternative tourism) they are being very narrow-minded. These are issues that will be examined in more detail in Chapter 8 on tourism planning.

A further complicating element in discussions of mass and alternative tourism is that the attributes of the tourist are usually interwoven with attributes of the destination and the supporting infrastructure for the trip along all its stages. However, such a combination of elements is highly problematic in at least two ways. First, tourism is co-produced, meaning that destinations should not be seen as passive elements in the development of tourism and are as much contributors to particular forms of tourism as well as the patterns and flows of visitors associated with them. Second, and even more significant, it is quite likely that in the same trip a consumer can move between different forms of tourism so that they are engaging in mass tourism at one point in time and alternative tourism at another. How would such a situation lead to an effective description of the tourist or might it actually reflect a characteristic of modern tourism?

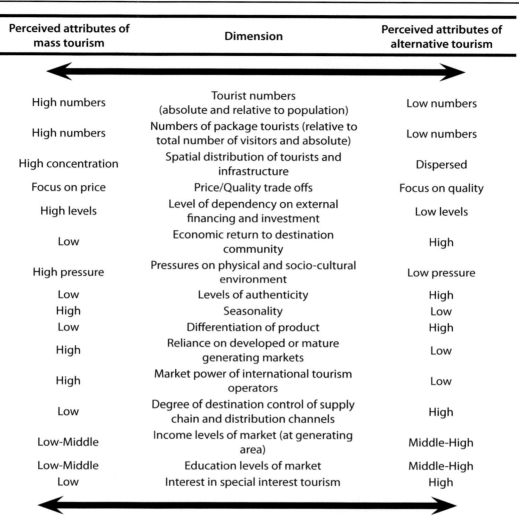

Perceived attributes of mass tourism	Dimension	Perceived attributes of alternative tourism
High numbers	Tourist numbers (absolute and relative to population)	Low numbers
High numbers	Numbers of package tourists (relative to total number of visitors and absolute)	Low numbers
High concentration	Spatial distribution of tourists and infrastructure	Dispersed
Focus on price	Price/Quality trade offs	Focus on quality
High levels	Level of dependency on external financing and investment	Low levels
Low	Economic return to destination community	High
High pressure	Pressures on physical and socio-cultural environment	Low pressure
Low	Levels of authenticity	High
High	Seasonality	Low
Low	Differentiation of product	High
High	Reliance on developed or mature generating markets	Low
High	Market power of international tourism operators	Low
Low	Degree of destination control of supply chain and distribution channels	High
Low-Middle	Income levels of market (at generating area)	Middle-High
Low-Middle	Education levels of market	Middle-High
Low	Interest in special interest tourism	High

Figure 3.1: Continuum of idealized attributes of mass and alternative tourism. Source: After Hall 1998, 2008

■ Special interest tourism

The confusion between description of *the tourist* and descriptions of *types of tourist* is also to be found in discussions of special interest tourism (SIT), a concept often closely associated with that of alternative tourism (e.g. Poon 1997). SIT occurs when travel motivation and decision making is primarily determined by a particular special interest, that is often associated with 'serious leisure' (Hall & Weiler 1992; Stebbins 1992; Hall 2005a; Brown & Smith 2010). Derrett (2001: 3) defined SIT as 'the provision of customised leisure and recreational experiences driven by the specific expressed interests of individuals and groups'. However, in a link to "alternative tourism" she also related the concept to the development of 'new tourism', defined by Poon (1997: 47) as the 'phenomenon of large scale packaging of non-standardised leisure services at competitive prices to suit demands of tourists as well as the economic and socio-environmental needs of destinations'. The 'new' and 'experiential' dimensions of SIT were also picked up on in Novelli's (2005) collection of studies on 'niche tourism' which arguably also has links to ideas concerning the experience economy (see Chapter 1).

Despite empirical and theoretical difficulties in categorising special interest travellers, SIT is often characterised, at least in part, by the tourists' search for novel, authentic, and quality tourist experiences (e.g. Derrett 2001). However, it is important to recognise that SIT needs to be related to the primary motivations of the tourist to participate in a particular trip or activity rather than just the provision of activities which meet such motivations (McKercher & Chan 2005). Otherwise, in the course of the same trip, even on the same day, and using categories to be found in the tourism literature, a visitor to a city such as London could be categorized as an urban tourist, a heritage tourist (when she goes to visit an historic site such as the Tower of London), a cultural tourist (when she goes to an art gallery such as the National Portrait Gallery), a sports tourist (when she goes to Stamford Bridge stadium to watch Chelsea thrash Manchester United in a game of football), a food tourist (when she goes to a Gordon Ramsay restaurant) and a shopping tourist (when she goes to Fortnum and Masons to purchase some Assam tea and a game pie). And potentially each time she undertakes one of these activities she may be added to the numbers of tourists that fit into that category.

Hall (1998) distinguished between special interest tourism which refers to cases in which the traveller's motivation and decision making are primarily determined by a particular special interest (the demand or consumption characteristics) and specialty tourism which refers to the supply characteristics of producing more specialised tourism experiences within the context of the setting (for example, rural tourism) and/or the activities (for example adventure tourism). Although there is an overlap between the two concepts, it is important to distinguish between the two because the size of the market that could be described under the rubric of special interest tourism is substantially smaller than that which participates in specialty tourism activities. For example, during the course of a trip a tourist could participate in a number of specialty tourism activities with none of them constituting either the primary or even a secondary motivation to undertake the trip or choose a particular destination. In the case of the tourist visiting London as described in the previous paragraph, her actual main reason to travel to London could have been to visit friends. Figure 3.2 illustrates the relationship between strength of motivation and number of tourists engaging in an activity with respect to different categories of what may be described as food tourism.

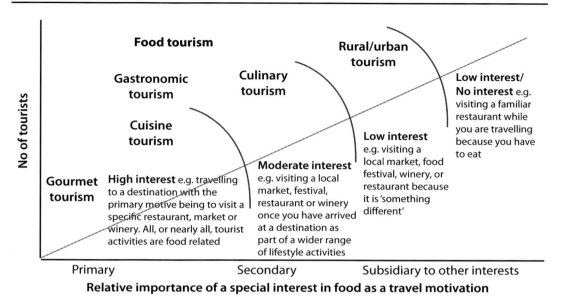

Figure 3.2: Food tourism as special interest tourism (Hall & Sharples 2003: 11)

■   Microscale approaches

Identifying and amalgamating the various motivations of travelers is a useful exercise in market segmentation but it is an exercise that is fraught with difficulties because it rests on assumptions of not only being able to adequately identify elements of another person's psychology but, in many cases, being able to rely on other people being willing and able to explain their motivations to someone else. Macrolevel constraints (see Chapter 1) such as money, time, culture, gender and health, are obvious influences on individual travel decision-making but this section focuses more on some of the psychological variables that are utilized to explain tourism flows and patterns.

Several influential typologies of tourists have been developed that focus on psychological types or personality traits. One of the first was that of Gray (1970) who identified pleasure travel as being grounded in two basis motivations, 'sunlust' or 'wanderlust'. Wanderlust is a 'basic trait in human nature which causes some individuals to want to leave things with which they are familiar and to go and see at first hand different exciting cultures and places... a desire to exchange temporarily the known workaday things of home for something which is exotic' (1970: 57). In contrast, sunlust depends on the existence elsewhere of different or better amenities for a specific purpose than are available locally. In 1972 Cohen created a typology of tourists that had four different categories; 'organised mass tourist', 'individual mass tourist', 'the explorer' and 'the drifter'. Perhaps more widely recognized in tourism marketing terms is Plog's typology of psychocentric, midcentric and allocentric tourists.

- Allocentrics are in line with Cohen's (1972) explorers and drifters and do not partake in mass tourism. Allocentrics tend to seek new and exciting destinations and are prepared to take risks (Ryan 2003).

- Psychocentrics however are akin with the organised mass tourist and the individual mass tourist. Psychocentrics include tourists who are self inhibited and have anxious or risk averse personalities. These tourists will seek the familiar and are happier in an urban environment. They are very conservative about their travel arrangements and select to stay close to home or, if they do travel abroad, will travel to destinations where tourists similar to themselves go (Ryan 2003).

Plog (2001, 2002) more recently reintroduced the psychographic scales but with changed descriptors: allocentric became 'venturer' and psychocentric became 'dependable'. Plog also asserts that the tourist population, like any population, is normally distributed with the true venturer segment representing about 4% of the population and the true dependable about 2.5%. Such personality and psychographic type models, which are highly influential in tourism studies, raise interesting questions about co-creation of tourism experiences particularly with respect to how destinations and their products adapt to leisure tourists over time. Plog, for example, in the original formulation of his work on psychocentrics and allocentrics believed the capacity to adapt, along with how tourists both perceived and experienced destinations, to be an important element in determining destination success.

Another way in which tourism patterns and flows are often described at the individual level is with respect to tourist motivations. Motivation refers to the process by which an individual will be driven to act or behave in a certain way (Decrop 2006). An example of a very common way of using travel motivations to identify tourism patterns and flows is the use of international and domestic visitor surveys and international visitor information from entry controls (Hall & Page 2006). Such surveys often ask visitors for the primary reason for travel and typically offer options such as leisure/holiday, convention, business, education and visiting friends and relations (VFR). An analysis of the results of such surveys will often reveal significant patterns in the seasonality of certain types of travelers (e.g. Spencer & Holecek 2007; Cuccia & Rizzo 2011). For example, in many western countries the peak period for VFR travel is Christmas with Easter also being significant, while in the United States the Thanksgiving Holiday is peak period for VFR often exceeding Christmas. Leisure holiday related travel flows tends to be strongly influenced by factors such as school holidays, and climate conditions in the destination as well as in the generating region. In contrast, business travel tends to demonstrate relatively little seasonality with the exception being that Christmas and New Year tends to be a low point in business related travel. Importantly, the patterns and flows of such motivationally categorized markets tend to demonstrate substantial inertia and significant rapid change only tends to occur at a time of external shocks (Hall 2010).

More detailed analyses of travel motivations often focus on the concept of push and pull factors (Decrop 2006; Bakir & Baxter 2011). These factors, that were originally derived from migration studies, seek to answer the question of 'why do people move?' Dann (1977) argued that push factors reflect the desire to travel while pull factors are concerned with destination choice. Push factors are 'internally generated drives causing the tourist to search for signs in objects, situations and events that contain the promise of reducing prevalent drives'. In contrast, pull factors are 'generated by the knowledge about goal attributes the tourist holds' (Gnoth 1997: 290-291). According to Dann (1976: 22), 'holidays are essentially experiences in fantasy... A certain picture is built up of a world that marks an escape from present reality, an environment for acting out psychic needs, and the playing of certain roles that cannot be fulfilled at home, and it is this which forms part and parcel of tourist motivation'. However, much of the research on tourism motivations does not account for change in motivation over time through the accumulation of experience and/or different stages in life. For example, Pearce and Lee (2005) observed that a core of travel motivation factors including escape, relaxation, relationship enhancement and self development seemed to comprise the core of motivation for all travelers that they surveyed in their research. However, they also noted that different motivational factors appeared related to different levels of travel experience with factors such as experiencing different cultures or being close to nature being more important for experienced travelers. For less experienced travelers, motivations such as nostalgia, personal development, romance, recognition, security, and stimulation were more significant.

■ Meso-level accounts of tourism

A key question in understanding and predicting individual travel behaviour is 'how do motivations and opportunities for travel and mobility change over time?' It has long been recognised that past travel and life experiences influence future travel destination choices (Pearce 2005). However, such changes are not easily captured without the use of longitudinal data. A key point of interest for tourism and travel research is the increased routinisation of longer-distance leisure and tourism mobilities (Hall 2005a; Frändberg 2006, 2010). Both transport and tourism researchers have identified the implications of the changing nature of social networks – larger and/or more dispersed set of social relationships – as being a critical factor in influencing travel behaviours that are undertaken in order to maintain such networks (Coles & Timothy 2004; Peeters & Landré 2012). The expansion of social and economic networks in terms of both activity and knowledge spaces has been referred to as the development of 'global generations' (Edmunds & Turner 2005) and is an important factor in distinguishing contemporary tourism from that of previous generations. Indeed, an important research question, with respect to describing tourism patterns, is the extent to which travel behaviours remain consistent over a generation.

One way in which generational change as well as individual changes in travel behaviour can be charted is through a life course approach. The life course paradigm emphasizes that changes in one dimension of the household-aging process, for example, are necessarily linked to changes in other dimensions, in seeking to explain behaviours. A life course approach suggests that the timing and order of major life events (e.g. partnership, separation, birth of children, retirement), be considered with respect to the relationships between the individual, age cohorts, and changing social structures. A life course approach also aims not to impose the idea of a normal life path as articulated in traditional life-cycle models; instead central to the concept of the life course is not the concept of stage but that of transition. Early transitions have implications for later ones with transitions occurring in 'personal time', 'historical time' and 'family time'. Warnes (1992) identified several transitions that affect travel careers:

- Leaving parental home
- Sexual union
- Career
- Family
- Children (income high/low)
- Career promotion
- Divorce or separation
- Cohabitation and second marriage
- Retirement
- Bereavement or income collapse
- Frailty or chronic ill health.

Membership in a cohort is a central factor in life course opportunities such as partnership, employment or the capacity to raise a family. However, the temporal category of birth cohort (or generation), which is a tool used by many researchers in examining consumer behaviour, may also be a factor related to value shifts (Mills 2000), including with respect to travel. As Mills (2000: 101) noted, 'Although one's spatial or physical location, for instance, may change as a consequence of migration, persons are born into not only a particular historical, but also a unique cultural and social context'.

A model for understanding the implications of a life course approach for understanding travel behaviour is illustrated in Figure 3.3 in which the life course domain is shown to be related to the accessibility domain and the mobility domain (Salomon 1983; Lanzendorf 2003; Hall 2005a). This has been done because lifestyle change is connected with changes in accessibility and mobility over the life course and the economic and time budgets that result, leading to different constraints on travel and changing motivations over time. In addition to indicating the factors that affect individual mobility, including with respect to tourism, life course approaches also highlight generational patterns in travel behaviour (Pennington-

Gray & Spreng 2002; Pennington-Gray et al. 2003; Leask et al. 2011). With the present generation of tertiary students (born late 1980s and later) arguably being the most mobile in terms of discretionary long-distance travel than any previous generation in terms of amount and distance of travel.

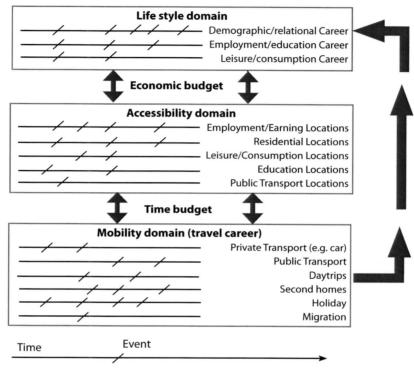

Figure 3.3: The construction of mobility biographies and life courses (after Hall 2003)

Summary

This chapter has described a range of different approaches to explaining contemporary tourism behaviour and flows. It started with an overview of growth in international tourism since 1950, with the remarkable factor in international tourism being the inertia in the tourism system. Several macro-level or structural economic, spatial and social explanations for international patterns and flows were provided with wildcard events being identified as key factors in affecting tourism growth.

The chapter then examined mass and alternative categories of tourism with particular attention being paid to the way in which such descriptions conflate consumption and production dimensions of tourism. In addition, the notions of mass and alternative tourism were also identified as having moral elements associated with them that may detract from their empirical dimension while, from a tourism system approach, the environmental benefits of mass tourism may be better in relative terms than previously recognised. Similarly, the categorization of various types of special interest tourism is also frequently confused.

Micro-level approaches that focus on describing individuals' travel behaviour were divided into psychographic and motivational approaches. Valuable as these approaches are, it was noted that they often do not sufficiently account for changes over the life course of an individual. Finally, it was noted that life course approaches may give an appreciation of cohort dimensions of tourism behaviour that highlight the fact that the younger contemporary tourist may well be the most mobile of any generation in terms of long distance travel.

Self-review questions

1   What have been the major trends in international tourism since the 1950s?

2   Why has international tourism been characterized as having considerable inertia?

3   To what extent does distance affect tourism flows and patterns?

4   What are the key characteristics of mass and alternative tourism?

5   Does the term 'mass tourism' have an elitist connotation?

6   What are the implications of categorizing different types of tourism by activity rather than motivation?

7   How might psychographic approaches to describing tourism be related to the success of destination in attracting tourists?

8   What are push and pull factors with respect to tourism behaviour?

9   What are some of the key transitions that affect travel careers?

10 What advantages may a life course approach have in explaining individual travel behaviour?

Recommend reading

Pearce, P.L. (2011). *Tourist Behaviour and the Contemporary World,* Bristol: Channel View Publications.
A good introduction to a number of significant topics in the study of tourist behaviour.

Hall, C.M. (ed.) (2011). *Fieldwork in Tourism: Methods, Issues and Reflections*. London: Routledge
An edited book with a range of chapters that discusses the difficulties of researching tourists in the field. Many of the chapters were written by then graduate students reflecting on the problems of research tourist behavior and flows.

Plog, S.C. (2001). Why destination areas rise and fall in popularity: An update of a Cornell Quarterly classic. *Cornell Hotel and Restaurant Administration Quarterly*, 42(3), 13-24.
> This update of a highly cited work on tourism psychographics outlines the inter-relationships between market and destination.

Pearce, P.L. (2005). *Tourist Behaviour: Themes and Conceptual Issues*, Clevedon: Channelview Press.
> Provides a good overview of contemporary understandings of tourism behaviour including the concept of travel careers.

Coles, T. & Timothy, D. (Eds.) (2004). *Tourism and Diaspora*, London: Routledge.
> Book focuses on the role of transnational networks as a factor in influencing tourism flows and hence is of particular interest for understanding both international flows of tourists but also the Visiting Friends and Relations market.

Hall, C.M. & Williams, A.M. (Eds.) (2002). *Tourism and Migration: New Relationships Between Production and Consumption*, Dordrecht: Kluwer Academic Publishers.
> A collection that examines the influence of migration on tourism flows and provides a complimentary approach to the work of Coles and Timothy.

Decrop, A. (2006). *Vacation Decision Making*. Wallingford: CABI Publishing.
> Book provides a useful overview of decision-making processes with respect to leisure travel.

Hall, C.M. & Page, S. (2006). *The Geography of Tourism and Recreation: Space, Place and Environment*, 3rd ed. Routledge, London.
> Chapter 2 provides a detailed account of issues associated with defining tourism demand and research on international and domestic tourism statistics.

Arlt, W. (2006). *Chinese Outbound Tourism*. London: Routledge.
> A benchmark study of one of the fastest growing international outbound markets that will dominate global tourism by 2030 and which also demonstrates different cultural behaviours in tourism from many Western tourists.

Williams, A.V. & Zelinsky, W. (1970). On some patterns in international tourist flows. *Economic Geography* 46(4), 549-567.
> Seminal article with respect to issues of inertia and change in international tourism flows.

References cited

Albayrak, T. & Caber M. (2012). The symmetric and asymmetric influences of destination attributes on overall visitor satisfaction. *Current Issues in Tourism* DOI: 10.1080/13683500.2012.682978.

Bakir, A. & Baxter, S.G. (2011). 'Touristic fun: Motivational factors for visiting Legoland Windsor theme park. *Journal of Hospitality Marketing & Management* 20, 407-424.

Bramwell, B. (2004). Mass tourism, diversification and sustainability in southern Europe's coastal regions. In B. Bramwell (Ed.), *Coastal Mass Tourism: Diversification and Sustainable Development in Southern Europe*, pp. 1-32. Clevedon: Channel View Publications.

Brown, C.A. & Smith, F.R. (2010). Wine tourism: A serious leisure approach. *Journal of Service Science* 3(1), 29-34.

Burns, P. (1999). *An Introduction to Tourism and Anthropology,* London: Routledge.

Butcher, J. (2003). *The Moralisation of Tourism,* London: Routledge.

Clarke, J. (1997). A framework of approaches to sustainable tourism. *Journal of Sustainable Tourism* 5(3), 224-233.

Cohen, E. (1972). Towards a sociology of international tourism. *Social Research* 39, 164-182.

Coles, T., Hall, C.M. and Duval, D. (2006). Tourism and post-disciplinary inquiry. *Current Issues in Tourism* 9(4-5), 293-319.

Coles, T. & Timothy, D. (eds.) (2004). *Tourism and Diaspora*, London: Routledge.

Conway, D. (2004). Tourism, environmental conservation and management and local agriculture in the Eastern Caribbean – Is there an appropriate, sustainable future for them? In D.T. Duval (ed) *Tourism in the Caribbean*, pp.187-204. London: Routledge.

Cuccia, T. and Rizzo, I. (2011). Tourism seasonality in cultural destinations: Empirical evidence from Sicily. *Tourism Management* 32, 589–595.

Dann, G. (1976). The holiday was simply fantastic. *Tourist Review* 31(3), 19–23.

Dann, G. (1977). Anomie, ego–enhancement and tourism. *Annals of Tourism Research* 4, 184–94.

Decrop. A. (2006). *Vacation Decision Making*. Wallingford: CABI Publishing.

Derrett, R. (2001). Special interest tourism: starting with the individual. In N. Douglas, N. Douglas and R. Derrett (Eds.), *Special Interest Tourism*, pp. 1-24. Brisbane: Wiley.

Duval, D.T. (2004). Trends and circumstances in Caribbean tourism. In D.T. Duval (Ed.), *Tourism in the Caribbean* pp.3-22. London: Routledge.

Dwyer, L. Kim, C. (2003). Destination competitiveness: Determinants and indicators. *Current Issues in Tourism* 6, 369-414.

Eadington, W.R. & Smith, V.S. (1992). Introduction: The emergence of alternative forms of tourism. In V.L. Smith and W.R. Eadington (Eds.), *Tourism Alternatives: Potentials and Problems in the Development of Tourism*, pp. 1-12. Philadelphia: University of Pennsylvania Press.

Edmunds, J. & Turner, B.S. (2005). Global generations: Social change in the twentieth century. *British Journal of Sociology* 56(4), 559-577.

Frändberg, L. (2006). International mobility biographies: A means to capture the institutionalisation of long-distance travel? *Current Issues in Tourism* 9, 320-334.

Frändberg, L. (2010). Activities and activity patterns involving travel abroad while growing up: The case of young Swedes. *Tourism Geographies* 12(1), 100-117.

Furlough, E. (1998). Making mass vacations: Tourism and consumer culture in France, 1930s to 1970s. *Comparative Studies in Society and History,* 40, 247-286.

Gabbat, A. (2010). Volcanic ash cloud cost European business up to €2.5bn, says EU. *The Guardian* 27 April. Online. Available HTTP: http://www.guardian.co.uk/world/2010/apr/27/iceland-volcano-cost-business-europe. (accessed 28 April 2010).

Gnoth, J. (1997). Tourism motivation and expectation formation. *Annals of Tourism Research* 24, 283-304.

Gray, H.P. (1970). *International Travel–International Trade,* Lexington: Heath Lexington.

Hall, C.M. (1998). *Introduction to Tourism.* South Melbourne: Longman.

Hall, C.M. (2003). Tourism and Temporary Mobility: Circulation, Diaspora, Migration, Nomadism, Sojourning, Travel, Transport and Home. Paper presented at the International Academy for the Study of Tourism (IAST) Conference, 30 June – 5 July, Savonlinna, Finland.

Hall, C.M. (2005a). *Tourism: Rethinking the Social Science of Mobility.* Harlow: Prentice-Hall.

Hall, C.M. (2005b). Time, space, tourism and social physics. *Tourism Recreation Research* 30(1), 93-8.

Hall, C.M. (2006). Tourism urbanization and global environmental change. In S. Gössling and C.M. Hall (Eds), *Tourism and Global Environmental Change: Ecological, Economic, Social and Political Interrelationships,* pp. 142-156. London: Routledge.

Hall, C.M. (2008). Of time and space and other things: Laws of tourism and the geographies of contemporary mobilities. In P. Burns and M. Novelli (Eds), *Tourism and Mobilities,* pp. 15-32. Wallingford: CABI.

Hall, C.M. (2008b). *Tourism Planning,* 2nd ed. Harlow: Prentice-Hall/Pearson Education.

Hall, C.M. (2010). Crisis events in tourism: Subjects of crisis in tourism. *Current Issues in Tourism,* 13, 401–417.

Hall, C.M. (2011). Yes, Virginia, there is a tourism class. Why class still matters in tourism analysis. In J. Mosedale (Ed.), *Political Economy and Tourism: A Critical Perspective,* pp. 111-125. London: Routledge.

Hall, C.M., Müller, D. & Saarinen, J. (2009). *Nordic Tourism.* Bristol: Channelview Press.

Hall, C.M. & Page, S. (2006). *The Geography of Tourism and Recreation: Environment, Place and Space,* 3rd ed. London: Routledge.

Hall, C.M. & Saarinen, J. (2010). Polar tourism: Definitions and dimensions. *Scandinavian Journal of Hospitality and Tourism* 10, 448-467.

Hall, C.M. & Sharples, E. (2003). The consumption of experiences or the experience of consumption? An introduction to the tourism of taste. In C.M. Hall, E. Sharples, R. Mitchell, B. Cambourne, and N. Macionis (Eds), *Food Tourism Around the World: Development, Management and Markets,* pp.1-24. Oxford: Butterworth-Heinemann.

Hall, C.M. & Weiler, B. (1992). Whats special about special interest tourism? In B. Weiler and C.M. Hall (Eds), *Special Interest Tourism,* pp.1-14. London: Belhaven Press.

Hunter, C. (2002). Sustainable tourism and the touristic ecological footprint. *Environment, Development and Sustainability* 4, 7-20.

3

Jóhannesson, G.T. (2010). Tourism in times of crisis: Exploring the discourse of tourism development in Iceland. *Current Issues in Tourism* 13, 419-434.

Khan, M.M. (1997). Tourism development and dependency theory: Mass tourism vs. ecotourism. *Annals of Tourism Research* 24: 988-991.

Lanzendorf, M. (2003). Mobility biographies. A new perspective for understanding travel behaviour. Conference paper in *Moving Through the Nets: The Physical and Social Dimensions of Travel, 10th International Conference on Travel Behaviour Research*, 10-15 August, Lucerne.

Leask, A., Fyall, A. & Barron, P. (2011). Generation Y: opportunity or challenge – strategies to engage Generation Y in the UK attractions sector. *Current Issues in Tourism* DOI: 10.1080/13683500.2011.642856.

Lee, H., Guillet, B.D., Law, R. & Leung, R. (2011). Robustness of distance decay for international pleasure travelers: A longitudinal approach. *International Journal of Tourism Research* DOI: 10.1002/jtr.861.

Lew, A., Hall, C.M. & Williams, A.M. (Eds), (2004). *A Companion to Tourism*, Oxford: Blackwell.

Marzouki, M., Froger, G. & Ballet, J. (2012). Ecotourism versus mass tourism. A comparison of environmental impacts based on ecological footprint analysis. *Sustainability* 4, 123-140.

McKercher, B. & Lew, A. (2003). Distance decay and the impact of effective tourism exclusion zones on international travel flows. *Journal of Travel Research* 42(2), 159-165.

McKercher, B. & Chan, A. (2005). How special is special interest tourism? *Journal of Travel Research*, 44(1), 21-31.

McKercher, B. & Decosta, P.L. (2007). Research report: The lingering effect of colonialism on tourist movements. *Tourism Economics* 13, 453-474.

McKercher, B., Chan, A. & Lam, C. (2008). The impact of distance on international tourist movements. *Journal of Travel Research* 47, 208-224.

Michael, E.J. with contributions from Frisk, L., Hall, C.M., Johns, N., Lynch, P., Mills, M. (2000). Providing space for time: The impact of temporality on life course research. *Time and Society* 9(1), 91-127.

Mitchell, R., Morrison, A. & Schreiber, C. (2007). *Micro-clusters and Networks: The Growth of Tourism*, Oxford: Elsevier.

Mittleberg, D. (1998). *Strangers in Paradise: The Israeli Kibbutz Experience*, New Brunswick: Transaction Publishers.

Novelli, M. (Ed.) (2005). *Niche Tourism: Contemporary Issues, Trends and Cases*, Oxford: Butterworth Heinemann.

Pearce, D.G. (1992). Alternative tourism: Concepts, classifications, and questions. In V.L. Smith and W.R. Eadington (Eds), *Tourism Alternatives: Potentials and Problems in the Development of Tourism*, (pp.15-30). Philadelphia: University of Pennsylvania Press.

Pearce, P.L. (2005). *Tourist Behaviour: Themes and Conceptual Issues*, Clevedon: Channelview Press.

Pearce, P.L. & Lee, U. (2005). Developing the travel career approach to tourist motivation, *Journal of Travel Research* **43**(3), 226-237.

Peeters, P. & Landré, M. (2012). The emerging global tourism geography—an environmental sustainability perspective. *Sustainability* **4**(1), 42-71.

Pennington-Gray, L. & Spreng, R. (2002). Analyzing changing preferences for pleasure travel with cohort analysis. *Tourism Analysis* **6**(1), 1–13.

Pennington-Gray, L., Fridgen, J.D. & Stynes, D. (2003). Cohort segmentation: An application to tourism. *Leisure Sciences* **25**, 341-361.

Plog, S.C. (1974). Why destination areas rise and fall in popularity. *Cornell Hotel and Restaurant Administration Quarterly*, **15**(Nov.), 13–16.

Plog, S.C. (2001). Why destination areas rise and fall in popularity: An update of a Cornell Quarterly classic. *Cornell Hotel and Restaurant Administration Quarterly* **42**(3), 13-24.

Plog, S.C. (2002). The power of psychographics and the concept of venturesomeness, *Journal of Travel Research* **40**(3), 244-251.

Poon, A. (1997). Global transformation: New tourism defined. In L. France (Ed.), *The Earthscan Reader in Sustainable Tourism*, pp.47-53. London: Earthscan Publications.

Romão, J., Guerreiro, J. & Rodrigues, P. (2012). Regional tourism development: culture, nature, life cycle and attractiveness. *Current Issues in Tourism*, DOI:10.1080/13683500.2012.699950.

Ryan, C. (2003). *Recreational Tourism,* Clevedon: Channel View Publications.

Salazar, N. (2010). Towards an anthropology of cultural mobilities. *Crossings: Journal of Migration & Culture* 1(1), 53-68.

Salomon, I. (1983). Life styles – a broader perspective on travel behaviour. In S. Carpenter and P. Jones (Eds.), *Recent Advances in Travel Demand Analysis*, pp. 290-310. Aldershot: Gower.

Scott, D., Amelung, B., Becken, S., Ceron, J-P., Dubois, G., Gossling, S., Peeters, P. & Simpson, M. (2008). Technical report. In UNWTO, UNEP, and WMO, *Climate Change and Tourism: Responding to Global Challenges*, pp. 23-250. Madrid: UNWTO; Paris: UNEP; Geneva: WMO.

Scott, D., Gössling, S. & Hall, C.M. (2012). *Tourism and Climate Change: Impacts, Adaptation and Mitigation*, London: Routledge.

Shaw, G. & Williams, A.M. (2004). *Tourism and Tourism Spaces*, London: Sage.

Spencer, D.M. & Holecek, D.F. (2007). Basic characteristics of the fall tourism market. *Tourism Management* 28, 491–504.

Stamboulis, Y. & Skyannis, P. (2003). Innovation strategies and technology for experience-based tourism. *Tourism Management*, 24, 35-43.

Statistics Iceland (2006). *Iceland in figures 2006-2007*. Online. Available at http://www.iceland.is/media/Utgafa/Iceland_in_figures_2006-2007.pdf (accessed 26 November 2008).

3

Statistics Iceland (2009). Statistics. Tourism, transport and information technology. Online. Available at http://www.statice.is (accessed 1 August 2009).

Statistics Iceland (2012). Statistics. Tourism, transport and information technology. Online. Available at http://www.statice.is/Statistics/Tourism,-transport-and-informati (accessed 1 July 2012).

Stebbins, R.A. (1992). *Amateurs, Professionals and Serious Leisure*. Montreal: McGill-Queens University Press.

Tobler, W.R. (1970). A computer movie. *Economic Geography,* 46, 234-40.

Tobler, W.R. (2004). On the first law of Geography: A reply. *Annals of the Association of American Geographers* 94(2), 304-310.

UNWTO (2006). *International Tourist Arrivals, Tourism Market Trends, 2006 Edition – Annex*. Madrid: UNWTO.

UNWTO (2010). International tourism on track for a rebound after an exceptionally challenging 2009, UNWTO Press Release, Madrid, Spain 18 January 2010. Online. Available at http://www.unwto.org/media/news/en/press_det.php?id=5361&idioma=E (accessed 25 January 2010).

UNWT O (2011). *Tourism Towards 2030 Global Overview, UNWTO General Assembly 19th Session, Gyeongju, Republic of Korea, 10 October 2011*. Madrid: UNWTO.

UNWTO (2012). *UNWTO Tourism Highlights, 2012 Edition – Annex*. Madrid: UNWTO .

Walton, J. (1983). *The English Seaside Resort: A Social History 1750–1914*. Leicester: Leicester University Press.

Walton, J. (2000). *The British Seaside: Holidays and Resorts in the Twentieth Century*. Manchester: Manchester University Press.

Warnes, A. (1992). Migration and the life course. In Champion, A. and Fielding, A. (Eds). *Migration Processes and Patterns, Vol.1, Research Progress and Prospects*, pp. 175-187. London: Belhaven.

Wearden, G. (2010). Airline industry takes $1.7bn hit from volcanic ash disruption: Trade body IATA says airlines should not pay the bill for poor decision making by European politicians. *The Guardian* 21 April. Online. Available HTTP: http://www.guardian.co.uk/business/2010/apr/21/airline-industry-cost-volcanic-ash (accessed 22 April 2010).

Weaver, D. (2011). Small can be beautiful, but big can be beautiful too - and complementary: towards mass/alternative tourism synergy. *Tourism Recreation Research* 36, 186-189.

Williams, A.V. & Zelinsky, W. (1970). On some patterns in international tourist flows. *Economic Geography* 46(4), 549-567.

World Tourism Organization (1997). *Tourism 2020 Vision*. Madrid: World Tourism Organization.

World Tourism Organization (WTO) (2001). *Tourism 2020 Vision – Global Forecasts and Profiles of Market Segments*, Madrid: World Tourism Organization.

4 Contemporary Tourism Marketing

Chapter objectives

After reading this chapter you will:

- Be aware of the scope and definition of contemporary tourism marketing.

- Be familiar with the evolution of marketing focus from goods to services.

- Understand the nature and dimensions of the contemporary tourism marketing environment.

- Appreciate the need for tourism market information and the role of research.

- Recognise the central role of relationship marketing in contemporary tourism marketing.

- Understand that technology is transforming the practice of contemporary tourism marketing.

- Realise the importance of innovation and new product development in tourism.

- Be aware that corporate social responsibility and ethics will play a growing role in contemporary tourism marketing.

Introduction

This chapter introduces the dimensions of contemporary tourism marketing. The chapter outlines current thinking in terms of the scope and definition of marketing and in particular charts the shift in focus from goods to services. Driving this shift has been the recognition that tourism marketing must focus on both the tangible and intangible nature of the service. But, as we have noted in previous chapters, above all it must focus on consumer needs and their involvement in the co-creation of the contemporary tourism experience and its products. We outline the dimensions of the increasingly turbulent and complex marketing environment for tourism, and conclude that particular types of organization will be best suited to success in this environment. This is a globalising environment, increasingly dominated by technology, and with demanding consumers interacting with connected knowledge-driven organizations. Finally, the chapter focuses on the contemporary tourism marketing practices that will be essential for success in this environment. These are research-driven market information delivering a deep knowledge of the consumer; relationship marketing focussing on the 'life time value' of a continuous relationship with market actors; the imperative for innovation through new product development; the smart use of technology to build relationships with customers and understand them; and finally, the evolution of tourism towards societal marketing. This involves the contemporary tourism marketers recognising the broader needs of society through ethical and socially responsible behaviour in their operations.

Definitions and contemporary tourism marketing approaches

Marketing as a concept is evolving quickly and, interestingly for tourism, there is a growing trend to conceptualise marketing based upon services rather than physical goods. There are many definitions of marketing and they all focus around the need to identify and supply customer needs. Inevitably, definitions tend to reflect the prevailing thinking of the time, with early definitions, for example, tending to stress the management of the marketing function. More recently, the focus is upon the many actors in the marketplace. Kotler et al's (2003) definitions are the most commonly used:

A market is:

'A set of actual and potential buyers who might transact with a seller. This market can be a physical or virtual space' (Kotler et al. 2003: 20).

Marketing is:

'A social and managerial process by which individuals and groups obtain what they need and want through creating and exchanging products and value with others' (Kotler et al. 2003: 12).

These definitions work well for tourism as they include the non-profit sector (such as destination marketing organizations (DMOs), but do not lose sight of the two central concepts of marketing – the concept of exchange and the imperative to supply consumer needs:

1   The concept of exchange states that exchange takes place when parties agree about a transaction and will be worse off without the exchange – it therefore creates value. Transactions are the way that tourism marketing managers calibrate exchange. Relationships in the tourism marketplace lead to exchanges and naturally have led to the concept of relationship marketing where the nurturing of the relationship is more important than single exchanges. Given

the nature of tourism as a high involvement product, relationship marketing plays an important role and is facilitated by technology.

2   The process of identifying and supplying consumer needs lies at the heart of tourism marketing. The marketing concept is tightly focussed on delivering value to the consumer, where value is viewed as the difference in the benefits that consumer receives from the product and the costs of obtaining it. There is an important difference here between the marketing of tourism and that of physical goods.

For tourism, a marketing orientation implies that an organization displays four characteristics:

1   A dominant marketing philosophy which demonstrates an unwavering focus on the consumer and which is underpinned by research.

2   It encourages exchange and strengthens both its networks and loyalty by recognising the importance of developing long-term relationships with customers.

3   A thought process accepting that strategic and tactical planning goes hand-in-hand and includes a tolerance of innovative thinking.

4   It demonstrates an integrated organisational structure geared to the organization's goals of delivering value to the consumer through business-to-customer, customer-to-business and business-to-business activities.

The road to achieving these characteristics is shown in Table 4.1.

Table 4.1: Translating the marketing orientation into action

Task	Marketing function
Identifying consumer needs	Marketing research
Analyzing marketing opportunities	Market segmentation and understanding relationships
Translating needs into products	Product planning and formulation
Determining product value in different seasons	Pricing policy and creation of value delivery
Making the product available	Distribution policy
Informing and motivating the customer	Promotion strategy and tactics

Source: Cooper et al. 2005: 583.

Evolution towards a services marketing approach

There are opposing views of the evolution of marketing:

■ Evolution by production orientation

Some authors have identified key stages of the evolution of marketing in terms of the orientation of production (see for example Kotler et al. 2010; Cooper 2011). These stages are:

- **Production orientation** The industrialisation of tourism in the 1960s and 1970s saw a focus on making products available (beds and airline seats). This bred an inward-looking producer approach that did not need to consider the consumer.

- **Sales orientation** Once more product was available, the emphasis switched to securing sales. The focus was on exchange rather than building a longer-term relationship, simply persuading consumers to buy rather than understanding their decision-making process.

- **Marketing orientation** The marketing approach is driven by research to understand the consumer in a competitive market place. Many tourism organizations have yet to move to this stage – particularly small businesses.

- **Societal marketing** Here marketing is done in a way that 'maintains or improves the consumer's and society's well-being' (Kotler et al. 2003: 25). It takes into account the broader needs of society rather than just the consumer, and is exemplified by the movement towards corporate social responsibility (CSR), which is dealt with at the end of this chapter.

Evolution by marketing thought

The second approach to evolution has been pioneered by authors such as Vargo and Lusch (2004) and Gummesson (2010). These authors chart the evolution of marketing thought and show how it has swung from one extreme to the other:

1 Nineteenth-century thinking viewed marketing as based upon the exchange principle inherited from economics. This focuses on the unit of output and places goods in the centre of the stage. When marketing is based upon goods, it focuses on tangibility, embedded value and transactions.

2 A new paradigm emerged in the 1970s and 1980s that viewed services as different from goods. This contemporary thinking shifted marketing thought to a service-oriented view where the key drivers are intangibility, co-creation of value and relationship marketing.

3 By the new millennium, the notion of goods versus services was increasingly unhelpful and services instead were seen more as processes where the application of competencies (knowledge and skills) are used for the benefit of another party (Gummesson et al. 2010).

Vargo and Lusch (2004) have articulated this third approach as the contemporary logic of marketing – the service dominant logic (S-D) and it is very helpful for contemporary tourism marketing. In fact, it could be argued that the S-D approach provides a reorientation of the market for the firm as a whole to include human resources, leadership, IT and operations (Gummesson et al. 2010) They state that whilst the 4 Ps are a handy framework, they are in fact meaningless in an age where marketing is seen as an innovating and adaptive force and where the focus is on the continuous nature of relationships between all market actors, facilitated by technology. Their view is shared by Lovelock and Gummesson (2004), who agree that the dominant logic of marketing is reflected in an emphasis on provision of service, a theme that we stress throughout this book.

However, it is dangerous to take this trend too far. A maturing view recognises that goods and services are both part of the marketing offering and in fact what has occurred is more of a paradigm shift away from manufacturing to a customer-centred approach (see also Chapter 12). Here tourism organizations are beginning to collaborate, adapt to and learn about customer needs. As Vargo and Lusch (2004) see it, value is then defined by and co-created with the consumer rather than embedded in output. This approach to the product as the sum of services and goods has been termed 'the molecular approach' by Shostack (1977). He views products as made up of many parts, some tangible, some intangible – in other words an amalgam that is exemplified by the fragmented nature of the tourism product. This 'molecular' approach allows managers to manage the total product and to realise the synergies between parts of the amalgam.

However, we question whether contemporary tourism marketing, and indeed marketing in general, has fully taken these ideas on board. The services sector is a fuzzy and fragmented concept and this has held back the implementation of the S-D approach. In tourism we can add to this the very strong traditions of custom and practice, reflected in the conservative nature of the industry, so that tourism organizations are often a number of years behind other economic sectors in terms of their place in these evolutionary schemes. We suggest that tourism marketing remains rooted in the twentieth century and traditional approaches. The tradition of promoting managers up through the ranks rather than educating them, the view that tourism products somehow need a different approach and the later adoption of technology in the sector are all factors which are in part to blame. However, as the tourism market matures, there will be less of a place for the entrepreneur and professional marketing managers will be more in demand. The question is then whether the tourism sector has the professional and technical capacity to cope with the contemporary marketing environment.

The contemporary marketing environment for tourism

In the twenty first century, the tourism sector operates within a turbulent environment of rapid and unpredictable change. In addition, advances in technology have led to time compression, where products are instantly available, fundamental shifts in the way that tourism products are promoted and distributed and a complete overturning of the relationship between customers and the firm through social media. Overlying this is the heightened security concerns following '911', the inherent lack of loyalty in price-led tourism markets and the challenges of a knowledge-rich environment. Tourism markets are maturing and fragmenting as growth slows and competition increases. This is compounded by the paradox that much of the product in tourism is in fixed plant such as hotels or theme parks, whilst demand is fickle and unstable. This section of the chapter is structured using Day and Montgomery's (1999) four characteristics of the contemporary marketing environment:

1 Demanding empowered consumers

2 The connected knowledge economy

3 Globalising markets

4 Adaptive organizations.

■ Demanding empowered customers

The contemporary tourism market is defined by the 'post-tourist' as noted in Chapter 2. The customers are demanding, empowered and knowledgeable travellers who understand the industry and know how to take advantage of ticketing and pricing flexibility. As a result of the fragmentation of supply, technology and new product development, consumers have more choice and more ways to purchase tourism. This group are time poor and demand on-time delivery of tourism products and services to a quality standard. As a group, they want more control, are less passive in the marketing process and, in effect, are the ideal group to work with, in the co-creation of products.

Technology however gives this group of travellers control over their purchasing decisions, turning on its head the traditional relationship between the tourist and the tourism sector as the market evolves from 'customer centric' to 'customer driven'. Buhalis and Jun (2011) observe that travellers can benefit hugely from the information-rich and interactive nature of the Internet. They have access to a wide range of comparable product information, including transparency of pricing, they can book quickly and, increasingly, do not need boarding cards as equivalent apps for mobile devices become more common. Web 2.0 technology now allows travellers to collaborate and share information on line – in effect to become a commentator and co-creator of the travel experience through social media sites. Social media can be thought of as:

> 'Internet-based applications that carry consumer–generated content encompassing media impressions created by consumers, typically informed by relevant experience and archived or shared online for easy access by other impressionable consumers' (Xiang and Gretzel 2010: 180).

In tourism, social media include (Kaplan & Haenlein 2010):

■ User generated review sites such as TripAdvisor. These are replacing 'word of mouth' (WOM) with e-WOM as the one of the most trusted sources of information that influences a purchase and include both quantitative (ratings) and qualitative (opinions) information (Sparks & Browning 2011).

■ Social networking sites such as Facebook which are replacing the postcard as a means of letting peers know that they are travelling.

- Blogs and micro-blogs such as Twitter, which are effectively online diaries and stories, have the potential to facilitate powerful and influential discussions about tourism experiences and to influence purchasing, images and destination communication networks (Banyai & Glover 2012).

- Online or virtual content communities of like-minded travellers such as The True Travellers Society (www.truetravellers.org) who exchange information and ideas through postings on bulletin boards and social networks.

- Collaborative projects, such as Wikipedia which contains substantial information on tourism destinations and companies.

- Virtual game worlds and virtual social worlds, such as Second Life, which itself has a tourism and travel realm.

Of course, the advantage here lies with the traveller, and the tourism sector is having to catch up quickly or risk being left behind by new technology. Indeed, technology has flattened access to information and so completely changed the balance of power between the tourism sector and the tourist, begging the question 'who is in control?'

These technological innovations mean that traditional models of consumer behaviour and segmentation may not apply. Tourism marketers therefore must devise new ways of understanding these consumers by rethinking traditional approaches to research, as outlined later in this chapter. Here research is uncovering typologies of social media users, based upon frequency of use and the impact of the user. Simply using frequency misses the point that whilst everyone has the right to contribute to conversations and that in theory, every post is of equal value, in fact some users have more impact than others – celebrities, for example. Gallup (2011) built upon this approach by adding in the order of magnitude of participation and whether it is active or passive. They have identified three distinct behaviours:

1 **Creation** – *Bohemian* creators initiate their opinions frequently online and offline. *Casual* creators share their opinions much less often and entirely offline.

2 **Consumption** – *Active* consumers talk about their organizations and brands on their social networks every day. *Passive* consumers do not engage in these types of conversations.

3 **Connection** – *Connectors* intentionally connect others with information about organizations and brands. *Non-connectors* do not do this.

The imperative of understanding the new consumers, and of working with them in the co-creation of products is clearly illustrated in the following case study.

Case study 4.1: Consumer behaviour and generation Y

Much is written about generation Y and the fact that their attitudes, values and behaviour in the marketplace are different from preceding generations. This is a significant generation, the largest since the baby boomers, and they represent the future of tourism consumption (Solnet & Hood 2011). As a result the realities of their behaviour must be taken into account and researched. Yet there is little in-depth research on the tourism behaviour of generation Y – what, for example, will be the tourism behaviour of China's generation Y as they begin to travel the world? This case study outlines the consumer behaviour characteristics of generation Y and poses questions as to how this will impact on tourism marketing.

Generational marketing?

A generation can be defined as an identifiable group that shares birth years, age, and significant life events at critical developmental stages (Kupperschmidt 2000). In terms of consumption we can think of three significant generations:

1   The baby boomers, born between 1945 and 1964.

2   Generation X, born between 1965 and 1978.

3   Generation Y born between 1979 and 1994.

We outlined the life course approach in Chapter 3 and a continuation of this theme is the robust debate over the usefulness of using generations as market segments:

■   Supporters of 'generational marketing' recognise that each generation has distinctive values and beliefs and these influence tourism demand. Generations also experience common environmental variables such as culture, politics, media and world events, which in a sense describe a generation socially rather than biologically. As a result each generation has specific consumer behaviours which allow targeting in terms of products, promotion and services.

■   On the other hand, Kotler et al. (2010) raise the question as to whether specific marketing approaches and campaigns need to be devised for different generations. They suggest that those generations themselves represent large groups in the population, and that it is perhaps difficult to devise marketing specifically for such a large group. This is supported when we consider the definition of a generation as the years between the birth of parents and the birth of their children, tending to average around 20 years. Add to this the fact that the pace of change in technology and society will change social values immensely in 20 years, and a single marketing approach may be seen as inadequate. Adding to this complexity of changing social trends, couples are having children later and the generational span in some countries is approaching 30 years.

Despite the argument against generational marketing, we believe that it has an important role to play in tourism marketing. Indeed, companies that have used the same marketing messages to different generations soon found that their approach was not working. Examples here include using the same marketing messages to generation Y that was used for their parents, or simply approaching generation Y as a linear extension of generation X.

Generation Y

There is a range of definitions of generation Y (Beckedorff 2009). Most definitions state that generation Y are those born from 1979 -1994. They have been variously labelled as the 'millennial generation', 'connexivity kids', or the 'dot-com generation', but generation Y is now the accepted label for this demographic cohort.

The consumer behaviour of generation Y

4

Generation Y have been born into a period dominated by technology and thus demand almost instant connection to friends and peers through mobile phones and the Internet, using wireless, VOIP and mobile technology. The media, particularly broadband Internet and television, are important to this group in terms of reality TV and the spontaneous availability of programming. Digital convergence will heighten generation Y's abilities to treat new technologies as their own. This allows them to be consistently in touch, communicate and to join global networks - whether with friends on mobile phone networks, or on community web sites such as Facebook. They are also the most formally educated generation in history, aware of opportunities, world geography and tourism destinations. In other words they are confident, smart and technologically savvy. Finally, they have grown up in an affluent world where economic prosperity has grown and unemployment has been low; but equally with terrorism and changing economic fortunes they have experienced an uncertain world.

There are two conflicting views here. One is that with the economic recession which began in 2008, we have a 'lost generation' who will struggle to recover financially in later life. On the other hand, studies show that members of generation Y, despite growing up in the midst of economic downturn, are relentlessly optimistic and do not share the financial concerns and priorities of their parents. From a market research perspective, it is interesting that few studies actually survey members of both generations X and Y.

Generation Y intuitively understand the importance of networks and how to leverage from them. They tire of well-known brands quickly and respond equally to adverts in media such as the Internet rather than in the usual press and television placement. In terms of promotion, they respond more to humour, irony and honesty rather than the messages of their parent's generation where tourism brands pushed lifestyle and image. In particular they are the vanguard of the ethical consumer, favouring tourism products and destinations with strong social or environmental values.

For tourism, this means that successful tourism products and destinations must 'connect' with these consumers. It is less important to build products *for* them, but to build products *with* them in the classic model of co-creation. Generation Y recognise that knowledge is power and have a new language rooted in the digital age. This implies that marketing must use this language and provide truthful and comprehensive information. To summarise, generation Y are:

- Interested in experiences.
- Opportunity focussed.
- Strongly influenced by their friends and peers.
- Influenced by viral marketing and word of mouth.
- Technologically literate favouring interactivity and selective on how they receive and seek out information.
- Short term-focussed.
- Not brand loyal, but respond to campaigns focussed on local values.
- Supportive of consensus and collaboration.
- Concerned to achieve a work/life balance.
- Concerned to be connected.
- Strongly opinionated on social and ethical marketing issues and supportive of causes such as fair trade and volunteering.
- Family rather than work-centric – they are loyal to parents, friends and peers. Indeed co-purchasing with parents is common.
- Practical in their world view.

As a target market for tourism, generation Y are racially more diverse than previous target markets such as the baby boomers. For example, Demoor and Zhang (2006) have done a ground-breaking study of generation Y in China. They see this generation as more aggressive and rebellious than previous generations, looking to enjoy life and to spend money. They are creative, and follow fashionable products, displaying the generational characteristic of low brand loyalty. This has important implications for countries marketing into China for the outbound market that is predicted to dominate world tourism flows in the first twenty years of this century.

Key sources

Beckendorff, P.J., Moscardo, G. & Pendergast, D. (2009). *Tourism and Generation Y*, Oxford: CABI.

Demoor, P. & Zhang, W. (2006), China's Y Generation. *Orion Journal of International Hotel Management* 2(1), 13-17

Kotler, P., Bowen, J. & Makens, J. (2010). *Marketing for Hospitality and Tourism*, 5th ed., New Jersey: Prentice Hall.

Kupperschmitt, B.R. (2000). Multi-generation employees strategies for effective management. *The Health Care Manager* 19, 65 – 76

Solnet, D. & Hood, A. (2011). *Generation Y as Hospitality Employees. An Examination of Work Attitude Differences,* Brisbane: School of Tourism, University of Queensland.

Discussion questions

1   Taking the characteristics of generation Y outlined in this case study, what strategies would you use to market a destination to this group?

2   List the pros and cons of taking a generational approach to tourism marketing.

3   Generation Y are characterised by their use of connections and technology – how can this be used to attract them to tourism products?

Globalising markets

Whilst tourism has always been an *international industry*, it has not necessarily demonstrated the characteristics of a *global industry*. These include the growth of large multi-national firms, the movement of resources across borders, and the increasing permeability of borders as we enter a 'borderless world'. Globalisation is seeing distinct national tourism markets blurring to become globally-linked markets, fuelled by the homogenisation of customer needs and low transport costs; the tourism market in Asia is a good example here. Globalisation imparts two opposing forces on the contemporary tourism market environment:

1   Homogenisation of consumer preferences with communication convergence and the mass marketing of brands and lifestyles.

2   Fragmentation as mass markets break into molecular markets with smaller and smaller segments.

The connected knowledge economy

The contemporary tourism marketing environment is characterised by inter-organizational networks in both tourism value chains and destinations. This emphasises the importance of collaboration between marketing organizations and the need to form alliances and partnerships. More than in most economic sectors, delivering the tourism product involves the development of formal and informal collaboration, partnerships and networks. In both the value chain and destinations, loosely articulated groups of independent suppliers link together to deliver the overall product. These networks of cooperative and competitive link-ages are used to exchange knowledge and resources for competitive advantage. However, the growth of alliances, particularly cross-border alliances, does mean that markets are blurring within tourism and across other industries (such as technology) and as a result competitors in the tourism market place are emerging from unlikely sources – technology-driven companies such as Travelocity are a good example here. Finally, these organizations are becoming learning organizations. Using technology, they can remember consumers and their responses, learning more and more with each interaction. They make decisions based more upon facts than conjecture and are developing databases capturing market structure, market responses and market economics.

■   ## Adaptive organizations

A particular type of organization is required to succeed in this contemporary tourism marketing environment. Achrol (1991) foresaw success in this environment based upon organizations that act on the basis of coalitions and exchange, and are ambidextrous and highly flexible to cope with complex and dynamic task environments. He sees these organizations as hubs of complex networks with boundary-spanning management, and in many respects these organizations have strong analogies with destinations. Achrol's (1991) organizations are of two types:

1   **Market exchange companies** These are organised around consumers and markets – effectively a grand marketing information system, brokering and clearing information, consumer needs, products and marketing services. Environmental scanning and adaptive mechanisms are driven by both consumers and the market. The quality of its market information network will be the primary source of coordinating power. Many DMOs operate in this way.

2   **Marketing coalition companies** These adapt to the turbulent environment by developing many different forms of functionally specialised organizations, working within alliances. Each organization is adapted to particular circumstances and is exemplified by specialist tour operators who can draw upon different elements of supply at different times to customise their product.

Both these types of organization will need to be directly wired into the pulse of their markets and be flexible enough to react to market signals with customisation and speed. This will require flat organizations that are dependent upon the skills and competencies of their employees. Whilst this is still an unusual format for many tourism organizations, it will become the model for the future, based on networks, knowledge and flexibility.

The practice of contemporary tourism marketing

Given the characteristics of the contemporary tourism marketing environment, what are the key techniques and approaches that tourism marketers need to utilise in the twenty first century? The final section of this chapter examines five of these approaches:

1   Research-driven tourism market information
2   Relationship marketing
3   The use of technology
4   New tourism product development
5   Corporate social responsibility and marketing ethics.

■   ## Research-driven tourism market information

A tourism marketing information system – or knowledge management (KM) approach – is a vital, yet unusual, step in the development of most tourism organizations. Such a system involves assessing information needs, and then developing and seeking that information to both underpin decisions and meet strategic priorities. There are a variety of sources of market information available to the tourism marketer including:

- Internal records such as guest histories, comment cards, or staff debriefs.

- External sources of market intelligence such as competitor information. In tourism, much information on competitors and the composition of their products is readily and easily available through brochures and Internet sites. Increasingly, because of the explosion of information, tourism organizations are placing more emphasis on market intelligence, often from secondary sources, rather than engaging in the expensive exercise of primary data collection.

- Information and trends gleaned from social media. Here a new generation of market research companies has arrived who specialise in extracting data from social networking sites such as Twitter, Youtube and Facebook.

Combined, these sources amount to a huge array of rich and meaningful data available to the marketer. Deep and meaningful research is the key to understanding the contemporary tourism consumers and their needs in tourism; it informs the marketer when and how to intervene in the purchasing decision process. Marketing research is therefore a key element in the total field of market information. It links the consumer with the marketer through information that is used to:

1 Identify and define marketing opportunities and problems

2 Generate, refine and evaluate marketing actions

3 Improve understanding of marketing as a process

4 Show how specific marketing activities can be made more effective (ESOMAR 1995: 4).

Marketing research rather than *market* research is relatively new in tourism compared to other economic sectors. In tourism, research on consumer behaviour is not well developed and research is not focused on model testing. There are two reasons for this:

1 Tourism itself is a difficult activity to research. This is the result of several compounding factors. Firstly tourism purchases are highly involving, with an emotional element; however tourism is also an ephemeral activity demanding sampling of a highly mobile population meaning that tourists may be interviewed about their holiday many weeks or months after the event. In addition, the location of tourism research is often noisy – in crowded airports or other tourism venues. The travel decision-making process is also complex and difficult to isolate for research purposes and, of course, domestic tourism is more difficult to measure than international travel as no national border is crossed. There also remains debate about definitions of tourism, the scope of the sector itself and the categories that should be used in research questions (such as for age) as we noted in Chapter 1.

2   Another reason for the research-averse nature of the tourism sector is due to the fact that it has not felt the need for deep and meaningful tourism marketing research until recently. We must remember that most tourism organizations are small firms which lack the resources and formal training to engage in research. Not only is good marketing research expensive, it is often poorly managed in tourism organizations. The key here is the reporting process and the legibility of the information that is delivered to managers. In tourism, this remains a huge problem, as often the reports of researchers have not been tailored for their audience or the research is reported to an inappropriate part of the organization. This is often due to a lack of understanding of the research needs of differing areas of management activity.

Nonetheless, continuous research is integral to the marketing information system of contemporary tourism organizations. It delivers competitiveness and profitability and is used for two main purposes.

Firstly, it is used to understand the following aspects of consumer behaviour:

- Market analysis and forecasting – market volumes, shares and revenues.
- Consumer research for segmentation and positioning – the quantitative measurement of customer profiles, awareness and purchasing habits; and the qualitative measurement of attitudes and perceptions of the tourism organization and its products.
- Service quality research to monitor service standards and satisfaction.

Secondly, it is used to underpin decisions on new products and new product opportunities:

- Product and price studies – product formulation, pricing, consumer testing and price sensitivity analysis.
- Investment analysis for new products.
- Promotions and sales research – efficiency of communication and consumer reaction to sales and advertising.
- Distribution research – distributor awareness of products.
- Evaluation and performance monitoring – for marketing control.

■ The future of research-driven market information

There are a variety of future trends evident in the world of tourism research, the first being the need for a deeper understanding of the contemporary tourist. Swarbrooke and Horner (2004) and the Marketing Science Institute (2012) recommend a clear research agenda to understand consumer behaviour. They say that research should:

1   Focus on tourism purchase decisions, rethinking the journey to purchase now that technology is so pervasive in the process, for example, asking where consumption starts – is it Web browsing?

2   Focus on perceptions of destinations and products.

3   Improve the use of qualitative research and new techniques using mobile devices and social media to capture rich tracking data.

4   Understand tourists' perception of quality and their satisfaction with tourism experiences.

5   Develop longitudinal research to allow temporal comparisons.

6   Ensure that market segmentation techniques are research-led.

7   Research tourists' evaluation of competing products.

8   Research reasons for non-purchase.

9   Research cultural and geographical differences in tourism behaviour.

10 Explore the linkages between tourism consumer-behaviour models and those in other sectors of the economy.

4

Technological development is radically changing tourism knowledge management and research as the ability of computers to cope with complex data analysis and complex consumer behaviour choice sets is improving exponentially. The Internet, email and social media offer dramatic new channels for collecting and disseminating market information. This does, however, raise ethical and technical issues and has led to the development of new codes of conduct and concern for the ethical responsibilities of researchers (see for example, ESOMAR 1995). Web-based surveys can be combined with easy-to-use survey analysis packages to allow tourism organizations to bypass commercial research companies. This delivers cost savings as well as more tailored research and reporting. In addition, we can add to this list the need to research the rich data available on social networking sites. Companies such as 'DataSift' and 'Gnip' analyse Tweets and blogs to track opinions of products in real time, whilst other research companies such as 'Klout' can analyse the influence of those who post on-line opinions. This is a new departure for market research and one that has moved rapidly from a cottage industry to the mainstream as the sophistication of the technology has improved.

Despite improvements in technology, tourism marketing research still draws upon more traditional, qualitative techniques such as focus groups, critical incident research and Delphi surveys. These techniques are used to develop, screen and position products; and to understand the consumer and their use of products. There is also a greater use of secondary sources as the public sector is increasingly called upon to provide data from large tourism surveys in a form that allows re-analysis.

■ Relationship marketing

A key strategy in the marketing approach of Vargo and Lusch (2004) is to build relationships across the marketing networks of an organization. For tourism marketers, relationship marketing plays an increasingly important role both with other organizations and with businesses. Kotler et al. (2003: 390) define relationship marketing as 'creating, maintaining and enhancing strong relationships with customers'.

Relationship marketing differs from transactional marketing because it:

- Takes a longer-term view.
- Emphasises the relationship not the transaction.
- Focuses on trust, partnership, and research into the characteristics of the customers.

Relationship marketing is ideally suited to the new marketing paradigm, is facilitated by technology and works well in tourism. It is suited to tourism as in this sector the customer controls the selection of the supplier, brand switching is common and both word of mouth and e-word of mouth are powerful promotional media. It also recognises that tourism organizations should work towards building the lifetime value (LTV) of a relationship. This allows organizations to build 'customer equity', representing the sum of the lifetime values of the organization's customers. As a result, one of the keys to success is the judicious identification of customer groups. Other keys to success are that tourism organizations must recognise that regular customers are not always profitable, and that relationship building will engender true loyalty. In turn this will deliver organisational growth and profitability for the organization because customer acquisition costs are reduced. As Kotler et al. (2010) state, customer satisfaction is a pre-requisite for loyalty, which can be built through relationship marketing. Classic 'customer binding' approaches that are used in tourism include:

1. Financial incentives such as frequent flier programmes, frequent guest schemes and car rental preferred customers.
2. Social benefits such as providing a personal shopper or a key executive who is applied to the customer.
3. Building structural ties such as reservation systems locked into particular suppliers or customers.
4. Utilising social media to get closer to customers, for example by developing organisational Twitter feeds and Facebook pages.

The success of relationship marketing can be measured through customer retention rates, or satisfaction surveys and recommendation rates - indeed customer relationship research is a growth sector in the research industry. This raises the issue of 'trust and fairness' in the relationship, a growing area of research in marketing. With the increased use of technology to manage relationships, different groups of customers are treated in particular ways and if they feel disadvantaged by, for example, treatment over frequent flier points, they are increasingly likely to know.

Fyall et al. (2003) note that relationship marketing for destinations can be viewed as:

1. A tactical promotional activity often tied to databases.
2. A strategic tool used to retain customers and lock them into particular products and brands.

3 A fundamental business philosophy leading to genuine customer involvement and co-creation. The philosophy is to establish, build and maintain successful life-long relationships with customers.

However, they also note that it is more difficult to apply relationship marketing to destinations, due partly to the nature of the destination product, but also the fact that to be successful it requires destination-level cooperation.

Many organizations are now into their third or fourth generation of CRM and there is a danger that they believe that CRM is now routine, but there are many challenges ahead, including how to deal with 'bad' customers, data safeguards and ethics, social media and effective return on investment for CRM systems. Here the growth of social media has greatly enhanced organizations' ability to build relationships with customers, as we explore in the next section.

4

■ The use of technology

Tourism has embraced technology for over three decades, beginning with development of computer reservation systems by the airlines. However, it is the Internet that has acted to revolutionise the way that tourism does business. The Internet influences every aspect of the contemporary tourism business and has changed the culture and behaviour of how people purchase, search, and communicate, as we saw above. It connects companies, customers and governments at low cost and without constraints of time or space and as such is a paradigm-breaking marketing tool. This is because it has significant advantages over traditional communication media; advantages such as reach, low cost, richness, speed of communication and interactivity.

As technology develops, it is having a profound impact upon how marketing is practiced. Indeed, technology facilitates many of the processes that are needed in the new marketing paradigm of relationship building and co-creation. These include communication with customers, interactivity, tools for research, massive data storage and the ability to build, track and maintain relationships through social media and web behaviour.

There is no doubt that the Internet is ideally suited to tourism. Indeed, it has created a whole new marketing industry – e-marketing, which can be defined as the promotion of a tourism product, company service or web site online and can include a variety of activities from online advertising to search engine optimisation. It also provides a medium and delivery mechanism for consumers to gather information and to make purchasing decisions. In effect, the tourism sector has gone through a major process of rethinking its approach and business model since the advent of the Internet, a process driven not only by the considerable cost advantages of the Internet, but also by the fact that customers have taken advantage of the medium, demanding a response from the sector.

E-marketing allows the development of online brochures that can deliver rich multimedia content, blending text, images, sound and video into multimedia documents to overcome the intangible nature of the product. Through video and interactivity it delivers the ability to 'test drive' the product. It also gives tourism organizations the ability to instantly change dates, prices and availability on-line so saving expensive brochure reprints. Technology also allows organizations to individually target customers through 'narrow casting' to customise messages, utilise email and web links to engage in 'viral marketing' and employ social media sites such as Twitter. As such, the Internet gives small businesses and destinations a degree of global market reach previously unheard of.

E-marketing in tourism aims to generate traffic to an organization's web site, to engage the customer's interest, encourage repeat visits to the site and to convert that traffic into sales. At the same time, the organisation can track the behaviour and preferences of users and so learn more about them to allow for more customised interactions (Park & Gretzel 2007). There is a range of mechanisms for closely engaging with the consumer through e-marketing and for tracking use of the web site. This includes how often they visit, for how long and which pages are browsed.

E-marketing involves three key principles (Nova Scotia Tourism Partnership Council 2003):

1   Generate traffic to the web site

2   Engage the customer on the site

3   Convert the visit to a booking or sale.

Generating traffic

Both new and returning customers will visit a tourism organization's web site. They may be attracted through traditional media or directed by other on-line marketing activities including social media.

Engaging the customer

Good e-marketing provides content and links to add value to customers and so begins the process of interacting with them. Increasingly, tourism companies are using social media to interact with their customers and potential customers. This ensures that the customer uses the site and therefore the site must be as intuitive and useful as possible. This can be measured by the time they spend on the site, on-line feedback, viral marketing through the links they follow, and as we saw above, by their posts and opinions on social media sites.

Conversion

Conversion is the measurable output of on-line marketing and can be measured by the number of links followed, a boost in awareness of a destination or actual bookings/sales. This can be tracked using research.

A major impact of technology has been upon the tourism distribution channel. Liu (2000) and Buhalis and Jun (2011) observe that electronic distribution has a number of advantages:

- Drastic cost reduction achieved through the electronic processing of bookings (such as e-tickets and electronic confirmations) and other transactions.
- Automation reducing labour costs and office space.
- All information is up to date.
- Direct and personal links to suppliers worldwide.
- Direct and personal links to the customer worldwide allowing customisation of the relationship.
- Business is open 24 hours a day.
- It encourages customer-driven distribution through blogs and web sites (such as Mytripadvisor.com).

Of course, the entry of electronic distribution companies such as Expedia and Travelocity has decimated traditional intermediaries such as 'bricks and mortar' travel agents and as such they are rethinking their roles as specialist travel advisors. Tour operators, on the other hand, are reinventing themselves with the ability to flexibly package the product (dynamic packaging) and to deal directly with their customers. This shows that electronic distribution works well for tourism where the product is fragmented and web portals allow companies to provide and deliver a dynamic assembly of all of the elements of the product (Expedia and Travelocity are good examples here). Buhalis (2003) suggests that in the future tour operators will fall into two distinct groups:

1 Multinational, large and vertically integrated operators with economies of scale, wide distribution and a global network, taking a high volume, low profit approach.

2 Small, niche differentiated operators focussing on particular destinations or products, taking a low volume, high profit approach.

Despite the obvious advantages of its use, technology does bring with it certain constraints when used in marketing. For example, there are concerns over the security of financial information and personal identity as online fraud increases and consumers lose confidence in the Internet as a place to do business. This is particularly the case as there are no international standards for quality or security (Buhalis & Jun 2011). Most web sites are in English so creating a barrier to access, and in some countries access to the Internet comes at a high cost. In the future the limits to this technology will be economic, in terms of investment; human, in terms of attitude and habits; and technological, in terms of computing power, storage and bandwidth.

Nonetheless, despite these limitations, the future is exciting. For example, digital convergence is beginning to provide overlapping and ubiquitous use of computer systems with other devices such as entertainment systems, phones, tablets MP3 players and other devices. Here tour operators can create pod and video casts of destinations, using sites such as Google Earth, effectively creating very rich, interactive brochures.

For tourism, one of the most exciting marketing innovations is the use of mobile devices to access web sites, deliver marketing messages through say, social media sites and to enable travel information at the destination. Mobile phones have evolved to be smart computers where a range of tourism information can be accessed anywhere and anytime, particularly as the devices are location aware and can be used as tourist guides. They provide instant answers to tourism queries, allow the tourists to share experiences and post information and evaluations in real time, as well as acting as storage devices (Wang et al, 2012) Yet, despite the potentially game changing innovation of mobile devices, mobile marketing expenditure is still relatively small compared with other technology.

New tourism product development

An imperative for contemporary tourism marketing is innovation through new product development (NPD) (Hall & Williams 2008; Hjalger 2010). Changing tastes, technology and heightened competition mean that NPD in tourism is vital. As products and destinations progress through the life cycle, they need to be continuously refreshed and revitalised. Moutinho (1994) states that new products are the lifeblood of tourism organizations, delivering increased revenue, competitiveness and facilitating market positioning, diversification and growth. Failure to innovate risks failing to meet consumer demands, engage with new technology and keep up with the competition. In the contemporary tourism marketing environment there are two key competitive pressures driving innovation:

1 Increased competition, market complexity, and differentiation.

2 Decreased lead times and shorter life cycles.

Hogdson (1990) states that tourism has a number of distinctive characteristics that need to be considered when developing new products. As a result, the classic processes and stages of NPD are not always appropriate. The distinctive characteristics of tourism are:

1 Government regulation of products such as air routes and fares. This takes marketing decisions away from the tourism organization.

2 Public ownership and control of tourism resources means that many destinations and organizations are not purely commercially-focussed.

3 The inward-looking nature of many companies and organization acts as a constraint upon NPD.

4 The intangible nature of the tourism product means it is difficult to test and communicate, but easy to copy.

5 Many tourism organizations are research averse and do not have sufficient knowledge for NPD, or the ability to monitor the success of the NPD process.

This means that for many tourism products the classic step-wise model of NPD is better replaced with the stage-gate process. The stage-gate process places a stronger element of risk control at each development stage and is increasingly preferred by practitioners (Figure 4.1). The advantages of the stage-gate process are that it allows a decision to be taken at each stage, it has a smaller number of stages than the classic step-wise model, and it is more suitable for the contemporary marketing approach because it can easily cross organisational boundaries of, say, finance and marketing.

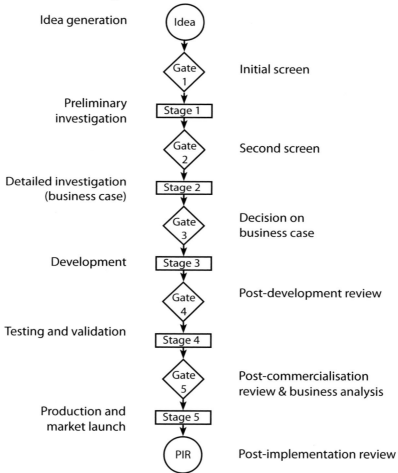

Figure 4.1: The stage gate process model.

An important consideration for NPD in the tourism sector is the organization's ability to integrate the NPD process and outcome with its existing products and marketing strategy. NPD must also consider the new product and its market placement. This will depend upon:

1 *Product newness.* There is a range here from completely new to supplements of existing products – the newer the product, the greater the unfamiliarity with the consumer and so the greater the risk of development (Table 4.2). In tourism there are few truly new products that demand a completely new marketing campaign. Indeed, because many tourism organizations follow a risk-averse path, real product innovation often comes from outside the tourism sector.

2 *Product complexity.* Complexity is measured by technology, number of product elements, functions and interfaces with customers and suppliers; and

3 *Commercial constraints.* These include investment available for NPD, consumer pressure for 'green' products, and legislation. In tourism, new products often have greater capacity. The new generation of Boeing and Airbus aircraft for example will require high levels of demand for viability.

Table 4.2: Degrees of product 'newness'

Definition of new product	Degree of 'newness'
New to the world	Entirely new
New product lines	New market entry
Additional lines	Supplements
Product improvements	Additional 'value'
Product re-positioning	Into new markets
Product cost reductions	For same performance

As a result of these pressures, Moutinho (1994) notes that many new products in tourism fail due to:

1 Poor assessment of consumer demand

2 Poor assessment of the competition

3 Poor planning and integration of the product into the organization

4 Poor positioning of the new product

5 Lack of resources to implement to NPD.

Up until this point we have discussed new 'products' rather than new 'services'. Here the question is whether 'new services development' is the same as 'new product development' or whether the processes are different. Of course there are similarities. For example, just as with products there are degrees of 'newness' of services. It is often more efficient to refresh or redesign services to serve customers better than to jettison and start again (see Berry and Lampo 2000). Nonetheless, we suggest that the two processes are different because new service development tends not to need large amounts of capital, but imitation and competition are more intense, demanding a speedier development process (Table 4.3). Finally, new service development suffers from the inherent conservatism of the sector and the fact that there is no tradition of new service design. For example when designing new tourism services, organizations:

1 Tend not to use customers or customer information

2 View the brand as less important

3 Are more likely to involve senior personnel

4 Develop a more formal process that requires greater organisational integration.

Table 4.3: A framework for service redesign

Service redesign concept	Potential customer benefits	Potential company benefits	Challenges/limitations
Self service: Customer assumes role of producer	Increases perception of control and speed of service; improves access; saves money	Lowers cost; increases productivity; enhances technology reputation; differentiates company	Requires customer preparation for the role; limits face to face interaction between customer and company; creates difficulty in obtaining feedback and establishing customer loyalty/relationships
Direct service: Service delivered to customer's location	Increases convenience; improves access	Eliminates store location limitations; expands customer base; differentiates company	Creates additional logistical burdens; may require costly investment; requires credibility/trust
Pre-service: Streamlines activation of service	Increases speed of service; improves efficiency; shifts task from customer to provider; separates service activation from delivery; customizes service	Increases ability to customize service; improves efficiency; increases productivity; differentiates company	Requires extra customer education and employee training to implement smoothly and effectively
Bundled service: Combines multiple services into a package	Increases convenience; customizes service	Creates opportunity to charge higher prices; differentiates company; aids customer retention; increases per-capita service use	Requires extensive knowledge of targeted customers; may be perceived as wasteful
Physical service: Manipulates the tangibles associated with the service	Increases convenience; enhances function; cultivates interest	Differentiates company; improves employee satisfaction; increases productivity	Can be easily imitated; requires expense to effect and maintain; raises customer expectation for the industry

Corporate social responsibility and marketing ethics

■ Corporate social responsibility

At the beginning of this chapter we identified an evolution of marketing towards 'societal marketing' which takes into account the broader needs of society rather than just the consumer. This is exemplified by the movement towards corporate social responsibility (CSR) which Dodds and Kuehnel (2010: 222) define as:

'A company's obligation to be accountable to all of its stakeholders in all its opera-tions and activities with the aim of achieving sustainable development not only in the economic dimension but also in the social and environmental dimensions'.

CSR can be viewed as pyramid where each element of social responsibility is important but where different organisations and different eras will emphasise one particular element (Carroll 1999). Figure 4.2 shows the pyramid, beginning with economic social responsibility for CSR as the foundation, moving up through the legal and the ethical social responsibilities and finishing with the philanthropic which can be seen as discretionary. There are four basic classifications of CSR ranging from the minimalist to the social activist (Table 4.4). Although it can be traced back to the 1930s, tourism has been slow to adopt CSR (Sheldon & Park 2011). Only in the twenty first century has CSR grown in profile in the tourism sector where it has tended to be driven by consumers and group pressure, rather than by tourism marketers. It represents a shift of marketing focus from an over-emphasis on profitable products and the consumer towards conducting business in the interests of the society in which an organization is based. Increasingly, organisations will be expected to undergo external audits of their CSR activity to prevent green-washing as an ethical approach to business becomes expected (Font et al. 2012). The following case study demonstrates an international initia-tive making considerable progress towards CSR in the supply chain.

Figure 4.2: The corporate social responsibility pyramid. Source Carroll, 1999

Table 4.4: Approaches to corporate social responsibility. *Source:* Hall and Brown (2012)

Minimalist	Philanthropic	Encompassing	Social activist
Basic stakeholder support	Project specific Related to specific issues relevant to the particular organisation	Looks beyond the immediate business stakeholder group to the broader community	Approach is the foundation of the business
Addressing aspects that are generally human resource-oriented	Donations and gifts	Embedded in company values and management style	Business is a catalyst for change
Tokenistic	Seeks to change	Seeks to lead change	Seeks to affect change in others

Case study 4.2: The tour operators' initiative for sustainable development

Corporate social responsibility (CSR) adds a new layer to the bottom line of tourism companies. Companies recognise that they must be accountable for their impacts upon society, the environment and the economy. There are two sides to CSR in tourism - some companies see it as a means of internalising sustainability with the potential for competitive advantage, whilst others see it as a means of avoiding regulation and managing risk (Schwartz et al. 2008). Essentially, CSR is about customer satisfaction, looking after the workforce and environmental protection. For most tourism organizations CSR is not yet part of their core business but there are efforts to integrate CSR throughout the supply chain.

Until recently, the tourism supply chain was a combat zone with members vying for dominance (Song 2011). Tour operators in particular are powerful in the supply chain, as they control the marketplace through directing tourist flows (Schwartz et al. 2008) Not only was this an issue between companies, such as accommodation providers and tour operators, but it was also an issue between tour operators and destinations themselves, with operators often seeing destinations as an asset to strip. A number of new initiatives have been taken to change these practices, and in the tour operator sector in particular there is a range of approaches to secure ethical behaviour along the supply chain. In addition there are moves to instil a sense of corporate responsibility for partners and destinations in the supply chain, particularly in terms of sustainability. Indeed, it can be argued that the supply chain is the perfect medium to communicate these messages to suppliers and integrate them into contracting practices. There have been both government initiatives to instil sustainability into the supply chain – the European Union's 'Travelife' project was one – and also initiatives from the industry itself. This case study outlines a highly successful industry initiative – the Tour Operators' Initiative for Sustainable Development (TOI).

The Tour Operator's Initiative for Sustainable Development

The Tour Operators' Initiative for Sustainable Development (TOI) was established in 2000 to catalyse action in the tour operation sector. The TOI aims to integrate sustainability as a guiding principle into all business practices and works to promote and disseminate methods and practices compatible with sustainable development. The TOI is a voluntary, non-profit organization open to all tour operators regardless of size. The initiative acts as a network and disseminates good practice and has the support of the United Nations Environment Programme (UNEP), UNESCO and the UNWTO. Their mission is twofold (www.toiinitiative.org):

1   To advance the sustainable development and management of tourism.
2   To encourage tour operators to make a corporate commitment to sustainable development.

This will be achieved by reducing the negative impact on host destination environments and communities through the design and process of tours and tour operators' business practices. The initiative recognises that suppliers and destinations are the core of a tour operator's product and that if those elements of the product are sustainable, with clean and pristine environments, then consumers will respond positively to their product. The approach has led to a range of benefits:

- Cost savings through efficient and reduced consumption of water and power.
- Increased revenues and shareholder value.
- Repeat custom and new business from clients who value a responsible tourism approach.
- Closer community relationships.
- A better image and reputation for tour operators.
- Enhanced brand values.
- Reduced risk of conflict with destination, governments and pressure groups.

As intermediaries, tour operators are unusual because unlike many other economic sectors, they directly influence the consumer's purchasing decision. They also have a major impact in the supply chain through supplier contracting (of airline seats or hotel beds, for example). It is this unique nature of the tourism supply chain that allows it to be such an important medium for the dissemination of good practice. The TOI has four key values:

1   Recognition of the importance of collaboration over competition in the supply chain.
2   A sustainable supply chain policy and management system.
3   Support for suppliers in reaching sustainability goals.
4   Integration of sustainability into supplier contracts.

The TOI approach

The TOI has three key objectives (www.toiinitiative.org):

1   Assist tour operators in implementation of sustainable tourism through adoption of best practices in their internal operations, the supply chain and in the destination.
2   Broaden the support for sustainable development among other players in the tourism sector including tourists.
3   Create the a critical mass of committed tour operators

This achieved through five groups of activities (www.toiinitiative.org):

1   Research and information exchange to share ideas.
2   Capacity building to assist members.
3   Technical support to further commitment to sustainable development.
4   Communication and PR to create awareness in both the public and the tourism industry.

5   Outreach to open dialogue with tour operators and stakeholders.

Responses to these activities vary across the sector and are summarised in a published set of case studies (TOI 2003). The TOI is at the cutting edge of cooperating with a number of pilot destinations (such as Side in Turkey and Punta Cana in the Dominican Republic) and is collaborating with the World Wide Fund for Nature on sustainable tourism in marine destinations.

Key sources

Dodds, R. & Kuehnel, J. (2010). CSR among Canadian mass tour operators: good awareness but little action. *International Journal of Contemporary Hospitality Management* 22(2), 221–244.

The Tour Operators Initiative (2003). *Sustainable Tourism: The Tour Operators' Contribution*, Paris: TOI.

Schwartz, K., Tapper, R. & Font, X. (2008). A sustainable supply chain management framework for tourism operators. *Journal of Sustainable Tourism* 16(3), 298-314.

Song, H. (2011). *Tourism Supply Chain Management*, London: Routledge.

Discussion questions

1   Why has this change in thinking amongst tour operators taken so long to emerge?

2   Draft the elements of sustainable practices that you might expect to see in a contract between a tour operator and a hotel supplier.

3   There are clear benefits for the tour operator in marketing their CSR to clients – what messages would form the basis of this promotion?

4

Green and ethical marketing

For a tourism organization, ethical values are the core beliefs and standards of that organization. Perhaps the best-known set of values is the global code of ethics for tourism developed by the UNWTO (WTO 2001). Ethics can relate to a variety of tourism issues and some examples include the impact of tourism on the environment, cultures and communities; the marketing of fast food; the invasion of privacy through tele-marketing or viral marketing; or the social impact of marketing alcohol. It can also relate to the relationship between the organization and the tourist in terms of fairness in trust in how tourists are managed by organizations and in social networks.

An ethical approach to the tourism market place may be cynically used to pre-empt the development of legislation applying to, say, responsible gambling. Indeed it could be argued that the tourism sector's uptake of green and ethical marketing has been at best tokenistic. However, there is no doubt that the ethical tourism market place also attracts particular groups of consumers. Goodwin (2003) for example, notes the growth of the ethical purchasing of tourism with an purchasing index which calibrates the ethical market place.

Fennell (2006) questions how easy it is for tourism organizations to market to the ethical tourist. He asks whether ethical holidays are just a ploy to increase the margins for certain target market groups and to exploit a trend in society. Often, the host community is closely involved in these ethically acceptable tours, but may in fact be exploited or, as in the case of the Tasmanian experience strategy case in Chapter 2, simply treated as the cast on the destination stage set. The ethical tourism market place can be used cynically to gain competitive advantage.

In the future the tourism sector will need to engage with 'deep ethics', the desire of the customer to 'do the right thing' (Fennell 2012). This will involve the need to understand their behaviour better by not simply researching their travel purchasing intentions (which are often altruistic and irrational) but focussing more on their actions when reality bites. It will also be important to consider the influences upon individual travel decisions by understanding the pressure from social networks and family to consume ethically.

Summary

This chapter began by conceptualising tourism marketing as involving exchange and a focus on the consumer. In terms of exchange, the contemporary approach demands a continuous relationship with marketing actors and has led to the development of relationship marketing and the notion of the co-creation of products and experiences with the consumer. This leads to the consumer focus. Over time, marketing theory has changed from a focus on output in the form of physical goods, to the idea of services, where the drivers are the co-creation of value, and the building of relationships with market actors through relationship marketing. For tourism marketers these new approaches are performed in a turbulent and complex global environment. This is characterised by empowered, demanding consumers, who are showing generational shifts in needs and wants, as outlined by the case study on generation Y. Suppliers are increasingly networked and knowledge-driven, leading to a particular type of flexible, loosely structured organization that is emerging as a way to compete in this contemporary tourism marketing environment. The chapter closed by considering five key contemporary marketing practices. In the knowledge economy, no organization can afford to ignore market information and not have a deep and meaningful understanding of their consumers. Tourism does not have a glowing record in this regard. Market information fuels the practice of relationship marketing, another concept explored in this chapter, where the life time value of the relationship is viewed as more important than individual transactions. Of course, technology, both computing power and the Internet, has facilitated both of these practices and will continue to pervade contemporary tourism marketing as e-marketing matures into its own science. The chapter outlined the imperative of innovation and new product development and the need to carefully structure and integrate that process into the organization. Finally, we illustrated the growth of ethical marketing and the role of corporate social responsibility, demonstrating this through a case study of CSR in the tourism supply chain.

Self review questions

1 List the actors in the tourism market place and classify their roles in the market.

2 How might companies engineer 'co-creation' of tourism products and experiences?

3 Debate the notion that tourism lags behind other economic sectors in its marketing thinking and approach.

4 Identify the factors that have changed the contemporary marketing environment since 1980.

5 Why is the knowledge economy so significant for contemporary tourism marketing?

6 Draft an approach for a museum to collect market information about their customers without resorting to primary data collection.

7 What do you understand by the term 'life time value'?

8 Why is the Internet so well suited to contemporary tourism marketing?

9 Is there a difference between new product development and new service development?

10 What do you understand by the term 'corporate social responsibility' in respect of contemporary tourism marketing?

4

Recommended reading

Buhalis, D. & Jun, S.H. (2011). E-Tourism. *Contemporary Tourism Reviews*, Oxford: Goodfellow Publishers.
A wide ranging and through review of the use and impact of technology on tourism marketing and the sector in general

Cooper, C.P. (2006). Tourism and knowledge management. *Annals of Tourism Research* 33(1), 47-64.
A review of the new science of knowledge management and its application to tourism, including marketing

Fennell, D. (2006). *Tourism Ethics*. Clevedon: Channelview.
Excellent overview of tourism ethics

Fyall, A and Garrod, B (2005) Tourism Marketing. A Collaborative Approach, Channelview, Clevedon
Edited volume thoroughly reviewing the use and role of collaboration and partnership in tourism marketing

There are an increasing number of excellent marketing texts with a tourism and hospitality flavour. These include:

Hudson, S. (2012). *Tourism and Hospitality Marketing. A Global Perspective*. London: Sage.

Morgan, M., Ranchhod. A. (2012). *Marketing in Travel and Tourism*. London: Routledge.

Kotler, P. Bowen, J. & Makens, J. (2010). *Marketing for Hospitality and Tourism*, 5th ed., New Jersey: Prentice Hall.

McCabe, S. (2008). *Marketing Communications in Tourism and Hospitality*, London: Routledge.

Tressider and Hirst (2012). *Marketing in Food, Hospitality, Tourism and Events*. Oxford: Goodfellow.

Moutinho, L. (1994). New product development. In S.F. Witt and L. Moutinho (Eds), *Tourism Marketing and Management Handbook*, pp. 350-353. Hemel Hempstead: Prentice Hall.
A clear and thorough review of NPD in tourism

Swarbrooke, J. & Horner, S. (2004). *Consumer Behaviour in Tourism*. Oxford: Elsevier Butterworth Heinemann.
Excellent review of consumer behaviour for tourism

The Tour Operators Initiative (2003). *Sustainable Tourism: The Tour Operators' Contribution*, Paris: TOI.
A thorough set of case studies and the principles of CSR in the supply chain

Vargo, S.L. and Lusch, R F (2004). Evolving to a new dominant logic for marketing. *Journal of Marketing* 68(January), 1-17.
Classic paper on the evolution of marketing thought towards services

Zeithmal, V., Bitner, M.J. & Gremler, D. (2006). *Services Marketing. Integrating Customer Focus across the Firm*, New York: Irwin McGraw Hill.
Excellent text on services marketing

Cooper, C.P. (2011). *Essentials of Tourism*, Harlow: Pearson.
Chapter 13 'Tourism Marketing' provides a thorough overview of the subject.

Recommended web sites

www.Expedia.com
www.Travelocity.com
DataSift.com

References cited

Achrol, R.S. (1991). Evolution of the marketing organization: new forms for turbulent environments. *Journal of Marketing* 55(4), 77-94.

Banyai, M. & Glover, T.D. (2012). Evaluating research methods on travel blogs. *Journal of Travel Research* 51, 267 – 277.

Berry, L.L. & Lampo, S.K. (2000). Teaching an old service new tricks. The promise of service redesign. *Journal of Service Research* 2(3), 265-275.

Buhalis, D. (2003). *eTourism: Information Technology for Strategic Tourism Management*. London: Prentice Hall.

Carroll, A.B. (1999). Corporate social responsibility: evolution of a definitional construct. *Business and Society* 38, 268 -295.

Cooper, C. (2011). *Essentials of Tourism*. Harlow: Pearson.

Day, G.S. & Montgomery. D.B. (1999). Charting new directions for marketing. *Journal of Marketing* 63 (Special issue), 3-13.

Demoor, P. & Zhang, W. (2006). China's Y Generation. *Orion Journal of International Hotel Management* 2(1), 13-17.

ESOMAR (1995). *ICC/ESOMAR International Code of Marketing and Social Research Practice*, Amsterdam: ESOMAR.

Fennell, D. (2006). *Tourism Ethics*. Clevedon: Channelview.

Fennell, D (2012). Tourism ethics needs more than a surface approach. In T.V. Singh (Ed.), *Critical Debates in Tourism*, pp.188-191. Bristol: Channel View.

Font, X., Walmsley, A., Cogotti, S., McCombes, S. & Hausler, N. (2012). Corporate social responsibility: the disclosure-performance gap. *Tourism Management* 33, 1544-1553.

Fyall, A., Callod, C. & Edwards, B. (2003) Relationship marketing: The challenge for destinations. *Annals of Tourism Research* 30(3), 644-659.

Gallup (2011). Making the most of social media. *Gallup Business Journal*. Online. Available at: http://businessjournal.gallup.com/content/149411/making-social-media.aspx

Goodwin, H. (2003). Ethical and responsible tourism: consumer trends in the UK. *Journal of Vacation Marketing* 9(3), 271-283.

Gummesson, E., Lusch, R.F. & Vargo, S.L. (2010). Transitioning from service management to service dominant logic. Observations and recommendations. *International Journal of Quality and Service Sciences* 2(1), 8-22.

Hall, C.M. & Williams, A.M. (2008). *Tourism and Innovation*. London: Routledge.

Hall, D. & Brown, F. (2012). The tourism industry's welfare responsibilities: an adequate response? In Singh, T V (ed.), *Critical Debates in Tourism*, pp. 175-183. Bristol: Channel View.

Hjalager, A.M. (2010) A review of innovation research in tourism. *Tourism Management* 31, 1-12

Hodgson, P. (1990). New tourism product development. market research's role. *Tourism Management* 11(1), 2-5

Kaplan A. & Haenlein, M. (2010). Users of the world, unite! The challenges and opportunities of social media. *Business Horizons* 53(1), 59-68.

Kotler, P., Bowen, J. & Makens, J. (2003). *Marketing for Hospitality and Tourism*, 3rd ed., New Jersey: Prentice Hall.

Liu, Z (2000). Internet Tourism Marketing: Potential and Constraints, Paper presented at the Fourth International Conference, Tourism in South East Asia and Indo China: Development, Marketing and Sustainability.

4

Lovelock, C and Gummesson E (2004). Whither services marketing? In search of new paradigm and fresh perspectives. *Journal of Service Research* 7(1), 20-41.

Marketing Science Institute (2012). *2012-2014 Research Priorities*. Cambridge, MA: MSI.

Moutinho, L (1994) New product development. In S.F. Witt and L. Moutinho (Eds), *Tourism Marketing and Management Handbook*, pp. 350-353. Hemel Hempstead: Prentice Hall.

Nova Scotia Tourism Partnership Council (2003). *E-Marketing Strategy for Tourism*, Halifax: Nova Scotia Tourism Partnership Council.

Park, Y.A. & Gretzel, U. (2007), Success factors for destination marketing web sites: a qualitative meta analysis. *Journal of Travel Research* 46, 46 – 63.

Ritchie, J.R.B. (1994). Roles of research in tourism management. In J.R.B. Ritchie and C.R. Goeldner (Eds.), *Travel, Tourism and Hospitality Research. A Handbook for Managers and Researchers*, pp. 13-21. New York: John Wiley.

Sheldon, P. & Park S. (2011). An exploratory study of corporate social responsibility in the U.S. travel industry. *Journal of Travel Research* 50, 392 – 407.

Shostack, G.L. (1977). Breaking free from product marketing. *Journal of Marketing* 41, 73-80.

Sparks, B. & Browning, V. (2011). The impact of on-line reviews on hotel booking intentions and perception of trust. *Tourism Management* 32, 1310–1323.

Swarbrooke, J. & Horner, S. (2004). *Consumer Behaviour in Tourism*. Oxford: Elsevier Butterworth Heinemann.

The Tour Operators Initiative (2003). *Sustainable Tourism: The Tour Operators' Contribution*, Paris: TOI.

Vargo, S.L. & Lusch, R.F. (2004). Evolving to a new dominant logic for marketing. *Journal of Marketing* 68 (January), 1-17.

Wang, D., Park, S. & Fessenmaier, D. (2012). The role of smartphones in mediating the touristic experience. *Journal of Travel Research* 51, 371 – 387.

World Tourism Organization (2001). *Global Code of Ethics for Tourism*, Madrid: WTO.

Xiang, Z. & Gretzel, U. (2010). Role of social media in online travel information search. *Tourism Management* 31, 179-188.

Section 3:
The Contemporary Tourism Destination

5 Delivering the Contemporary Tourism Product: the Destination

Chapter objectives

After reading this chapter you will:

- Understand the core elements in the destination concept.

- Be able to identify the key elements that make up 'place'.

- Understand the concepts of landscape, servicescape, and experiencescape.

- Understand the concept of a tourism resource and its dynamic nature.

- Recognise the cultural basis for tourism resources and attractions.

- Identify tourism attractions as a specific type of tourism resource.

- Appreciate the specific challenges facing destination management and marketing organisations with respect to controlling the destination product.

The destination concept

The notion of a destination lies at the heart of tourism. The concept that people travel from home to a destination, stay there for a limited period of time, and then return is how the phenomena of tourism is generally understood. The destination concept is one of the most important, yet also most complex, aspects of tourism (Saraniemi & Kylänen 2011). It is complex because people, including marketers and researchers, refer to destinations of different scale. For example, Metelka (1990: 46) defined a destination as the 'geographic location to which a person is traveling'; Vukonic (1997) equated the term to that of a 'resort', while Gunn (1994: 107) saw a destination as being a 'travel market area' and referred to destination zones that are geographic areas 'containing a critical mass of development that satisfies traveller objectives' (Gunn 1994: 27). The varying approaches to the destination concept reflects Saarinen's (2004: 164) observation:

> Destination is by nature a problematic concept. It refers to a varying range of spatial scales (i.e. levels of representation) in tourism: continents, states, provinces, municipalities and other administrative units, tourist resorts or even single tourist products. Spatial scales and definitions of destinations based on administrative or other such units ... tend to approach tourism as a spatial and geographical phenomenon from a technical and static viewpoint.

Tourism destinations are therefore described at different scales ranging from the country level to regions, towns or resorts, specific sites and even specific attractions that are visited by tourists. A destination is a spatial or geographical concept that is primarily defined by visitors from outside the location, although many places seek to make themselves destinations for visitors in order to be able to benefit economically from tourism. A destination therefore, by definition, comes to exist by virtue of the people that visit it. If people from outside a location do not visit a place it is not a destination. That may seem like stating the obvious but it is actually an extremely important point because it forces us to ask: how do places become destinations? And, as a follow up to that, what are the implications of becoming a destination?

The above two questions serve as the focal point for this and the following chapters. This chapter examines how places become destinations and the elements that then make up a destination. The following chapters examine how destinations are governed, managed, planned and marketed.

From places to destinations

Three principle meanings of the idea of place can be distinguished, all of which are important to understanding the nature of destinations:

- Location
- Locale
- Sense of Place

■ Place as location

In locational terms, a place is a specific point on the earth's surface. This not only means that such a location has fixed geographical coordinates so that we can find them on maps, but that it helps us to place locations in relation to each other. New York is 'there', London is 'here'. Obviously mapping locations is important for tourism, but more significantly the location of where somewhere is in relation to other places will determine how relatively accessible it is and therefore its potential market for visitors.

■ Place as locale

This refers to place as a material or physical setting for people's daily social relations, actions and interactions. The physical aspects of places are obviously important in terms of their capacity to manage visitors as well as providing resources and attractions for tourists. Place in this sense not only refers to urban settings, such as ethnic neighbourhoods and arts and heritage precincts, but also to various kinds of 'scapes', including landscapes, servicescapes, streetscapes and experiencescapes (Figure 5.1).

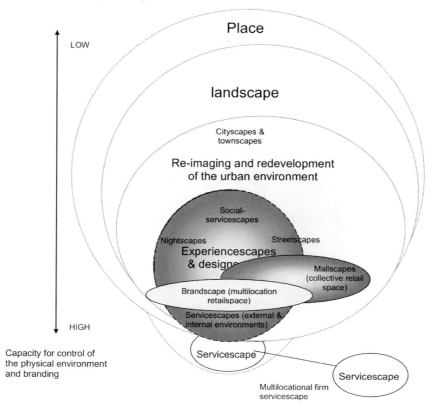

Figure 5.1: Elements of place as locale: locating scapes

The word 'scape' refers to a view or a scene as well as to realist and abstract representations of a view. In marketing and related literature the notion of a scape has been utilized to refer to the physical environment that a consumer experiences and which is, often, deliberately produced so as to encourage consumption, provide a specific set of experiences, or at least satisfy a consumer's desires (Hall 2008). Julier (2005), for example, refers to the notion of designscapes to describe the use of the regeneration of areas within cities to create a place-identity. Urban designscapes are defined as 'the pervasive and multilevel use of the symbolic capital of design in identifying and differentiating urban agglomerations' (Julier 2005: 874) with reference not only to brand design, architecture, events and urban planning; but also to the productive processes of design promotion, organization and policy-making (Hall 2008). Undoubtedly, the numerous scapes of the city may be somewhat confusing. However, they highlight the way in which 'the conscious design and manipulation of the physical environment in order to enhance atmospherics for consumers is not just internal to retail environments but is being extended to the fabric of space itself and the aesthetic experiences and social interactions that occur within it' (Hall 2008: 237).

Landscapes

Landscapes are a visual idea and refer to how a portion of the earth's surface is socially constructed and perceived. Importantly, in most ideas of landscape it is something the viewer is outside of whereas place tends to be something that one is inside of. Nevertheless, landscapes are clearly an important element for the image of place to outsiders such as tourists, which they may then want to experience or gaze upon. The experience of landscape is determined not only by the cultural background of the consumer but also by the environmental, political and cultural processes that lead to the creation of particular landscapes. Saarinen argues that rather than destinations being static spatial structures they are better conceived as a 'cultural landscape subject to continual transformation and reformation, in which it emerges, changes, disappears, and re-emerges in varied forms' (1998: 160).

Servicescapes

Servicescapes refer to the physical facility in which a service is delivered and in which the service provider (firm or other organization) and the customer interact, and to any material or tangible commodities that facilitate the service (Bitner 1992). The idea of servicescapes was originally primarily applied to the immediate physical environment provided by firms in which they sought to use design principles to reinforce brand as well as provide positive service encounters. However, for some businesses, particularly in the tourism industry, the firm servicescape is multilocational. For example, the servicescape for an airline includes not only the aircraft but also the gate and ticketing area for arrival and departure. In addition, for those booking direct with airlines, the airline company's internet portal represents a virtual servicescape while uniforms, food, and tickets are also tangible elements of the service experience. Some firms, for example some hotel and fast-food chains, present their servicescapes in the virtually the same format no matter what the location, so as to reinforce their presentation as a global brand. However, in order to appeal to local markets, marginal changes may be made in design and presentation so as to appeal to local consumers. For example, the design of McDonald's restaurants has undergone significant changes around the world in recent years so that while there is still great consistency in menus (with some local variation) and operating procedures there is greater variation in design. In Israel, several outlets serve Big Macs without cheese so as to permit the separation of meat and dairy products required of kosher restaurants, while in India McDonald's serve vegetable McNuggets and a mutton-based Maharaja Mac so as to meet the religious requirements of Hindus (do not eat beef), Muslims (do not eat pork), and Jains (do not eat any meat) (Watson 1997).

Although originally primarily focused on the internal built environment, the servicescape context has since been extended to include the external built environment and concepts of place experience, as well as the social environment created in spaces of consumption, otherwise referred to as the social-servicescape (Tombs and McColl-Kennedy 2003). To this can be added the concept of the brandscape, which Sherry (1998: 112) uses to refer to the 'material and symbolic environment that consumers build with marketplace products, images, and messages, that they invest with local meaning, and whose totemic significance largely shapes the adaptation consumers make to the modern world.' Brandscapes are utilized by transnational leisure and hospitality companies such as Disney and Starbucks to provide a symbolic retail space that is familiar and comfortable for consumers no matter where they are in the world, and which also enables them to physically inhabit and experience brandspace (Thompson & Arsel 2004). Thereby, experiencing what Guliz and Belk (1996) refer to as a 'consumptionscape'. Similar, strategies are also employed by international hotel chains such as Marrott and Hyatt with respect to the creation of brandscapes.

Many firm servicescapes are also extremely complex environments. Resort complexes or theme parks, for example, have many design elements that ideally need to be brought together to establish a coherent servicescape for the consumer. A tourism destination is typically an amalgam of the many servicescapes of different firms and their facilities. In some cases the landscapes within which the firm servicescapes are embedded are also subject to the control and regulation of destination authorities, in order to satisfy the perceptions of the consumer. For example, land use regulation is used in many parts of the world to maintain rural landscapes in a particular fashion, similarly in many heritage precincts there are often restrictions on building and development, so that new structures will be architecturally sympathetic to the old. This deliberate shaping of environments to make places more appealing as destinations has become an integral component of place promotion and marketing and the development of a destination servicescape that transcend the boundaries of individual firms.

Experiencescapes

Experiencescapes are landscapes of produced experience. They are physical spaces of market production and consumption in which experiences are staged and consumed and are, in effect, in effect, stylized landscapes that are strategically planned and designed with market imperatives as the key design goal. According to O'Dell (2005: 16), experiencescapes 'are not only organized by producers (from place marketers and city planners to local private enterprises) but are also actively sought after by consumers. They are spaces of pleasure, enjoyment and entertainment…'. Experiencescapes serve to connect the servicescapes of different firms within a specific location. They are one of the means by which place is transformed into a destination product by virtue that experiencescapes have been consciously packaged through public-private partnerships. In one sense, the design and packaging of a place in order to produce a desired set of experiences is a logical expression of what Pine and Gilmore (1999) referred to as 'the experience economy' in which 'experiences drive the economy and therefore generate much of the base demand for goods and services' (Pine and Gilmore 1999: 65) (see also Chapter 2).

Examples of experiencescapes include themed waterfronts and former industrial precincts, although many previously existing distinct communities may become transformed into packaged experiencescapes as a result of destination development and promotion processes. The thematic development of parts of a city for tourism and leisure purposes is an extremely common urban tourism strategy. Many cities, for example, have Chinatowns or other ethnic districts such as a 'Little Italy' or 'Little India' even though the social, political and economic processes that originally led to the creation of such ethnically distinct locations has long since past. Indeed, a major challenge in packaging destinations is then to not damage the characteristics that differentiated it from surrounding places. For example, Chang's (2000) study of Singapore's Little India Historic District suggested that its redevelopment had led to the taming of at least three dimensions of what had made the area distinctive: a decline in traditional Indian-owned retail outlets and services (change in activities), the transformation from a place of permanent residence into a retail attraction (change in community), and a dimming of its Indian cultural identity (changes in identity). Nevertheless, the identification of specific districts and quarters as part of urban redevelopment strategies has clearly become significant for the creation of urban leisure and tourism space along with place promotion. Case Study 5.1 details the influence of the SoHo project in New York as an example of such an urban redevelopment.

Case study 5.1: SoHo, urban redevelopment and place branding

An influential example of an urban area that was redeveloped with a strong brand name and image is South of Houston, or SoHo, located in Manhattan, New York. In the late 1960s and early 1970s SoHo was a run-down industrial area that proved attractive to the arts community and became the home of loft living. According to the Top New York City Apartments (2006) description of the area, the renaissance of SoHo 'has made the area into an upscale residential neighborhood and one of the most desired areas to live. The once industrial buildings have been lovingly restored and renovated into luxurious loft homes with many of the tenants having boutiques and galleries located in the same buildings at street level.'

A lead actor in the redevelopment and branding of SoHo was Tony Goldman, Chairman of the Goldman Properties Company founded in 1968. Goldman gives three criteria for a successful rebranding of an urban area; the place must be urban, pedestrian, and have historic architecture (Brown 2004). When undertaking a revitalization project Goldman attempts to 'preserve historic architecture, establish local community organizations and business improvement districts, and finally rebrand neighborhoods' (Brown 2004: 9). Goldman observes that is crucial to create an identity and a brand for a nondescript area, and stresses the importance of historical architecture which areas already have to offer, saying they are a point of differentiation which give a sense of place and is invaluable in terms of differentiating a servicescape offering, and ultimately creating a unique brand and image (Hall 2008).

Tourism and hospitality benefit from, and are integral to, such redevelopments. According to the Goldman Properties Group (n.d.) which, in addition to the SoHo development, have also been involved in urban revitalization and development projects in Miami, Baltimore, Newark and Philadelphia, the company:

- Strives to elevate the quality of life in select cities by revitalizing historic architectural districts in critical mass, restoring existing landmark structures, and building new and appropriate infill.

- Recasts historic structures, recycling them, preserving them aesthetically and adapting them for profitable commercial and residential use.

- Sets a taste level and established a standard that begins to remarket depressed and deteriorated communities.

- Develops, operates, and owns its own self-styled restaurants and hotels in the areas that they reinvent using 'their hospitality units to ignite the first changes that occur'.

- Focuses on establishing and developing urban self help programs that recycle human resources and improve neighborhoods. The corporate objective is to discover, enhance, and articulate the community identity, and the quality

5

of life in historic and industrial neighborhoods, for the public good and for commercial gain.

Such an approach highlights that place branding is dependent on both *hardware* (servicescape), the architectural design of buildings and use of space, which can be used as a differentiator and to communicate an image to a target audience; and *software* (marketing and promotion) which incorporates marketing strategies to create a place identity through the use of slogans, brand identity programs, and other traditional marketing tools being applied to a place (Hall 2008). These elements are common to a number of urban projects that seek to develop, brand and promote urban quarters and districts as part of urban revitalization strategies and plans (Table 5.1).

Table 5.1: Place attributes of urban districts and quarters

Activity	diversity of primary and secondary land uses
	extent and variety of cultural venues and events
	presence of an evening economy, including restaurants and cafe culture
	strength of small-firm economy, including creative businesses
	managed workspaces for office and studio users
	access to education providers
	development of 'third spaces'
	significant hospitality industry presence in hotels, restaurants and cafés
Built form	fine-grain urban morphology
	variety and adaptability of building stock
	permeability of streetscape
	legibility
	amount and quality of public space
	utilization of heritage attributes
	active frontages
Meaning	important meeting and gathering spaces
	sense of history and progress
	area identity and imagery
	knowledgeability
	design appreciation and style
	brand identification and communication strategies

Sources: Montgomery, 2003, 2004; McCarthy 2005a, 2005b; Hall 2008

The SoHo approach has been influential around the world. For example, in New Zealand the SoL (South of Litchfield) lane developments in Christchurch were strongly influenced by the architectural strategies by SoHo (Hall 2008). SoHo also served as the basis for the invention of SoFo (South of Folkungagatan) as a district within a district (Södermalm) of Stockholm in Sweden.

The brand SoFo was invented in 1998 by three friends (Henrik Borggren, Fredrik Glejsner, and Per Holm) who were involved in helping friends renovate cafés and the like in the area. They felt a need to name the area where they were hanging out, and inspired by SoHo in New York they invented the idea of SoFo. ... The idea behind the slogan was to re-brand the previously working class quarter as a 'hip', gentrified, and vibrant urban area (Jansson & Power 2006: 34).

Key sources

Julier, G. (2005). Urban designscapes and the production of aesthetic consent. *Urban Studies* 42(5/6), 869-887.

Goldman Properties: http://www.goldmanproperties.com/

SoHo Alliance (community organization): http://www.sohoalliance.org/

SoHo Travel Guide (wikitravel): http://wikitravel.org/en/Manhattan/SoHo

Discussion questions

1   As neighbourhoods develop and become cultural quarters and districts property and rental prices increase, to what extent may this affect the values and attributes that made a neighbourhood attractive in the first place?

2   To what extent may the replication of urban development approaches lead to the homogenization of urban tourism and leisure products? Is this actually an issue for either neighbourhood or destination branding?

5

The Little India and SoHo experience suggest that while the influence of such projects may contribute to 'good practice' their emulation may lead to an essentially similar mix of architectural, branding, design, and planning elements in very different economic and socio-cultural contexts, 'with the associated risk of homogeneity and loss of local identity or distinctiveness' (McCarthy 2005a,:300). Such issues raise questions about how people experience place and this leads us to our third meaning of place.

■ Sense of place

This is the term used to refer to the subjective, personal and emotional attachments and relationships people have to a place. The notion of sense of place is usually applied in the context of people who live in a location on a permanent basis and reflects how they feel about the physical and social dimensions of their community. People might only consciously notice the unique qualities of their place when they are away from it, when it is being rapidly altered, or when it is being represented or marketed and promoted in a way they do not relate to. From this perspective, senses of place are extremely important when examining the affects of tourism development on a location, as tourism-related changes may leads to changes in sense of place, possibly then leading to resentment towards tourism and even visitors. However, people can have multiple senses of places, derived from the various places they have lived in or visited. Tourists may also develop a sense of places with respect to destinations. Perhaps the most obvious situation in which this occurs is when tourists have a second home in a location or they visit the same location on a regular basis as return visitors. In such a situation, the second home, which is often a place of relaxation, fun and social togetherness, can be regarded as more of a home than the place of 'permanent' residence, particularly when the second home has been passed down several generations of family (Hall & Müller 2004). Nevertheless, many visitors feel that they gain a sense of place when visiting tourism destinations as they experience the landscape and the people. Furthermore, some visitors may feel that they have a sense of place of a destination even before they have visited as a result of meetings with people from the location, other personal conversations, and what they have seen or heard in the media. Of course, the sense of place of a visitor to a destination may be substantially different from someone who lives there.

The resource base of tourism

From the above discussion we can see that various elements of place, some of which are purposively defined for visitor consumption, act as resources for tourism. A tourist resource is that component of the environment (physical or social) which either attracts the tourist and/or provides the infrastructure necessary for the tourist experience (Hall 2007: 34). Tourism resources can be categorized as scarce (e.g. capital, labour, land) or free (e.g. climate, culture). Yet resources are an entirely subjective, relative and functional concept.

What actually constitutes a tourism resource depends on the motivations, desires and interests of the consumer, and the cultural, social, economic and technological context within which those motivations occur. To repeat the frequently quoted words of Zimmermann's seminal work on resources, 'resources are not, they become; they are not static but expand and contract in response to human wants and human actions' (Zimmermann 1951: 15). A tourism resource therefore becomes a resource only if it is seen as having utility value, and different cultures and nationalities can have different perceptions of the tourism value of the same object. What may be a resource in one culture may be 'neutral stuff' in another. Or in other words, what may be a tourist attraction in one culture or location may not be recognized as an attraction in another. Tourism resources can therefore encompass a wide range of settings associated with different physical, topographical and climatic characteristics. For example, people from a farming area in rural New Zealand see sheep as an agricultural resource, whereas for visitors from urban China or Japan they constitute a tourism resource as they see sheep as an attractive element of the landscape. Similarly, for people living in London, the underground railway or 'tube' is primarily a means to commute to work although for many people from outside London taking a ride on the tube is an attraction in its own right, so for those people the underground represents a tourism resource as well as a means of transport. Indeed, a challenge for many destinations is how to commodify tourism resources so that an economic return can be gained for their use. In the case of sheep in New Zealand note above, one means has been to establish businesses that allow Chinese and Japanese tourists to experience sheep directly by seeing sheep being shorn and rounded up by dogs, touch animals directly, and purchase sheep products, such as wool and lanolin, or even eat sheep.

A tourist attraction is a specific type of tourism resource. An attraction is a resource that tourists are prepared to experience for a purpose other than to support their travel, e.g. provision of accommodation, transport or other hospitality services. From this perspective, a hotel in which tourists stay the night because it is convenient within the context of their overall trip is not an attraction, but if the same tourists choose to stay the night in a specific hotel because of, for example, its historic associations, then it is an attraction. Because attractions are a tourism resource this also means that what is attractive to one tourist may not be to another. However, some locations come to be widely regarded as attractions by virtue of the large numbers of people who visit them and have reached an 'iconic' status or because they are commercial operations. Classification of attractions is sometimes determined along the lines of:

- *Cultural or human-made*, e.g. townscapes, museums, national monuments
- *Natural*, e.g. wilderness areas and national parks

Yet, such a division between natural and cultural attractions is extremely problematic given that all tourism resources are inherently cultural. Indeed, a decision to set aside an area as national park is as much of a reflection of culture as it would be to farm the same area of land (Frost & Hall 2009).

Resources are therefore inherently dynamic. New technologies or cultural appraisals can lead to the recognition of new tourism resources. For example, the development of new recreational technologies such as mountain bikes or sailboards meant that the tourism capacities of existing natural resources were considerably expanded and allowed some resort locations to overcome seasonal limitations. Indeed, natural tourism resources are often seasonal in nature. Some destinations (e.g., beach, mountain, skiing, hunting, or fishing destinations) are especially seasonal because of either the nature of the main resource used by visitors or the environment in which the resource is located. Furthermore as consumer preferences change, so does the perceived utility of particular tourism resources. For example, although the beach is seen as a primary tourism resource in many destinations, in western societies it only became an attractive place to go swimming at the turn of the Twentieth Century. Few countries have sought to promote beach tourism as much as Australia, yet it only became legal to swim during the day at Manly Beach, arguably one of Sydney's main tourist attractions, in 1903. Furthermore, such sea bathing needed to be undertaken with substantial clothing on and not in mixed (i.e. male and female) company. As Archbishop Kelly commented in 1911 (*The Sun*, Sydney, 14 August 1911 in Hall 2007: 74-5):

> *I think promiscuous surf-bathing is offensive in general to propriety, and a particular feature of that offensiveness is the attraction it has for idle onlookers...There is no border-line between vice and virtue. Our worst passions are but the abuse of our good ones. And I believe that the promiscuous intermingling of sexes in*

surf-bathing makes for the deterioration of our standard of morality...Woe betide Australia if she is going to encourage immodesty in her women.

Not only has what people wear when they go swimming changed but also other aspects of tourism fashion. For example, until the late 1920s having a suntan was not seen as fashionable. However, in 1929 a great shift occurred in popular taste with suntans starting to be seen by many westerners as being desirable. The growth in popular media had much to do with this shift. In the northern summer of 1929 the fashion magazine *Vogue* featured models with a sun tan for the first time as the models and the film stars of the then new Hollywood film industry had been holidaying in the South of France. At the same time as fashion setters in the film and entertainment industry started to wear a tan so was there a wider social and design movement, referred to as Art Deco, which featured houses and hotels with large windows that allowed light into rooms. In addition, the overall health benefits of sun and light came to be advocated as increasingly numbers of people worked inside factories and offices. For the first time having a tan was seen as an indication of being wealthy and having leisure time as opposed to earlier perceptions of a tan being associated with manual labouring in the outdoors. All these elements came together to make the tan desirable and those destinations and attractions where a tan could be gained also became desirable. Such a shift in fashion and cultural taste clearly had enormous implications for many locations. For example, it is hard to imagine destinations on the Mediterranean or island resorts in the Caribbean or the Pacific being as attractive as they are unless exposure to the sun is seen as relatively desirable. Indeed, the phrase of 'sun, sand and surf' is often equated as a description of mass tourism destinations.

The massive shift in Western consumer tastes in the late 1920s and early 1930s with respect to the sun and the human body is one example of the implications of changes in culture affecting perceptions of what constitutes a tourism resource and therefore potential leisure attractions and destinations. Another example, which arguably had equally dramatic affects of leisure travel, was the shift that occurred in the late Eighteenth and early Nineteenth Centuries in relation to landscape. Up until this time, mountains or wild rural landscapes were seen in Western culture as being not worthy of places to visit. Instead, the ideal landscape was regarded as being urban areas or well managed and highly designed gardens. However, with the arrival of the Romantic movement in art, literature and design in the late Eighteenth Century, and the consequent reaction to the rapidly industrializing towns, all began to change. Painting started to feature wild seas and mountain ranges often shrouded in mist. Poets, such as Wordsworth and Coleridge, also started to write of waterfalls, lakes and hill country. Such artistic reactions were highly significant as they had considerable influence on the popular taste of the upper-class and the emerging and increasingly literate middle classes. Again, the implications for leisure travel in the early Nineteenth Century were staggering. Destinations such as Scotland, the Lake District of England, Wales, and the alpine areas of Switzerland and Austria suddenly became desirable landscapes to visit and experience whereas for most of the preceding history of European civilization they had been cast in a negative light.

The Romantic movement laid the groundwork upon which a popular appreciation of the value of wild land and nature would come to be based. For example, artistic, literary and political perceptions of the importance of contact with wild nature provided the stimulus for the creation of positive cultural attitudes towards wilderness in the United States and elsewhere and arguably laid the foundations for the creation of national parks and the development of ecotourism. In the United States, artist George Catlin called for the establishment of 'a nation's park' in 1832 to preserve the wilderness and its human and non-human inhabitants (Catlin 1968). Thoreau, in 1858, repeated these demands for preservation of wilderness 'for modesty and reverence's sake, or if only to suggest that earth has higher uses than we put her to' (cited in Nash 1982: 103). Once positive attitudes towards primitive, unordered nature had developed, the emergence of individuals and societies dedicated to the preservation of wilderness values as well as the development of a tourism industry to take people to see wild land was only a short step away.

This transformation in landscape taste, as with the change in fashion with respect to having a sun tan, was incredibly dramatic, with enormous implications for what was perceived as a resource. Changes in taste meant that some locations that were previously avoided now became highly fashionable, and still are to the present day. Niagara Falls in the United States, the Swiss Alps and the highlands of Scotland are all locations that are now seen as significant tourist attractions and destinations to the stage where most people do not even realize that their value as a tourism resource was contingent on changed in landscape preferences. These examples are important as they highlight the cultural base of resources for tourism. Different cultures will have different understandings of what is a tourism resource and therefore what constitutes a tourist attraction. Just as significantly we must recognize that even within cultures, changes occur and therefore perceptions of resources will also change.

Perceptions of resources change as a result in shifts in cultural taste. However, the attractiveness of locations will also be affected by more short-term factors such as perceptions of how safe a destination is or the extent to which resources exist following a natural disaster. Because perceptions determine understanding of resources so it becomes important to realise that there are often significant differences between reality and how potential tourists understand a destination or attraction. Therefore, the media play a critical role in influencing tourist understandings of place not only through formal travel programmes and documentaries but also through general news stories and coverage as well as film and television entertainment.

Some destinations deliberately seek to utilize film and media as a way of positioning their destination through certain images (see Chapter 9 for a more detailed account of destination marketing). For example, Tourism New Zealand extensively assisted in the promotion of the film trilogy of *Lord of the Rings* as well as *The Hobbit* films and promoted itself as 'Middle Earth' in much of its publicity in an effort to reinforce New Zealand's natural images. In July 2012 Tourism New Zealand reemphasized the link between *The Hobbit* films and the branding and promotion of New Zealand.

> '100% Middle-earth,100% Pure New Zealand' will underpin Tourism New Zealand's campaign work to promote New Zealand as a visitor destination through its association with the upcoming film releases of The Hobbit: An Unexpected Journey and The Hobbit: There and Back Again, productions of New Line Cinema and MGM.
>
> The aim is to take advantage of that global profile by showing how easily the fantasy of The Hobbit movies can become reality in the form of a New Zealand holiday.
>
> Many movie goers would probably consider the landscapes of 'Middle-earth' to be a fantasy, only made possible thanks to the talents of film makers. Not so.
>
> Marketing work will show potential travellers that the fantasy of Middle-earth is in fact the reality of New Zealand – and that there is a whole world of experiences to be had and people to meet within the movie-scene style landscapes.
>
> Marketing activity will show how easy it is to come here, see Middle-earth first-hand, and enjoy all the exciting and fun experiences New Zealand has to offer (Tourism New Zealand 2012).

The New Zealand government promoted the tourism and high-technology aspects of *Lord of the Rings* after the first film in the trilogy was released late in 2001 and likewise with the first Hobbit film in 2012. Such was the perceived economic importance of having *The Hobbit* filmed in New Zealand that the National Party led government even changed the country's labour laws in 2010 in order to be able to weaken union negotiated employment terms and conditions as well as providing further subsidies for production. The importance of the media in changing perceptions of destinations is reflected in the comments of the then responsible minister, Peter Hodgson, who noted that the movie had the potential to rebrand New Zealand: 'This [film] has come out of a country which a lot of viewers might associate with sheep' (Campbell 2001: 24). As such, the nature of the New Zealand landscape as a tourism resource has also changed.

Although many destinations seek to proactively influence their image and perception of their attractions and resources, in many cases destinations have to be reactive, particularly at times of natural disaster or political insecurity. The growth of global media, such as the Internet and satellite television, has meant that events in a location can be seen almost instantaneously in other parts of the world. Therefore, as well as focusing on ensuring that the desired physical and cultural resources are in place for visitors, destinations also need to try to influence the relevant information resources. This situation is analysed in more detail with respect to the example of crisis management and the impact of Hurricane Katrina on New Orleans detailed below (Case Study 5.2).

From this understanding of tourism resources we can see that if a destination seeks to attract tourists, at least four things need to be available from the destination:

1 Resources in the form of physical and cultural attractions to induce people to visit.

2 Resources in the form of facilities and services, including human resources, that enable tourists to stay at the destination.

3 Resources in the form of infrastructure and services that makes the destination accessible as well as the various attractions, facilities and services within the destinations accessible.

4 Information provision so that the consumer actually knows about the destination and its resources. From this perspective, information is itself also a tourism resource and a gateway resource, in that it creates awareness of the other types of resources that a destination has.

Given that consumption and production are simultaneous in tourism as a service industry, in addition to destination resources, consumer resources are also essential for tourism to occur. As Chapter 1 highlighted, in order to be able to engage in leisure travel, some of the resources that people need include, time, money, the political rights to travel, and health. The accessibility of a destination, and its relative potential to attract visitors, is going to be dramatically impacted by the resources in its market area. The capacity of a destination to attract visitors is therefore a function of the resources that exist within the destination, the resources in the transit region, and the resources of the generating region, including the personal resources of potential travelers.

Case study 5.2: Hurricane Katrina and New Orleans tourism

On the early hours of August 29, 2005, the Gulf Coast region of the United States was hit by what is considered to have been one of its most destructive hurricanes ever. Hurricane Katrina, a Category 4 storm, made landfall on the Louisiana coast and travelled northeast through Mississippi and Alabama before being downgraded to a tropical storm in Tennessee the following day. A category 4 storm implies:

■ Winds 210-249 km/hr (131-155 mph).

■ Storm surge generally 4 to 5.5 metres above normal.

■ More extensive curtain wall failures with some complete roof structure failures on small residences.

■ Shrubs, trees, and all signs are blown down. Complete destruction of mobile homes. Extensive damage to doors and windows.

■ Low-lying escape routes may be cut by rising water 3-5 hours before arrival of the centre of the hurricane.

- Major damage to lower floors of structures near the shore.
- Terrain lower than 3 metres above sea level may be flooded requiring massive evacuation of residential areas as far inland as 10 kilometres.

The final characteristic greatly increased the severity of the impact of the hurricane in New Orleans, Louisiana, as the city sits between 3m below to 4m above sea level. Unfortunately, many residents ignored or were unable to fulfill the evacuation order and remained in New Orleans, while the major flood-control levees were breached covering approximately 80% of the city in water. Hurricane Katrina triggered the city's ultimate 'worst-case-scenario' and the chain of events that followed indicated a general lack of preparedness even though the likelihood of such a disaster occurring had been predicted by many scientists and had also been the subject of several television documentaries.

The impact of Hurricane Katrina on tourism in Louisiana and New Orleans was dramatic. In 2005, U.S. resident visitors to Louisiana numbered 17.3 million, a decline of 23% from 2004. In the fourth quarter alone, visitors declined by 76%. Total inquiries to the Louisiana Office of Tourism via the internet, telephone and mail also plummeted immediately after Hurricane Katrina and the subsequent Hurricane Rita which affected southwest Liousiana (from over three million in fiscal year 2004-05 to just under two million in fiscal year 2005-06). Not surprisingly visitor spending in Louisiana dropped US$1.9 million in 2005 to $8 billion (Department of Culture, Recreation and Tourism 2006b). However, New Orleans is the focal point for the state's tourism industry. In 2004 more than 10 million visitors to New Orleans spent US$5billion, with 40% of revenues being generated by business conventions and meetings which made New Orleans the eighth-largest US market for business conventions. The New Orleans Convention and Visitors Bureau (NOCVB) estimated lost tourism revenues of approximately US$500 million (Euro411m, £277m) each month the city could not open for visitors (Yee 2005). Nevertheless, even with the cancellation of all city-wide conventions (using the convention centre and three or more hotels) scheduled for the city between September 2005 and April 2006 the NOCVB maintained its business operations by setting up a temporary office in Baton Rouge and with 90 staff working remotely across the USA. Indeed, a scaled down version of Mardi Gras, New Orleans' icon event was still scheduled for February as a means of reviving the city's tourism industry, with Donna Karl, vice president of NOCVB proclaiming, 'Mardi Gras is on... We're thinking that the city will be up rocking and rolling in the first quarter'. In addition, it was reported that where possible meetings were being swapped with New Orleans with the city being promised events for 2008 and beyond (Yee 2005: 8).

In addition to the damage that Hurricane Katrina caused to the physical and human resources of New Orleans, the media reporting on the hurricane also had substantial effects on the perception of New Orleans as a destination. A study conducted by Cunningham Research (2005) indicated that travellers were most concerned over their personal safety and their finances related to a trip to New Orleans. Fifty percent of travellers who stated they were interested in visiting New Orleans were somewhat or extremely concerned over a hurricane being predicted before they leave home, and an equal number were just as concerned over losing money from pre-paid travel expenses and additional costs from delays. An overall negative impact on confidence with leadership at all levels of government was also regarded as influencing the attractiveness of New Orleans as a destination (CBS 2005). Indeed, a year after Hurricane Katrina hit, many problems still remained that not only affected the people of New Orleans but also the city's image. For example, an Australian newspaper article read: 'From the ghostly streets of New Orleans' abandoned neighbourhoods to Mississippi's downtrodden coastline, the first anniversary of Katrina's onslaught arrives with emerging signs of federal money at work: rented caravans parked in driveways of flood-ravaged homesteads, teams of army engineers overseeing levee repairs, beaches swept clean of debris' (Simmons and Fausset 2006). Despite four emergency spending bills approved by Congress to provide more than $US110 billion ($A145 billion) in aid, federal agencies had spent only $US44 billion with many displaced home-owners still waiting for temporary caravan accommodation (Simmons & Fausset 2006).

By mid-2006 the Louisiana Department of Culture, Recreation and Tourism (2006a: 1) reported that 'negative images of affected areas portrayed by the media... had resulted in a significant loss of interest in tourism'. Louisiana was expected to have lost 20 percent of its visitor spending in one year, (approximately US$2.2 billion) and New Orleans an average of $15.2 million per day, with a consequent loss of state tax dollars of approximately US$125 million per annum. Indeed, the state acknowledged that not only were tourists' image of the state and city affected but also 'The State's image after the hurricanes has weakened investor confidence with regards to spending money in Louisiana' (Department of Culture, Recreation and Tourism 2006a: 3).

Nevertheless, though negative aspects of the impact of Katrina were affecting the city's and state's image and economy, the media was seen as part of the solution with respect to redeveloping tourism. According to Louisiana State Senator Ann Davis Duplessis:

> I am afraid when the lights go off, when something will no longer be there and our people are no longer being talked about in the media constantly, others will feel less and less sympathetic. The world will become less sympathetic of our condition. If in the next catastrophe, damage reaches this stage or worst, hundreds of thousands people who are still trying to recover will not be ready. It is imperative therefore, the media continues the coverage at a level that it is 'in our face' and 'in the face' of the world. We need that sympathetic heart to be able to repair the level of this damage, so that we can rebuild. If news goes away in 2-3 months, I don't know how long it will take for us to go back to any semblance of normality. (in Heyer 2005)

In response to the damage wrought by Hurricane Katrina on the physical and image dimensions of New Orleans and Louisiana tourism, the State of Louisiana launched a 'Rebirth plan' (Department of Culture, Recreation and Tourism 2005; State of Louisiana, Office of the Lieutenant Governor 2005). Employment, housing, and the rebuilding of physical and social infrastructure were seen as important but so too was the provision of information and the development of a public relations campaign. According to the plan, 'People need new images of Louisiana, to replace the weeks of negative images on television' (Department of Culture, Recreation and Tourism 2005: 3). With respect to tourism five strategies were identified:

1   *Public relations campaign* – 'Immediately and aggressively promote those areas of the state currently open for business. An aggressive public relations campaign will be implemented'

2   *Business assistance* – 'Rapidly develop and implement a statewide tourism small business assistance program, utilizing any and all available federal, private and state funds'

3   *Infrastructure* – 'Facilitate the rapid rebuilding and improvement of the state's infrastructure'.

4   *Image* – 'rebuild and enhance Louisiana's national and international image as an attractive, compelling, unique tourism destination...'

5   *Lead agency* – The Office of Lieutenant Governor to serve as the lead agency with respect to policy setting , intergovernmental relations, and as an information clearing house (Department of Culture, Recreation and Tourism 2005: 7)

In 2006 the state amended its tourism marketing plan so as to increase the number of visitors in the areas impacted by Katrina. The State proposed that US$28.5 million be invested in a national campaign and other initiatives designed to bring out-of-state travelers back to the New Orleans region, and Southeast and Southwest Louisiana with the primary targets being leisure travelers as well as convention and business travelers. The initiative included:

1   Convention and interactive marketing, promotions to travel agents, and related activities.

2   An awareness campaign focusing on New Orleans, Southeast Louisiana, and Southwest Louisiana. This campaign will target drive-in and national travelers as well as international travelers.

3   Niche marketing programs designed to promote family activities and festivals and cultural attractions unique to the areas most affected by the storms.

4   Coordinated marketing efforts between the Department of Culture, Recreation, and Tourism and the Louisiana Department of Economic Development to regain investor confidence for spending money and creating jobs in Louisiana (Department of Culture, Recreation and Tourism 2006a: 4).

By September 2006 significant progress had been made in restoring the tourism resources of New Orleans and Louisiana. Prior to Hurricanes Katrina and Rita, 21% of the nation's travelers and 53% of Louisiana's regional market expressed an intent to travel to Louisiana in the next 24 months. Immediately after the hurricanes, the national number dropped to 13% and the regional market dropped to 37%. As of May 2006, the regional number had increased to 47% (Department of Culture, Recreation and Tourism 2006b: 4). Other changes in infrastructure are noted in Table 5.2. A year after Katrina almost two-thirds the number of flights pre-Katrina were flying out of Louis Armstrong International Airport to 77% the number of destinations. However, substantial growth was expected into the future as attractions were being reopened and convention and business travel started to return to the city. Nevertheless, in July 2008 30% of respondents to a Louisiana tourism tracking survey still said that the 2005 hurricanes had made them want to change their plans to visit Louisiana (Department of Culture, Recreation & Tourism 2008).

By 2010 total spending by domestic and international visitors in Louisiana was estimated at $9.3 billion, a figure that was still just below pre-Katrina levels and which had also been affected by the BP oil spill in the Gulf of Mexico (Louisiana Office of Tourism 2011), while annual visitor spending in New Orleans had reached $5.3 billion, the highest in the city's history, although visitor numbers were still at a pre-Katrina level (New Orleans Convention and Visitors Bureau 2011) (Table 5.3). In January 2010, New Orleans' hospitality leaders announced a strategic, unified master plan for the tourism industry, the goal of which is to attract 13.7 million annual visitors by the city's 300th anniversary in 2018 (New Orleans Convention and Visitors Bureau 2011). Nevertheless, the long-term future of tourism in New Orleans and the state will likely be affected by the redevelopment of the city, including the development of new flood protection practices and infrastructure, as well as the impact of any future hurricane on the city.

Table 5.2: Key for New Orleans and Louisiana pre- and post- Katrina

Indicator	Pre-Katrina	Sept 2005	Sept 2006	Aug 2011
Daily commercial flights from Louis Armstrong New Orleans	162	19	112[1]	119
Statewide hotel availability (rooms)	80,000	42,000[2]	70,000	
New Orleans hotel availability	38,000	20,000[2]	28,000	35,550
New Orleans metropolitan area hotels (no.)	140		103	
New Orleans, number of restaurants	3,400		1,562	
New Orleans Parish Police Force, no. of officers	1,680		1,469	
Parish Police Force, ratio of police/citizens	1/289		1/157	
New Orleans Parish, no. of citizens	485,000		220-235,000	
Metropolitan New Orleans, no. of citizens	1.3 million		1.1 million	

1 This figure represents 13,185 seats or 59% of pre-Katrina level of seats per day

2 January 2006 figures

Source: derived from Department of Culture, Recreation and Tourism 2006b; New Orleans Metropolitan Convention & Visitors Bureau 2006, 2011.

Table 5.3: Leisure and Business Travel to New Orleans 2003-2010

Year	Visitors (million)	Annual Visitor Spending (billion)	CVB booked meetings & conventions	Number of attendees
2003	8.5	$4.5		
2004	10.1	$4.9	1 299	1 253 848
2005 (Jan. - June)	5.3	$2.6		
2006	3.7	$2.8	360	428 922
2007	7.1	$4.8	607	647 516
2008	7.6	$5.1	704	789 333
2009	7.5	$4.2	661	838 875
2010	8.3	$5.3	726	893 427

Source: derived from New Orleans Metropolitan Convention & Visitors Bureau (CVB) 2011.

Key sources

Louisiana Office of Tourism: www.crt.state.la.us/tourism

Louisiana Rebirth Plan, Louisiana Department of Culture, Recreation and Tourism: www. crt.state.la.us

Louis Armstrong Airport: www.flymsy.com/

New Orleans Convention & Visitors Bureau: www.neworleanscvb.com

New Orleans Convention Center: www.mccno.com

New Orleans Superdome: www.superdome.com/

Discussion questions

1   How might marketing best contribute to disaster management for tourism destinations?

2   With reference to the websites, discuss the further progress the city has made with respect to regaining tourism numbers and the extent to which hurricanes and tourist safety and security are noted in tourist information?

3   How does the New Orleans example highlight the extent to which image and perception, as well as infrastructure and attractions, constitute a tourism resource?

Summary

The different dimensions of place are a critical element in understanding the contemporary destination. Places become destinations by virtue of their being visited. Places seek to become destinations so as to reap the economic benefits of attracting visitors, as well as promote a destination for purposes of investment and migration. Yet as the destination product is the sum of all experiences the tourist has at the destination as a result of encounters with a variety of tourism resources including firms, people, communities and the destination environment (see Chapter 1), this is an extremely difficult product to manage. As the service dimensions outlined in Chapters 1 and 2 indicated, tourism as a service is a very difficult product to control in the manner that the quality of a physical product could be controlled. Indeed, the destination product that is promoted by DMOs is quite different from many other commercial products, in that the DMO does not 'own' the product it is promoting, while the development of the product is itself the result of an amalgam of different public and private firms and organizations, many of which may not even be aware of each other's existence.

The concepts of servicescape and experiencescape highlight the extent to which firms and destinations will seek to produce experiences that consumers desire, through design and regulation of the physical environment that visitors experience. Yet the service encounters through social interactions between producer and consumer are far harder to control. To an extent, these can be managed within the firm via training programmes, although outside of the commercial environment social interactions between visitors and members of the destination community are impossible to control except in the most totalitarian states. This situation illustrates the difficulties associated with the notion of destination management, as destination management or marketing organizations in liberal democracies have only a limited degree of control over the encounter between consumers and producers of the tourist experience. An exception may be the case of visitors who have purchased an all inclusive package tour at a destination where they do not speak the local language. Nevertheless, for all visitors, social interactions are also defined partially by the configuration of the servicescapes encountered in destinations.

The issue of control of all elements of the tourist destination product, or rather the relative lack of control, clearly lies at the heart of understanding the contemporary destination. Unlike many other business products or services, destination management or marketing organizations do not own the product that they are managing or marketing. This constitutes a significant point of difference in the business and organizational dimensions of tourism from that of many other commercial and public sectors. Destination management is therefore focused on the gaining of control, or at least seeking to increase the levels of certainty of appropriate provision, in relation to the delivery of the key elements of the tourism product to the consumer. Ideally, destination management is concerned not just with the consumption of the tourism product but also with how the tourist gains value from each element of the value chain and how producers also add value, and therefore increase returns to the destination, to the supply chain. This broader perspective on what destination management is seeking to achieve cannot be stressed enough, as it influences how destinations are governed with respect to tourism (Chapter 6), the effects of tourism on destinations (Chapter 7), and the planning of tourism in destinations (Chapter 8). It also highlights the importance of understanding the wide array of factors that affect the viability of tourism destinations.

Self-review questions

1 Why is the question of what constitutes a *destination* determined by the visitor?

2 How does *scale* affect the ways in which destinations are usually described?

3 What are the three main approaches to describing *place*?

4 Why might it be difficult to manage visitor experiences in a *servicescape* or *experiencescape*?

5 Why are all tourism resources *cultural* in origin?

6 Why is *information* a tourism resource?

7 What is the term that is used to refer to the subjective, personal and emotional *attachments* and *relationships* people have to a place? Is it possible for people to have multiple place attachments?

8 For some people a *second home* or holiday destination might feel more like a home than their place of permanent residence. Why might this be the case?

9   Why is the issue of *control* such an important element in understanding contemporary destination management?

Recommended reading

Framke, W. (2002). The destination as a concept: A discussion of the business-related perspective versus the socio-cultural approach in tourism theory. *Scandinavian Journal of Hospitality and Tourism* 2, 93-108.
Article describes two idealized approaches in describing the destination concept.

Leiper, N. (2000). Are destinations 'the heart of tourism'? The advantages of an alternative description. *Current Issues in Tourism* 3, 364-68.
A critical perspective of the destination concept and its utility in tourism studies.

Cresswell, T. (2004) *Place: A Short Introduction*, Blackwell, Oxford.
Provides a good introduction to the main themes in the study of place including current debates over supposed non-places, such as airport terminals.

Saraniemi, S. (2010). Destination brand identity development and value system. *Tourism Review* 65(2), 52–60.
Proposes a model of destination brand identity and value system that takes a holistic view of destination branding.

Bitner, M.J. (1992). Servicescapes: The impact of physical surroundings on customers and employees. *Journal of Marketing* 56, 57-71.
A seminal article with respect to the notion of servicescapes which has had a substantial impact in the marketing literature.

Singh, S., Timothy, D. & Dowling, R. (Eds) (2003). *Tourism in Destination Communities*, Wallingford: CAB International.
An edited collection that provides a range of perspectives with respect to destination communities and the issues that tourism raises within them.

Ringer, G. (ed.) (1998). *Destinations: Cultural Landscapes of Tourism*, New York: Routledge.
Edited book that provides a useful collection of readings on the cultural construction of destinations.

Hall, C.M. (2005). *Tourism: Rethinking the Social Science of Mobility*, Harlow: Prentice-Hall.
Chapter 6 provides a detailed discussion of the production of tourism destinations.

Saraniemi, S. & Kylänen, M. (2011). Problematizing the concept of tourism destination: An analysis of different theoretical approaches. *Journal of Travel Research* 50(2), 133-143.
Identifies four major approaches to defining tourism destinations and proposes a new definition.

Lew, A., Hall, C.M., & Williams, A.M. (Eds) (2004). *A Companion to Tourism*, Oxford: Blackwell.
Provides a detailed collection of review chapters on key aspects of tourism destinations, including specific destination types and attractions such as the tourist-historic city.

References cited

Bitner, M.J. (1992). Servicescapes: The impact of physical surroundings on customers and employees. *Journal of Marketing* 56: 57-71.

Brown, S. (2004). 15 Minutes with… Tony Goldman: The urban visionary behind Soho and South Beach tells all. *The Next American City* 5 (January), 9.

Campbell, G. (2001). Planet Middle Earth. *Listener*, 15th December: 16–24.

Catlin, G. (1968). An artist proposes a national park. In R. Nash (ed.) *The American Environment: Readings in the History of Conservation*, pp. 5-9. Reading: Addison-Wesley Publishing.

CBS (2005). Poll: Katrina Response Inadequate. Online. Available at: http://www.cbsnews.com/stories/2005/09/08/opinion/polls/main824591.shtml (accessed August 23, 2006)

Chang, T.C. (2000). Theming cities, taming places: Insights from Singapore. *Geografiska Annaler* 82B, 35-54.

Cunningham Research (2005). *Study of 2005 Hurricane Impacts on Tourism*, http://www.cunninghamresearch.com/release.html (accessed July 17, 2006)

Department of Culture, Recreation and Tourism (2005). *Louisiana Rebirth: Restoring the Soul of America*. Baton Rouge: Department of Culture, Recreation and Tourism.

Department of Culture, Recreation and Tourism (2006a). *Tourism Action Plan Amendment: Louisiana Tourism Marketing Program*. Baton Rouge: Department of Culture, Recreation and Tourism.

Department of Culture, Recreation and Tourism (2006b). *Louisiana Rebirth Scorecard*. Baton Rouge: Department of Culture, Recreation and Tourism.

Department of Culture, Recreation and Tourism (2008). *Final Report Perceptions of New Orleans/Louisiana, Tracking Study, August 14, 2008,* Market Dynamics Research Group. Baton Rouge: Department of Culture, Recreation and Tourism.

Frost, W. & Hall, C.M. (Eds) (2009). *Tourism and National Parks: International Perspectives on Development, Histories and Change*, London: Routledge.

Goldman Properties (n.d.). Overview. Online. Available at: http://www.goldmanproperties.com/ (accessed 1 April 2012).

Guliz, G. & Belk, R.W. (1996). I'd like to buy the world a Coke: Consumptionscapes in the less affluent world. *Journal of Consumer Policy* 19, 271-304.

Gunn, C.A. (1994). *Tourism Planning*, 3rd ed. London: Taylor and Francis.

5

Hall, C.M. (2007). *Introduction to Tourism in Australia: Development, Issues and Change*, 5th ed. South Melbourne: Pearson Education Australia.

Hall, C.M. (2008). Servicescapes, designscapes, branding and the creation of place-identity: South of Litchfield, Christchurch. *Journal of Travel and Tourism Marketing* 25(3/4), 233-250.

Hall, C.M. & Müller, D. (Eds) (2004). *Tourism, Mobility and Second Homes: Between Elite Landscape and Common Ground*. Clevedon: Channelview Publications.

Heyer, H. (2005), New Orleans needs 10 years minimum. *Travel Wire News* November 22, http://www.travelwirenews.com/cgi-script/csArticles/articles/000066/006625.htm

Julier, G. (2005). Urban designscapes and the production of aesthetic consent. *Urban Studies* 42(5/6), 869-887.

Louisiana Office of Tourism (2011). *Louisiana Tourism By Numbers*. Baton Rouge: Office of Tourism.

McCarthy, J. (2005a). Cultural quarters and regeneration: The case of Wolverhampton. *Planning, Practice & Research* 20(3), 297-311.

McCarthy, J. (2005b). Promoting image and identity in 'cultural quarters': The case of Dundee. *Local Economy* 20(3), 280-293.

Metelka, C.J. (1990). *The Dictionary of Hospitality, Travel and Tourism*, 3rd. ed., Delmar Publishers, Albany.

Montgomery, J. (2003). Cultural quarters as mechanisms for urban regeneration. Part 1: Conceptualising cultural quarters. *Planning, Practice & Research* 18(4), 293-306.

Montgomery, J. (2004). Cultural quarters as mechanisms for urban regeneration. Part 2: A review of four cultural quarters in the UK, Ireland and Australia. *Planning Practice & Research* 19(1), 3-31

Nash, R. (1982). *Wilderness and the American Mind*, 3rd ed. New Haven & London: Yale University Press.

New Orleans Metropolitan Convention & Visitors Bureau (2011). *New Orleans Tourism Industry Fact Sheet: Six-Year Anniversary of Hurricane Katrina, August 2011*. New Orleans: New Orleans Metropolitan Convention & Visitors Bureau.

New Orleans Convention & Visitors Bureau (2006). *New Orleans Metropolitan Convention and Visitors Bureau Issues 'State of the City' Report*. New Orleans: New Orleans Convention & Visitors Bureau.

Pine, J. & Gilmore, J. (1999). *The Experience Economy: Work is Theatre & Every Business a Stage*. Boston: Harvard Business School Press.

O'Dell, T. (2005). Experiencescapes: Blurring borders and testing connections. In T. O'Dell and P. Billing (Eds.), *Experiencescapes: Tourism , Culture and Economy*, pp. 11-33. Copenhagen: Copenhagen Business School Press.

Saarinen, J. (1998). The social construction of tourist destinations: The process of transformation of the Saariselkä tourism region in Finnish Lapland. In G. Ringer (Ed.), Destinations: Cultural landscapes of tourism, pp. 154-172. London: Routledge.

Saarinen, J. (2004). Destinations in change: The transformation process of tourist destinations. *Tourist Studies* 4, 161-179.

Saraniemi, S. & Kylänen, M. (2011). Problematizing the concept of tourism destination: An analysis of different theoretical approaches. *Journal of Travel Research* 50(2), 133-143.

Sherry, J.F., Jr. (1998). The soul of the company store: Nike Town Chicago and the emplaced brandscape. In J. F. Sherry, Jr. (Ed.), *Servicescapes: The concept of place in contemporary markets*, pp. 109-150. Lincolnwood, IL: Nike Town Chicago Business Books.

Simmons, A. & Fausset, R. (2006). New Orleans disaster still overwhelms. *The Age*, August 29.

State of Louisiana, Office of the Lieutenant Governor (2005). *Lt. Gov. Landrieu Unveils Plan to Rebuild Tourism and Cultural Industries. Press Release*, September 20. Baton Rouge: State of Louisiana, Office of the Lieutenant Governor.

Thompson, C. J. & Arsel, Z. (2004). The Starbucks brandscape and consumers (anticorporate) experiences of glocalization. *Journal of Consumer Research* 31(3), 631-642.

Tombs, A. & McColl-Kennedy, J. R. (2003). Socialservicescapes conceptual model. *Marketing Theory* 3, 447-475.

Top New York City Apartments. (2006). SoHo Neighborhood, 2 May. Online. Available at: http://www.topnycapts.com/blog/Neighborhood-Guide.php?cat5135 (accessed 1 April 2008).

Tourism New Zealand (2012). 100% Middle-earth, 100% Pure New Zealand, 24 July 2012. Online. Available HTTP: http://www.tourismnewzealand.com/sector-marketing/the-hobbit/100percent-middle-earth/ (accessed 28 July 2012).

Vukonic, B. (1997). Selective tourism growth: Targeted tourism destinations. In S. Watson, J.L. (Ed.) (1997). *Golden Arches East: McDonald's in East Asia*. Stanford: Standford University Press.

Wahab and J. Pigrim (Eds), *Tourism, Development and Growth: The Challenge of Sustainability*, pp. 95-108. London: Routledge.

Yee, A. (2005). New Orleans vows to let the carnival go on – but will anybody come? *Financial Times* (Europe) 21 September: 8.

Zimmermann, E.W. (1951). *World Resources and Industries*, Rev. Ed. New York: Harper and Brothers.

5

6 Governing the Contemporary Tourism Product: the Role of the Public Sector and Tourism Policy

Chapter objectives

After reading this chapter you will:

■ Understand the development of the concept of governance.

■ Identify the key characteristics of governance.

■ Understand the reorganisation of the state along new functional and territorial lines.

■ Recognise the importance of multi-level governance, particularly in policy areas that have become highly globalised.

■ Appreciate the complexity of governance in tourism.

■ Understand the major roles of government in tourism.

■ Identify different types of tourism policy.

Introduction

Governance is the act of governing. The focus of this chapter is the government and governance of tourism, an issue that has become a major concern to stakeholders in tourism in recent times. That is, the design, implementation and monitoring of public policies and strategies with respect to how the state intervenes in tourism.

This involves the horizontal and vertical coordination of government at various levels, the private sector, and non-government organizations, as well as the wider population. This occurs over scales ranging from the global through to the local. It has assumed importance as researchers have sought to understand how the state can best act to mediate contemporary tourism-related social, economic, political and environmental policy problems at a time when the role of the state has itself changed, given the dominance of neoliberal policy discourse in many developed countries (Hall 2011a). The chapter also discusses the various roles of the public sector and the changing nature of government intervention in tourism that may be described as a shift from government to governance. Nevertheless, the nation state and its national government are still extremely important sovereign actors in tourism policy.

'The value of the governance perspective rests in its capacity to provide a framework for understanding changing processes of governing' (Stoker 1998: 18).

The various ways in which the term 'governance' is used in tourism studies can therefore not be fully understood unless we also know its theoretical underpinnings and context (Bramwell & Lane 2011; Hall 2011a). In this chapter, different roles of government and the state in tourism are described and then analysed via different policy typologies, to enable the reader to understand the various means by which governments approach tourism policy in order to achieve policy objectives. The chapter will then examine the importance of cooperative strategies as a means of gaining producer support in the overall marketing, planning and development of a destination.

From government to governance

In public policy terms there has been a substantial transformation of the perceived role of government in general, and in tourism in particular, in recent years. This shift is sometimes referred to as a move from government to governance. Central to this shift has been a change in the relative role of state institutions, i.e. government agencies, in securing state-sponsored economic, environmental and social projects. For example, in developed countries many of the activities of the welfare state approach that existed until the beginning of the 1980s, including management of leisure and cultural facilities, are now operated and implemented by private sector providers or non-government organizations. Therefore, rather than the implementation of government policies being undertaken by a sole government agency, there is now a greater emphasis on partnership between government departments, state-owned or part-owned organizations that operate on a commercial basis (para-governmental organizations), the private sector and non-governmental organizations, in which the roles of government agencies and departments are to steer organizational networks and partnerships in a required direction (Hall 2005, 2011a; Bramwell & Lane 2011).

There is no single accepted definition of governance. This is reflected in Kooiman's (2003: 4) concept of governance as 'the totality of theoretical conceptions on governing'. Definitions tend to suggest a recognition of a change in political practices involving, amongst other things, increasing globalisation, the rise of networks that cross the public-private divide, the marketization of the state, and increasing institutional fragmentation (Hall 2011a). Nevertheless, the term tends to be used in two inter-related ways. The first describes contemporary state adaptation to its economic and political environment with respect to how it operates. The second meaning of governance is that it denotes a conceptual and theoretical representation of the role of the state in the coordination of socio-economic systems. Within this meaning two main strands can be identified. The first focuses on the capacity of the state to 'steer' the socio-economic system and therefore the relationships between the state and other policy actors (Pierre & Peters 2000, 2005). The second focuses on coordination and self-government, especially with respect to network relationships and public-private partnerships. For example, Rhodes (1996, 1997) identified a number of characteristics of governance:

- Interdependence between organizations.

- The concept of governance is broader than that of government and includes a role for non-state actors (i.e. private sector, non-government organizations and interest groups, including organisations in the voluntary sector).

- The boundaries between the public and other sectors are now far more opaque.

- The need to exchange resources and negotiate shared purposes between organization members of networks leads to ongoing interaction between those members.

- The rules of interaction within a network is set by its members, with trust being critical for the maintenance of network relationships.

- Many networks have a significant degree of autonomy from government and are self-organising.

- Although the state does not necessarily occupy a privileged position it can imperfectly and indirectly steer networks.

The latter characteristic of governance identified by Rhodes, and the significance of partnership relations between state agencies and other organizations has meant that both the development and the implementation of government policies has become extremely complex. Jessop (1997) referred to situation as one of 'meta-governance' as it requires the steering of multiple agencies and organizations, which although operating autonomously of one another, remain linked together through their involvement in common policy issues and associated funding and benefits. This situation is extremely relevant to tourism as it well describes the problem of many destination tourism organizations, which are often part or fully funded by government or even a part of the formal structure of the state, i.e. a government agency, and their role in trying to bring together other public agencies, tourism producers and even destination communities in common causes with respect to destination marketing and/or development. As noted frequently in this book, one of the key management characteristics of DMOs is that they do not own the products they are selling or promoting. Therefore, it is perhaps not surprising that ideas of partnership and collaboration are extremely important to understanding the relationships between individuals and organizations that exist in tourism networks.

Another important element in the development of the concept of governance is the changing nature of the nation state with state roles being reorganized functionally and territorially along sub-national, supranational and even trans-territorial lines.

- *Sub-national* state refers to the role of the local state (city, local or regional government) as a political actor at both domestic and international levels. For example, there is the development of a new regionalism in many parts of Europe and North America by which regional governments have acquired new rights and responsibilities and become more aggressive in seeking to acquire economic benefits. A good example of sub-national state activity in tourism is international destination marketing and promotion even when national tourism organizations may already be involved in such activities.

- *Supranational* states and organisations refers to organizations such as the European Union in which there are considerable regulatory capacities, and which also seeks to steer member government policies in certain directions. There are many supranational organizations that influence tourism at global or international levels. At a global level, organizations such as the UNWTO, IATA (International Aviation Transport Association) and the WTTC (World Travel and Tourism Council) affect various dimensions of nation-state tourism policies as well as the sub-national state. The WTTC, a private sector based organisation with membership by invitation only, has been extremely influential in achieving its policy goals, including adoption of tourism satellite accounts and liberalisation of the tourism sector as part of its overall policy positioning (Hall 2005).

- *Trans-territorial* states and organizations are those that have boundaries that include the territories of constituent members. For instance a number of trans-border regional agencies have been established within Europe with the support of the European Union and national and regional governments. One of the best examples of such a development in both general and tourism terms is the Øresund region of Denmark and Sweden.

Case study 6.1: Øresund: 'One Destination, Two Countries'

The Øresund region links the region of Skåne County in south-western Sweden with Region Zealand and the Capital Region in Denmark. It is centred on the cities of Copenhagen, the capital of Denmark, and Malmö in Sweden. The Øresund region has a combined population of approximately 3.75 million. The most concrete, as well as symbolic, example of the Øresund region was the construction of the cross-border Øresund bridge, across the Øresund Strait between Denmark and Sweden, which links Malmö and Copenhagen by road and train, although ferries still operate between Helsingborg in Sweden and Helsingør in Denmark to the north of the region.

Although a physical connection between Denmark and Sweden had been mooted since the Nineteenth Century, a new governance structure of an integrated region did not appear until the 1950s. Various economic and political factors delayed both the physical and political connection of the cross-border region until the convergence of a number of economic, political and intellectual interests in the late 1980s. These interests found organizational manifestation in a number of institutions that promoted the Øresund concept. Foremost among these is the region's governing body the Øresund Committee (Øresundskomiteen) which is a forum for local and regional politicians and authorities from both sides of the Øresund Strait. The Committee has been described as a 'classic example' of governance without government (Pike et al. 2006: 139). According to the OECD (2003):

> The committee is composed of local and regional bodies from both sides of the sound and – which is quite exceptional for transnational regionalism – by the two national ministries... The process of integration in Øresund is therefore achieved not through the set up of an additional government layer but through the voluntary coordination of policies of its members (OECD 2003: 160).

The key institutions of the Committee are the Copenhagen Regional Authority and the region of Skåne. Also of great importance are a number of other organizations that contributed to the institutionalization of the Øresund Region concept. These include:

- Scandinavian Academy of Management (a business and economics think tank)
- Medicon Valley Academy (a network organization that facilitates the collaboration of educational institutions and biomedical, biotechnological and pharmaceutical firms)
- Copenhagen Capacity (a marketing organization aimed at attracting and retaining firms and industries)
- Wonderful Copenhagen (a tourism marketing organization; Copenhagen has the region's international airport hub)
- Øresund University (a network composed of universities in the region with a secretariat based at Lund University and the University of Copenhagen)

■   Øresund Science Park (a network of the various science parks in the region)

According to Tangkjær (2000; Berg et al. 2000) the establishment of different institutions and organizations followed an 'open house' strategy in which every organization interested in contributing to cross-border integration was welcomed into the broader network so long as they followed some basic rules, such as not questioning the actual vision of regional integration. The development of such networks was regarded as important part of the regional strategy as it was seen as a way to not only mobilize support but also manifest the idea of an integrated region (Berg et al. 2000; Ek 2005). According to Ek (2006) the public discourse on and region building practices in the Øresund region can be characterised through the concept of simplicity.

The Øresund region process is to a high degree regarded by its advocates as simple in the sense of not being complicated or complex (but not in any way in the sense of being gullible or feeble-minded). It is regarded as a difficult process, as the region builders are up against sinewy national institutions and regulations as well as intangible national cultural differences. It is regarded as a heterogeneous process as it involves a multitude of different actors (even if the actors that set the tone are quite few) from local football clubs to the Chambers of Commerce. But still, the integration process is regarded as simple, imagined as similar to an organic process and possible to fulfil through an almost causal formula: 'better infrastructure, communications and transportation → higher mobility and interaction → regional integration' (Ek 2006).

Network development has practical implications for tourism as it encourages greater mobility within the region, both directly through requirements for business travel and meetings but also as a justification for further transport provision to support regional integration. In addition, running parallel to the institutionalization of the Øresund regional concept was the development of place marketing and promotional strategies that sought to reinforce an Øresund place identity internally and externally.

In business and industrial terms the region was marketed as a European 'hub of excellence', with the region being branded a 'human capital' so as to reinforce the positive social, economic and natural environment of the region, including a well-educated workforce and the geographic concentration of certain industries. In addition, other programmes, some of which were funded by the EU, were also created to reinforce regional identity. These included language and cultural programmes, including 'Cultural Bridge 2000' to parallel the opening of the Øresund Bridge. According to Ek (2005: 79):

> Through the use of maps and regional statistics, the Øresund region was represented as a fact rather than a vision or dream, and the 'Øresund citizen' was characterized as a well-off, mobile, postmodern cosmopolitan with a high degree of cultural capital and a larger curiosity about the world inherited from the Vikings and their interest in trade and travel (the common image of the Vikings as ravagers and warriors is quite misleading.

Nevertheless, even though the notion of a human capital is used in external advertising and promotion, Ek (2005) argues that this brand/identity has never successfully been adopted by the citizens of the region (see also Hospers 2008). Indeed, the Visit Øresund website now redirects to the Visit Copenhagen website. This situation perhaps reflects Ek's (2006) observation with respect to the 'simplicity' of the discourse of the Øresund region and region building in two ways. First, because the Øresund region has not been considered as a political project, the political and democratic consequences have not been appreciated. Second, the geographical imagination of the Øresund region is simplistic and has not been sensitive towards intra-regional political geographies. This has had the consequence that intra-regional tensions have not been addressed and handled in a thorough way and disputes have emerged around specific geographically-based projects and co-operative arrangements (Ek 2006; Collinge & Gibney 2010).

Key sources

Berg, P., Linde-Laursen, A. & Lofgren, O. (2000). *Invoking a Transnational Metropolis: The Making of the Øresund Region*. Lund: Studentlitteratur AB.

Collinge, C. & Gibney, J. (2010). Place-making and the limitations of spatial leadership: reflections on the Øresund. *Policy Studies* 31(4). 475-489.

Ek, R. (2005). Regional experiencescapes as geo-economic ammunition. In T. O'Dell (Ed.) *Experiencescapes: Tourism, Culture and Economy* (pp.69-89). Copenhagen: Copenhagen Business School Press.

Øresund region: www.oresund.com

Øresund tourism: www.visitoresund.info (opens the Visit Copenhagen site: http://www.visitcopenhagen.com/)

Øresund history and tourism: http://www.oresundstid.dk/kap/start.aspx

Skåne region: www.skane.com

Wonderful Copenhagen: www.visitcopenhagen.com

Discussion questions

1   What are the advantages and disadvantages of a cross-border approach to destination promotion and management?

2   On what basis is Øresund an example of transterritorial and supranational governance?

3   Why might the Øresund integrated region serve to increase human mobility, including tourism, within the region?

Multilevel governance

Although the regional scale has clearly emerged as an important one with respect to governance, 'determining the actual impact of the new regional governance is fraught with difficulty because it requires us to isolate the effects of one actor or set of actors among others' (Pike et al. 2006: 141). For example, the nation state is still the key element in international policy making and regulation and national governments remain central to the formulation of public policy. Yet there is little doubt that the processes of globalization have created a situation in which some policy areas that were at one time the sole realm of national governments in the developed countries have become internationalized, while other policy concerns have been translated down to the regional level.

Examples of policy fields that have become increasingly internationalized include aviation, environment, human rights, international trade and migration. These represent areas that by their nature pose problems that cross international boundaries. Therefore, one of the best ways in which they can be dealt with is the development of international institutions such as international law and regulation as well as the development of formal management agencies. Environmental issues, for example, such as climate change, marine pollution and the loss of biodiversity, are policy matters that cross national boundaries, because what happens in one country with respect to pollution or greenhouse gas emissions can have effects in other countries. Although tourism is limited as an international policy field, there are numerous policy areas that are subject to international convention that directly or indirectly affect the flows of tourists or tourism development. Tourism has therefore become subject to what is described as multilevel governance, in which destinations, as well as individual tourism products, are now subject to multilevel governance structures in which local, regional, national and supranational institutions and agencies all have a role. The complex nature of emergent levels of institutions and relations is illustrated in Figure 6.1.

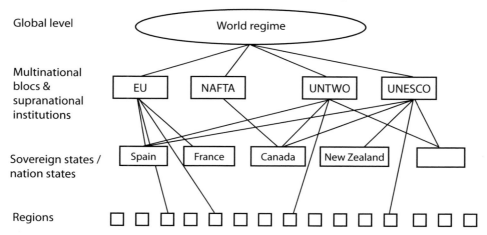

Figure 6.1: Elements of multilevel governance institutions and relations affecting tourism

According to Marks and Hooghe (2004: 16):

The dispersion of governance across jurisdictions is both more efficient than, and normatively superior to, central state monopoly. Most important is the claim that governance must operate at multiple scales in order to capture variations in the territorial reach of policy externalities. Because externalities arising from the provision of public goods vary immensely – from planet-wide in the case of global warming to local in the case of many city services – so should the scale of governance. To internalize externalities, governance must be multilevel.

However, the growth of new supranational and regional institutions is not without its critics, given that in many cases they are not democratically accountable to wider populations even though their decisions may have tremendous economic, social and environmental impacts. The complexity of multilevel governance is further complicated by the existence of private representative organizations, transnational businesses and non-governmental organizations that also act at domestic and international scales. For example, in tourism campaigns organized by non-government organizations to encourage people not to visit particular countries because of their human rights or environmental record.

The development of supranational institutions, such as international conventions, may also have significant long-term implications for tourism. For example, when international commercial aviation agreements were first being negotiated there was a divergence between the United States which advocated a free market and Britain and many other countries, particularly from Europe which argued for tight political restrictions, in part because of concerns that the market would become too dominated by American airlines. Governments secured the right to control all aspects of air travel to their country, including airline ownership, by allowing the country to set rules saying that only nationals of a given country could own and control an airline based in that country. However, the economic globalization of the aviation sector via improvements in transport technology and changes in constraints on trade and human mobility has meant that in many cases national airlines may be uneconomic to operate without there being direct government support. As Giovanni Bisignani, Director General of the International Air Transport Association stated 'Airline ownership restrictions became national rights… Now the flags on our aircraft are so heavy they are sinking the industry' (quoted in Phillips 2005: 13).

Regional changes in aviation regulation have occurred. American aviation has been relatively deregulated since the early 1980s, although considerable direct and indirect federal government exists for major carriers. Aviation in Europe was opened to limited competition in the mid-1990s when the European Union ended restrictions on cross-border operations with the EU. Australia and New Zealand also have a deregulated internal aviation market although international aviation rights beyond their borders remain substantially regulated, especially on key routes. Nevertheless, despite a degree of deregulation of the aviation regime that was developed in the post-Second World War era and the increasing financial pressures on airlines, particularly since 2001, the preeminence of national governments in determining international aviation flows remains. For example, prior to going bankrupt in 2008, Alitalia (Linee Aeree Italiane) was only kept afloat via large amounts of state aid. The 'new' Alitalia that re-launched operations in 2009 is 25% owned by Air France-KLM. Air France controls KLM (Netherlands) and Lufthansa (Germany) controls Swiss (the successor to Swissair the national airline of Switzerland), but in both cases KLM and Swiss have maintained their national identities as condition imposed by the Dutch and Swiss governments. In addition, they must maintain a major hub in each country.

Case study 6.2: World Heritage and issues of multilevel governance

The Convention for the Protection of the World's Cultural and Natural Heritage, to give the World Heritage Convention (WHC) its full name, was adopted by a United Nations Scientific, Education and Cultural Organisation (UNESCO) Conference on 16 November 1972. The Convention is designed to enable nations to cooperate in the protection of cultural and natural sites of outstanding value to humanity. It is often regarded as one of the pinnacles of world conservation (Hall 2000). 'The philosophy behind the Convention is straightforward: there are some parts of the world's natural and cultural heritage which are so unique and scientifically important to the world as a whole that their conservation and protection for present and future generations is not only a matter of concern for individual nations but for the international community as a whole' (Slatyer 1983: 138).

The Convention came into force in December 1975, when twenty nations had ratified it. The vast majority of the world's countries have either ratified or accepted the Convention. The signatories commit themselves to assist in the identification, protection, conservation and preservation of World Heritage properties. They undertake to refrain from 'any deliberate measure which might damage directly or indirectly' cultural or natural heritage (Art. 6(3)), and to 'take appropriate legal, scientific, technical, administrative and financial measures necessary for [its] identification, protection, conservation, presentation and rehabilitation' (Art. 5d).

World Heritage Sites are cultural (monuments, groups of buildings or sites) and natural (natural features, geological and physiographical features and sites) items which are selected by the definition of the Convention because they are judged to display universal value. Under the terms of the WHC each cultural property nominated should therefore:

(i)   represent a masterpiece of human creative genius; or

(ii)   exhibit an important interchange of human values, over a span of time or within a cultural area of the world, on developments in architecture or technology, monumental arts, town planning or landscape design; or

(iii)   bear a unique or at least exceptional testimony to a cultural tradition or to a civilization which is living or which has disappeared; or

(iv)   be an outstanding example of a type of building or architectural or technological ensemble or landscape which illustrates (a) significant stage(s) in human history; or

(v)   be an outstanding example of a traditional human settlement or landuse which is representative of a culture (or cultures), especially when it has become vulnerable under the impact of irreversible change; or

(vi)   be directly or tangibly associated with events or living traditions, with ideas, or with beliefs, with artistic and literary works of outstanding universal significance (the Committee considers that this criterion should justify

6

inclusion in the List only in exceptional circumstances and in conjunction with other criteria cultural or natural) (UNESCO 1999: Sec.24).

In addition cultural sites have to meet the test of authenticity in design, material, workmanship or setting and, in the case of cultural landscapes, their distinctive character and components, and have adequate legal and/or contractual and/or traditional protection and management mechanisms to ensure the conservation of the nominated cultural properties or cultural landscapes.

Natural sites must:

i)   be outstanding examples representing major stages of earth's history, including the record of life, significant ongoing geological processes in the development of land forms, or significant geomorphic or physiographic features; or

(ii)   be outstanding examples representing significant ongoing ecological and biological processes in the evolution and development of terrestrial, fresh water, coastal and marine ecosystems and communities of plants and animals; or

(iii)   contain superlative natural phenomena or areas of exceptional natural beauty and aesthetic importance; or

(iv)   contain the most important and significant natural habitats for insitu conservation of biological diversity, including those containing threatened species of outstanding universal value from the point of view of science or conservation (UNESCO 1999: Sec.44).

In addition, they should also fulfil a number of conditions regarding their integrity. These include: containing all or most of the key interrelated and interdependent elements in their natural relationships; should have sufficient size and contain the necessary elements to demonstrate the key aspects of processes that are essential for the longterm conservation of the ecosystems and the biological diversity they contain; should be of outstanding aesthetic value and include areas that are essential for maintaining the beauty of the site; should contain habitats for maintaining the most diverse fauna and flora characteristic of the biographic province and ecosystems under consideration; a management plan; adequate longterm legislative, regulatory, institutional or traditional protection; and should be the most important sites for the conservation of biological diversity (UNESCO 1999).

The WHC is widely regarded as one of the most significant and successful international heritage agreements. Unlike many international treaties that deal with environmental issues it is widely ratified. Ratification of the Convention imposes obligations on those that sign it. The WHC is an example of 'hard' international law. Hard international law refers to firm and binding rules of law such as the content of treaties and the provisions of customary international law to which relevant nations are bound as a matter of obligation. However, 'soft' international law is also significant for World Heritage. Soft law refers to regulatory conduct which, because it is not provided for in a treaty, is not as binding as hard law (Hall 2000). Examples of soft law include recommendations or declarations which are made by international conferences, agencies and associations.

The nature of the WHC makes it a very good example of the significance of multilevel governance. In the case of the WHC, nominations must be put forward by national governments to the World Heritage Committee where they are then analysed by experts from non-government heritage organizations. If site nominations are accepted, then national governments in concert with regional governments and various management agencies have a responsibility to appropriately manage sites. International law cannot be enforced in the same manner as domestic law, because nations can only rarely be compelled to perform their legal obligations. For example, in a study of World Heritage sites van der Aa (2005) found that while most sites have some degree of local or national legal protection, designation does not necessarily lead to an increase in legal protection under domestic law. Of the 64 sites he studied only 39% (25 sites) received further protection under law although, in certain situations, increased protection may be a precursor to nomination so as to ensure that a site has suitable protected status to enable appropriate management strategies. The complexity of multilevel governance is further evidenced in the case of the WHC as there is no standard legislative or regulatory approach that nations use to ensure that their obligations to the Convention are met, although the vast majority of sites are protected under existing national and local legislation and regulation. There is no common approach to developing participatory structures in the nomination and management process. In numerous cases listing is not fully supported by people at the local or regional level who may be directly affected by listing, with some stakeholders opposing nominations or the boundaries of nominated sites (e.g. van der Aa et al. 2004) particularly if they believe that it may restrict land use or development options. Instead, there is a vastly different array of regulatory and institutional instruments that parties to the World Heritage Convention use to manage sites. ranging from national park acts and heritage law through to planning ordinances and policy statements (Hall 2006).

In England planning policies were changed in 1994 so as to protect World Heritage properties from inappropriate development (Rutherford 1994; Wainwright 2000). No additional statutory controls follow from the inclusion of a UK site in the WH list. However, inclusion 'highlights the outstanding international importance of the site as a key material consideration to be taken into account by local planning authorities in determining planning and listed building consent applications, and by the Secretary of State in determining cases on appeal or following call-in' (Office of the Deputy Prime Minister 2005: para.2.22). This has already occurred with respect to an application to engage in mining activities near Hadrian's Wall (Rutherford 1994). Under the Policy Guidance from the Office of the Deputy Prime Minister, each local authority, as well as other interested parties, such as other public authorities, property owners, developers, amenity bodies and all members of the public, has to recognise the implications of World Heritage designation as well as other statutory designation, in the formulation of

> ... specific planning policies for protecting these sites and include these policies in their development plans. Policies should reflect the fact that all these sites have been designated for their outstanding universal value, and they should place great weight on the need to protect them for the benefit of future generations as well as our own.

6

Development proposals affecting these sites or their setting may be compatible with this objective, but should always be carefully scrutinised for their likely effect on the site or its setting in the longer term. Significant development proposals affecting [World Heritage Sites] will generally require formal environmental assessment, to ensure that their immediate impact and their implications for the longer term are fully evaluated (Office of the Deputy Prime Minister 2005: para.2.23).

Such an approach means that in England development projects that affect World Heritage sites, 'should always be carefully scrutinized for their likely effect on the site or its setting in the longer term' (Cookson 2000: 698) before planning approval can be given. Significantly, the English planning guidance with respect to World Heritage specifically refers to the Convention's *Operational Guidelines for the Implementation of the World Heritage Convention* (first produced in 1978 and revised regularly) as a document that local authorities should refer to with respect to the planning and management of World Heritage sites. In addition, local planning authorities are encouraged to work with owners and managers of sites in their areas, and with other agencies, to ensure that comprehensive management plans are developed. According to the planning guidance (Office of the Deputy Prime Minister 2005) these plans should:

- Appraise the significance and condition of the site;
- Ensure the physical conservation of the site to the highest standards;
- Protect the site and its setting from damaging development; and
- Provide clear policies for tourism as it may affect the site.

Key sources

Aa, B.J.M. van der, Groote, P.D. & Huigen, P.P.P. (2004). World heritage as NIMBY: The case of the Dutch part of the Wadden Sea. *Current Issues in Tourism* 7(4-5): 291-302.

Hall, C.M. (2006). World Heritage, tourism and implementation: What happens after listing. In A. Fyall & A. Leask (Eds) *Managing World Heritage Sites*, (pp.18-32). Oxford: Butterworth Heinemann. (The above UK example is abstracted from this chapter)

Rodwell, D. (2002). The World Heritage Convention and the exemplary management of complex heritage sites. *Journal of Architectural Conservation* 3: 40-60.

Discussion questions

1   How might local communities and stakeholders be able to influence decisions taken at the international level with respect to the World Heritage Convention?

2   Given that World Heritage sites are meant to be universally significant to humankind should the heritage interests of the global community have precedence over concerns of the local community or even national governments with respect to heritage management?

3   On what basis might it be possible to compare management strategies and their effectiveness at different World Heritage sites?

The roles of government in tourism

The exact nature of the roles of government in tourism changes from jurisdiction to jurisdiction and through the various scales at which governance occurs. Different countries will have constitutions and legislative frameworks that will give different powers over different topics to different levels of government. Furthermore, to make the picture even more complicated the role of government has changed over time. This has meant that in some countries government responsibility for tourism is clearly defined, while in others responsibility is taken up to varying degrees at different levels of government. Nevertheless, in general seven roles of government with respect to tourism can be identified. The forerunner to the UNWTO, the International Union of Tourist Organisations (IUOTO) (1974) in their discussion of the role of the state in tourism identified five areas of public sector involvement in tourism: coordination, planning, legislation and regulation, entrepreneur, and stimulation. To this may be added two other functions, a social tourism role, and a broader role of public interest protection (Hall 2008). These roles are outlined in more detail below.

■ Coordination

Coordination is necessary both within and between the different levels of government in order to avoid duplication of resources between the various government tourism bodies and the private sector, and to develop effective tourism strategies. Government often takes a major coordination role or facilitation role in bringing various tourism stakeholders together for common goals. The importance of government's coordination role has arguably increased in recent years as a result of the focus on governance.

■ Planning

Planning is the process of preparing a set of decisions for action in the future, directed at achieving identified goals by preferable means. Government planning for tourism occurs over different scales as well as different forms (economic, social, environmental, regional, urban, rural, land use, promotion and marketing, labour force) and is a major focus of government activity with respect to the development of tourism. However, many of the most significant planning activities that affect tourism often occur outside of tourism specific agencies, which usually only have a very limited legal mandate that concentrates on promotional activity. Therefore, much of the most important tourism planning occurs in agencies such as national parks, environment, culture and heritage or in the context of broader urban and rural planning at the regional level (see Chapter 8).

■ Regulation

One of the most important aspects of government as a sovereign institution is its legislative capacities. Therefore government's regulatory role with respect to tourism is critical. The regulation of tourism ranges from the authorisation of who can leave or enter countries, through to environmental, land use and health and safety issues. However, again, the vast majority of laws and regulations that affect tourism are actually not tourism specific. Therefore, policy decisions undertaken in other policy jurisdictions, e.g. economic policy, and conservation policy, may have substantial implications for the effectiveness of policy decisions undertaken in tourism. For example, general regulatory measures such as industry regulation, environmental protection, and taxation policy will significantly influence the growth of tourism. The level of government regulation of tourism tends to be a major issue for the various components of the tourism industry. Although industry recognises that government has a significant role to play, particularly when it comes to the provision of infrastructure, promotion or research from which industry benefits, the predominant argument by industry throughout most of the world is that the tourism industry must be increasingly deregulated so as to reduce compliance costs and therefore increase firm and destination competitiveness. However, from a broader public interest perspective, governments simultaneously have to manage demands from industry for deregulation with calls from some interest groups for increased regulation of tourism, e.g. in relation to conservation and environmental protection, and, increasingly, human rights and social justice.

■ Entrepreneur

Governments have long had an entrepreneurial role in tourism. Not only do they usually provide basic infrastructure, such as roads and sewage, or manage attractions, such as national parks and museums, but they may also own and operate tourist ventures including airlines, hotels and travel companies. Increasingly the role of government as entrepreneur has broadened to include the provision of event and sport facilities as well as sponsoring urban redevelopment projects. At the national level, government ownership of airlines, railways and hotel chains has diminished in recent years as such public assets have been privatized or corporatised. However, the local state has arguably increased its entrepreneurial role, particularly in respect to financially supporting hallmark events or major urban development programmes as part of a regional competitiveness strategy.

■ Stimulation

The stimulation role of government is similar to that of entrepreneurship but is more intangible because of the focus on services. Three major sources of stimulation exist.

1   The provision of financial incentives such as low cost loans, depreciation on capital or even direct subsidies to private investors.

2   Government funding of research, often at low or nil cost, which is then available to the private sector.

3 Financial support or the direct undertaking of marketing and promotion, generally aimed at generating tourism demand, although it can also take the form of promotion aimed at encouraging investment in tourism attractions and facilities. However, such is the size of the role that government plays in promotion that it is usually recognised as a separate function.

■ Promotion

Marketing and promotion has long been one of the main activities of government in tourism. This is possibly because of the territorial relationships between government and destinations. although it is also closely related to arguments that tourism promotion represents a 'public good' given the high degree of fragmentation between the various elements of the tourism industry and the various economic and social benefits that are accrued by wider society. Given the extent of producer fragmentation in tourism and the substantial degree of market failure that exists with respect to generic destination promotion, government has therefore supported destination promotion, particularly at the national level. In Australia a number of different means to fund national tourism promotion were examined (Hall 2000) including:

- Forcing businesses to pay a funding levy.
- 'User pays'/cooperative funding systems.
- Levies on foreign exchange earnings.
- Making government funding conditional on industry funding.
- Levies on tourism investment.
- Funding from a passenger movement charge.
- A commercial bed tax.
- Funding out of consolidated revenue.
- Funding out of a Goods and Services Tax (GST) [similar to VAT].

After examining the different potential forms of national government intervention, it was concluded that the most appropriate form to fund national tourism promotion was the appropriation of funds from consolidated revenue funds through normal budget processes. Several reasons for this conclusion were put forward:

- The inability to capture the benefits of generic marketing activity is severe given the fragmented nature of the tourism industry.
- Levies, user pays charges and business tax arrangements, including bed taxes, will institutionalise the 'freerider' or 'freeloader' problem whereby firms that do not financially support destination campaigns may benefit as much as those that do.
- The benefits of successful generic promotion as a travel destination are dispersed across the community (Hall 2008).

■ ## Social tourism

Social tourism refers to the provision of tourism opportunities for those that are otherwise economically or otherwise disadvantaged. During the period of welfare state provision in many western countries, holidays were often provided by governments or by unions or other non-government organisations, often at holiday camps and with subsidized transport. However, this function has declined dramatically over the past 25 years in Western society although some remnants still remain with respect to the roles of charities that often receive a degree of government funding.

■ ## Public interest

The final role of government in tourism is with respect to the traditional role of government in many societies to act as a protector of community or public interests, as opposed to just being willing to protect tourism interests. Furthermore, tourism policy needs to be understood in the context of broader economic, social and environmental policies that a government is trying to achieve for its polity, in that tourism should ideally be seen as a means to an end rather than an end in its own right. Although it is somewhat debatable as to whether it is a particular subset of the public interest role of government or a separate role in its own right, concern over the rights of the environment is an increasingly important public interest role of government. Several national jurisdictions have legislation that gives rights of conservation to rare and endangered species for example which means that development projects may not go ahead if they are a threatened species.

Types of regulation

Although identifying the different categories of government's involvement in tourism is a useful exercise in terms of differentiating the roles of government between levels of governance and between jurisdictions, it is not very helpful in assessing the nature of tourism public policy. One general model that assists in distinguishing between different policies is that of Anderson (1994) who identified four different policy types: regulatory, self-regulatory, distributive, redistributive. These four policy types can be combined in a matrix with the roles of government in tourism as a means of assessing tourism policy (Table 6.1)

■ *Regulatory policy* refers to the placement of restrictions and limits on the actions of individual persons or organizations. Regulatory provisions may include restrictions on individual mobility for either political or environmental reasons; restrictions on land use; or jurisdiction-wide resource protection laws (Parker 1999).

■ *Self-regulatory policy* is similar to regulatory policy in that it refers to controls on the behaviour of identified groups or individuals but is undertaken by the regulated group or non-government organization. Self-regulation may be utilized as a government policy so as to reduce its own costs of policy implementation or to satisfy the demands and needs of particular producer groups to reduce their compliance costs. However, self-regulation, like regulation, is only as effective as the extent to which compliance with regulations is sought. Unfortunately, the tourism industry are often poor self-regulators, particularly with respect to environmental concerns.

■ *Distributive policies* involve the distribution of benefits to particular groups in society. Parker (1999: 320) argues that distributive policy is 'fundamentally promotional in nature and governments rely heavily upon it to stimulate the tourism and ecotourism industries', although he also gives examples such as the use of investment tax credits, accelerated depreciation, leasing of property, subsidization and market support as exogenous distributive policies that are typically used to attract investment from external interests. Such measures may also be made available to domestic interests as well.

■ *Redistributive policies* are specific policies that government utilize to shift the distribution of wealth or other resources from one group in society to another. This may be undertaken on the basis of income levels, wealth, class, ethnicity or region. For example, in the 1980s ecotourism was conceived as a means of improving the level of economic well-being of otherwise marginal communities in peripheral areas. More recently, the notion of pro-poor tourism has become increasingly significant as it reflects a policy idea that tourism can be used as a targeted means of redistribution of wealth through encouraging consumers to undertake certain tourism activities in specific locations that require increased income and/or job creation.

Table 6.1: Policy matrix: Roles of government in tourism and policy types

Role of government	Regulatory policy	Self-regulatory policy	Distributive policy	Redistributive policy
Coordination				
Planning				
Entrepreneur				
Stimulation				
Promotion				
Social tourism				
Public Interest				

Frameworks of governance

As well as identifying the distributive nature of government policy it is also possible to categorise the nature of state intervention and the assumptions that underlie them. Hall (2011a) developed a framework that identified the variables that best clarify the core concepts of governance. This was done by reference to the relative use of hierarchical forms of regulation, i.e. legislation, and the relative power balance in the relationship between the state and other policy actors as categorical variables (Figure 6.2). Critical to the value of the different modes of governance are the relationships that exist between public and private policy actors and the steering modes that range from hierarchical top down to non-hierarchical approaches. Significantly, each of the modes of governance is related to the use of particular sets of policy instruments as well as different conceptual approaches to implementation (Hall, 2009) (Table 6.2).

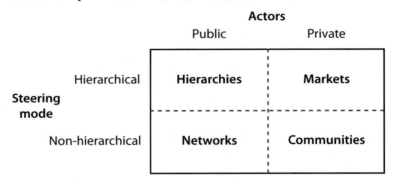

Figure 6.2: Frameworks of governance. Source: After Hall 2011a.

From politics to partnership?

The recent focus on ideas of governance in tourism (Hall 2005, 2011a) within a multi-scaled and multi-dimensional policy environment has focused attention on concepts such as partnership and cooperation, implying that if governance is the 'steering' of policy then stakeholders need to be working in the same direction. Partnerships are perceived as 'a search for efficiency within an organizationally fragmented and fiscally discontinuous landscape' (Lowndes 2001: 1962) as well as presenting new opportunities for uniting additional human and financial resources to build the capacity of tourism development. The notion of partnerships reflects the ideas of governance discussed above, that no single organization is capable of tackling messy policy problems, such as those which occur in tourism, by itself (Bramwell & Lane 2000). As Deas (2005: 205) states, the policy-making consensus within government managerial thinking increasingly sees 'cross-sector, inclusive partnership working as itself inherently preferable to the narrower, outmoded styles characteristically pursued by local government'. Partnership has become the dominant 'common-sense' of tourism policy in ways that make it a taken-for-granted element of governance either within tourism marketing and development, i.e. between public tourism organization and private tourism firms, or in regional development or promotion programmes that utilize tourism as an element, e.g. urban redevelopment projects in which tourism is integrated with retailing, sport, entertainment and property development (Bramwell & Lane 2000).

Table 6.2: Frameworks of governance and their characteristics. consumers and producers. Source: After Hall 2008, 2009, 2011a

	Hierarchies	Communities	Networks	Markets
Classificatory type characteristics	- Idealised model of democratic government and public administration - Distinguishes between public and private policy space - Focus on public or common good - Command and control ('top-down' decision-making) - Hierarchical relations between different levels of the state	- Notion that communities should resolve their common problems with minimum of state involvement ('bottom-up decision making) - Builds on a consensual image of community and the involvement of its members - Governance without government - Fostering of civic spirit	- Facilitate coordination of public and private interests to enhance efficiency of policy implementation and resource allocation - Range from coherent policy communities/ policy triangles through to single issue coalitions - Regulate and coordinate policy areas according to the preferences of network actors - Mutual dependence of network and state	- Belief in the market as the most efficient and just resource allocation mechanism - Belief in the empowerment of citizens as consumers - Use of monetary criteria to measure efficiency - Policy arena for economic actors where they cooperate to resolve common problems
Governance / policy themes	Hierarchy, control, compliance	Complexity, local autonomy, devolution, decentralised problem-solving	Networks, multi-level governance, steering, bargaining, exchange and negotiation	Markets, bargaining, ex change and negotiation
Policy standpoint	Top: policy makers; legislators; central government	Bottom: implementers; local officials and bureaucrats	Where negotiation and bargaining take place	Where consumers and producers bargaini
Underlying model of democracy	Elitist	Participatory	Hybrid/stakeholder; significant role given to interest groups	Consumer determined; citizen empowerment
Primary focus	Effectiveness: to what extent are policy goals actually met?	What influences action in an issue area?	Bargained interplay between goals set centrally and actor (often local) innovations	Efficiency: markets will provide the most efficient outcome
Criterion of success	When outputs / outcomes are consistent with a priori objectives	Achievement of actor (often local) goals.	Difficult to assess objectively; success depends on actor perspectives	Market efficiency
Implementation gaps/deficits	Occur when outputs / outcomes fall short of a priori objectives	'Deficits' a sign of policy change, not failure. They are inevitable	All policies are modified as a result of negotiation (there is no benchmark)	Occur when markets are not able to function
Reason for gaps/deficits	Good ideas poorly executed	Bad ideas faithfully executed	'Deficits' are inevitable as abstract policy ideas are made more concrete	Market failure; inappropriate indicator selection
Solution to implementation gaps/deficits	Simplify the implementation structure; apply inducements and sanctions	'Deficits' are inevitable	'Deficits' are inevitable	Increase the capacity of the market
Primary policy instruments	- Law - Regulation - Allocation and transfer of power between different levels of the state - Institutional arrangements - Licensing, permits, consents and standards - Removal of property rights - Regulatory based development guidelines and strategies	- Self-regulation - Public participation - Non-intervention - voluntary instruments - Information, education and social marketing - Direct democracy (referenda) - Community opinion polling - Capacity building of social capital	- Self-regulation and coordination - Accreditation schemes - Codes of practice - Industry associations - Non-government organisations - social marketing	- privatisation and/or corporatisation of state bodies - Use of pricing, subsidies and tax incentives to encourage desired behaviours - Voluntary instruments - Non-intervention - Education and training to influence behaviour

6

Many partnership programmes have been criticized for not bringing benefits to the communities they were meant to help (Cochrane 2007; Zapata et al. 2012). Instead, some potential stakeholders are often left out of partnership arrangements, particularly with respect to urban redevelopment schemes. Therefore, as Healey (1997: 70) noted, 'unless all stakeholders are acknowledged in the process, policies and practices will be challenged, undermined and ignored'. Genuine collaboration and partnership therefore operates on a model of power which is in keeping with the idea of the existence of a shared or public interest. A number of benefits of collaboration can be identified (Hall 2008):

- Broad comprehensive analysis of the domain improves the quality of solutions
- Response capacity is more diversified
- It is useful for reopening deadlocked negotiations
- The risk of impasse is minimised
- The process ensures that each stakeholder's interests are considered in any agreement
- Parties retain ownership of the solution
- Parties most familiar with the problem, not their agents, invent the solutions
- Participation enhances acceptance of solution and willingness to implement it
- The potential to discover novel, innovative solutions is enhanced
- Relations between the stakeholders improve
- Costs associated with other methods are avoided
- Mechanisms for coordinating future actions among the stakeholders can be established.

Yet critical to the collaborative process is the opportunity and capacity to participate. Genuine partnership in tourism development therefore may not mean the end of politics, but instead provide a structure by which the full range of opinions and perspectives of those impacted by tourism can be heard and addressed (Zapata et al. 2011). The inclusiveness of collaborative approaches may therefore help assist in dealing with some of the key problems of implementation in an increasingly complex environment for tourism policy and governance.

- Many tourism policies represent compromises between conflicting values of stakeholders.
- Many tourism policies involve compromises with key stakeholders and interests within the policy development and implementation structure.
- Many tourism policies involve compromises with key stakeholders and interests upon whom implementation will have an impact.
- Many tourism policies are framed without attention being given to the way in which underlying forces (particularly economic ones) and policy decisions outside of tourism will affect them

Such policy making difficulties for a field as full of diverse stakeholders as tourism are further complicated by the range of impacts that tourism has on destinations and the range of planning approaches that exist. These are issues that we will go on to examine in the next two chapters.

Summary

This chapter has examined the issues associated with governing the contemporary tourism product. Central to this has been the attention given to the changing role of government – the public sector – in governing tourism and the changing notion of governance itself. The concept of governance has been shown to refer to the capacity of government to steer the amalgam of public, private and third sector stakeholder organisations in the pursuit of tourism policies. The task of government with respect to tourism and tourism destinations is demonstrated to be more complex than ever, with increased potential for conflicts not only between different government roles and different forms of regulation with respect to tourism, but also different stakeholders. The nature of governance was also demonstrated to be multiscale in nature, whereby policy connections exist between international, national, regional and destination scales of governance. Nevertheless, despite the complexities and difficulties associated with governance of tourism and of destinations the state still continues to have a significant role with respect to both tourism policy and, perhaps more importantly for the nature and direction of tourism development, policies that affect tourism.

6

Self review questions

1   What are the seven *roles* of government in tourism identified in this chapter?

2   What justifications may be given for government subsidy of *destination promotion*?

3   Why has the extent of *multiscaled governance* increased, especially at the *supra-national* level?

4   What are the key characteristics of *governance*?

5   What are the differences between the four *policy types*?

6   What are the main differences between the four different *modes of governance*? To what extent do they reflect different philosophies about the appropriate role of the state?

7   What are the main benefits of *collaboration*?

8   Why is governance increasingly *complex* in tourism?

9   Does the *nation state* still have a role with respect to tourism?

Recommended reading

Pierre, J. & Peters, B.G. (2005). *Governing Complex Societies: Trajectories and scenarios.* Basingstoke: Palgrave.
An excellent overview of governance within the broader political science and public policy literature.

Journal of Sustainable Tourism, 2011, Volume 19 (numbers 4-5).
This is a special issue on governance with a focus on sustainable tourism. However, it provides an excellent range of perspectives on the subject.

Hall, C.M. (2008). *Tourism Planning,* 2nd ed. Harlow: Prentice-Hall.
Provides an account of tourism policy at various scales of analysis as well as the importance of cooperative approaches in tourism destinations.

Hall, C.M. & Jenkins, J.M. (1995). *Tourism and Public Policy.* London: Thomson.
A seminal work on theories of tourism public policy that remains relevant today.

Dredge, D. & Jenkins, J.M. (2007). *Tourism Planning and Policy.* Milton: John Wiley.
A good introduction to policy making issues in tourism.

Dredge, D. & Jenkins, J.M. (2003). Federal-state relations and tourism public policy, New South Wales, Australia. *Current Issues in Tourism* 6(5): 415-43.
A good analysis of multi-level policy and governance issues within federal systems.

Hall, C.M. (2011). A typology of governance and its implications for tourism policy analysis. *Journal of Sustainable Tourism.* 19(4-5), 437-457.
Provides a framework for the analysis of governance issues in tourism along with identifying different forms of state intervention.

Schilcher, D. (2007). Growth versus equity: The continuum of pro-poor tourism and neoliberal governance. *Current Issues in Tourism,* 10, 166–193.
Influential analysis of neoliberal approaches to governance and their implications for the poverty-tourism relationship.

Bramwell, B. & Lane, B. (Eds.) (2000). *Tourism Collaboration and Partnerships: Politics, Practice and Sustainability.* Clevedon: Channel View Publications.
One of the best collections of works on collaboration and partnership issues in tourism. This was also a special issue of *Journal of Sustainable Tourism.*

Zapata, M.J. & Hall, C.M. (2012). Public-private collaboration in the tourism sector: balancing legitimacy and effectiveness in Spanish tourism partnerships, *Journal of Policy Research in Tourism, Leisure and Events* 4(1), 61-83.
Analysis of public-private collaboration in tourism in a Spanish context that draws strongly on public policy and public administration literature.

References cited

Aa, B.J.M. van der (2005). *Preserving the Heritage of Humanity? Obtaining World Heritage Status and the Impacts of Listing*, Doctoral Thesis, Faculty of Spatial Sciences, University of Groningen, Groningen.

Aa, B.J.M. van der, Groote, P.D. & Huigen, P.P.P. (2004). World Heritage as NIMBY: The case of the Dutch part of the Wadden Sea. *Current Issues in Tourism* 7(4-5), 291-302.

Anderson, J.E. (1994). *Public Policymaking: An Introduction*. Dallas: Houghton Mifflin.

Berg, P., Linde-Laursen, A. & Lofgren, O. (2000) *Invoking a Transnational Metropolis: The Making of the Øresund Region*. Lund: Studentlitteratur AB.

Bramwell, B. & Lane, B. (Eds.) (2000). *Tourism Collaboration and Partnerships: Politics, Practice and Sustainability*, Clevedon: Channel View Publications.

Bramwell, B. & Lane, B. (2011). Critical research on the governance of tourism and sustainability. *Journal of Sustainable Tourism* 19(4-5), 411-421.

Cochrane, A. (2007). *Understanding Urban Policy: A Critical Approach*. Oxford: Blackwell Publishing.

Collinge, C. & Gibney, J. (2010). Place-making and the limitations of spatial leadership: reflections on the Øresund. *Policy Studies* 31(4). 475-489.

Deas, I. (2005). Synchronization, salesmanship and service delivery: governance and urban competitiveness. In N. Buck, I. Gordon, A. Harding and I. Thurok (Eds), *Changing Cities: Rethinking Urban Competitiveness, Cohesion and Governance* (pp. 204-222). Basingstoke: Palgrave Macmillan.

Ek, R. (2005). Regional experiencescapes as geo-economic ammunition. In T. O'Dell (Ed.) *Experiencescapes: Tourism Culture and Economy*, pp. 69-89. Copenhagen: Copenhagen Business School Press.

Ek, R. (2006). The Öresund region – six years with the bridge. Paper presented at Towards a New Nordic Regionalism? Conference arranged by the Nordic Network of the Regional Studies Association in Balestrand, Norway, 4-5 May 2006

Hall, C.M. (2005). *Tourism: Rethinking the Social Science of Mobility*, Harlow: Prentice-Hall.

Hall, C.M. (2006). World Heritage, tourism and implementation: What happens after listing. In A. Fyall and A. Leask (Eds), *Managing World Heritage Sites*, pp. 18-32. Oxford: Butterworth Heinemann.

Hall, C.M. (2008) *Tourism Planning* (2nd ed.). Harlow: Pearson.

Hall, C.M. (2009). Archetypal approaches to implementation and their implications for tourism policy, *Tourism Recreation Research*, 34(3): 235-245.

Hall, C.M. (2010). Tourism and the implementation of the Convention on Biological Diversity, *Journal of Heritage Tourism*, 5(4), 267-284.

6

Hall, C.M. (2011a). A typology of governance and its implications for tourism policy analysis. *Journal of Sustainable Tourism.* 19(4-5), 437-457.

Hall, C.M. (2011b). Policy learning and policy failure in sustainable tourism governance: From first and second to third order change? *Journal of Sustainable Tourism* 19(4-5), 649-671.

Healey, P. (1997). *Collaborative Planning: Shaping Places in Fragmented Societies,* Basingstoke: Macmillan Press.

Hospers, G-J. (2008). Governance in innovative cities and the importance of branding. *Innovation: Management, Policy & Practice* 10,. 224-234.

Jessop, B. (1997). Capitalism and its future: Remarks on regulation, government and governance. *Review of International Political Economy* 4(3), 561-581.

Kooiman, J. (2003). *Governing as Governance.* Los Angeles: Sage.

Lowndes, V. (2001). Rescuing Aunt Sally: Taking institutional theory seriously in urban politics. *Urban Studies* 38(11), 1953-71.

Marks, G. & Hooghe, M. (2004). Contrasting visions of multi-level governance. In I. Bache & M. Flinders (Eds) *Multi-level Governance.* Oxford: Oxford University Press.

Maskell, P. & Törnqvist, G. (1999). *Building a Cross-border Learning Region: Emergence of the North European Øresund Region.* Copenhagen: Handelshøjskolens Forlag.

OECD (2003). *OECD Territorial Reviews: Øresund, Denmark/Sweden.* Paris: OECD.

Office of the Deputy Prime Minister (2005). *Planning Policy Guidance 15: Planning and the Historic Environment,* London: Office of the Deputy Prime Minister.

Parker, S. (1999). Ecotourism, environmental policy and development. In D.L. Soden and B.S. Steel (Eds.), *Handbook of Global Environmental Policy and Administration,* pp. 315-345. New York: Marcel Dekker.

Phillips, D. (2005). National pride, missed connections. *International Herald Tribune* 11-12 June: 13, 15.

Pierre, J. & Peters, B.G. (2000). *Governance, Politics and the State.* New York: St. Martin's Press.

Pierre, J. & Peters, B.G. (2005). *Governing Complex Societies: Trajectories and Scenarios.* Basingstoke: Palgrave.

Rhodes, R. (1996). The new governance: governing without government. Political Studies 44, 652-667.

Rhodes, R.A.W. (1997). *Understanding Governance: Policy Networks, Governance, Reflexivity and Accountability.* Buckingham: Open University Press.

Rodwell, D. (2002). The World Heritage Convention and the exemplary management of complex heritage sites. *Journal of Architectural Conservation* 3, 40-60.

Rutherford, L. (1994). Protecting World Heritage sites: Coal Contractors Limited v Secretary of State for the Environment and Northumberland County Council. *Journal of Environmental Law* 6(2), 369-84.

Slatyer, R.O. (1983). The origin and evolution of the World Heritage Convention. *Ambio* 12(3-4), 138-9.

Stoker, G. (1998). Governance as theory. *International Social Science Journal* 50(155), 17–28.

Tangkjær, C. (2000). *'Åbent Hus': Organiseringen Omkring Øresundsregionen.* Copenhagen: Handelshøjskolens Forlag.

UNESCO Convention for the Protection of the World Cultural and Natural Heritage [adopted on November 16, 1972], UNESCO Document 17 c/106 of 15 November, 1972.

United Nations Educational, Scientific and Cultural Organisation (Unesco) Intergovernmental Committee for the Protection of the World Cultural And Natural Heritage (1999). *Operational Guidelines for the Implementation of the World Heritage Convention.* Paris: UNESCO.

Wainwright, G.J. (2000) The Stonehenge we deserve. *Antiquity* 74, 334-342.

Zapata, M.J., Hall, C.M., Lindo, P. & Vanderschaeghen, M. (2011). Can community-based tourism contribute to development and poverty alleviation? *Current Issues in Tourism* 14, 725-749.

Zapata, M.J. & Hall, C.M. (2012). Public-private collaboration in the tourism sector: balancing legitimacy and effectiveness in Spanish tourism partnerships, *Journal of Policy Research in Tourism, Leisure and Events* 4(1), 61-83.

6

7 Consequences of Visitation at the Contemporary Destination

Chapter objectives

After reading this chapter you will:

- Be able to appreciate some of the positive and negative perceptions of tourism's effects.

- Appreciate that although the destination is a focal point of attention to the impacts of tourism, effects occur over all stages of the geographical tourism system.

- Understand that the consequences of tourism are *contextual* and *situational*.

- Understand the potential significance of change for the consumption and production of tourism.

- Be able to identify some of the key factors that affect the assessment of the effects of tourism.

Introduction

Being aware of the consequences of visitation is not just important in terms of environmental and social responsibilities but also in terms of good business practice (Gössling et al. 2009). As has been stressed throughout this book, the multiple layers of the tourism product, especially with respect to the destination product, means that consideration needs to be given to the people and environments that are packaged as part of that product as otherwise the various qualities of a place that make it attractive to visit will be eroded. Therefore, an appreciation of the effects of tourism is vital to understanding the contemporary business environment of tourism as well as its relationship to destinations.

One of the most significant debates in contemporary tourism centres on the positive and negative dimensions of tourism development. For many years tourism was generally seen in a favorable light and regarded as having a benign influence on destinations. However, with the advent of a new generation of jet aircraft in the late 1960s and early 1970s, and a consequent massive year on year growth in international travel which continues to the present day, tourism has now come to be seen as possibly having undesirable effects for destinations, in addition to its potential economic benefits.

This chapter discusses some of the effects of tourist visitation. These impacts are discussed under various headings but the chapter emphasises that these are not discrete categories. It first examines some of the positive and negative dimensions of tourism before going on to outline some of the issues that arise in assessing tourism. These issues are important because they represent a vital step in being able to accurately assess the consequences of tourism on people and places. The chapter then concludes by outlining different forms of the relationship between tourism and its various environments.

The positive and negative consequences of tourism

7

One of the significant dimensions in assessing the consequences of tourism is that its effects are often interpreted differently by different people at different times. For example, increases in property values as a result of tourism development are often regarded positively by property owners and municipalities who gain income from property taxes, but negatively by those who rent properties as they often lead to increased rents as well as making it more difficult to buy into the property market. In addition, perceptions and understandings of the consequences of tourism will also be different between destinations depending on the different attitudes towards tourism and the changes it is related to and broader values and goals in society.

Within the tourism literature the impacts of tourism have usually been divided into three main categories: environmental (referring to the physical environment), social and economic (e.g. Matheson & Wall 1982; Hall & Lew 2009). These categories are not mutually exclusive and have a significant degree of overlap but they serve as reasonable semantic devices by which to discuss tourism's effects (Figure 7.1). The interrelationships and interdependencies between economic, environmental and social dimensions means that they also act as the main categories around which the notion of sustainable development is considered (see Chapter 8).

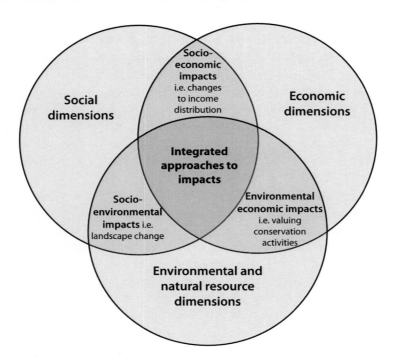

Figure 7.1: Interrelationships between traditional categorization of tourism's impacts

   For consequences of tourism to be visible, change has to occur. Therefore change is an integral concept for understanding the impacts of tourism. Where change occurs very slowly and is incremental in nature, there are usually relatively few negative attitudes towards tourism. Most circumstances in which negative attitudes towards tourism develop are usually related to rapid rates of change that is seen to be tourism induced. Although change is normal, rapid change makes it difficult for people to adapt to their new economic, social and physical environments. However, in recent years the rapid growth of tourism and tourism-related infrastructure and facilities has meant that the perceived consequences of tourism have been steadily increasing. Tourism is no different from any other form of industrial development in terms of its potential for change. Indeed, some may argue that it may even have greater potential to contribute to change in some areas, such as with respect to culture and social relations, because the co-creation of tourism experiences intrinsically requires social exchange.

   An additional issue with respect to assessing the consequences of tourism is that they occur at different scales and at different stages of the tourist trip. For example, with respect to the elements of the geographical tourism system (Figure 1.2, page 4) many of the effects of tourism occur outside of the destination. The generation of greenhouse gas emissions from transport primarily occurs along the transit route, but has effects on all elements of the system (Scott et al. 2012). At the individual level, people living at all stages of the production of trip are affected by the consumption and production of the tourism experience. This includes people working in the tourism industry, such as those involved in enabling the tourist to get to and from the destination, as well as in the destination themselves as part of the tourism labour force. However, importantly, this will also include the tourists themselves who will be affected by the travel experience. Indeed, one of the most significant insights of understanding that tourism experiences are co-created (Chapter 1) is that this invariably means that there are social exchanges between consumer and producer, as well as, of course, economic and environmental exchanges, although the latter is often not so visible. This observation does not mean that such exchanges will be equal in terms of such factors as, for example, power, roles, income, language or status, but it does mean that such exchanges occur and that both parties will be affected in some way.

People living along transit routes and in the generating region near major transport connections, such as airports, will also be affected by tourism. This is often most visible in terms of their reaction to noise and other pollution as a result of tourism transport, but will also include significant economic impacts because of the contribution of tourism to employment along transit routes, even if people do not stay overnight on their way to their main destination. Although tourism has consequences at all stages of the trip, the greatest concentration of impacts usually occurs at the destination (Figure 7.2). The next section will discuss some of the key dimensions of destination effects.

Relative tangibility of consequences of tourism to external view	Examples of dimensions in which effects of co-creation of tourism are observed	Generating Region	Transit Region	Destination	Environment external to tourist trip
HIGH ↑↓ LOW	Physical environment				
	Built environment				
	Economic environment				
	Socio-cultural environment				
	Product / service environment				
	Personal - consumer	consumer	consumer	consumer	
	Personal – producer	producer	producer	producer	

Figure 7.2: Change matrix of consequences of tourism. Shading indicates relative change as a consequence of the consumption and production of tourism. The darker the shading the more apparent the consequences.

Within the tourism literature, several key themes emerge (see Lew et al. 2004 for a selection of review chapters that detail some of these themes). The economic dimension is obviously significant as it is the potential income and employment aspects of tourism that drive government and destination policy with respect to tourism marketing and management. In the economic sphere, primary concerns are with the economic contribution of tourism to destination and national growth and economic development and employment generation. Secondary issues focus on the opportunity costs of tourism development, linkages with other sectors and the implications of foreign investment.

With respect to environmental consequences, attention has focused on tourism contribution to a loss of naturalness, landscape changes, changes to physical environmental systems and habitats and their consequences and issues of biodiversity. Secondary concerns have often focused on specific environments, such as alpine areas or coral reefs, as well as the relationship between tourism and conservation. Perhaps most significantly with respect to the environmental consequences of tourism is the realisation that the impacts of tourism occur at more than just the destination and this has therefore led to a substantial reevaluation of the environmental dimensions of contemporary tourism (see Chapter 13 for a fuller discussion of the implications of this).

The social and cultural consequences of tourism are extremely complex as they relate not only to the different scales at which change occurs: cultures, communities, and individuals; but also to particular categories of individuals: tourists and the producers of the tourism experience whether they be formally a part of the tourism industry or of the broader human resource base by belonging to the destination. To complicate matters still further the same individual will often fulfill different roles at different times over their life course, at one time being a tourist and at another time being a producer. Indeed, in some situations it is possible that an individual may be both a tourist and a part of the tourist experience for someone else.

At the destination level, a key theme is the extent to which tourism leads to changes in the sense of place of a community (see also Chapter 5) as well as to its culture. Such changes are usually seen in a negative light, however in some instances tourism has been credited with helping to conserve culture by providing a market for cultural activities that otherwise had little external value outside of that culture. In one sense this is similar to the value that tourism can bring to the environment by creating a market for national parks and ecotourism products that otherwise may have only limited market value. However, change is individual as well as collective, therefore there is also significant interest in how tourism has consequences for personal values and attitudes and how these may change. For tourists many of these consequences will usually be felt back in their home environment after they have had the opportunity to reflect on their experiences, in terms of the encounters that occurred on the trip, but also how such experiences may cast new light on their social relations at home or work and on concepts and understandings of self. For individuals who are part of the tourism product, the service experience may have tasks of performance and emotional labour that also lead to reassessment of notions of self and personal relations.

Indeed, the nature of the tourist experience also leads to considerable interest in the values that are exchanged, and their appropriateness, as well as on the very authenticity of the experiences that all parties have, but particularly from the consumer's perspective.

Table 7.1 details some of the main positive and negative effects of tourism that have been detailed in the tourism literature, organized by six different categories of primarily collective impact. One of the immediate observations that can be made of the consequences of tourism is that the same consequence can be seen as either positive or negative – even in the same destination – depending on the perspective of the viewer and the situation in which it occurs. A fundamental element of understanding contemporary tourism is that the consequences of tourism are *contextual* and *situational*. This does not mean that they do not occur in an empirical sense nor that they are unimportant. Instead, it highlights the fact that from a services perspective, in which we have the co-creation of tourism experiences as the core of our understanding of contemporary tourism phenomenon, then what is critical for managing those consequences is knowing how and why they are identified as consequences over which stakeholder concern is expressed and action may be required.

Table 7.1: Perceived impacts of tourism on destinations identified in tourism literature.

Positive	Negative
Economic	
Increased expenditures	Localised inflation and price increases
Creation of employment	Replacement of local labour by outside labour
Increase in labour supply	Greater seasonal unemployment
Increased value of real estate	Real estate speculation
Increase in standard of living	Increased income gap between wealthy and poor
Improved investment in infrastructure and services	Opportunity cost of investment in tourism means that other services and sectors do not get support
Increased free trade	Inadequate consideration of alternative investments
Increased foreign investment	Inadequate estimation of costs of tourism development
Increased free trade	Increased free trade
	Loss of local ownership
Tourism/Commercial	
Increased destination awareness	Acquisition of a poor reputation as a result of inadequate facilities, improper practices or inflated prices
Increased investor knowledge concerning the potential for investment and commercial activity in the destination	Negative reactions from existing enterprises due to the possibility of new competition for human resources and state assistance
Development of new infrastructure and facilities, including accommodation and attractions	Inappropriate destination images and brands are used

7

Increase in accessibility

Improvements in destination image	Negative effects on destination image

Environmental/Physical

Changes in natural processes that enhance environmental values	Changes in natural environmental processes
Maintenance of biodiversity	Loss of biodiversity
Architectural conservation	Architectural pollution
Preservation of natural and built heritage	Destruction of heritage
Maintenance and recreation of habitat and ecosystems	Destruction of habitat and ecosystems / competition for existing land uses
Conservation measures to reduce impact	Exceeding physical carrying capacity / reducing natural capital
Biosecurity measures	Introduction of alien species
Improved sewage systems	Increased run-off leading to eutrophication and algal blooms
Water conservation	Increased demand on water supply

Social/Cultural

Increased local participation in destination activities and events	Commercialisation and commodification of activities, events and objects that may be of a personal nature
Community renewal	Changes in community structure
Strengthening of community values and traditions	Weakening or loss of community values and traditions
Exposure to new ideas through globalization and transnationalism	Increases in criminal activity
Creation of new community space	Loss of community space
	Social dislocation
	Exceeding social carrying capacity
	Loss of authenticity

Psychological

Increased local pride and community spirit	Tendency toward defensive attitudes concerning host regions
Tourism as a force for peace	High possibility of misunderstandings leading to varying degrees of host/visitor hostility
Increased awareness of non-local values and perceptions	Increased alienation as a result of changes to what was familiar

Political/Administrative

Enhanced international recognition of destination region	Economic exploitation of local population to satisfy ambitions of political elite / growth coalitions
Greater political openness	Use of tourism to legitimate unpopular decisions or regimes
Development of new administrative institutions	Tourism used to fund repressive regimes and legitimate their ideologies

Source: Mathieson & Wall 1982; Ritchie 1984; Krippendorf 1987; Hall 1992, 2005; Lew et al. 2004; Gössling & Hall 2006; Hall & Page 2006.

Case study 7.1: Economic impact of the Football World Cup

Football (soccer) is the world's favorite sport. The Football World Cup is one of the world's largest sporting hallmark events which has significant impacts on the host nation as well as on participating countries. For example, research by ABN-AMRO (van Leeuwen & Kalshoven 2006) suggested that a World Cup winner enjoys an average economic bonus of 0.7% additional growth, while the losing finalist suffers an average loss of 0.3% compared to the previous year. However, the demands of hosting a World Cup are substantial (Table 7.2). For example, in the case of the FIFA World Cup: 'Any host country requires a comprehensive tax exemption to be given to FIFA and further parties involved in the hosting and staging of an event'. Guarantee no.3 requires 'Full tax exemption of FIFA and FIFA subsidiaries' and 'is not limited to the events and is not limited time-wise' (in Pollock 2010).

The exemption stated in this section shall encompass all revenues, profits, income, expenses, costs, investments and any and all kind of payments, in cash or otherwise, including through (i) the delivery of goods or services, (ii) accounting credits, (iii) other deliveries, (iv) applications, or (v) remittances, made by or to FIFA and/or FIFA subsidiaries (in Pollock 2010).

This means that to be successful in its bid, a government must agree to forgo large amounts of tax revenue for the benefit of FIFA, a charitable organization that pays little tax in its home country Switzerland.

Table 7.2: FIFA requirements for government guarantees and infrastructure technical requirements for a World Cup (abridged)

- Entry and exit permits are to be issued to all officials related to FIFA and national organisations, and to media representatives and visitors.

- Work permits (if required by local law) are to be provided to all officials and staff related to FIFA and finalist teams, and media representatives.

- Customs duty and taxes are not to be raised for the temporary import and subsequent export of goods, supplies, personal belongings, gifts and equipment of players, officials and the media.

- Security shall be provided by the host country, including at airports, city centres, anti-terrorist activities etc., and a guarantee of safety and personal protection shall also apply to the FIFA delegation, media representatives and spectators during, before and after matches, including when travelling around the country.

- Government shall guarantee unrestricted import and export of all foreign currencies as well as the exchange and re-conversion of these currencies into US dollars or Swiss Francs.

- The Government shall guarantee the installation of a telecommunications network.

- The host country shall assist the organising association in setting up an international broadcast centre and a media centre.
- The national transport network shall provide the transport necessary for the technical organisation of a FIFA World Cup.
- A hotel pricing policy is required, that freezes hotel prices for officials related to FIFA and accredited media at the level of the beginning of the year that the World Cup competition will be held.
- The host country shall not exact any kind of taxes, charges, duties or Government levies from FIFA or the team delegations.
- Commissions on tickets shall not exceed 10 per cent of the face value of the ticket.
- The host country shall guarantee that all national anthems and flags will be provided at matches.
- The host country shall guarantee the availability of comprehensive medical care including an emergency service for every participant.
- The following stadium infrastructure specifications are likely to be required in a future World Cup bid:
  - eight to twelve stadia are required;
  - prospective stadia must have the following capacity:
  - for group matches, the round of 16 and the quarter finals (excluding media and VIPs) – a minimum of 40,000 people; and
  - for the opening match, semi-finals and final (excluding media and VIPs) – a minimum of 60,000 people;
  - prospective stadia must be seated with no perimeter fences;
  - there must be a natural turf pitch measuring at least 105x68 metres, with a further 7.5 metres between the pitch and spectators behind each goal and 6 metres around the side touchlines;
  - a minimum of 10 technical and administrative rooms must be available; and
  - a choice of training grounds, in good condition, close to competitor's living quarters must be available.

Source: HM Treasury (2007) *Hosting the World Cup: A Feasibility Study*, HMSO: 17, 18, 19, Crown copyright.

In the 2010 competition in South Africa, a 'tax-free bubble' was established around the tournament at FIFA's request, relieving FIFA, its subsidiaries, and foreign football associations which are taking part, of income tax, customs duties, and VAT (Pollock 2010). This also applied to the various organisations designated as FIFA's commercial affiliates, licensees, host broadcasters, broadcast rights agencies, merchandise partners, service providers, concession operators and providers of hospitality. It also means that the tournament income of the players, some of whom are among the highest paid earners in the world, were exempt from tax for World Cup related activities in South Africa (Hall 2012). According to Moray Wilson, from the professional advisory firm Deloitte in Cape

Town 'The host government has given away almost the entire tax-take to FIFA' (in Pollock 2010). Given the public costs of staging hallmark events, it is therefore perhaps not surprising that when people were surveyed as to whether Britain should bid to host a World Cup that slightly more people were against a bid because of concerns over costs as those who believed that it would be good for the economy (Table 7.3).

Table 7.3: Reasons for being in favour of or against World Cup bid

Main reasons for being in favour of a bid	% of those in favour
'Good for the economy'	42
'National pride'	39
'Interest in football'	31
'Better chance that England will win'	9
'Motivating others to play football'	9
'Good for the country'	5

Main reasons for being against a bid	% of those against
'Costs'	49
'Not interested in football'	26
'Football hooliganism/trouble'	19
'Not very good at organising such things'	5

Source: HM Treasury (2007) *Hosting the World Cup: A Feasibility Study*, HMSO: 17, 18, 19, Crown copyright.

Hallmark sporting events have long been recognized as being significant for the promotion of sports tourism, urban regeneration strategies and reimaging (Ritchie & Adair 2004; Hall 2005; Hinch & Higham 2011) and being part of a broader political economy of sport (Nauright & Schimmel 2005). According to the UK Treasury ,cities and countries bid to host global sporting events for a variety of reasons, other than the pure sporting spectacle:

- The positive economic impact of visitors during the event and potential for new tourism markets.
- As a catalyst for the economic regeneration of a city or region.
- The intangible benefits often associated with sporting events including increases in national pride and strengthened identity.
- The opportunity to showcase an emerging nation or city – this has become especially relevant in recent years with the awarding of the Summer Olympics in 2008 to Beijing and the 2010 Football World Cup to South Africa (HM Treasury 2007: 5).

The 2006 FIFA World Cup in Germany provides a range of positive perspectives of the value of hosting the event. A study for Postbank, a German bank that was one of the 2006 World Cup's competition sponsors, reported that the 2006 World Cup in Germany should create 40,000 jobs in the country and that GDP should rise by about €10 billion (approximately US$12 billion) (Milne 2005a), a figure representing 0.5% of the German economy's total domestic productivity. The study also said that World Cup 2006 could help create 10,000 to 20,000 permanent jobs (Davis 2006). The World Cup was also regarded as important for the morale of German industry given the then downturn of the German economy. According to Herbert Heiner, chief executive of Adidas, the world's second largest sporting goods manufacturer and an official World Cup sponsor for which it paid approximately US$56.5 million for exclusive marketing rights (Davis 2006), 'It is a very good chance for us and the whole of Germany to push us out of the agony we have in the country... With a positive World Cup we can bring some optimism to the country and to the economy in general' (in Milne 2005a: 20). In order to maximize returns from the Cup, Adidas brought together 100 people to work solely on preparations for the World Cup with the aim of achieving soccer sales of €1 billion in 2006, up from €900 million in 2004. However, actual results were even better with Adidas reporting a 37% rise in sales in first quarter 2006 and reported sales of US$1.5 billion during World Cup 2006, an increase of 30% on the previous Cup (Davis 2006). An example of the impact of a World Cup on Adidas is that Adidas reported sales of 15 million replica footballs – over double the sales of the six million official World Cup soccer balls of the 2002 World Cup (Milne 2005b).

Other companies also believed they would benefit. For example, Jochen Zeitz, head of the world's number three sporting goods manufacturer, Puma, stated, that 'it will have a lot of impact on confidence in our industry and in the retail sector' (in Milne 2005a: 20). This was despite the fact that Puma could not be an official sponsor of the World Cup and instead sponsored players, e.g. Freddie Ljungberg of Sweden, and national teams, e.g. Cameroon and Italy. An indication of the commercial importance attached to the World Cup was that Puma even brought forward the launch of its strategic plan by a year so that it coincided with the 2006 competition and ends with the 2010 Cup in South Africa.

The worldwide interest in the World Cup explains its attraction to both government and industry alike. According to FIFA (2007) 'the FIFA World Cup™ represents one of the most effective global marketing platforms which offers sponsors unmatched opportunities for reaching out to the consumer. ... [and] ... reaches an audience of a size and diversity that is unrivalled by any other single-sports body'. The 2006 World Cup in Germany was covered by 500 television broadcasters and generated total coverage of more than 73,000 hours, equivalent to over eight years of broadcasting. Media interest is also indicated by the 18,850 accredited journalists the tournament hosted. Of these, 13,400 were television and radio representatives, 4,250 print journalists and 1,200 were photographers. The official website FIFAworldcup.com registered 4.2 billion page views in total during the competition (FIFA 2007).

The 64 matches at the 2006 World Cup had a total attendance of 3.36 million people with an average attendance per game of 52,491. This was the second-biggest attendance in World Cup history with the largest being the 1994 Cup in the United States which attracted 3.59 million people to games with an average attendance of 68,991 (there were 52 matches in the 1994 event). Nevertheless, in the German tournament many international visitors still traveled to Germany even though they would never get to tickets to see a game live in order to experience the atmosphere and watch the game on giant screens at 'Fan Fests' which had been organized by the World Cup host cities.

The 2006 World Cup was undoubtedly an opportunity for substantial investment in sport and other infrastructure with investment having substantial legacies with respect to employment, infrastructure, and tax benefits (Ahlert 2000). €1,510.4 million was invested in stadium development for the World Cup of which €575.9 million was public financed. €124.6 million was invested in new media facilities though the greatest amount of investment was on transport infrastructure. Within the 12 regions in which World Cup matches were staged €3,577.1 million was invested in transport infrastructure, with total supplementary public investment in transport infrastructure of around €5,600 million. The majority of this came from the German federal government and was primarily put into motorways and traffic information and control. Ahlert (2006) forecast that the macroeconomic impact due to World Cup induced inbound tourism consumption would lead to increases in GDP and consumption in 2006, but that impacts would be almost negligible by 2008. In 2006 under favorable conditions, Ahlert (2006) estimated the World Cup induced supplementary inbound tourism consumption (approximately €1 billion) would lead to an increase in the annual German GDP growth rate of up to 0.07%. Ahlert (2006: 10) identified six positive 'sustainable impacts' for Germany of hosting the FIFA World Cup 2006:

- Upgrade of the national transportation system (railway & land transport; traffic steering systems)
- Update of the German football stadium facilities
- Update of the national tourism information system as a multilingual interactive platform using the internet
- New alignment of Germany as a modern and hospitable destination in international tourism with cultural and regional diversity
- Promotion of the German tourism industry with a relatively low price level and perfect service and shopping facilities
- Promotion of Germany as an excellent place for international investors.

The range of benefits of hosting World Cup matches and visitors was also recognized by Karl-Heinz Merfield, head of Cologne Tourism, in whose city five games were played. According to Merfield:

> In the short term, our city's economy will directly benefit from fans and visitors spending money in hotels, shops, restaurants and bars as well as on transport. This will produce an estimated additional income for Cologne's local economy of some 10 million Euro. In the long term, Cologne will benefit from an improved reputation of being an international city of sport and events.

The World Cup represents fantastic public relations opportunity for our city. Tour operators, travel agencies and the whole tourism industry in Cologne and the region will benefit. In addition, the City of Cologne and the German Government are investing millions on public transport, improvement of roads and other areas of infrastructures. Cologne's sports infrastructure is being improved greatly - not only for our guests but also for residents. All of these measures will contribute to the success of the games as well as having long-lasting economic benefit (City Mayors 2006).

However, the long-term benefits of hosting a World Cup at a national level are seen as rather mixed. As Holger Schmieding an economist in the Bank of America stated, 'It is an opportunity… But I don't think on its own it will make a difference, although it could contribute' (in Milne 2005c: 9). An analysis of the Football World Cups held from 1954 to 1998, indicated that eight of the host countries witnessed increased economic growth after the competition while four had lower growth. While in a study of the 1994 World Cup in the United States, the estimated losses of the host cities amounted to US$4 billion as opposed to a predicted gain of US$4 billion (Milne 2005c). For Germany, Otto Schilly, the Interior Minister, stated that he expected GDP to be boosted by €8-10 billion over several years as a result of hosting the event.

The construction industry was clearly a major beneficiary with the World Cup being estimated to be worth €3.5 billion and the creation of 20,000 jobs in the sector. Tourism was also expected to benefit with the German Tourism Office forecasting an extra 5.5 million overnight stays during the month of the competition, an increase of one-sixth above the normal levels for June, leading to approximately a million Euro increase in tourist spending. Nevertheless, overall benefits might not have been as great as expected. Despite double the expected number of tourist visits (approximately two million tourists spending €600 million (approximately US $766 million), German economic growth was approximately 0.25%, half of the expected amount as a result of hosting the Cup (Davis 2006). German Economic Minister Michael Glos wrote in the business daily *Handelsblatt* that 50,000 jobs had been created with only half being temporary, slightly more than planned. However, the best results he believed were that World Cup 2006 '[marked] an enormous gain in Germany's image' (Davis 2006). An observation no doubt encouraged not only by the overall positive media coverage of the management and planning of the event, but also be the perhaps unexpected success of the German team on the football field. Indeed, much of the impact is psychological, a 'feel-good' factor. As van Leeuwen and Kalshoven (2006: 1-2) observed: 'Happier consumers are more inclined to spend more. Leaving aside the fact that the parties in the winning country will last longer (which means higher turnovers at bars and supermarkets) and that there will be a market for souvenirs of the sweet victory (DVDs, shirts and other merchandising), it is undeniable that confident consumers spend more'.

For the 2006 World Cup the German Football Association announced that a profit before tax of €135 million had been made from staging the 2006 competition. Net of tax and after repaying the FIFA contribution of €40.8 million, the €56.6 million net profit will be shared between the German Football Association (DFB) and the German Football league (DFL) (HM Treasury 2007). However, the operating costs and therefore operating profit exclude any major capital infrastructure costs associated with the tournament which, as noted above, were substantial. Of course all the above fails to answer a key economic question, 'what were the opportunity costs of hosting the World Cup?' i.e. what would the costs and benefits have been if the funding was invested in other parts of the economy, such as health, education, or science rather than sport?

Key sources

Ahlert, G. (2005). *What does Germany expect to gain from hosting the 2006 Football World Cup – Macroeconomic and Regional Economic Effects*. GWS Discussion Paper 2005/4. Osnabrück: Gesellschaft für Wirtschaftliche Strukturforschung mbH.

Hinch, T. & Higham, J. (2011). *Sport Tourism Development* (2nd ed.). Bristol: Channelview.

Nauright, J. & Schimmel, K. (Eds) (2005) *The Political Economy of Sport*. London: Palgrave Macmillan.

HM Treasury (2007). *Hosting the World Cup: A Feasibility Study*. Norwich: HMSO.

Ritchie, B. & Adair, D. (2004). *Sports Tourism: Interrelationships, Impacts and Issues*, Clevedon: Channelview Publications.

Official site of the Fédération International de Football Association (FIFA): www.fifa.com

Discussion questions

1   What are the benefits and costs of hosting a major sporting event such as a football World Cup or an Olympic Games?

2   What are the economic advantages and disadvantages of already having stadia in place when hosting a major sporting event?

3   Should government be financially supporting the hosting of major sporting events if the income from the event goes to the sporting association?

4   What role might major sporting events have in urban reimaging and regeneration strategies?

7

Assessing the consequences of tourism

As noted above the consequences of tourism are contextual and situational. This means that there are a number of issues that must be clarified in seeking to identify and understand the consequences of visitation (Hall 2008) (Figure 7.3).

■ Definition

Given the problems inherent in identifying tourism phenomenon and tourists, and in distinguishing tourism from other forms of mobility and leisure behaviour (see Chapter 1), it can be difficult to isolate the impacts of tourism from other forms of human mobility or economic and social behaviour. In public policy terms for example, most of the effects of tourist visitation are managed under general planning and impact law rather than regulation that is tourism or tourist specific.

■ Differentiation

Following on from the previous issue, in many social and ecological environments it can be difficult isolating the impacts of tourism from other industrial and cultural impacts. Nevertheless, tourism has long been 'blamed' for changing places, particularly in destinations in the development world. For example, one of the first books on tourism planning, by Baud-Bovy and Lawson (1977: 183) commented that tourism: 'degrades irreversibly the very attractions which justi-fied and attracted it, eroding natural resources, breaking up the unity and scale of traditional landscapes and their characteristic buildings, polluting beaches, damaging forests and rendering banal under the inundation of alien facilities of often mediocre uniform design a formerly unique country'. However, any form of development can affect the physical and social environment – for good or for worse. Criticism of tourism has been particularly strong with respect to the effects of tourism on culture yet even though tourism is clearly a part of processes of cultural globalization its effects may be difficult to separate from those of the media and the internet or even religion. In such a situation it may be that the very visibility of tourists and tourism facilities may serve to focus attention on tourism as a potential change agent rather than other factors.

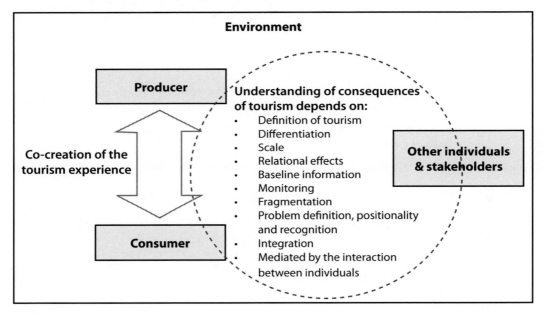

Figure 7.3: Understanding the consequences of tourism

■ Scale

Tourism has impacts over different scales, from the individual through to com-munities and destinations and beyond. In addition, tourism has impacts over time. Therefore in seeking to assess the impacts of tourism it is extremely important to clearly identify the boundaries of analysis and the advantages and disadvantages of the boundaries used. For example, the majority of studies of the effects of tourism are at site or destination level which may mean that some of the global effects of tourism may be missed (Gössling & Hall 2006; see Chapter 13) and, just as significantly, many tourism studies are one-offs rather than being a part of a longitudinal or time series study – this latter situation therefore potentially affecting our understanding of how tourism affects a place over time.

The issues of scale and the delimitation boundaries of analysis have a major effect on studying the economic impacts of tourism. There has been a failure in many studies to delimit implications of the size of the regional economy that is to be studied – the smaller the area to be analysed, the greater will be the number of 'visitors' and hence the greater is the estimate of economic impact. However, this issue of delimitation will also influence what is included and excluded in social and environmental impact assessment.

Case study 7.2: The climate impact of international travel by Swedish residents

The scale of analysis will affect the results of any impact study. In studying the environmental effects of tourism it is increasingly important to understand that the effects of emissions, for example, clearly go beyond that of the destination. The tourism systems approach discussed in Chapter 1 highlighted the significance of 'whole system' approaches to climate change (see also Scott et al. 2012).

Many countries are seeking to reduce their carbon and other greenhouse gas emissions from travel and tourism. Using data from a 2006 Swedish national travel survey based on 27,000 telephone interviews, Åkerman (2012) estimate that international travel by the Swedish resident population amounted to 37 billion passenger-km, or 4,100 km per capita in 2006. This corresponded to 22.5% of total travel by Swedes, representing a significant increase from 16.6% in 1994. Emissions of greenhouse gases from international travel by the Swedish population in 2006 were estimated at 8.5 million tons of CO_2 equivalents, of which 92% came from air travel. This figure represents approximately 11% of total Swedish emissions including international transport. As with other authors (Gössling & Hall 2008; Gössling et al. 2010, 2012; Scott et al. 2012), Åkerman (2012) concluded that a continued growth of international travel at its current pace is difficult to reconcile with long-term climate targets.

Key sources

Åkerman, J. (2012). Climate impact of international travel by Swedish residents. *Journal of Transport Geography*, 25, 87–93.

Dubois, G., Peeters, P., Ceron, J.P. & Gössling, S. (2011). The future tourism mobility of the world population: Emission growth versus climate policy. *Transportation Research Part A*, 45, 1031–1042.

Gössling, S. & Hall, C.M. (2008). Swedish tourism and climate change mitigation: An emerging conflict? *Scandinavian Journal of Hospitality and Tourism* 8(2), 141-158.

Gössling, S., Hall, C.M., Peeters, P. & Scott, D. (2010). The future of tourism: A climate change mitigation perspective. *Tourism Recreation Research*, 35(2), 119-130.

Gössling, S., Scott, D., Hall, C.M., Ceron, J-P. & Dubois, G. (2012). Consumer behaviour and demand response of tourists to climate change. *Annals of Tourism Research*, 39(1), 36-58.

Scott, D., Gössling, S. & Hall, C.M. (2012). *Tourism and Climate Change: Impacts, Adaptation and Mitigation*, London: Routledge.

Discussion questions

1   Will people voluntarily change their travel behavior so as to reduce emissions?

2   How should the emissions from international travel be treated in a country's emissions budget and associated reduction targets? Should the emissions be included in the emissions budget of the generating country, the destination, or should they be split 50:50?

■ Relational effects

Tourism is often discussed as if it had a one-way impact, i.e. tourism affects a destination, without it being highlighted that in reality the impacts, effects or consequences are two-way, in that tourism affects a destination and vice versa, the destination affects tourism. This is also an important issue as it stresses that there is an exchange process occurring at all levels with respect to tourism, i.e. from personal exchange between visitors and members of the destination community through to economic and environmental flows. This relational dimension is integral to understanding how tourism systems actually work, but is often not sufficiently stressed in discussions of tourism in many texts (Hall 2008) or in discussion of tourism impacts (Hall & Lew 2008). The relational aspect of tourism impacts are illustrated in Figure 7.4.

■ Baseline information

In order to understand the effects of tourism it is desirable to understand what a location was like before tourism was developed. Unfortunately, in all but a very few circumstances, such base line data does not exist. Therefore, in some cases an approximate estimate may be made. For example, in some locations that have previously had little human impact, it may be possible to approximate environmental conditions such as biodiversity and geomorphology.

■ Monitoring

There is often little ongoing monitoring of the specific consequences of tourism. Instead, any monitoring is often part of a broader programme of assessment of economic, social, and/or environmental change. For example, in a review of the environmental impacts of tourism developments in Australia, Warnken and

Buckley (2000) noted that only 7.5% of Australian developments were subject to a formal monitoring process. When monitoring did occur there was a greater use of BACIP environmental impact assessment designs (Before, After, Control, Impact, Paired Sampling). However, Warnken and Buckley observed that there was often a lack of control sites, and the implementation of monitoring programs was often subject to constraints in time and finance (2000: 459–60):

> One common deficiency is the absence or inadequacy of predevelopment baseline monitoring; the before, after (BA) comparison in the BACIP design. Some human disturbances are unforeseen, and monitoring can take place only after the event. More commonly, however, entrepreneurs are simply reluctant to invest in monitoring until development approvals have been granted, and then want to commence construction immediately after having received approval, without time for predevelopment baseline monitoring.

Tourism as a one-way affect or unidimensional relationship

Tourism 'impacts' as a relationship in which tourism not only affects something but is also affected itself. In this case the physical environment

Recognition of tourism 'impacts' as change over time in the relationship between tourism and the environment. The state of tourism and the environment are constantly influencing and affecting each other with each observation at any given time being a different expression or situation of the relationship between them

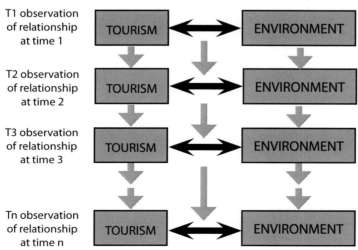

Figure 7.4: The relational nature of tourism impacts (After Hall & Lew 2009)

■ Fragmentation

Our knowledge of the consequences of visitation is extremely fragmented. This is partially because of some of the problems outlined above, but also because tourism research is often concentrated on some locations or environments and not on others. This has meant that there is arguably a disproportionate amount of research at some places, such as the Great Barrier Reef Marine Park or Yellowstone National Park, or on some types of tourism, such as ecotourism, when compared to mass tourism destinations, which the bulk of leisure tourists engage in. The reason for this is unknown but, at the destination level at least, there is often a significant disconnect between the number of visitors to a destination and the level of research that is conducted. Alternatively, it could be argued that researched could be prioritized by other means such as the relative economic or environmental significance of a development project or location. However, as discussed earlier in the chapter, the relative values of different locations for research and monitoring will vary according to the different perspectives of individuals as well as other rationales such as funding availability and the priorities and policies of different government and private organisations.

■ Problem definition, positionality and recognition

Although it may sound somewhat strange, one of the most significant issues with respect to understanding what the consequences of tourism are is being able to perceive what constitutes a problem in terms of tourism's effects. Chapter 5 emphasised that tourism resources constitute a resource because they are recognized as such in terms of a utility value. In exactly the same way, many problems are also perceptual in nature. Many of the consequences of tourism may not be recognized or may be recognized by some and not others. Furthermore, one's position in the tourism system may also affect how you perceive the consequences of tourism, with those working in the industry often having very different understandings of its effects from those who work outside it – a situation that clearly raises challenges for assessing the consequences of tourism.

To rework the insights of Zimmermann (1951) with respect to resources (noted in Chapter 5) in the case of the consequences of tourism: Problems are not, they become; they are not static but expand and contract in response to human actions, perceptions and wants. Different people, cultures and nationalities can have different perceptions of the consequences of tourism often as a result of different sets of values or aesthetic judgements. A resort or tourism development may be architectural pollution to one person and deemed as beautiful and aesthetically pleasing to another. Therefore, what is a problem or valuable for one person or in one culture may be 'neutral stuff' to another. Or in other words, what may be a recognized as a consequence of tourism in one culture or location or group of stakeholders may not be recognized as a problem in another. For example, in September 2012 a major controversy broke out in the Italian media over the future of the Sistine Chapel in the Vatican City, Rome, after one of Italy's most respected writers slammed it as an 'unimaginable disaster' where tourists resemble 'drunken herds' (Kingston 2012) (See Case Study 7.3).

Case study 7.3: Tourism and the Sistine Chapel

The Sistine Chapel (Sacellum Sixtinum in Latin) is the best-known chapel in the Apostolic Palace, the official residence of the Pope in the Vatican City, Rome. The chapel receives over five million visitors a year to see its Renaissance frescoes and especially the iconic image of the Hand of God giving life to Adam which is part of the ceiling painted by Michelangelo between 1508 and 1512 (Graham-Dixon 2008). Although heavily visited, the Chapel is still used for religious services, and is well known as the location for the Papal Conclave of the College of Cardinals that selects new popes.

The number of tourists and pilgrims that visit the chapel is estimated at 20,000 per day. This number is acknowledged as affecting the art works in the chapel, serving to both increase the air temperature and humidity as well as create dust and other pollution (Kingston 2012), and previous restorations of works in the chapel have caused substantial controversy (Graham-Dixon 2008).

In an article in *Corriere della Sera* in September 2012, Pietro Citati, a leading literary critic and biographer, demanded that the Vatican limit access to the Sistine chapel, claiming it would save the frescoes from damage and restore some decorum to the consecrated site. Describing a visit, Citati claimed that 'in the universal confusion, no one saw anything' and 'any form of contemplation was impossible'. The answer, he said, was to reduce the number of visitors drastically. 'The church needs money for its various activities, but these monstrous conditions are not possible'. Antonio Paolucci, the manager of the Vatican museums, which include the Sistine chapel, replied in the pages of the Holy See's daily paper, *L'Osservatore Romano*: 'The days when only Russian grand dukes and English lords or [American art expert] Bernard Berenson could gain access to the great masterpieces are definitely over… We have entered the era of large-scale tourism, and millions want to enjoy our historical culture … Limiting numbers is unthinkable' (Kingston 2012).

Paolucci said because the chapel was a place of prayer, timed visits were impossible. 'This chapel is a compendium of theology, a catechism in images. Could you limit access to Lourdes?' But Citati told the *Observer* newspaper: 'Why can't you limit numbers at a holy place if it is at risk? We are condemning it to disaster' (Kingston 2012).

Key sources

Graham-Dixon, A. (2008). *Michelangelo and the Sistine Chapel*, London: Weidenfeld & Nicolson.

Vatican Museums Online, the Sistine Chapel: http://mv.vatican.va/3_EN/pages/CSN/CSN_Main.html

Discussion questions

1   Is it appropriate to limit visitor access to religious sites only to people on a pilgrimage or from that religion?

2   Is charging an appropriate way to limit access to sites with high visitor numbers?

■ Integration

The majority of studies have examined the impacts of tourism and recreation on a particular environment or component of the environment rather than on a range of environments, and there has been little attempt to present an integrated approach to the assessment of the impacts of tourism, which requires consideration of its economic, social and environmental dimensions as part of 'solving' impact issues. (Hall & Härkonen 2006) (This point is taken up further in Chapter 8 in discussing different approaches to tourism planning). This has meant that problems associated with the consequences of tourism are often treated in a one-dimensional, often disciplinary, fashion rather than seeing issues as being intertwined. For example, environmental problems are usually a result of underlying economic and social issues, and physical measures to manage an environmental issue may not work unless the reasons underlying the problem is fully understood in the first place.

Approaches to integrative assessment

In order to address issues of integration two related approaches are increasingly being utilised. First, the development of new institutional approaches and methods to encourage integrated problem solving (Hall & Lew 2009). Second, the utilization of post-disciplinary approaches to tourism issues (Coles et al. 2006). The former is especially strong in resource management and connects to the ideas of governance and stakeholder relations outlined in Chapter 6.

Collaborative strategies are increasingly used to manage significant environment and resource problems that have multiple stakeholders and hence multiple perspectives on what actually constitutes both the problem and, potentially, the solution. Collaboration is a process through which 'parties who see different aspects of a problem can constructively explore their differences and search for solutions that go beyond their own limited vision of what is possible' (Gray 1989: 5). It is a process driven by multiple stakeholders that usually involves several components:

1   Agreeing on a common purpose;

2   Ensuring the process is both inclusive and transparent;

3   Allowing participants to design the process;

4   Promoting joint fact finding and creative problem solving;

5   Insisting on accountability;

6 Developing an action plan; and

7 Developing collaborative leadership (Margerum 1999; Margerum & Whitall 2004).

In the case of lake tourism, a type of tourism that clearly has implications for a natural resource and its multiple users, Hall and Härkonen (2006) identified four reasons why collaborative and integrated approaches were required in the management of lake systems in which tourism was significant:

■ Increased competition for natural resources, including the recognition of ecological uses, has led to increased conflict in natural resource management with collaborative approaches being seen as an alternative to expensive legal approaches to resolving conflict.

■ As understanding of the complexity of natural and social systems increases, more integrated responses to management must be developed that include a wider range of government and non-government decision makers and their associated capacities for information and analysis.

■ Many current environmental problems are a result of diffuse actions such as stormwater runoff, land use change and habitat modification, which are not well addressed through traditional regulatory actions, therefore a collaborative approach that generates broad scale participation is often better suited to fostering understanding and commitment among a large number of decision makers.

■ There are many different agencies and organizations with overlapping responsibilities, and it is argued that a collaborative approach offers an opportunity to reduce waste and duplication, reduce conflict and share data and expertise.

Along with changes in governance and institutional approaches, integrated approaches also have a different philosophical base with respect to problem solving. The complexity of many impacts associated with tourism development suggests that more than one disciplinary viewpoint is required to help solve problems. In resource management this has led to calls for interdisciplinary and transdisciplinary approaches in which the problem rather than disciplinary orientation is the key concern (Mitchell 1989). In tourism there have been calls for such approaches as well as postdisciplinary perspectives (Coles et al. 2006). For example, Coles et al. (2006: 18) observed that the emergence of new forms of tourism and mobility as well as the increasing mobility of some segments of society necessitates multiple approaches ,with contributions from fields outside of the immediate realm of tourism studies. They argued that the unprecedented levels of human mobility and its consequences were such that the complexity of tourism relationships to global environmental change exceeded the capabilities of an individual disciplinary approach (see also Chapter 13) and endorsed the perspective of Visnovsky and Bianchi (2005: no pages), the editors of *Human Affairs: A Postdisciplinary Journal for Humanities & Social Sciences*. They argued: 'Postdisciplinarity in our understanding does not mean that the traditional disciplines have disappeared or indeed should disappear, but rather that they are changing and should change in order to solve complex issues of human affairs. It is not sufficient to approach such complex issues from any single discipline'.

In a seminal paper that sought to describe the connections between tourism and conservation Budowski (1976) identified three different relationships between tourism and the environment that can usefully be employed to describe the relationships between tourism and all dimensions of the destination environment, including the social and economic: *conflict, coexistence* and *symbiosis*. Tourism and the environment are in *conflict* when tourism is regarded as having a detrimental impact on the environment by those at the destination. Tourism and the environment are in a state of *coexistence* when tourism does not have negative effects on the environment but neither does it positively contribute to the environment. This situation rarely remains static however as it implies a state of very slow change. Finally, there is a *symbiotic* relationship, in which tourism positively contributes to the environment and vice versa. This is a classic win-win situation in which tourists benefit and the overall quality of life of destinations improves as the social, economic and physical environments are all enhanced by tourism. This last state is obviously regarded as the ideal when it comes to assessing the consequences of tourism and it is the one that requires not only integrated assessments of tourism's effects but also an integrated planning strategy. And it is to this issue that the next chapter will turn.

Summary

This chapter has provided a review of some of the consequences of visitation to destinations and the effects of tourism overall. As part of a services approach to contemporary tourism, the chapter highlighted the fact that the co-creation of tourism experiences means that consequences are situational and contextual, but stressed that this does not mean that such effects are any less real. Rather it depends on a number of factors including the perspective and values of the viewer and their location within the tourism system as to whether they are (a) observed as occurring and (b) regarding as positive, negative or neutral. This means that the same consequence of tourism in the same location can be regarded simultaneously as positive by one person and negative by another. Indeed, as the chapter also noted it is even possible that over time an impact may also be perceived differently. Therefore, in understanding the impacts of tourism it was stressed that it was not just the impact that is significant but more importantly how it is perceived and understood. The tourist experience is potentially co-created or co-produced but the results of that co-creation are perceived differently by the parties involved.

Self-review questions

1 Why has *concern* over the consequences of tourism appeared to have become more significant since the 1970s?

2 Why are the *same* consequences of tourism seen *differently* by different people?

3 What did Budowski (1976) describe as the three different *relationships* between tourism and the environment?

4 What are the two main dimensions of *integrative assessment?*

5 What are the seven main components of *collaboration*?

6 What are the nine key issues that must be clarified with respect to the *assessment* of the consequences of tourism?

7 What is the relationship between our understanding of *resources* (Chapter 5) and understanding the consequences of tourism?

8 What does it mean to say that the consequences of tourism are *contextual* and *situational*?

Recommended reading

Hall, C.M., & Lew, A.A. (2009). *Understanding and Managing Tourism Impacts: an Integrated Approach*. London: Routledge
Provides an overview of the key concepts associated with tourism impacts as well as examples.

Lovelock, B. (Ed.) (2008). *Tourism and the Consumption of Wildlife: Hunting, Shooting and Sport Fishing*. Abingdon: Routledge.
The way in which wildlife is consumed is one of the more controversial areas of tourism impact. The chapters in the book examine the tourism and wildlife relationship from a variety of positions highlighting that different perspectives lead to different understandings of impact.

Coles. T., Hall, C.M. & Duval, D. (2006). Tourism and post disciplinary enquiry. *Current Issues in Tourism* 9(4-5), 293-319.
Details the nature of a post-disciplinary approach to examining issues within tourism and some of the implications this would have for the study of tourism.

Dovers, S. (2005). *Environment and sustainability policy: Creation, implementation, evaluation*. Sydney: Federation Press.
Although not written specifically for a tourism audience, the book highlights the difficulties in assessing environmental impacts and change.

Hall, C.M. & Page, S. (2006). *The Geography of Tourism and Recreation: Space, Place and Environment*, 3rd ed. Routledge, London.
Details the social, economic and environmental consequences of tourism from a geographical perspective over a range of different environments.

7

Newsome. D., Moore. S.A. & Dowling, R.K. (2012). *Natural Area Tourism: Ecology, Impacts and Management,* 2nd ed. Bristol: Channelview Press.
Updated second edition of one of the best accounts of the effects of tourism in natural areas.

Margerum, R.D. (1999). Integrated environmental management: The elements critical to success. *Environmental Management* 65(2): 151-66.
Although not tourism specific, the paper is a seminal work that provides a good overview of an integrated approach to environmental problems that remains relevant to the present day.

Buswell, R.J. (2011). *Mallorca and Tourism History, Economy and Environment.* Bristol: Channelview Press.
A very good destination level study of the effects of tourism at a major European island tourism destination.

Butcher, J. (2003). *The Moralisation of Tourism,* London: Routledge.
A thought provoking book that discusses how the consequences of tourism are often stereotyped.

Gössling, S. & Hall, C.M. (eds) (2006) *Tourism and Global Environmental Change,* Routledge, London.
Provides a sobering account of the impacts of tourism over all the elements of the tourism system and beyond

References cited

Ahlert, G. (2001). The economic effects of the Soccer World Cup 2006 in Germany with regards to different financing. *Economic Systems Research,* 13(1), 109-127.

Ahlert, G. (2005) *What does Germany expect to gain from hosting the 2006 Football World Cup – Macroeconomic and Regional Economic Effects.* GWS Discussion Paper 2005/4. Osnabrück: Gesellschaft für Wirtschaftliche Strukturforschung mbH.

Ahlert, G. (2006). FIFI World Cup Germany 2006™: Perspectives for Tourism. Paper presented at 1st ASEM Seminar on Tourism, Lisbon, Portugal, 8 May.

Åkerman, J. (2012). Climate impact of international travel by Swedish residents. *Journal of Transport Geography,* 25, 87–93.

Baud-Bovy, M. & Lawson, F. (1977). *Tourism and Recreational Development,* London: The Architectural Press.

Budowski, G. (1976). Tourism and conservation: Conflict, coexistence or symbiosis. *Environmental Conservation* 3(1), 27–31.

City Mayors (2006). For one month Cologne will be home from home for Brazilian football fans: An interview with Karl-Heinz Merfield, Head of Cologne Tourism, 15 January, http://www.citymayors.com/tourism/cologne_worldcup.html

Coles. T., Hall, C.M. & Duval, D. (2006). Tourism and post disciplinary enquiry. *Current Issues in Tourism* 9(4-5), 293-319.

Davis, O. (2006) *World Cup 2006 Economics: Winners and Losers Beyond Italy and Zidane.* AC Associated Content Media Company, July 26.

Dubois, G., Peeters, P., Ceron, J.P. & Gössling, S. (2011). The future tourism mobility of the world population: Emission growth versus climate policy. *Transportation Research Part A*, 45, 1031–1042.

FIFA (2007) Mass appeal of the FIFA World Cup™. FIFA.com – Marketing & TV, The Official Website of the Fédération Internationale de Football Association, http://www.fifa.com/en/marketing/concept/index/0,1304,22,00.html (accessed 01/25/2007).

Graham-Dixon, A. (2008). *Michelangelo and the Sistine Chapel*, London: Weidenfeld & Nicolson

Gray, B. (1989). *Collaborating: Finding Common Ground for Multiparty Problems*, San Francisco: Jossey-Bass.

Gössling, S. & Hall, C.M. (2008). Swedish tourism and climate change mitigation: An emerging conflict? *Scandinavian Journal of Hospitality and Tourism* 8(2), 141-158.

Gössling, S., Hall, C.M., Peeters, P. & Scott, D. (2010). The future of tourism: A climate change mitigation perspective. *Tourism Recreation Research*, 35(2), 119-130.

Gössling, S., Hall, C.M. & Weaver, D. (2009). Sustainable tourism futures: perspectives on systems, restructuring and innovations. In S. Gössling, C.M. Hall and D. Weaver (eds) *Sustainable Tourism Futures: Perspectives on Systems, Restructuring and Innovations*, pp. 1-18. New York: Routledge.

Gössling, S., Scott, D., Hall, C.M., Ceron, J-P. & Dubois, G. (2012). Consumer behaviour and demand response of tourists to climate change. *Annals of Tourism Research*, 39(1), 36-58.

Hall, C.M. (1992). *Hallmark Tourist Events: Impacts, Management and Planning*, London: Belhaven.

Hall, C.M. (2005). Selling places: Hallmark events and the reimaging of Sydney and Toronto. In J. Nauright and K. Schimmel (Eds), *The Political Economy of Sport*, pp.129-151. London: Palgrave Macmillan.

Hall, C.M. (2008). *Tourism Planning*, 2nd ed. Harlow: Prentice-Hall.

Hall, C.M. (2012). Sustainable mega-events: beyond the myth of 'balanced' approaches to mega-event sustainability. *Event Management*, 16(2), 119-131.

Hall, C.M. & Härkonen, T. (2006). Lake Tourism: An introduction to lacustrine tourism systems. In C.M. Hall and T. Härkönen (Eds.) *Lake Tourism: An Integrated Approach to Lacustrine Tourism Systems*, pp.3-26. Clevedon: Channel View Publications.

Hall, C.M. & Lew, A.A. (2009). *Understanding and Managing Tourism Impacts: an integrated approach*. London: Routledge.

Hall, C.M. & Page, S. (2006). *The Geography of Tourism and Recreation: Space, Place and Environment*, 3rd ed. Routledge, London.

HM Treasury (2007). *Hosting the World Cup: A Feasibility Study*. Norwich: HMSO.

7

Kingston, T. (2012). Vatican in row over 'drunken tourist herds' destroying Sistine Chapel's majesty. Author Pietro Citati calls for limit on crowd numbers to preserve Michelangelo's art in Vatican City, Rome. *The Observer*, 29 September 2012. Online. Available at: http://www.guardian.co.uk/world/2012/sep/29/sistine-chapel-tourist-row (accessed 29 September 2012).

Krippendorf, J. (1987). *The Holiday Makers: Understanding the Impact of Leisure and Travel*, Oxford: Heinemann Professional Publishing.

Lew, A., Hall, C.M. & Williams, A.M. (Eds) (2004). *A Companion to Tourism*, Oxford: Blackwell.

Margerum, R.D. (1999). Integrated environmental management: The elements critical to success. *Environmental Management* 65(2), 151-66.

Margerum, R.D. & Whitall, D. (2004). The challenges and implications of collaborative management on a river basin scale. *Journal of Environmental Planning and Management* 47(3), 407-27.

Mathieson, A. & Wall, G. (1982). *Tourism: Economic, Physical and Social Impacts*, London: Longman.

Milne, R. (2005a). World Cup could bring a German net gain. *Financial Times* 15 June, 20.

Milne, R. (2005b). Operation World Cup: war begins. *Financial Times* 15 June, 9.

Milne, R. (2005c). Germany gets in training to host month of Games. *Financial Times* 15 June, 9.

Mitchell, B. (1989). *Geography and Resource Analysis*. London: Longmans.

Nauright, J. & Schimmel, K. (Eds) (2005). *The Political Economy of Sport*. London: Palgrave Macmillan.

Pollock, I. (2010). World Cup: To tax or not to tax? BBC News Business, 11 May. Online. Available at: http://www.bbc.co.uk/news/10091277

Ritchie, B. & Adair, D. (2004). *Sports Tourism: Interrelationships, Impacts and Issues*, Clevedon: Channelview Publications.

Ritchie, J.R.B. (1984). Assessing the impact of hallmark events: Conceptual and research issues. *Journal of Travel Research* 23(1), 2–11.

Scott, D., Gössling, S. & Hall, C.M. (2012). *Tourism and Climate Change: Impacts, Adaptation and Mitigation*, London: Routledge.

van Leeuwen, R. & Kalshoven, C. (2006). *Soccer and the Economy. Soccernomics 2006*, ABN AMRO Economics Department, March.

Visnovsky, E. & Bianchi, G. (2005). Editorial. *Human Affairs* 15/2005, available at http://www.humanaffairs.sk/editorial.htm. (Accessed 15 April 2006).

Warnken, J. & Buckley, R. (2000). Monitoring diffuse impacts: Australian tourism developments. *Environmental Management* 25(4), 453–61.

Planning and Managing the Contemporary Destination

After reading this chapter you will:

- Understand the key questions facing tourism planning as a field of planning.

- Recognise the five different traditions of tourism planning and their key features.

- Appreciate the difficulties of developing a sustainable approach to tourism.

- Recognise how changes in planning approaches may be related to changes in the intellectual and physical environment.

- Understand the differences between low- and high-road approaches to regional competitiveness and development.

Introduction

Given the inherent characteristics of destination products in terms of their being an amalgam of separate firm and public products, and public and privately owned tourism resources, it may seem unusual to some readers to be able to discuss destination management and planning. However, as the previous chapter indicated, it is the very nature of a destination that actually makes planning processes so important. Although the desirability for tourism planning is generally accepted in most jurisdictions, the form and method of the most effective method of planning is a highly contested concept (Dredge & Jenkins 2007; Hall 2008). One of the seminal works on tourism planning by Gunn (1979) identified a number of foundation points for the development of an overall approach to tourism destination planning that still remain significant to contemporary tourism.

1   Only planning can avert negative impacts, although for planning to be effective, all 'actors' must be involved – not just professional planners.

2   Tourism is symbiotic with conservation and recreation, not a conflicting use with irreconcilably incompatible objectives or effects.

3   Planning today should be pluralistic, involving social, economic, and physical dimensions.

4   Planning is political, and as such there is a vital need to take into account societal objectives and to balance these with other (often conflicting) aspirations.

5   Tourism planning must be strategic and integrative.

6   Tourism planning must have a regional planning perspective – as many problems arise at the interface with smaller areas, a broader planning horizon is essential.

Tourism planning occurs at various scales from individual firms, to regions, nations and even on an international basis. Although such planning activities are interrelated, the focus of this chapter is on planning at the destination level. It first examines different traditions of destination planning and their relationship to other forms of planning. It then goes on to discuss the importance of sustainability as a part of the planning agenda. Finally the chapter examines some of the planning strategies that assist in the achievement of planning objectives.

The development of destination planning

Destination planning is a relatively recent concept that has emerged only since the late 1960s. Prior to that time planning for tourism was primarily seen within the context of broader urban and regional planning activities (Hall 2008). However, the rise of international tourism, with the advent of a new generation of jet aircraft and the consequent recognition of the real economic importance of tourism to places in terms of development and employment, saw the development of the first comprehensive attempts to plan for tourism. Nevertheless, destination planning remains very much connected to some of the broader issues and questions that occur within planning in its wider sense. Campbell and Fainstein (2003) identified five questions with respect to planning theory, all of which should also be of concern in tourism planning.

1 What are the historical roots of planning?

This first question is one of identity and therefore history. Reflecting on the history of a field not only helps answer how did we get to where we are now in terms of applications and intellectual developments but also helps to understand the implications for planning practice (Hall and Page 2006; Dredge & Jenkins 2011), including being able to learn from previous planning mistakes. Arguably, in the case of tourism planning, one of the biggest issues is that most planning texts fail to acknowledge that tourism planning is grounded within contemporary capitalist society and that there are winners and losers in various types of developments. Furthermore, as Campbell and Fainstein (2003: 6) observed, 'an effective planning history helps the contemporary planner shape his or her complex professional identity'.

2   What is the justification for planning?

The issue of justification raises the key question of why and when should the state intervene in order to change or modify an existing course of events? Planning, in the sense used in this chapter with respect to destinations, is primarily a public (state) activity that may be done in concert with private and other bodies but for which the original rationale lies within the broader issue of the role of the state. The question over what is the justification for planning therefore also raises issues as to the justification for state intervention (Bramwell 2005; Hall 2011).

From the late 1920s on, planning in terms of intervention was often seen as a means to counter the effects of the market. This notion of a dualism between planning and the market continued through to the 1980s when, in light of the failure of much centralized planning to achieve desired societal goals, the market came to be championed as a resource allocation mechanism to replace planning activities. This perspective had substantial impact on government in many developed nations as many government assets and authorities were privatized or corporatised in order to meet political demands for 'smaller' government. Tourism was not immune to such changes. In countries such as Australia, Canada and New Zealand, government's development function in tourism came to be replaced with a far stronger marketing role along with the development of new cooperative structures with the private sector (Dredge & Jenkins 2007; Hall 2008).

More recent developments with respect to notions of governance (see Chapter 6) have also led to a rethink of the planning - market dualism. The necessity of steering hybrid public-private relationships and the growth of non-government non-profit 'third sector' organizations mean a significant reinterpretation of the relationship between planning and the market is required (Beaumont & Dredge 2010; Hall 2011). Because tourism is a significant area of public-private relationships with respect to urban regeneration projects or infrastructure, such as airports, destination planning is strongly influenced by debates over the nature of govern ment intervention in destinations with respect to tourism.

3   What are the rules of the game for planning in respect of ethics and values?

The breakdown of the dualism between planning and the market, and the development of extensive public-private relationships raise substantial questions with respect to planning. When planning could be clearly interpreted as acting in the public interest such dilemmas were not so significant. However, the reinterpretation of government's role in the economy and in society as well as the creation of new government corporate bodies have meant that the idea of public interest is often interpreted in terms of economic interest or sectional interests (Zapata & Hall 2012). In the case of tourism, this can mean, for example, debates over the extent to which destination planning is about serving the needs of the tourist as opposed to the needs of the local community. Furthermore, ethical issues are also raised with respect to the role of expert knowledge in the planning process and the extent to which expert technical knowledge, and the values that underlie it, can be accommodated by other value positions that exist in destinations (Schilcher 2007; Zapata et al. 2011).

4   How can planning be effective in a mixed economy?

Planning intervention raises questions about the authority and power of those who seek to intervene (Dredge & Jenkins 2007; Hall 2011). The authority of the planner is constrained by economic and political power of various stakeholders and interests as well as by the vagaries of democracy. In such a situation, the goals of planners, for example with respect to sustainability and the physical and social environment, may have only a low position within the political issue-agenda where immediate economic and employment concerns may be given far greater priority in decision-making. Arguably within tourism planning, economic goals have typically been given priority over social goals despite planning traditions that go back to the early 1980s with respect to the importance of the community in tourism (Murphy & Murphy 2004) and which remain important to the present day (Zapata et al. 2011).

5   What do planners do?

As Campbell and Fainstein (2003: 9) noted, comprehensiveness of approach has often been a main justification for undertaking planning. Yet the comprehensive approaches have suffered serious criticism on several counts. First, the extent to which planners have the necessary capacities of analysis, coordination and knowledge to effectively develop comprehensive approaches to complex situations. Second, ideas of comprehensiveness often assume an ideal common public interest, whereas in reality planning may only give voice to more powerful political and economic interests if other interests or stakeholders are unable or unwilling to participate (Pforr 2001; Timothy & Tosun 2003; Treuren & Lane 2003; Wesley & Pforr 2010; Zapata & Hall 2012).

Within tourism planning, the issue of comprehensiveness is extremely significant because tourism planning is often justified on the basis of integrating economic, social and environmental goals (Murphy & Murphy 2004; Ruhanen 2004; Dredge & Jenkins 2007; Hall 2008). However, the likelihood of actually being able to achieve this level of integration in tourism planning is extremely problematic. Indeed, the criticism of Campbell and Fainstein (2003) with respect to comprehensive planning in general could easily be applied specifically to tourism planning:

> Planners often argued about the proper role of planning based simply on the merits of the concepts themselves (e.g. large- versus small-scale; top-down versus bottom-up), while ignoring the vaster political and economic forces that shaped and

constrained planning. The articulation and eventual challenge to comprehensive planning was thus part of a broader expansion of planning theory beyond land-use planning into social and economic policy (Campbell & Fainstein 2003: 9).

The latter point is extremely important as tourism destination planning has also expanded substantially from land-use based approaches to ones that seek to enhance economic and social policies, e.g. with respect to the growth of interest in pro-poor tourism in developing countries and the interest in developing competitive cities and destinations in the developed world. The expansion of approaches to destination planning is therefore the subject of the next section.

Changing approaches to destination planning

Approaches to destination planning change over time as a result of:

- Changes in ideas with respect to planning, e.g. 'new' theoretical insights and developments that transform planning thinking such as sustainability or creative cities, or conceptual developments such as that associated with the concept of governance.

- Changes in the destination's external environment, e.g. new issues and challenges to destinations that emerge as a result of developments outside of the destination such as competition from other destinations as well other forms of social, economic, and environmental change.

- Changes in the destination itself, e.g. environmental or land use change or political change that may affect the resource base of the destination or its relative accessibility.

Importantly, the different types of change are typically interrelated and rarely occur in isolation. A good example of this in the context of tourism planning is with respect to the environment.

■ Changing understanding of the environment in tourism

Our understanding of environmental change and its importance as a factor in destination planning has developed not just as a result of change to the physical environment per se, because such changes have often been occurring for much longer than a place has been a tourism destination, but also because our understanding of the importance of the physical environment has also changed with the development of a stronger environmental ethic in tourism studies (Gössling & Hall 2006; Hall & Lew 2009).

In the 1950s, when tourism started to grow rapidly in the post-World War Two period following greater personal car access and higher personal disposable income, it was mainly seen as an economic sector with great potential for national and regional economies, and providing increased leisure opportunities to large parts of the working population in the industrialized countries. It was not until the rise of a significant environmental conservation movement in the 1960 and

1970s that the negative environmental impacts of industrial development and urbanisation began to receive publicity. However, even here tourism was seen as a relatively benign form of economic development as compared with the more obvious pollution and impacts of heavy industries. In addition, at this time the impacts of tourism were perceived as being local in character (e.g. focusing on erosion problems or beach crowding), rather than the more global perspective of present-day analyses of tourism, which highlight impacts such as climate change, marine pollution, and biodiversity loss.

Gössling and Hall (2006) argue that it was not before the publication of the Swiss tourism academic and environmentalist Krippendorf's (1975) Die Landschaftsfresser (The Landscape Eaters), that the environmental impacts of tourism began to be perceived by a broader public in mainland Europe. Although there was earlier English language on the impacts of tourism in specific environments 'there has not been a publication, similar to that of Krippendorf, that has encouraged a wider public debate on tourism's environmental impacts. Instead, tourism often remains something that impacts negatively "somewhere else"' (Gössling & Hall 2006: 13).

In the late 1970s and 1980s new methodological tools for analyzing environmental change came to be developed as tourism brought increasing human pressure to bear on local natural environmental resources, particularly national parks and reserves. For example, concepts such as carrying capacity became increasingly important as did the use of environmental impact assessment or limits of acceptable change assessment (Hall & Lew 2009; Newsome et al. 2013). Significantly, the 1980s also saw the development of new tourism concepts such as sustainable tourism and ecotourism. The term sustainable development became widely used in relation to tourism following the publication of the 'Brundtland report' in 1987 (WCED 1987), although it had first been used in relation to tourism and the World Conservation Strategy prior to the WCED (Hall 2008). Nevertheless, the concept of sustainable tourism became a significant new approach to tourism planning, particularly as it emphasised the interrelationships between environmental change and social, economic and political factors that affect change (Hall & Lew 2009). But just as importantly it provided a new way to see the nature of environmental problems, as such problems were not just an issue of the physical environment but were instead embedded in social and economic factors. Arguably, the international issue of sustainability also raised questions about the scale at which the impacts of tourism needed to be understood (see Chapter 8) so rather than just regarding environmental issues as being just a concern to tourism at the destination level, it highlighted how tourism both contributed to and was affected by environmental change at a global scale (Gössling & Hall 2006; Scott et al. 2012).

Our understanding of the role of the environment in tourism has therefore changed over time, simultaneously with a change in the empirical impact of tourism and the development of new management techniques (Newsome et al. 2013). This is important as it has also meant that the planning problem, in terms of what planning is trying to solve, has also shifted over time. However, while change has undoubtedly been significant in our understanding of destination planning issues, there has also been continuity, with perhaps the most important ongoing concern being how to find a balance between economic development and public welfare concerns (including the quality of the physical environment). Nevertheless, while some concerns have remained constant for public planners' perspectives on the best means to accomplish planning goals, particularly with respect to what the relative role of the public and private sectors should be, there have been changes in the light of broader shifts in the understanding of the capacities of government (see Chapter 6).

Five traditions of tourism planning

Five approaches or traditions of tourism planning at the destination level can be recognised (Hall 2008):

- 'Boosterism'
- An economic, industry-oriented approach
- A physical/spatial approach
- A community-oriented approach
- A sustainable tourism approach.

The traditions are broadly sequential although they are not mutually exclusive and also occur simultaneously (Table 8.1). This section will briefly outline each of these approaches and their implications for destination planning.

Boosterism

Boosterism is in one sense a form of non-planning. It refers to the simplistic attitude that tourism development is inherently good and will be of automatic benefit to the destination. Boosterism is characterized as being part of an attitude to development that 'growth is good' and that any negative externalities of tourism development will be outweighed by positive benefits. From a boosterist perspective the primary planning problem is one of how to attract as many people as possible to a given location.

Economic approach

The economic tradition in tourism planning constructs the tourism planning problem around economic questions in terms of tourism's role in regional and national economic growth and development. The economic approach has been dominant in destination planning since places first consciously sought to attract visitors and develop a tourist industry. However, while the role of economic analysis as the main arbiter in destination planning has continued, there have been changes in the scale of analysis.

Table 8.1: Timelines for traditions of tourism planning. Source: After Hall 2008

Dates	Boosterism	Eeconomic	Physical/spatial	Community	Sustainable tourism
1850s	Established with the advent of industrialized mass tourism				
1890s	Established by the late 1890s with respect to discussions of development alternatives of natural area destinations		Antecedents emerge with respect to the conservation of natural areas, secondary to economic approaches		Debates over 'sustained yield' forestry antecedent for sustainable development
1930s		State's role in managing the economy becomes extremely important	Land-use zoning becomes established in urban and regional planning	Idea of planner as expert well established in urban and regional planning	
1960s		Economic analysis of development decisions becomes more common-place	Emergence of modern conservation movement with environmental agencies established for the first time	Idea of planner as expert comes to be challenged in the late 1960s and early 1970s	UN Habitat and Man and Biosphere programmes begin to be developed in the late 1960s
1980s	Neoconservative political approaches to role of state give boosters a stronger role in destination growth coalitions	Economic analysis dominant in public planning and decision-making	Spatial approaches are weakened as public-private approaches become a popular planning strategy	Increased application of community approaches to tourism through public participation exercises	Sustainable development key concept in World Conservation Strategy and the Brundtland report
2000	Continued role of growth coalitions reinforced by rise of concept of place wars and destination competition	Economic analysis remains dominant. Tourism satellite accounts become important evaluation tool while idea of competitiveness influences destination planning	Spatial planning tools remain important especially as a result of new geographic information technologies; spatial planning approached at multiple scales	Participation standard in much destination planning although extent to which it affects planning outcomes problematic	Sustainable tourism a significant planning concept but application is contested; increased concern over global environmental change
2010s	Neoliberal dominance of tourism planning in many jurisdiction leading to emphasis on market-based planning interventions	Economic concerns key in much planning as a result of global financial uncertainty. Continued belief in growth based planning models including 'green economic growth' approaches	Spatial planning increasingly integrated with market-based approaches to planning intervention	Increased cynicism over public participation exercises and democratic processes in many countries	Climate change, energy security and biodiversity core environmental issues. Emergence of transition management and steady-state destination planning

Within the economic approach, the planning emphasis is on the economic impacts of tourism and the most efficient and effective use of tourism to create income and employment benefits for regions, communities or countries as a whole. Particular attention has been given to the means by which the economic impacts of tourism can be measured. In recent years this has meant the development of a series of tourism satellite accounts at national and regional levels. In addition, there has been a focus on the competitiveness of destinations and the development of approaches that support competitiveness such as clustering and networks (Michael 2007). However, the role that tourism actually plays in regional development is regarded as somewhat problematic as it is possible that a focus on tourism development may not be the most appropriate strategy in terms of regional competitiveness (Malecki 2004).

Despite the development of new techniques for the economic analysis of tourism, many studies of tourism at the destination level focus on its gross impacts rather than taking a more sophisticated approach that evaluates the benefits and costs of tourism development and the opportunity costs of tourism. In addition, economic approaches are often criticized for failing to adequately account for environmental and social values that, from the perspective of some stakeholders, may not be easily assessed within an economic paradigm (Hall and Lew 2009).

■ Physical/spatial tradition

The physical/spatial approach has its origins in the work of urban and regional land-use planners, geographers and environmental scientists who advocate an approach to the planning of tourism destinations based on consideration of the renewability of natural resources; spatial interactions, spatial organization, and regional planning and development. Although economic considerations are important, economic development is regarded as being dependent on the 'wise use' or stewardship of natural resources. Therefore, environmental considerations may be given priority over immediate economic ones in order to keep longer-term management options open. Key planning approaches from this perspective include: carrying capacity; hazard and risk assessment; understanding stakeholder attitudes, behaviour and perceptions; resource and landscape evaluation; resource appraisal and allocation; decision-making and evaluation; and the development of appropriate institutional arrangements. However, many of the planning techniques within the physical/spatial tradition have tended to be applied more in natural areas, such as national parks and protected areas (Newsome et al. 2013). In contrast, the economic traditions of planning has tended to have substantial sway in urban destinations and in broader policy approaches of national and regional governments that embrace notions of place competition.

8

■ Community oriented tourism planning

The community based tourism approach emerged in the 1970s and was influenced by two main factors. First, an increased recognition that tourism development was not benign and had negative socio-cultural, economic and environmental impacts on some members of destination communities. Second, a realization in urban and regional planning, that community stakeholders often needed to be involved in decision-making if planning interventions were to be successful. Although community oriented tourism planning was actually being undertaken by practitioners prior to its recognition in the tourism research literature, one of the most influential statements of the community approach to tourism development was found in Murphy's (1985) book *Tourism: A Community Approach*. Murphy advocated the adoption of an 'ecological' approach to tourism planning that emphasised the need for local control over the development process. A key component of the approach was the notion that in satisfying local needs it is possible to satisfy the needs of tourists. Despite the undoubted attraction of a 'win-win' concept to many destinations, the approach was not adopted as widely as it might have been. This was because:

- The approach was seen as being more time consuming and expensive than other approaches.
- It blurred where control lay in decision-making processes.
- The outcomes of the consultation processes and the consequent plans often did not meet the more economically oriented agendas of the tourism industry and government.

Nevertheless, the approach has still had significant influence on destination planning (Timothy & Tosun 2003) through:

- Encouraging at least some degree of consultation and public participation in destination planning (even if sometimes perceived as tokenism where consultation occurs just with industry stakeholders rather than the wider community).
- In some jurisdictions, encouraging the conduct of social impact assessments on large tourism developments.
- More recently, highlighting the significance of empowerment and equity issues as factors in tourism development, which has been particularly important to the concept of pro-poor tourism (Zapata et al. 2011).

This latter dimension is an area in which there has been overlap between the community and economic approaches. Interrelationships between the community and spatial approaches is best seen with respect to regional and local planning initiatives as well as in consultation exercises in the case of use of natural areas or heritage management (Singh et al. 2003).

■   # Sustainable tourism

The fifth approach to destination planning is the sustainable approach. Although having historical antecedents that go back to the 1870s, the sustainable tourism approach is seen as entering its current interpretation from the 1980s on following the emergence of the sustainable development paradigm (Hall & Lew 2009). According to Brake and Newton (1995: 117) 'the transitive verb "to sustain" is derived from the Latin *sustineo* meaning to hold up and is variously interpreted as also meaning to bear or support, to relieve or to prolong.' Sustainability has come to incorporate all of these meanings (Hall 2010). The primary objective of sustainable development is the provision of lasting and secure livelihoods that minimise resource depletion, environmental degradation, cultural disruption, and social instability. The report of the World Commission of Environment and Development (WCED) (Bruntland Commission) (1987) extended the basic objective of sustainable development that had previously been expressed in the World Conservation Strategy to include concerns of equity; the needs of economically marginal populations; and the idea of technological and social limitations on the ability of the environment to meet present and future needs.

Ideas of sustainable development have been hugely influential in destination planning discourse as well as affecting planning legislation. However, the transformation of the principles of sustainable development into successful planning interventions has been extremely difficult. Key issues include (Hall & Lew 2009) (see also Chapter 7):

■   The time scale in which sustainable approaches operate is greater than usual planning and policy timelines.

■   The spatial scale is also greater as sustainable approaches highlight the internationalization of many factors that affect sustainability, such as climate change and economic globalization, which therefore means that these are issues that are multi-jurisdictional and therefore require international cooperation (see Chapter 6).

■   Sustainability is an integrative approach that brings together socio-cultural, environmental and economic planning methods. This situation requires careful management and new sets of planning skills that allow for multi-disciplinary or post-disciplinary problem setting as well as new sets of institutional arrangements.

■   Sustainable development for a location is different from sustainable tourism development. While tourism may be sustainable it is quite possible that in some destinations it may not be a contributor to the overall sustainability of the location or may even contribute to a non-sustainable situation in other locations. For example, as indicated in Chapter 1, the greenhouse gas emissions from tourism transport affects climate change throughout the world not just at the destination of tourists (Scott et al. 2012). This situation therefore provides a significant challenge to the tourism industry.

8

Several planning strategies have been put forward as integral to a sustainable tourism approach (Hall 2008):

1 *Cooperative and integrated control systems.* Integrated planning seeks to coordinate planning processes at different scales in a more cooperative manner. In part the notion of 'steering' within contemporary governance is an important part of such processes (see Chapter 6)

2 *Development of industry coordination mechanisms.* Tourism has historically been a fragmented industry. The development of improved coordination mechanisms is regarded as a mechanism to improve firm and destination collaboration towards common goals as well as being a means by which the concerns of industry stakeholders can be better articulated to decision-makers.

3 *Raising consumer awareness.* The nature of tourist consumption obviously affects the resource base of destinations therefore alterations in consumption patterns may lead to better economic, social and environmental outcomes. In recent years there has been a growth in 'conscious consumption' in which consumers have thought about their purchases with respect to such factors as organic foods, environment conservation and human rights. Such conscious consumerism has influenced tourism with respect to the growth of ethical tourism considerations, codes of tourism conduct, types of tourism such as volunteer tourism as well as destination boycotts.

4 *Raising producer awareness.* Making tourism production more sustainable can be undertaken through a combination of regulatory and voluntary approaches. Educating producers to make their products more sustainable is one way of seeking to ensure that destinations benefit, however in some cases having more sustainable product may also increase the product appeal in certain markets. Many producer groups have developed codes of conduct and good practice in an effort to make their businesses more environmentally friendly.

5 *Strategic planning.* This requires a process that is integrative in terms of bringing stakeholders together and is also well structured in terms of effective analysis, the development of clear goals and measurable objectives, evaluation and monitoring, and a clear implementation strategy. One of the most important factors in strategic planning for sustainability is the identification of relevant indicators for sustainability which are measurable, meet objectives, and on which stakeholders agree as to their relevance and as to how results should be interpreted. When this is done acceptance of intervention and change management by stakeholders is far greater than with a non-strategic approach.

6 *Increased regulation.* Where voluntary procedures to promote sustainability have failed, then increased regulation may be the only option available. A range of potential regulatory measures exist but some of the more popular approaches include increased charging, new taxation regimes, licences and permits. However, governments are often fearful of industry and consumer backlash with respect to increased regulation, particularly if it also increases the cost of travel or products (Scott et al. 2012).

Responsibility for destination planning

As the above discussion illustrates, contemporary tourism is characterised by there being no single agreed approach to destination planning, as there is often no fixed agreement as to what the best methods are or what tthe role of the public sector should be. Instead, there are a number of different approaches that are utilised by different agencies that have different jurisdictions and agenda. Indeed, it is often the case that different organisations involved with destination planning fit within particular traditions making decision-making potentially problematic. For example, economic development agencies will usually embrace the economic approach, environmental agencies a physical/spatial approach, public interest groups a community based approach; with sustainable approaches often being part of the mandate and culture of regional planning agencies

Few destinations have a single body that is specifically responsible for destination planning from a tourism perspective. Most destination management or regional tourism organisations have a marketing function, with planning being a secondary and often only advisory role. Instead destination planning tends to be undertaken by a combination of urban and regional planning bodies and economic development organisations for which tourism is only a part of its overall brief. This situation therefore means that destination planning occurs in a complex set of institutional arrangements that include many different organisations. At one level such a perspective might be seen as a positive as it might encourage greater cooperation between different public, private and non-government organisations, although it may also means that planning for tourism 'falls between the gaps' as no one is clearly responsible. Indeed, even in those organisations that have a clear designated responsibility for planning tourism activities, such as national park and conservation bodies, this may only be a part of their mandate.

Case study 8.1: Planning for tourism in Finland's national parks

National parks are broadly recognized as extremely important attractions for tourism. As well as being important for domestic tourism, nature is an extremely important part of Finland's international tourism promotion and positioning as a destination (Tuohino & Patkinen 2004; Hall et al. 2009). There are 37 national parks in Finland with the Bothnian Sea and Sipoonkorpi parks established in 2011. The combined area of Finland´s national parks is 9,789 km² although the overall amount of protected areas is much greater (Table 8.2). All the national parks are managed by Metsähallitus, the Finnish Forest and Park Service.

The average number of visits to Finnish national parks has doubled since the 1990s and in peripheral economic areas, such as northern Finland, the national park associated tourism development has been even stronger (Saarinen 2003). Such has been the

8

recognized tourism significance of national parks that regional and local stakeholders and policy actors usually support the plans for opening parks, and for the national park status as they believe it increases the attractiveness of the area and promotes nature-based tourism. Consequently, national parks have become a significant tool for regional development and positive image building in numerous peripheral areas that otherwise have limited means of economic development (Saarinen 2003; Hall & Boyd 2005). As a result, several municipalities and organisations have proposed that further national parks should be designated in Finland (Hall et al. 2009).

Table 8.2: Protected areas managed by Metsähallitus. Adapted from Metsähallitus (2012).

Type of area	Number	Size (km2)
Statutory Protected Area		
National parks	37	9 807
Strict nature reserves	19	1 536
Mire reserves	171	4 618
Herb-rich forest reserves	51	12
Old-growth forest reserves	91	97
Seal reserves	7	188
Other state-owned protected areas	38	479
Privately-owned protected areas	106	83
Protected areas established by Metsähallitus	24	8
Total	544	16 828
Other areas		
Areas reserved for conservation programmes	1 708	7 665
Protected forests	327	515
Other protected sites	576	1 930
Wilderness areas	12	14 903
National hiking areas	7	355
Other recreational areas	22	1,406
Other areas (not included above)	45	3 683
Public water areas (where not included above)	-	23 730
All areas of land and water		**71 015**

However, while tourism is obviously important for national parks in Finland it is not the sole rationale for their establishment ,with biodiversity and landscape conservation obviously being important factors. As in other national park jurisdictions, the original Finnish legislation included provision for both conservation and visitation, a balance that has become increasingly difficult given the growth in tourist numbers in recent decades. The original 1923 *Nature Conservation Act* had an aim to preserve untouched nature, though it also stated that national parks were meant for pleasure and enjoyment for all citizens, that they should have value as an attraction and be easily reached by people (Sorsa 2004). Nevertheless, present-day park planning considerations give a substantial weight to nature conservation. Metsähallitus, the Finnish Forest and Park Service, reports that the role of the Finnish network of protected areas can be defined as:

Finland's protected areas form a varied network intended to preserve for present and future generations a suitable number of representatives and ecologically viable areas of all the ecosystems and natural habitat types occurring in Finland, taking into account geographical variations and the various stages of natural succession. Protected areas also have a very significant role in achieving and maintaining the favourable conservation status of habitat types and species (Metsähallitus 2000: 6).

Under the guidelines on the aims, function and management of public controlled protected areas the network of Finnish protected areas must primarily preserve (Metsähallitus 2000: 7): 'areas of natural habitat, particularly habitat types characteristic of the Finnish landscape, and habitats, land forms and features which are endangered'. As part of the primary aim, or additionally, the following should be preserved:

- Natural gene pools and ecosystem diversity.

- Species, geological and geomorphological features, especially species and features which are either naturally rare, or threatened or declining as a consequence of human activity.

- Landscapes and habitats shaped by previous generations, including the cultural heritage associated with the Finnish countryside, along with endangered domesticated plant and animal breeds.

- The natural succession of ecosystems and other natural processes at various stages.

- Areas of outstanding natural beauty.

- Wild areas ((Metsähallitus 2000: 7).

- The guidelines then go on to note that only 'within the limitations set by the requirements of conservation, the network of protected areas should also aim to facilitate': (Metsähallitus 2000: 7):

- Research and monitoring work on the state of the environment

- Environmental education, promoting understanding and interest towards nature

- Outdoor recreation.

Significantly, the guidelines state that 'the economic utilisation of protected areas for ecotourism, for example, is permissible where it does not endanger the achievement of conservation aims' (Metsähallitus 2000: 7). Indeed, earlier in the guidelines, it is noted that the growth of ecotourism and an increase in the number of visitors to protected areas is indicative of a more favourable opinion towards nature conservation. Yet tourism is regarded as only one out of ten different uses of the Finnish protected area system that require a policy statement (the others being everyman's right, fishing and hunting, photography, local residents, traffic, forestry, mineral prospecting and mining and leasing land). Indeed, ecotourism is not explicitly defined within the guidelines, although its economic dimension is noted, which therefore suggests that ecotourism is regarded as commercial tourism use of protected areas by firms as opposed to access by independent travellers. A clear policy boundary is also established by Metsähallitus with respect to tourism planning. According to Metsähallitus (2000: 42) the agency does not intend to develop its own activities in the field but instead will 'aim to provide a framework and opportunities for independent enterprises in the field of ecotourism. The aims of sustainable ecotourism must be agreed upon with all interested parties (local residents, the tourism sector, other local organisations) by drawing up a strategy for tourism following the principles of participatory planning'. For example, Metsähallitus (2010) developed a set of nine principles that are intended to guide its operations in protected areas (Table 8.3), although as they noted:

Sustainable nature tourism is promoted in co-operation with local residents, the local authorities, firms offering tourist services, and other organisations. These principles for sustainable nature tourism are not simply a list of "dos and don'ts", but rather represent jointly agreed practical guidelines that will help to promote sustainability. These guidelines may be followed in different ways by different organisations, according to local conditions (Metsähallitus 2010).

Table 8.3: Metsähallitus Principles for Sustainable Nature Tourism, Source: Summarised from Metsähallitu s (2012).

1	Natural values are preserved and all activities promote nature conservation.
2	The environment is subjected to as little pressure as possible.
3	Local traditions and cultures are respected.
4	Visitors increase their understanding and appreciation of nature and cultures.
5	Improved recreational facilities are provided for visitors.
6	Visitors are encouraged to enjoy both mental and physical recreation.
7	Local economies and employment are promoted.
8	Publicity materials are produced responsibly and carefully.
9	Activities are planned and organised co-operatively.

For the full details of the principles, visit: http://www.metsa.fi/sivustot/metsa/en/NaturalHeritage/ ProtectedAreas/SustainableNatureTourism/Sivut/SustainableNatureTourisminProtectedAreas. aspx

Nevertheless other dimensions of tourism are included in other sets of plans. The above sets of aims and principles are intended to serve as a guide for the development of management and land use plans for protected areas, which may be laid out in a master plan for a given protected area as well as cooperative arrangements. Planning is therefore regarded as an integral measure to preserving the natural qualities of protected areas along with specific management strategies such as restrictions on access, supervision of visitors, influencing human behaviour, and research and monitoring. However, planning in this context is interpreted both as the process of developing a plan as well as the production and implementation of a plan that sets out 'land use and the location and organization of activities, through the provision of services and facilities. For example, according to the principles of land use zoning and distribution' (Metsähallitus 2000: 16).

With respect to participatory planning processes for the development of tourism in protected areas, Metsähallitus (2000: 42-3) identified three main requirements:

1   Survey the problems and opportunities presented in the protected area being planned from a tourism perspective, and set economic, social and ecological aims for ecotourism, i.e. encouraging certain activities, identifying preferred routes, and minimizing littering and disturbance. In addition, special consideration is meant to be given to local communities and employment generation. Special ecotourism plans can be drafted for areas used intensively for tourism purposes.

2   The tourism sector should seek to develop products that meet client expectations and interests. This should be supported by the undertaking of marketing research on new consumer markets and their level of satisfaction. Infrastructure and facilities built as part of tourism product development should aim to support the preservation of biodiversity.

3   Tourism operators should promote conservation aims. 'The attractiveness of an area should not be prejudiced through its use for tourism, and the overall environmental impact of tourist activities should otherwise be minimised' (Metsähallitus 2000: 43).

To a great extent the Finnish experience mirrors the approaches of the Nordic countries and other national park agencies in the developed world with respect to the relationship between tourism and national park and protected area planning (Gössling & Hultman 2006; Hall et al. 2009). The difficult task of balancing conservation aims while still encouraging visitation is one that is almost universal at destinations that are either national parks or have a significant area set aside as protected area. The Finnish approach of land use zoning, with particular zones providing for specific activities and visitor experiences, is an extremely common strategy. However, the development of principles for sustainable nature tourism is also significant for cooperative arrangements between Metsähallitus and other stakeholders such as local governments and tourism operators. According to Metsähallitus (2010):

The increasing use of protected areas for nature tourism means that clear rules must be jointly agreed by everyone concerned. Written agreements are made between Metsähallitus Natural Heritage Services and local firms, to define acceptable and sustainable practices. In addition to the contracts entitling firms to organise activities in protected areas, even more detailed co-operation may be established through co-operation and partnership agreements. Sustainability can only be achieved through co-operation.

The recognition of participatory planning approaches that seek to include the local community, tourism industry, and other planning agencies as well as an understanding of the market, reflect both a greater public-private approach to destination planning and the increased complexity of the planning process. Tourism planning by national park and protected area agencies in many jurisdictions is therefore likely to be based on a combination of statutory based spatial planning and market-oriented cooperative and public-private partnerships in the foreseeable future.

Key sources

Frost, W. & Hall, C.M. (eds) (2009). *Tourism and National Parks: International Perspectives on Development, Histories and Change*, London: Routledge.

Heinonen, M. (ed) (2007). *State of the Parks in Finland. Finnish Protected Areas and Their Management from 2000 to 2005. Nature Protection Publications of Metsähallitus. Series A 170*. Vantaa: Metsähallitus. Available: http://www.metsa.fi/sivustot/metsa/en/Natural-Heritage/ProtectedAreas/StateoftheParksReporting/Sivut/StateoftheParksReporting. aspx

Metsähallitus (Forest and Park Service) (2000). *The Principles of Protected Area Management in Finland: Guidelines on the Aims, Function and Management of State-owned Protected Areas*. Metsähallituksen luonnonsuojelulkaisuja Sarja B No.54. Vantaa: Metsähallitus – Forest and Park Service, Natural Heritage Services.

Metsähallitus (2010). Sustainable Nature Tourism in Protected Areas. Available at: http://www.metsa.fi/sivustot/metsa/en/NaturalHeritage/ProtectedAreas/SustainableNatureTourism/Sivut/SustainableNatureTourisminProtectedAreas.aspx (accessed 18 Sept 2012)

Metsähallitus Natural Heritage Services (NHS), State of the Parks Reporting: http://www.metsa.fi/sivustot/metsa/en/NaturalHeritage/ProtectedAreas/StateoftheParksReporting/Sivut/StateoftheParksReporting.aspx

Saarinen & Hall, C.M. (Eds) (2004) *Nature-based Tourism Research in Finland: Local Contexts, Global Issues*. Finnish Forest Research Institute, Research Papers 916. Rovaniemi: Rovaniemi Research Station, Finnish Forest Research Institute.

National parks in Finland: http://www.outdoors.fi/destinations/nationalparks/Pages/Default.aspx

Discussion questions

1   To what extent might planning be able to reconcile the twin objectives of national parks to conserve natural heritage and to provide a source of enjoyment for visitors?

2   With reference to national park destinations in your own country (a) to what extent are master plans developed for parks?; (b) how often are they updated and what might be the implications of planning timetables?; and (c) what are the commonalities and differences in planning priorities for different parks?

3   How does national park planning processes in your country seek to be inclusive of stakeholders in the planning process?

4   Should all stakeholders have an equal say in park planning or should some stakeholders, e.g. the local community or park users, have a greater say than other stakeholders?

5   Are non-users stakeholders in national park planning?

Planning sustainable destinations and sustainable regions

At the destination level, a sustainable approach to tourism is concerned with tourism being the most appropriate form of development of the economic, social and physical resources of a region in a manner which conserves the social and physical environment and which promotes the long-term goals of the community. Such a perspective highlights that there is a difference between focusing on tourism development for its own sake, which is how sustainable tourism may be interpreted, versus looking at sustainability within the totality of a regional jurisdiction. While a concern with the sustainability of tourism is obviously important, the adoption of an integrative planning perspective means that tourism's contribution to regional sustainable development needs to be understood within a 'whole of government' or 'whole of region' approach that assesses what can be achieved for a place as a whole, rather than just in terms of tourism.

Within studies of regional planning the contribution of tourism to sustainable place development is often questioned. Tourism is primarily seen as part of an imitative 'low road' policy in contrast to 'high road' knowledge based policies (Table 8.4) (Malecki 2004; Hall 2008). Low-road strategies are focused on 'traditional' location factors such as land, labour, capital, infrastructure and locational advantage with respect to markets or key elements of production as well as direct state subsidies to retain firms: more intangible factors, such as intellectual capital and institutional capacity are secondary (see Chapter 6 and the discussion of government's role on tourism development). Low road strategies are tied into property-oriented growth strategies linked to urban and regional reimaging strategies (Judd 2003; Hall 2005). However, low road strategies tend to lead to the serial replication of urban tourism infrastructure such the waterfront marketplace, heritage precinct, art gallery, museum, casino, marina, and retail centre because of the belief of some destination planners that this is what required for tourism induced economic development. Such factors were described by Harvey (1989: 12) as being a part of 'urban entrepreneurialism' whereby, 'many of the innovations and investments designed to make particular locations more attractive as cultural and consumer centers have quickly been imitated elsewhere, thus rendering any competitive advantage within a system of cities ephemeral.' Yet the sustainability of such serial place competitive strategies is increasingly questionable. The requirements of having to constantly develop and upgrade visitor facilities and infrastructure has meant that places 'face the possibility of being caught in a vicious cycle of having to provide larger subsidies to finance projects that deliver even fewer public benefits' (Leitner & Garner 1993: 72).

Table 8.4: Low, middle and high road regional competitiveness strategies

Low Road	Middle Path	High Road
Zero sum	*Growth enhancing*	*Network enhancing*
Place promotion	Training	Internal networks
Capturing mobile investment	Fostering entrepreneurship	External (non-local) networks
Firms and capital	Helping and mentoring new firms and entrepreneurs	Benchmarking assessments
Focus on visitors on the basis of numbers	Coordination	Investing in superstructure
Subsidised investment and means of production, e.g sites and premises	Business advice	Transport links, especially airline and airfreight links
	Reducing uncertainty	Scanning globally for new knowledge
	Investment in infrastructure	Information and communications links
Long term contribution to sustainable regional development		
Marginal	Moderate	High

Source: After Cheshire and Gordon 1998; Malecki 2002, 2004; Hall 2008

In contrast to the low road approach, Malecki (2004) argues that a high road approach of regional innovation and entrepreneurship is possible, although it is a much more difficult path to follow as it requires more of a focus on 'soft infrastructure' (also described as superstructure) and the development of regional innovation and knowledge economies that utilize agglomeration economies, institutional learning, associative governance, proximity capital and interactive innovation (Cooke 2002). Therefore, a high road approach stresses that regional infrastructure both hard (communications, transport, finance) and soft (knowledge, intellectual capital, positive and trustful labour relations, mentoring, worker-welfare orientation) is required in order to encourage innovation rather than adaptation (Malecki 2004). As Malecki (2004: 1109) observes, in smaller urban centres that cannot really afford the highly visible development projects of larger 'global' cities, even though they may try, it is the 'soft' cultural and social variables that 'matter most for regional development: institutions, leadership, culture and community.' Such elements have been strongly emphasized within the community and sustainable traditions of tourism planning and development. Nevertheless, it is important to recognize that many such high road strategies are not as immediately tangible and visible to stakeholders as compared with, for example, the construction of a new stadium, museum or convention centre.

Tourism does have a part to play in high road strategies for sustainable regional development. High road strategies emphasise connectivity, through transport and aviation as well as communication linkages, and high levels of amenity that may attract visitors as well as being important for residents. In addition, high road approaches tend to place value on cultural diversity and on the co-creation of services. This means that within the high road context, tourism is clearly seen as a subset of a broader understanding of human mobility, networks, planning and regional development, and services rather than a more simplistic notion of how many visitors have been attracted. At a broader planning level, debate now focuses on the fundamental questioning of economic growth as an end in itself or as an inevitable means to achieve higher standards of living (Pike et al. 2006). Indeed, new planning metrics for local and regional development reflect a broader notion of 'development' that include metrices of well-being and quality of life (Morgan 2004; Chase et al. 2012). Therefore, as Pike et al. (2006: 114) highlight, 'Recent approaches to sustainable local and regional development seek to integrate economic, environmental and social outcomes together rather than compromise through trade-offs and balances'.

Summary

Contemporary tourism planning is strongly oriented towards the notion of sustainable tourism development. The chapter has noted that the ideal planning style is integrative – in that it seeks to combine, social, environmental and economic planning goals and also seeks to satisfy a range of stakeholder aspirations. However, integrative planning is extremely difficult to achieve and often different organizations and individuals work within particular tourism planning traditions within the same destination. Understanding the different traditions is regarded as important because each approach defines the central planning problem in different ways. Nevertheless, changes in approach have occurred over time.

The chapter concluded by stressing how, from a regional planning perspective, sustainable tourism needs to be seen within the context of sustainable regional development rather than just from an industry perspective. In many cases tourism has unfortunately been regarded as a contributory to low road regional development rather than a high road path that emphasizes the role of soft infrastructure. Nevertheless, tourism does have a significant role in high road strategies, especially with respect to access, amenity and services.

8

Self-review questions

1 What are the five *traditions* of tourism planning identified in this chapter?

2 Why is *boosterism* sometimes described as a form of non-planning?

3 What are the key elements of a *sustainable* approach to tourism planning?

4 What are the five questions with respect to planning theory that are of concern in tourism planning?

5 Why do approaches to destination planning *change* over time?

6 What is the *justification* for planning?

7 What are the differences between *low-road* and *high-road* approaches towards regional competitiveness and development?

8 How do *low-road* approaches to regional development fit in with our understandings of *sustainable development*?

9 What *metrics* would you chose in helping to determine an understanding of sustainable tourism development?

Recommended reading

Michael, E.J. (2007). *Micro-clusters and Networks: The Growth of Tourism*, Oxford: Elsevier.
One of the best accounts of the role of state with respect to the promotion of tourism clusters and networks

Murphy, P.E. & Murphy, A.E. (2004). *Strategic Management for Tourism Communities*, Clevedon: Channel View Publications.
Updates some of Murphy's earlier work on community tourism within a more contemporary strategic planning perspective.

Hall, C.M. (2008). *Tourism Planning* (2nd ed.). Harlow: Prentice-Hall.
Provides an account of tourism planning at different scales and the influence of the different traditions of tourism planning

Dredge, D. & Jenkins, J. (Eds.) (2011). *Stories of Practice: Tourism Policy and Planning*, Farnham: Ashgate.
Provides a collection of different tourism planning case studies.

Gössling, S. & Hall, C.M. (Eds.) (2006). *Tourism and Global Environmental Change*, London: Routledge.
Provides an account of the development of tourism planning issues that are global in scope

Beaumont, N. & Dredge, D. (2010). Local tourism governance: A comparison of three network approaches. *Journal of Sustainable Tourism* 18, 7–28.
A good overview of some of the issues of governance associated with tourism planning.

Dredge, D. (2001). Local government tourism planning and policy-making in New South Wales: Institutional development and historical legacies. *Current Issues in Tourism* 4, 355-380.
Case study identifies some of the factors that influence tourism planning processes. The entire issue of the journal is devoted to tourism planning and policy

Hudson, R. (2001). *Producing Places*. New York: Guilford.
An excellent general overview of the issues involved in place planning and regional development.

Hall, C.M. 2009, Archetypal approaches to implementation and their implications for tourism policy, *Tourism Recreation Research* 34(3), 235-245.
Outlines the different idealized approaches to the implementation dimension of tourism planning and policy.

Frost, W. & Hall, C.M. (eds) (2009). *Tourism and National Parks: International Perspectives on Development, Histories and Change*, London: Routledge.
Provides a good account of the history of the national park concept and its relationship to tourism and the different approaches to tourism in different national jurisdictions.

References cited

Beaumont, N. & Dredge, D. (2010). Local tourism governance: A comparison of three network approaches. *Journal of Sustainable Tourism* 18, 7–28.

Brake, M. & Newton. M. (1995). Promoting sustainable tourism in an urban Context: Recent developments in Malaga City, Andalusia. *Journal of Sustainable Tourism*, 3: 115-134.

Bramwell, B. (2005). Interventions and policy instruments for sustainable tourism. In W. Theobold (Ed.), *Global Tourism* (3rd ed.), pp. 406–426. Oxford: Elsevier.

Bramwell, B. & Lane, B. (Eds.) (2000). *Tourism Collaboration and Partnerships: Politics, Practice and Sustainability*, Clevedon: Channel View Publications.

Cajander, V-R. (2003). Suomalaiset rakastavat suojelualueitaan! *Ympäristö* 3, 20–24.

Campbell, S. & Fainstein, S. (2003). Introduction: The structure and debates of planning theory. In S. Campbell and S. Fainstein (Eds), *Readings in Planning Theory*, pp.1-16. Oxford: Blackwell.

Chase, L.C., Amsden, B. & Phillips, R.G. (2012). Stakeholder engagement in tourism planning and development. In M. Uysal, R. Perdue & M.J. Sirgy (Eds) *Handbook of Tourism and Quality-of-Life Research: Enhancing the Lives of Tourists and Residents of Host Communities*, pp 475-490. Heidelberg: Springer Science+Business Media B.V.

Cheshire, P.C. & Gordon, I.R. (1998). Territorial competition: Some lessons for policy. *Annals of Regional Science* 32, 321-346.

Dredge, D. & Jenkins, J. (2007). *Tourism Planning and Policy*. Brisbane: Wiley.

Dredge, D. & Jenkins, J. (Eds.) (2011). *Stories of Practice: Tourism Policy and Planning*, Farnham: Ashgate.

Frost, W. & Hall, C.M. (eds) (2009). *Tourism and National Parks: International Perspectives on Development, Histories and Change*, London: Routledge.

Gössling, S. (2002). Global environmental consequences of tourism. *Global Environmental Change* 12: 283-302.

Gössling, S. & Hall, C.M. (Eds.) (2006). *Tourism and Global Environmental Change*, London: Routledge.

8

Gössling, S. & Hultman, J. (Eds) (2006). *Ecotourism in Scandinavia.* Wallingford: CAB International.

Gunn, C.A. (1979). *Tourism Planning.* New York: Crane Russak.

Hall, C.M. (2005) *Tourism: Rethinking the Social Science of Mobility.* Harlow: Prentice-Hall.

Hall, C.M. (2008). *Tourism Planning,* 2nd ed. Harlow: Prentice-Hall.

Hall, C.M. (2010). Changing paradigms and global change: From sustainable to steady-state tourism. *Tourism Recreation Research* 35(2), 131-145.

Hall, C.M. (2011). A typology of governance and its implications for tourism policy analysis, *Journal of Sustainable Tourism* 19, 437-457.

Hall, C.M. & Lew, A. (2009). *Understanding and Managing Tourism Impacts: An Integrated Approach,* London: Routledge.

Hall, C.M., Müller, D. & Saarinen, J. (2009). *Nordic Tourism,* Clevedon: Channelview Press.

Hall, C.M. & Page, S. (2006). *The Geography of Tourism and Recreation: Place, Space and Environment,* 3rd ed. London: Routledge.

Hall, D. & Brown, F. (2006). *Tourism and Welfare: Ethics, Responsibility and Sustained Well-Being,* Wallingford: CABI.

Harvey, D. (1989). From managerialism to entrepreneurialism: the transformation in urban governance in late capitalism. *Geografiska Annaler* 71B, 3-17.

Judd, D.R. (2003) Building the tourist city: editor's introduction. In D.R. Judd (Ed.), *The Infrastructure of Play: Building the Tourist City,* pp. 3-16. Armonk: M.E. Sharpe.

Krippendorf, J. (1975). *Die Landschaftsfresser: Tourismus und Erholungslandschaft, Verderben oder Segen?* Schönbühl, Switzerland: Hallwag.

Leitner, H. & Garner, M. (1993). The limits of local initiatives: a reassessment of urban entrepreneurialism for urban development. *Urban Geography* 14, 57–77.

Malecki, E.J. (2002). Hard and soft networks for urban competitiveness. *Urban Studies,* 39: 929-945.

Malecki, E.J. (2004). Jockeying for position: What it means and why it matters to regional development policy when places compete. *Regional Studies* 38, 1101-20.

Metsähallitus (Forest and Park Service) (2000). *The Principles of Protected Area Management in Finland: Guidelines on the Aims, Function and Management of State-owned Protected Areas.* Metsähallituksen luonnonsuojelulkaisuja Sarja B No.54. Vantaa: Metsähallitus – Forest and Park Service, Natural Heritage Service.

Metsähallitus (2010). Sustainable Nature Tourism in Protected Areas. Online. Available at: http://www.metsa.fi/sivustot/metsa/en/NaturalHeritage/ProtectedAreas/SustainableNatureTourism/Sivut/SustainableNatureTourisminProtectedAreas.aspx (accessed 18 September 2012)

Metsähallitus (2012) Protected Areas managed by Metsähallitus 1.1.2012. Online. Available at: http://www.metsa.fi/sivustot/metsa/en/NaturalHeritage/ ProtectedAreas/SizesofProtectedAreas/ProtectedAreasmanage/Sivut/ProtectedArea (accessed 18 September 2012).

Michael, E.J. (2007). *Micro-clusters and Networks: The Growth of Tourism*, Oxford: Elsevier.

Morgan, K. (2004). Sustainable regions: governance, innovation and scale. *European Planning Studies* 12(6), 871-889.

Murphy, P. (1985). *Tourism: A Community Approach*. London: Methuen.

Murphy, P.E. & Murphy, A.E. (2004). *Strategic Management for Tourism Communities*, Clevedon: Channel View Publications.

Newsome, D., Moore, S.A. & Dowling, R. (2013). *Natural Area Tourism: Ecology, Impacts and Management*, 2nd ed. Bristol: Channel View Publications.

Pforr, C. (2001). Tourism policy in Australia's Northern Territory: A policy process analysis of its tourism development masterplan. *Current Issues in Tourism* 4, 275-307.

Pike, A., Rodríguez-Pose, A. & Tomaney, J. (2006) *Local and Regional Development*, London: Routledge.

Ruhanen, L. (2004). Strategic planning for local tourism destinations: an analysis of tourism plans. *Tourism and Hospitality: Planning and Development* 1(3), 239-253.

Saarinen, J. (2003). The regional economics of tourism in northern Finland: The socio-economic implications of recent tourism development and the possibilities for regional development. *Scandinavian Journal of Hospitality and Tourism* 3(2), 91-113.

Schilcher, D. (2007). Growth versus equity: The continuum of pro-poor tourism and neoliberal governance. *Current Issues in Tourism* 10, 166–193.

Scott, D., Gössling, S. & Hall, C.M. (2012). *Tourism and Climate Change: Impacts, Adaptation and Mitigation*, London: Routledge.

Singh, S., Timothy, D. & R.K. Dowling, R.K. (Eds) (2003) *Tourism in Destination Communities*. Wallingford: CAB International.

Sorsa, R. (2004). The role of tourism in Finnish nature conservation from the nineteenth century to the present. In J. Saarinen and C.M. Hall (Eds) *Nature-based Tourism Research in Finland: Local Contexts, Global Issues*, pp.33-46. Finnish Forest Research Institute, Research Papers 916. Rovaniemi: Rovaniemi Research Station, Finnish Forest Research Institute.

Thorne, R. & Munro-Clark, M. (1989) Hallmark events as an excuse for autocracy in urban planning: A case history. In G.J. Syme, B.J. Shaw, D.M. Fenton and W.S. Mueller (Eds), *The Planning and Evaluation of Hallmark Events*, pp. 154–72. Aldershot: Avebury.

Timothy, D. & Tosun, C. (2003). Appropriate planning for tourism in destination communities: Participation, incremental growth and collaboration. In S. Singh, D. Timothy and R.K. Dowling (Eds), *Tourism in Destination Communities*, pp. 181-204. Wallingford: CAB International.

8

Treuren, G. & Lane, D. (2003). The tourism planning process in the context of organised interests, industry structures, state capacity, accumulation and sustainability. *Current Issues in Tourism* 6, 1-22.

Tuohino, A. & Patkinen, K. (2004). The role of tourism in Finnish nature conservation from the nineteenth century to the present. In J. Saarinen and C.M. Hall (Eds), *Nature-based Tourism Research in Finland: Local Contexts, Global Issues*, pp.129-50. Finnish Forest Research Institute, Research Papers 916. Rovaniemi: Rovaniemi Research Station, Finnish Forest Research Institute.

Wesley, A. & Pforr, C. (2010). The governance of coastal tourism: Unravelling the layers of complexity at Smiths Beach, Western Australia. *Journal of Sustainable Tourism* 18, 773–792.

World Commission on Environment and Development (WCED) (1987) *Our Common Future*. New York: Oxford University Press.

Zapata, M.J. & Hall, C.M. (2012). Public-private collaboration in the tourism sector: balancing legitimacy and effectiveness in Spanish tourism partnerships, *Journal of Policy Research in Tourism, Leisure and Events* 4, 61-83.

Zapata, M.J., Hall, C.M., Lindo, P. & Vanderschaeghen, M. (2011). Can community-based tourism contribute to development and poverty alleviation? *Current Issues in Tourism* 14, 725-749.

9 Marketing and Branding the Contemporary Destination

Chapter objectives

After reading this chapter you will:

- Understand the process and outcomes of contemporary destination marketing

- Appreciate the importance of engaging with all stakeholders in contemporary destination marketing

- Understand the formation and characteristics of the destination image

- Be aware of strategic approaches to contemporary destination marketing

- Understand the formation and characteristics of destination brands

- Recognise the role that technology, particularly the Internet, can play in contemporary destination marketing

- Appreciate the structure and roles of destination marketing organizations

- Recognise that destination marketing is surrounded by a range of issues and questions relating to the ability of a destination to be marketed as the equivalent of a product or brand

Introduction

This chapter provides an overview of the marketing and branding of contemporary destinations. It demonstrates that one of the major issues for destination marketers is the destination image, yet this is something that is very difficult to influence and to change. The significance of the destination image shows that destination marketing is as much a strategic process as it is a tactical one. Indeed, destination branding has to be viewed as a strategic activity as it is closely linked to the destination image and demands the close involvement of destination stakeholders in the design and acceptance of the brand. Of course, this process is now facilitated by technology and the Internet provides a cheap and effective marketing medium for destinations, as well as the opportunity to develop destination portals which provide a sense of ownership for stakeholders. Destination marketing organizations (DMOs) spearhead the technological developments for destinations and the marketing process generally; they act as umbrella marketing agencies and consolidate the role of destination partners. The chapter closes by identifying a range of key issues relating to destination marketing, including the role of the public sector, involvement of destination stakeholders, the very nature of the destination as a product and the question as to whether the theory of marketing can – or should – be extended to places and destinations.

Contemporary destination marketing and branding

Contemporary destination marketing and branding is both a process and an outcome (Pike, 2008). The process of destination marketing involves dealing with the complexities of destinations and their myriad stakeholders, whilst the outcome is the brand or image of the destination (Yang and Pizam, 2011). In other words a good destination marketer will focus upon two key operations. First, managing the destination's many stakeholders and networks; and second, formulating and managing the destination brand. Definitions of destination marketing clearly distinguish between the process of destination marketing and the outcome, as shown in Table 9.1.

Ward (1998) observes that place marketing dates back to the selling of the frontier to the American people in the mid-nineteenth century. Destination marketing came later in the late nineteenth century, when destinations sought to attract visitors in an increasingly competitive market. However, the actual term 'destination marketing' and the formal process of engaging in a disciplined marketing approach are more recent. They can be traced back to the 1970s when the advent of mass international tourism enhanced competition between destinations and prompted the beginnings of destination marketing as a practice. The concept continues to evolve and, increasingly there is a view that it is 'branding' that is the glue that holds the marketing of the destination together. Indeed, some now use the term 'destination branding' in place of 'destination marketing'. Tourism agencies are not alone in their practice of destination marketing – it is also practiced by urban planners who tend to take a broader, more holistic view and include economic and social objectives (see Chapter 8).

Table 9.1: Definitions of the process and the outcome of destination marketing

The process
'Destination branding is (the) process used to develop a unique identity and personality that is different from all competing destinations' (Morrison & Anderson 2002: 17)
'Place branding is an extremely complex and highly political activity that can enhance a nation's economy, national self-image and identity' (Morgan et al. 2004: 14).
Place marketing is 'the conscious use of publicity and marketing to communicate selective images of specific geographic localities or areas to a target audience' (Gold & Ward 1994: 2)
Destination marketing can be defined as the promotion of appealing images to attract visitors to a defined destination area (Middleton, 2000, p378).
Selecting a consistent element mix to identify and distinguish it [a destination] through positive image building (Cai 2002: 722)

The outcome
'A destination brand is a name, symbol, logo, word mark or other graphic that both identifies and differentiates the destination; furthermore it conveys the promise of a memorable travel experience that is uniquely associated with the destination; it also serves to consolidate and reinforce the recollection of pleasurable memories of the destination experience' (Ritchie & Ritchie 1998: 17).
A country image is 'the sum of beliefs and impressions people hold about places Images represent a simplification of a large number of associations and pieces of information connected with a place' (Kotler et al. 1993).

Contemporary destination marketing operates at a variety of scales from the international to the very local. It is central to the activities of tourism organizations, delivering destination competitiveness and a range of benefits to the destination. These benefits focus around the issue of differentiation and competitiveness and include:

- Securing the emotional link to, and loyalty of, visitors.
- Coordination of the private sector and other stakeholders through cooperative marketing.
- Acting as a base for promotion of other products such as investment, economic development, film, and TV.
- Facilitating and encouraging the use of local products and design.
- Facilitating seamless market communication of the destination.

However, to be successful, contemporary destination marketing must engage with the complexities of the destination itself, not only in terms of the necessity to be inclusive in the development of the brand, but also to get to grips with the nature of the destination product and the consumption process. Morgan et al. (2011) for example state that destinations are lifestyle indicators for aspirational visitors, communicating identity, lifestyle and status. Their consumption is a highly involving experience that is extensively planned and remembered, in contrast to the purchase and consumption of fast moving consumer goods (FMCG). A destination is therefore more than a product – it is the physical space

9

in which tourism takes place, where communities live and work and is imbued with symbols and images of culture and history. It is also the space within which tourists and suppliers interact to deliver the tourist experience. This context makes destination marketing so different from marketing FMCGs and is illustrated by the following case study, focussing on a DMO that takes a 'whole of destination' approach to its operation.

Case study 9.1: Place-making: The Blackstone Valley Tourism Council

The Blackstone Valley Tourism Council is an award winning DMO, having won a range of accolades, including the first ever Ulysses prize for innovation in destination management awarded by the UNWTO in 2006. This case study outlines key features of the Council's award winning approach. First, the Council's commitment to the local community and its development (Billington et al. 2008), and second, the Council's innovative approach to strategic destination marketing and product formulation.

The destination

Blackstone Valley is in Rhode Island, USA. It is the birthplace of the American industrial revolution, dating from 1790. By the nineteenth century it was dominated by up to one thousand textile mills. Poor economic decisions in the early twentieth century exposed the valley's over-dependence on textiles and the region became depressed with a 14% unemployment rate in 1982, and the river was the most polluted in America.

The Blackstone Valley Tourism Council is using tourism to spearhead the economic regeneration of the Valley. In addition, the Blackstone River Valley National Heritage Corridor was created in 1986 to preserve and interpret 46 miles of significant historic and cultural lands, waterways and structures in the Valley, and to boost the economy. The Corridor is managed by the National Park Service, which coordinates federal, state and local agencies. Congress established the 'Corridor Commission' to act as the umbrella agency to develop the vision of the corridor through innovative partnerships. The goal of the Corridor is to create a park system linking parks, historic sites and recreational facilities for locals and visitors along the Valley (Billington & Manheim 2002).

In the early years of the twenty first century, the valley had a population of half a million people living in 24 cities, and attracted around 3 million visitors each year. They visit the valley's attractions, which include:

- Historic sites and museums
- River tours
- Vineyards, farms and orchards
- Events and the arts
- Education and the River classroom.

The DMO

The Blackstone Valley Tourism Council was founded in 1985 as a not for profit educational organisational, professionally staffed and governed by a board of directors representing tourism interests in the Valley. It is one of seven tourism councils in the State and is the state-designated tourism development agency for the National Heritage Corridor.

The Council has a portion of public funding (a state hotel tax) and donations, but operates a large proportion of its budget through running events and private funding. The Blackstone Valley Tourism Council won its awards by demonstrating leadership, innovation and commitment to its mission. It is strongly influenced by the application of sustainable tourism principles in all its actions as a platform for resilience and flexibility. As part of this mission it has developed the Sustainable Tourism Planning and Development Laboratory that brings other communities to Blackstone and shares the Blackstone know-how of sustainable tourism planning in structured workshops.

The Council's main functions are:

■   Administration - running and coordinating tourism.

■   Visitor information services – face to face, mail and telephone enquires from the two Blackstone Valley Visitor Centres.

■   Special events and programmes – working with partners.

■   PR and communication – dealing with the media on behalf of the valley and working with partners.

■   Group travel – working with tour operators and easing packages.

■   River programmes – using council owned heritage boats for accommodation and interpretation.

■   Educational programmes – an educational coordinator managing programmes across the Valley.

Strategic destination marketing

The Council works to develop the Valley as a prime visitor and cultural destination. According to the Council's web site (www.blackstonevalleytourismorganisation.org), the mission of the Council is:

'To create positive change, with regard to community values, by developing coordinated responsible and sustainable tourism in Rhode Island's Blackstone Valley communities'.

And the purpose of the Council is place making:

'To create positive change with regard to community values by developing and promoting coordinated, responsible and sustainable tourism in Rhode Island's Blackstone Valley Communities. To plan and collaborate with intra-state, state, regional, national and international organizations to sustain and enhance the character of our destination, and to develop the public and private natural, historic, cultural, ethnic, industrial, recreational, educational, special events, artistic and commercial resources'.

The marketing of the Blackstone Valley is focussed on the river corridor and demands collaboration across a range of stakeholders at international, national and regional level as well as those in the Valley itself. In the Valley the two key agencies are:

■   Blackstone Valley Chamber of Commerce, which is focussed on the economic development of the valley.

■   The Corridor Commission, which is focussed on managing relationships in the National Heritage Corridor.

The Council's key objectives are framed around a strategic plan that focuses on the marketing of the Valley to create a unified vision. This plan aims to boost visitation and economic yield from tourism by:

■   Improving the tourism product.

■   Coordinating attractions and their operation across the Valley through linked trails and bikeways.

■   Encouraging more support services for tourism.

■   Better promoting the valley.

■   Coordinating marketing actions by collaborating with all stakeholders.

This is being achieved through:

■   Designation of tourism development zones with high potential to deliver a critical mass of attractions and support services.

■   Attraction of entrepreneurs through a tourism development programme with incentives.

In implementing the strategy, the Council has developed two key innovative concepts:

■   **The Blackstone Valley product** The Council has formulated the Valley's tourism product through the concept of 'geotourism' to sustain and enhance the authentic character of the Valley. Geotourism is defined as 'tourism that sustains or enhances the geographical character of a destination through its environment, culture, aesthetics, heritage and the well being of its residents'. The principles of geotourism are to attract those market segments most appropriate to the destination and to develop an authentic destination with a sense of place involving and benefiting the local community. Sustainability and interactive interpretation are central to the concept. The challenge faced by the Council in this vision is to balance economic regeneration with the socio-cultural authenticity of its local communities and the environmental and preservation needs of the region.

■   **The Blackstone Valley market** The Council engages overtly in relationship marketing by building strong relationships with visitors through its activities, communications and web site. This relationship is then used to encourage 'visitor payback' whereby visitors can pay back the destination for their experience there. This is done though a donation scheme developed by the Council through the Blackstone Valley Legacy Trust. In addition, visitors are encouraged to come back to the Valley as volunteers or employees.

By the early years of the twenty first century the Blackstone Valley Tourism Council had seen a valley-wide regeneration with a drop in unemployment across the region, an improved quality of life for local communities and return of pride of place in the destination. The Council demonstrates the fact that tourism is but one element of complex functioning communities and destinations and it has successfully balanced the economic, preservation and environmental needs of the region by weaving in an innovative approach to managing tourism. Above all the Council has kept the needs of local residents in mind by enhancing their quality of life, and thus the quality of the destination, as happy residents are more likely to encourage people to visit.

Key sources

Billington, R.D. & Manheim, P. (2002). Creating sustainable tourism development – The Blackstone River Valley Heritage Corridor - America's first industrialised valley: the role of leadership - creativity, cooperation and commitment. In K. Chon, V. Heung and K. Wong (Eds), *Tourism In Asia: Development, Marketing and Sustainability Fifth Biennial Conference*, pp. 25-33. New York: Haworth Press.

Billington, R.D., Carter, N. & Kayamba, L. (2008). The practical application of sustainable development principles: a case study of creating innovative placemaking strategies. *Tourism and Hospitality Research* 8, 37-43.

Blackstone River valley National Heritage Corridor, http://www.nps.gov/blac

Blackstone Valley Chamber of Commerce, http://www.blackstonevalley.org

Blackstone Valley Tourism Council, http://www.tourblackstone.com

Yaeger Communications (2001). *Blackstone Valley Tourism Strategic Plan*. Massachusetts: Yaeger Communications.

Discussion questions

1   Visit the Council's web site and map the stakeholders involved in the Blackstone Valley tourism sector – how could they be grouped?

2   What strategies should the Council consider to balance the needs of tourism development to regenerate the Blackstone Valley, with the imperative to preserve a unique historic industrial landscape?

3   What might be the drawbacks with the Council's concept of 'geotourism'?

9

Destination image

Understanding the formation and characteristics of the destination image is central to contemporary destination marketing. Destination image can be defined as:

'The attitude, perception, beliefs and ideas one holds about a particular geographic area formed by the cognitive mage of a particular destination' (Gartner 2000: 295).

In effect, the destination image is a simplified version of reality, a way of making sense of the many destination stimuli received and processed by the visitor or potential visitor. In other words, the image of a destination is critical to marketing as it affects both an individual's perception of a destination and their choice of destination. The generation of the image is different for destinations to many other products – such as FMCG, for example. This is because it is the tourists themselves who generate a destination image by selecting different sources of information. As a result, destination marketeers have much less influence on images, despite their critical importance to destination choice. The image is particularly critical for tourist destinations as:

1   The intangible nature of the destination product means the image is the only evidence that a visitor has of the destination before they visit. For the tourist, the destination promise is inherently uncertain and decisions depend upon the tourist's mental construct, which on effect acts as a surrogate for evaluating the product. The challenge for marketing lies in understanding the complex link between consumer decision-making and the destination image.

2   The inseparable nature of the production and consumption process of tourism means that once they visit, the tourist's image of the destination is immediately changed by the experience.

Whilst image formation is not the same as branding, it is closely related. This is because the choice of branding and brand attributes of a destination reinforce the destination image.

Components of the destination image

The theories of destination image are divided into two camps. The first suggests that the destination image can be disaggregated into many attributes and elements that can be measured. The second, gestalt approach, says that the image is a whole, or holistic concept and cannot be disaggregated.

Gartner (1993) provides an attractive framework for understanding destination image and its link to destination branding. He argues that a destination image comprises three distinct, but hierarchical related elements – components, formation and characteristics:

■ Components

There are three components of the image - cognitive, affective and conative:

■   *The cognitive component* comprises the beliefs and attitudes towards the destination and leads to the internal evaluation of the destination's attributes. This is based on fact, or what are believed to be the facts, acquired over time from many sources. From the tourist's point of view, the perceived image is reality.

■   *The affective component* represents the value of the destination in terms of what the tourist is looking for from the destination based on personal feelings or motives. It is this comparison of the image with the tourist's needs that determines value.

■ *The conative component* is the action component. This is the decision to visit and is based upon evaluation and the value of the first two components.

■ Formation

Formation of the destination image is based upon information acquired by the tourist from three sources:

■ *Induced agents* are generally controlled by sources external to the individual, such as advertisements.

■ *Organic agents* are sources acquired through personal experience. These are normally the most trusted sources of information.

■ *Autonomous agents* are media sources or popular culture (such as films or documentaries). They are powerful because they can quickly alter a tourist's image of a destination.

■ Characteristics

Destination images are characterised by certain features:

■ Distance blurs the image of a place such that distant destinations have a fuzzier image than closer destinations.

■ Images change continuously but slowly.

■ The smaller the destination image, the more likely its image will be based on its larger political parent.

■ The larger the image the more slowly it changes.

The role of images in destination marketing

9

Destination images are pervasive and powerful and clearly they play an important role in contemporary destination marketing and branding. As noted already, destination image has a profound effect on visitor behaviour and decision making with respect to destinations. Destination marketing therefore focuses on the deceptively simple approach of developing a positive image through promotion. In this process, images are used to achieve the following:

■ Communicate messages about destinations.

■ Redefine and reposition destinations.

■ Counter negative, and enhance positive, perceptions about destinations.

■ Target key market areas.

Marketing then, attempts to manage the image through researching perceptions of the destination, segmenting and targeting image audiences, and positioning destination benefits to support the image. In Table 9.2 the UNWTO shows how images can be classified and appropriate marketing action taken to reinforce or change the image.

Table 9.2: Destination image and marketing actions. Source UNWTO (2006)

Destination image	Marketing action
Positive	Focus on amplifying and delivering image to target groups
Weak	Places that are small lack attractions or do not promote
Negative	Requires fundamental change prior to image development
Mixed	Emphasise selected elements and rectify others
Contradictory	Different groups with opposing images – stress positive points to groups with negative images
Overly attractive	Withdraw publicity

Contemporary destination marketing strategy

Destination marketing is a strategic activity, linked not only to tourism but also to sustainability, economic development, investment and residential lifestyle. The goal of destination strategy is to convert current conditions at the destination into desired situations using strategic marketing and planning. Pike (2004) breaks this down further by identifying four thematic goals of DMOs:

1 Enhancing destination image

2 Increasing industry profitability

3 Reducing seasonality

4 Ensuring long-term funding.

Whilst this can be done by applying standard strategic marketing approaches to the destination – such as the Boston Consulting Matrix or Porter's Strategic Forces – these approaches do not translate well to the complexity of destinations. This is partly because destination-marketing agencies do not control the product that they are dealing with.

Two approaches merit consideration here. Gilbert (1990) takes the approach of classifying destinations along a continuum from commodity to status area. The destination's position on the continuum assists in developing an appropriate marketing strategy and can be used to strategically reposition a destination, as was done by Spain in the 1990s. The strategic process is as follows:

1 Assess current position.

2 Select desired position.

3 Strategy to achieve desired position.

4 Implement strategy.

However, Gilbert's approach suffers from the fact that most destinations lie between the two extremes and it omits the evolution of destinations. Instead, the approach devised by Jain (1985) works well and has been adapted for destinations by Cooper (1995). He classifies the strategic options for destinations according to a two dimensional matrix that takes into account the competitive position of the destination and the stage on the destination life cycle (Table 9.3). This is useful in locating the strategic response of destinations to the wider competitive environment. Jain's framework is linked to a comprehensive research and environmental scanning process, which is essential for destinations to understand not only the competitive environment and the consumer, but also the positive and negative associations of the destination brand.

Table 9.3: Jain's matrix of strategic action. Source: Cooper (1995), based on Jain (1985)

Competitor position	Stage on life cycle			
	Embryonic	Growth	Mature	Ageing
Dominant	Fast grow Start up	Fast grow Cost leadership Renew Defend position	Defend position Cost leadership Renew Fast grow	Defend position Focus Renew Grow with industry
Strong	Start up Differentiate Fast grow	Fast grow Catch up Cost leadership Differentiate	Cost leadership Renew, focus Differentiate Grow with industry	Find niche Hold niche Hang in Grow with industry Harvest
Favourable	Start up Differentiate Focus Fast grow	Differentiate, focus Catch up Grow with industry	Harvest-hang in Find niche, hold niche Renew, turnaround Differentiate, focus Grow with industry	Retrench Turnaround
Tenable	Start up Grow with industry Focus	Harvest, catch up Hold niche Find niche Turnaround Focus Grow with industry	Harvest Turnaround Find niche Retrench	Divest Retrench
Weak	Find niche Catch up Grow with industry	Turnaround Retrench	Withdraw Divest	Withdraw

■ Positioning

A key component of destination strategy is the positioning of the destination against the competition. This ensures that the destination delivers a unique position in relation to its competitors and occupies a particular place in the minds of potential tourists. Positioning of destinations is based upon differentiation, cost and developing a unique focus. Positioning must be consistent with cost and value for money, market trends and consumer preferences, convenience of purchase, technology and demographic trends. Finally, positioning must take into account the capability and resources of the destination to deliver the promise.

Destination branding

Destination branding is central to the contemporary destination marketing process – to quote Kotler (2003: 418) 'branding is the art and cornerstone of marketing'. The role of a brand is to:

> 'identify the goods or service of either one seller or a group of sellers and to differentiate those goods and services from those of competitors' (Aaker 1991: 7).

Brands can be approached from two viewpoints. First, the *product plus approach* views the brand as an addition to the product (along with say, price) and concerned with communication and differentiation. Second, the *holistic approach* views the brand as greater than the sum of its parts, such that brands reside in the minds of consumers. It is this second approach, which is most common in destination marketing.

Brands signify identity and originated as a means of ownership and identification by farmers or craftsmen. Merz et al. (2009) identify four eras of brand thinking:

1   The first era is based on individual goods. Brands became important as mass markets developed for products in the twentieth century. This was for two reasons: first, consumers became more sophisticated and were faced with greater product choice; and second, branding was developed for FMCG as they are characterised by low involvement products, with the need for branding to build loyalty and communicate benefits over competitors.

2   Second came the era of 'value' where brand image became important. It is this era that has been the focus of much of the destination branding literature.

3   Third came the focus on brands and relationships, where the brand was the promise made to the consumer.

4   The final era of brand thinking is the stakeholder focus. This is the most relevant to destination branding because here there is a dynamic relationship between the brand and destination stakeholders (residents, industry, DMO) such that the brand is co-created.

In other words brands assure quality, reduce the consumers' need for search and aid in product differentiation. Nonetheless, whilst it may appear that brands are fabricated, they are real entities, based upon products, resistant to change and dependent upon occupying defensible niches within product categories. Developing and managing destination brands is therefore as much a strategic operation as it is tactical (UNWTO 2009).

Blain et al. (2005) define the process of destination branding as:

> 'The set of marketing activities that (1) support the creation of a name, symbol, logo, word mark or other graphic that readily identifies and differentiates a destination; that (2) consistently convey the expectation of a memorable travel experience that is uniquely associated with the destination; that (3) service to consolidate and reinforce the emotional connection between the visitor and the destination; and

that (4) reduce consumer search costs and perceived risk. Collectively, these activities serve to create a destination image that positively influences consumer destination choice' (Blain et al. 2005: 337).

According to Hankinson (2004) destination brands:

- Communicate identity and are therefore of strategic importance.
- Are perceptual entities in themselves and so the issue of destination image is central to destination branding.
- Enhance value.
- Can be used to build a relationship with the visitor or supplier.

The link between destination brand and destination image is clear. Like images, brands are created by consumers, but at the same time, brands fast track the information processing of consumers by acting as a means of differentiation and a guarantee of quality. However, here consumers' needs for, uses of, perceptions and expectations of, and communication about brands is changing rapidly, prompted by social media, digital communication and changing values and lifestyles. Therefore to be successful a destination brand should:

- Be credible.
- Be deliverable.
- Be differentiated.
- Convey powerful ideas.
- Enthuse destination partners.
- Resonate with the visitor.

Formulating the destination brand is more complex for destinations than for say, FMCG. This is because the destination comprises many stakeholders, including local residents, and the branding process must be inclusive of these groups, as discussed later in this chapter. Destination branding serves two masters:

1 *The local community* where resident receptiveness is a major element of destination branding.

2 *The tourist* who in turn receives information and market stories about the destination from a variety of sources, including social media. When they visit they interact with destination products and services and evaluate the brand.

This raises the question of whether destination-marketing organizations can in fact control the brand to the same degree that marketers act as the custodian of FMCG brands. In other words, can all the actions that affect visitor perceptions at a destination be managed and coordinated, when many dimensions of destination brands are beyond the control of the marketer? This has been clearly demonstrated in the period since '911' with the many terrorist attacks on destinations.

9

Designing the destination brand

The destination brand enhances the favourability, strength and uniqueness of the destination and so must demonstrate consistency and clarity of design. Designing the destination brand delivers the blueprint for the branding, development and marketing of the destination. This includes:

■ Positioning.

■ Product formulation and composition (such as seaside, city or heritage destinations).

■ The nesting of the brand in terms of identifying a supra-brand (such as Australia) and sub-brands based on geography and products (Queensland, Gold Coast).

■ The communication strategy reflected in destination logos, insignia, and marketing collateral advertising concepts.

This can be seen as a four-step approach.

Brand assessment

This begins with an assessment of the current situation of the destination brand including a review of the marketplace, visitors, stakeholders, influencers, competitors and industry conditions as well as the demographic and social setting of the destination. It will be based on facts and research on visitor perceptions, influencers and stakeholders. The stages will include:

■ A review of all previous research.

■ A review of all brand communications and marketing plans.

■ Analysis of data on competitors and visitor research.

Brand promise

The brand promise is the essence of the commitment to visitors and the benefits (emotional and functional) that visitors can expect throughout the destination experience. The entire destination must commit to the brand if the promise is to be delivered, hence the need for the branding process to be inclusive of all stakeholders, including local residents. The promise is normally expressed in a few sentences to communicate brand attributes:

■ Something will be done.

■ An expressed assurance.

■ A perception of future excellence and achievement.

All destination brand communication is then consistent with the promise. However, it must be recognised that the destination brand promise will often reflect a compromise between the aspirations of the destination brand and the reality of what the brand can deliver to visitors.

Brand architecture

The architecture of the brand outlines the various messages to communicate the promise and the essence of the destination brand. This process attempts to signal the destination's values and positioning and increasingly tends to stress more emotional than functional benefits. The process also signals what the destination can deliver using a five-stage approach:

1 Choice of a destination brand name that resonates with the visitor and sets the tone of the destination.

2 Graphics such as logos or visual symbols.

3 A by-line that describes what the destination brand is all about.

4 A tag line that clarifies the destination's emotional and functional benefits.

5 The brand story, which is used to inspire visitors and explains how the brand came about.

In other words, brand architecture provides a framework within which to communicate the destination brand. It often utilises events or theming (linking to TV, seasons, history, film or literature).

Internalising the brand

This is the road map for how the destination organization delivers the brand promise on the ground at the destination through influencing and training employees, partners, stakeholders and residents. This enables and empowers the delivery of the brand promise at the destination. This is critical as the products delivered at the destination are often the strongest manifestation of brand identity. Brand internalisation comprises four stages:

1 Creation of brand principles.

2 Establishment of brand equity goals.

3 Outlining and communicating the brand plan to all stakeholders.

4 Completing a culturalization plan for all stakeholders.

The destination branding process therefore delivers a carefully crafted and conceptualised branding strategy that encompasses the entire destination experience reflecting visitor needs and being inclusive of destination stakeholders. Destinations are places where visitors have experiences, therefore brands have to capture visitor imagination and resonate with the market, whilst also being sensitive to, and inclusive of, the local community and destination stakeholders.

Technology

The Internet has revolutionised destination marketing, branding and image formation. At a stroke it has given small destinations with tiny budgets the same market reach as the largest destinations in the world (UNWTO 2008). It brings other advantages too. Internet technology is ideally suited to products such as

9

tourism, where the product is intangible and cannot be pre-tested. Indeed, the decision to visit is increasingly influenced by (i) the quality of a destination web site and the degree that it allows interaction and flexibility (Park & Gretzel 2007); (ii) Internet search engines which are a valuable tool connecting the traveller with destination organisations (Pan et al. 2010); and (iii) design of a flexible web presence that incorporates social media and the ability to interact with visitors and potential visitors (Milano 2011). Destination marketing organizations (DMOs) can use technology to:

- Provide destination information to travellers, saving on print and distribution costs, yet providing content of great depth and visual quality.
- Communicate and manage customers through email and social media.

Yet, whilst the Internet has been available for destination marketing since the mid-1990s, many destinations have been slow to take advantage of the cost savings and potential that it provides, and it is a common criticism that content provision by destinations lags behind the technology available to deliver it.

Destination web sites

DMOs now use the Internet as a central part of their marketing strategy. Here the key is to have a strategic e-marketing plan to direct traffic to a destination web site and to then capture the visitor (UNWTO 2005). Such web sites service visitors, local industry, media and professionals. The structure of a destination web site will depend upon two sets of factors:

- *Destination factors* – destination size, the variety of destination products, the number of web updates required, and the role of e-commerce on the site.
- *Technical factors* – the importance of position on search engines, whether the site is on a hosted or a purchased server, and the screen resolution required.

The WTO (2001) identified the following key features of web site functionality for destinations:

- Accessibility and readability – does the site reach all potential users.
- Identity and trust – trust on the Internet is fragile, especially if e-commerce is involved through online booking. Strong branding, use of logos and a clear statement of purpose all help here.
- Degree of customisation and interactivity.
- Ease of navigation.
- Finadability and search engine optimisation.
- Technical performance – lack of functionality is frustrating for users.
- The quality of the services offered via the web site:
  - ☐ Promotion
  - ☐ Information
  - ☐ Transactions.

Increasingly destination web sites are being used for more than the straightforward delivery and presentation of destination information. Many sites now include the ability to customise the site and for tourists to interact with the information. As destination web sites have evolved, their levels of flexibility and interactivity have improved and grown. This has been captured by Doolin et al. (2002) in their 'Extended Model of Internet Commerce Adoption' (eMICA).

The eMICA model demonstrates a staged approach to the evolution of destination web sites and provides a destination with a roadmap of its web site development. The model shows how web sites add layers of complexity and functionality as they develop (Table 9.4).

Table 9.4: The eMICA model. Source: Doolin et al. (2002)

eMICA	Examples of functionality
Stage 1 Promotion Layer 1 Basic information	Company name, address and contact details
Layer 2 Rich information	Annual report, email contact
Stage 2 Provision Layer 1 Low interactivity	Basic product catalogue, hyperlinks, online enquiry form
Layer 2 Medium interactivity	Higher level product catalogues, customer support (FAQs)
Layer 3 High interactivity	Chat room, newsletters and email updates
Stage 3 Processing	Secure online transactions, order status and tracking

Good web site design encourages the building of relationships between the destination and the tourist and leads to 'e-satisfaction' on behalf of the traveller. At the time of writing, contemporary destinations are increasingly achieving this by the development of a web-based interface, or destination portal, which can deliver tangible benefits to both the supplier and the tourist. In effect, destination portals become the digital version of the destination, unifying web access to the destination, integrating all aspects of the value chain and allowing communication amongst stakeholders.

On the supply side, destination portals allow the integration of destination management systems to draw together all elements of supply at the destination. They allow the identification of high quality content providers at the destination and can manage them by grouping, categorizing, and providing simplified navigation and straightforward accessibility. Portals also have the advantage of acting to encourage virtual destination communities and cooperation amongst stakeholders.

On the demand side, portals act as an interface with the consumer and have the ability to include e-commerce functions through integrated information management systems. These functions are achieved by the presence of both a customer database and a product database with an interface between the two.

DMOs must evaluate their web sites given the levels of investment in their development, and their critical dependence upon them in destination marketing strategies. Whilst this is still a relatively new science, there are a variety of approaches to web site evaluation (Law et al. 2010). These include:

- Best practice-based evaluations and measurements that use experts based on a set of quality criteria.
- Online surveys that evaluate the needs, satisfaction and opinions of users.
- Web analytics which track and trace user behaviour.
- Online experiments and laboratory testing of behaviour where visitors to sites are analysed and their behaviour in, say, searching is used to devise online market segmentation approaches.

These approaches evaluate web sites in terms of:

- Design, content and simplicity.
- Search engine compliance.
- Navigation and speed.
- Customer relationship management and links.
- E-commerce, advertising and response.
- Performance tracking and management.

The role of the destination marketing organization (DMO)

Given the investment needed for a destination to develop a fully-fledged e-marketing strategy, this is often led by the destination management organization. There are two forces at work here.

1 DMOs face the threat of disintermediation as their role becomes redundant in the face of Internet bookings and tourist information delivered by the Internet. DMOs typically provide information for the early stages of destination decision-making, but other web-based companies are now moving in to occupy that role (such as Expedia, Travelocity).

2 Coordination and leadership is needed at the destination level, and it is this strategic role that can be taken by the DMO. DMOs are often public sector funded agencies and therefore have the mandate to develop IT systems and leverage funding from destination partners. However, DMOs do not provide the final tourism service and therefore have to forge collaborations and partnerships with commercial firms to deliver and implement a seamless experience for the visitor (Zach 2011).

These two factors mean that the DMO must evolve beyond being a simple marketing organisation into an agency that manages the whole of the destination.

Destination marketing organizations (DMOs)

Destination marketing is normally spearheaded and implemented by a destination marketing organization (DMO) or a convention and visitor bureau (CVB). Funding tends to be secured by the public sector with additional funds from private sector partners, often on a membership basis. DMO structures vary considerably and continue to evolve; traditionally they were departments or agencies funded by government to market the destination but increasingly they involve the private sector in a partnership arrangement (Pike 2004). The International Association of Convention and Visitor Bureaus (IACVB) characterises DMOs as not for profit organizations representing a specific destination, offering a full range of unbiased information for both the trade and consumer and promoting the long-term marketing and development of the destination. In other words, DMOs have both a strategic aim and a range of tactical activities. Their strategic aim is to act as an umbrella-marketing agency by promoting the long-term development and marketing of the destination and consolidating the role of destination partners in this process. This strategic aim is achieved through a variety of tactical activities, which include:

- Creating the destination brand to deliver awareness of the destination.
- Coordinating destination stakeholders.
- Acting as an unbiased information clearinghouse for both the public and the travel trade.
- Commissioning research.
- Developing the destination-marketing plan.
- Developing funding resources to support the operation of the DMO.
- Developing the destination product and packaging.
- Monitoring service and quality standards.

The IACVB profiled 222 American CVBs in 2005 and summarised their characteristics as follows:

- On average each destination has two visitor centres.
- The average visitor centre utilises both paid staff (76%) and volunteers.
- Almost half of all visitor centres have a shop.
- Almost two thirds of CVBs are independent, not for profit organizations whilst 18% are government agencies.
- CVBs source their funding from a mix of government support and membership dues.
- Half of all CVBs are membership organizations.
- Average staffing of a CVB is 12-13 full time equivalent staff.

The survey also found that the average age of a CVB is 39 years, with the first being established in Chicago in 1896. In the twenty first century, more than 100 years later, some key trends can be identified in the way that DMOs are operating. These include an observable trend towards destination management and away from simply focussing on marketing. This reflects the fact that the DMO is seen to have to manage the product and to generate strategies that resonate with visitors. It is also linked to a trend for professionalism amongst DMOs as administrative structures flatten and the DMO is held accountable to the community. This is changing the way that DMOs report and measure their performance, with statistics of enquiry conversions more important than simply the number of enquiries. Finally, all DMOs are recognising that innovation and partnerships are a key aspect of their work. Case study 9.2 illustrates how partnerships across destinations can deliver an enhanced product and more effective marketing.

Case study 9.2: Marketing Australian cattle station destinations

The Australian Government is keen to spread the benefits of tourism to regional Australia and away from the state capitals of Sydney and Melbourne and the beaches of the Gold Coast. A number of initiatives have been tried including road tours, indigenous tourism and campaigns for Australians to see their home country. These include private sector initiatives such as Outback Beds – a web portal for touring and booking accommodation ahead (outbackbeds.com.au).Yet these campaigns have not been particularly successful because, as a destination, regional Australia lacks the infrastructure expected by the twenty first century tourist and also struggles to put together a coherent and attractive tourism product.

One aspect of tourism in regional Australia that is proving a success is visits to cattle stations. Here the investment in infrastructure such as spas and resorts on the cattle stations, and the attraction of a visit to an authentic working cattle station begin to create the ingredients for a successful destination product. As a result, a growing number of cattle stations are developing a sideline in pastoral tourism, representing a contemporary diversification of the use of these vast land holdings.

However diversification into tourism demands particular marketing and product development skills, and these are skills not always present in regional Australia. As a result, innovative owners and managers have developed collaborative networks to both share expertise in tourism and to pool resources. Before moving onto these collaborative destination marketing initiatives, we firstly profile some distinctive cattle station destinations:

Cattle Station Products

Home Valley Station, The Kimberley, Western Australia (http://www.hvstation.com.au)

The unique aspect of Home Valley Station is the focus on training of indigenous men and women from the local area. Home Valley Station is owned by Australia's Indigenous Land Corporation (ILC). The ILC is keen to create jobs for indigenous people through the development of sustainable land enterprises and in the case of Home Valley Station does so by working with the indigenous people from the region. Training includes both pastoral and tourism skills.

The Station is vast, covering over 1.4 million hectares of the Kimberley region of Western Australia with gorges, waterholes, beaches, rivers and spectacular ancient landscapes. The challenge is therefore to create appropriate tourism products for this this huge area. The managers of Home Valley Station have achieved this through:

- Use of indigenous guides to unlock the destination for the visitor
- Fishing tours
- Horse trekking
- Boating
- Cattle musters
- Walking tours

Bullo River Station, Northern Territory (www.bulloriver.com)

This station demonstrates small scale authentic outback tourism. It extends over 200,000 hectares of Australian Outback savannah landscape and is rich in wildlife. The accommodation is in a 12-room annexe surrounding the homestead.

Tourism products include:

- Aborigine rock art
- Cattle ranching
- Fishing
- Barbecues
- Pastoral skills

El Questro, Western Australia (www.elquestro.com.au)

The distinctive feature of this cattle station is the contrast of the realties of the station's life with a luxury tourism experience. It is a 400,000 hectare cattle station set in the Kimberley. The tourism business is operated very separately from the cattle business. It has adopted a contemporary approach with activities menus and a range of accommodation products:

- Six luxurious, fully catered rooms in the homestead itself.
- Three rooms on the edge of the Chamberlain Gorge.
- Emma Gorge Resort: 60 tented cabins offering a faux camping experience with swimming pool, bar, restaurant and landscaped gardens.
- The Station Township offers campsites or motel-style bungalows.

Wrotham Park, Queensland (www.wrothampark.com.au)

Wrotham Park's claim to fame is the level of luxury of the accommodation. It is an upscale cattle ranch experience, based around 10 luxury guest lodges on the edge of the Mitchell River ravine. The luxury is augmented by the homestead itself with a swimming pool.

9

Tourism products include:

- Quad bike tours
- Fishing
- Horse riding
- Helicopter tours

Burrawang West Station, New South Wales (www.burrawangwest.com.au)

This station used to be part of a larger cattle station until it was purchased by a Japanese corporation. The company created a plush bush retreat for its top executives. The station was given an extensive makeover to create a traditional homestead (complete with swimming pool and sauna), with guest accommodation in four double-bedroom cottages. Now no longer owned by the company, the present owner has opened it as a luxury retreat for visitors to experience life on a cattle station. Tourism products include:

- Quad bike tours
- Archery
- Tennis
- Canoeing
- Swimming

Collaborative destination marketing

To add to the significant investment required to develop tourism, and the risks involved in diversifying, cattle stations are also geographically remote and do not always have the professional tourism expertise to develop their tourism business successfully. Individually, the stations do not have the capacity to market themselves, are often family run and do not have significant resources to invest in marketing and product development

Nonetheless, these cattle stations occupy vast tracts of spectacular Australian landscape and are large enough to become destinations in their own right. Hence it makes sense for them to work together, share ideas, discuss common issues, develop web portals and create a business cluster. In effect, cattle stations have recognised the logic of cooperation rather than competition at the destination level – the concept of 'co-opetition'. Initiatives amongst clusters of cattle stations include:

- Developing touring resources such as maps
- Rostering attendance at trade shows
- Funding a marketing representative
- Developing joint web sites
- Developing collaborative marketing material
- Developing web sites to enable touring and accommodation booking (for example www.stationstayssa.com.au).

Conclusion

Cattle stations are very varied in their level of service and the products they offer. However, after only a few years in tourism, they are creating their own destination and collaborating across cattle station and state boundaries to market and develop their products as they diversify. Cattle stations present a particular problem for destination marketing – they are remote, occupy huge areas of land so touring is less easy and they are not owned and run by managers who understand tourism. The notion of collaboration across these varied products, and of assistance from Government agencies which are encouraging tourism into the regions, is a good example of how tourism destination marketing only works with cooperation and a full understanding of the product.

Key sources

http://www.desertknowledge.com.au/Our-Programs/Outback-Business-Networks/
  Case-Studies

http://www.outbackbeds.com.au

http://www.stationstayssa.com.au

Discussion questions

1   Visit a site such as Trip Advisor and collate the reviews of cattle and sheep stations in Australia. Using this information, design a tourism product development guide for cattle and sheep stations.

2   Attracting visitors to remoter parts of any destination is always a challenge. In class, brainstorm the options available for destinations managers to attract visitors to these regions.

3   Cooperation in destinations makes sense but the nature of tourism entrepreneurs often prevents true cooperation. How might you overcome resistance to cooperating with 'competitors'?

9

Contemporary destination marketing issues

This chapter has provided a synoptic view of destination marketing and branding. This is a controversial and relatively new area of academic focus and one that generates a range of significant questions and issues. This final section identifies and discusses three key issues relating to contemporary destination marketing and branding.

■ The role of the public sector

Gold and Ward (1994) identify a contradiction at the heart of place marketing; namely that the public sector tends to treat the process as one involving a policy dimension and also treats the destination as a public good – this of course, contrasts with the marketing approach where destinations overtly compete. This raises the significant issue as to whether government is the appropriate agency to deliver destination marketing and branding. In addition to the basic conflict of philosophies noted above, the public sector may not be the right agency for destination marketing because it:

- Controls neither destination product quality nor the private sector.
- Cannot address deficiencies in the product such as the accommodation mix.
- Has to be even-handed in its dealings with stakeholders and cannot be seen to 'back winners'.
- Tends not to be entrepreneurial.
- Often lacks marketing expertise and is more focussed on economic development and investment.
- Can only facilitate bookings and often cannot close a sale.
- Often has budgets that are inadequate for significant promotion and market research and the typical 12 monthly budgeting cycle is problematic.
- Views the destination as bounded by political boundaries which makes a cooperative or regional approach to marketing difficult.

■ The role of destination stakeholders

A second key issue for destination marketing is to ensure involvement and commitment by all stakeholders in the strategy and branding process. Stakeholders play a critical role in the branding of a tourism destination. Yet, destination politics are notoriously destructive of the marketing process and it is therefore vital to be inclusive from the outset. Here, Gnoth (2002) extends the concept of the destination brand to that of supply-driven destination brand communities. These provide a platform for connectivity, trust building and decision making at the destination to develop and maintain a sustainable brand strategy amongst all stakeholders.

The key here is to manage the relationship between collaboration and power and to recognise that the views of the local community must be included in destination marketing as destinations are places where people live work and play. Collaboration can be seen to encompass four further issues:

Creation of a shared brand

Creation of a shared brand ensures that the destination brand image is built on shared destination attributes. In other words, there is a need to 'internalise the destination brand' and to ensure that its authenticity is shared and believed in by all stakeholders. This allows citizens to be brand champions (but also enemies if they do not subscribe to the brand). DMOs often use leadership figures to communicate and advocate the brand within the destination.

Collaboration and inclusiveness

It is essential that the destination brand is the positive outcome of the achieve-ment of unity and collaboration amongst stakeholders; indeed it could be argued that effective destination marketing hinges on relationship building with stake-holders. Yet collaboration across destination stakeholders is a complex and politi-cised process. Destinations are often crucibles of conflict and stakeholders do not always agree. The danger for branding is that larger stakeholders will take their own brands and brand attributes to market, which damages the smaller players and the overall destination brand. In other words, support offered by stakehold-ers makes or breaks the destination marketing process.

Destinations as loosely articulated networks

Collaboration recognises that destination stakeholders are critically depend-ent upon each other. This involves joint decision-making with individuals and interest groups operating at different levels of the destination. In seeking agree-ment amongst groups, destination marketing can recognise that destinations are informal flexible networks based on trust and common interest. This can be encouraged through the use of destination portals as noted above, combined with training and innovative destination business models to connect and coordinate stakeholders.

Relationship versus transactional marketing

Of course, this begs the question as to whether DMOs should engage strongly in 'relationship' marketing with the destination community, rather than focussing on the more traditional 'transactional' marketing approach. Fyall et al. (2003) note that in theory, relationship marketing transforms a satisfied customer into a loyal customer and could be extended to the concept of destination loyalty by market-ing to all destination stakeholders, ensuring quality and targeting and retaining key markets. Relationship marketing is ideally suited to situations where the customer controls supplier selection, there is little loyalty, brand switching is common and word of mouth is a powerful form of communication. It works less well for markets characterised by infrequent purchases and environments where cooperation is difficult.

As a result, relationship marketing is difficult to apply at the destination level. This is because of the difficulty of achieving a clear vision, mission and cooperative organisational culture at destinations, which provide the environment of trust, direction, and long-term stability necessary to implement relationship market-ing. This means that the contemporary destination still engages in 'transactional' rather than 'relationship' marketing. However, as this chapter has shown, it is vital that destination marketing takes into account not just the 'transaction, but also the 'framework' or 'context' within which the transaction takes place.

9

■ The nature of the tourist destination

The two key questions that this chapter poses are:

1 Should the places where people live, work and play be transformed into brands and products?

2 Does the very nature of the tourist destination run counter to the ability to transform it into a brand?

Taking the first of these questions, the development of destination brands may conflict with the community's perception and feelings for the place where they live, work and play. This can be exacerbated by the delivery of the brand on the ground through the use of signage, street furniture and landscaping. Destinations are contested spaces and the various users of this space each hold their own images, identities and interests. They also have their own experiences and perceptions of the history and antecedents of the destination. It is extremely difficult to factor this into the destination marketing process.

Second, the theory and growing literature on branding is built largely upon the experience of FMCGs and tangible products. It could be argued that this theory cannot be simply transferred to the marketing of destinations. The nature of the destination as a fragmented and complex amalgam of attractions and support facilities, delivered by many different providers, means that the definition and formulation of the destination product is problematic. If it is to succeed, destination marketing must recognise that it is a more collective activity than is normally found in marketing. It can be argued that the branding theory embraced by tourism researchers has been extended beyond its original intent. Quite simply it is a challenge to build and manage destination images and brands, and when this has been done, they are in danger of failing due to the fact that the tourism sector will not take direction and politicians do not recognise link of tourism and economy. Hankinson (2004) adds to this view by arguing that the dominance of the perceptual aspect of destination branding – particularly the focus on destination image – has held back the further development of destination marketing in terms of management structures, stakeholder relationships and marketing control.

Summary

Growing competition in the tourism sector has demanded that destinations differentiate themselves through developing strong, unique and competitive destination brands. This is the key to destination marketing and, as has been demonstrated in this chapter, the process is one of branding that takes into account the formation and nature of the destination image. Yet, destination marketing is about more than just increasing visitation; it also has a regional development and investment role and is therefore strategic in nature, as demonstrated by the Blackstone Valley case. It has an imperative to engage closely with destination stakeholders to deliver a brand that has been derived by consensus and which has the support of the whole community. Of course, this is much more difficult than it sounds, as destinations are typically crucibles of conflict and the marketing process is therefore inherently political. Nonetheless, destination marketing now has a long history, in its current form dating back to the mid-1970s. DMOs tend to be the implementing agencies and increasingly they are reliant upon technology to reach the consumer, deliver tourist information and, through destination portals, provide a complete digital representation of the destination. Finally, as this chapter has shown, destination marketing is not without controversy with many significant questions – is the public sector the appropriate agency to lead the marketing process; just how does the process engage all destination stakeholders and perhaps most fundamental, are we confident that marketing theory and approaches can be extended to destinations and the places where people live, work and play.

Self-review questions

1　Distinguish between the *process* and the *outcomes* of destination marketing.

2　What are the *benefits* of destination marketing?

3　Identify the major categories of *destination stakeholder*. For each, what might be their role in the destination marketing process?

4　Why is the *destination image* largely out of the control of the destination marketer?

5　What are the characteristics of a *successful brand*?

6　How might the *brand architecture* of a particular destination be communicated?

7　Identify a destination web site of your choice. How does it perform on the UNWTO's features of *web site functionality*?

8　Recall the key *marketing roles* of a DMO.

9　Is *the public sector* the appropriate agency for destination marketing?

10　Is marketing theory overstretched when applied to destinations?

Recommended reading

Buhalis, D. (2000). Marketing the competitive destination of the future. *Tourism Management* 21, 97-116.

A comprehensive overview of the factors relating to destination marketing

Cai, L. (2002). Cooperative branding for rural destinations. *Annals of Tourism Research* 29(3), 720-742.

An excellent review of the nature of cooperation at the destination

Hankinson, G. (2004). Relational network brands: towards a conceptual model of place brands. *Journal of Vacation Marketing* 10(2), 109-121.

Thought provoking paper challenging the translation of branding theory to places

Harrill, R. (ed.) (2005). *Fundamentals of Destination Management and Marketing*, Michigan: Educational Institute of the American Hotel and Motel Association. Solid introduction to destination marketing in an easily accessible form

Heath, E. & Wall, G. (1992). *Marketing Tourism Destinations*. Chichester: Wiley. A well-structured approach outlining an approach to destination marketing and planning

Law, R., Qi, S. & Buhalis, D. (2010) Progress in tourism research management: a review of web site evaluation. *Tourism Management* 31, 297-313. Excellent review of the state of the art of web site evaluation for tourism sites

http://www. iacvb.org
Comprehensive web site with rich sources of information on the structure and operation of destination marketing organizations.

Morgan, N., Pritchard, A. & Pride, R. (2011). *Destination Brands*, 3rd ed. London: Routledge. Thorough, advanced overview of destination branding

Pike, S. (2004). *Destination Marketing Organizations*, London: Routledge. Excellent overview of destination marketing organizations

Pike, S. (2008). *Destination Marketing*, London: Routledge. Excellent overview of the process and issues of destination marketing

Blain, C., Levy, S.E. & Ritchie, J.R.B. (2005). Destination branding: Insights and practices from Destination Management Organizations. *Journal of Travel Research* 43, 328-338. Comprehensive paper outlining the theory of destination branding

UNWTO, Madrid - two excellent reports on marketing destinations online:
Evaluating and Improving Destination Web Sites - the Destination Web Watch (2005)
Handbook on E-Marketing for Tourism Destinations (2008)

Recommended web sites

Visit Scotland: http://www.visitscotland.com/

Destination Marketing Association International: http://www.iacvb.org/

Department of Tourism and Commerce Marketing, Government of Dubai: dubaitourism.co.ae/

Alberta Travel: www.albertatravel.ca/

Tourism British Columbia: www.hellobc.com/

References cited

Aaker, D. (1991). *Managing Brand Equity.* New York: Free Press.

Cai, L. (2002) Cooperative branding for rural destinations. *Annals of Tourism Research* 29(3), 720-742.

Cooper, C. (1995). Strategic planning for sustainable tourism: The case of offshore islands in the UK. *Journal of Sustainable Tourism* 3(4), 191-209.

Doolin, B. Burgess, L. & Cooper, J. (2002). Evaluating the use of the web for tourism marketing: a case study from New Zealand. *Tourism Management* 23, 557-561.

Fyall, A., Callod, C. & Edwards, B. (2003). Relationship marketing. The challenge for destinations. *Annals of Tourism Research* 30(3), 644-659.

Gartner, W.C. (1993). Image formation process. In D. Fessenmaier and M Uysal (Eds), *Communication and Channel Systems in Tourism Marketing*, pp. 191-215. New York: Horwath Press.

Gartner, W.C. (2000) Image. In J. Jafari (ed.), *Encyclopedia of Tourism*, pp. 295-296. London: Routledge.

Gilbert, D. (1990). Strategic marketing planning for national tourism. *The Tourist Review* 45(1), 18-27.

Gnoth, J. (2002). Leveraging export brands through a tourism destination brand. *Brand Management* 9(4-5), 262-280.

Gold, J.R. & Ward, S.V. (1994). *Place Promotion. The Use of Publicity and Marketing to Sell Towns and Regions.* Chichester: John Wiley.

Hankinson, G. (2004). Relational network brands: Towards a conceptual model of place brands. *Journal of Vacation Marketing*, 10(2), 109-121.

Jain, S.C. (1985). *Marketing, Planning and Strategy.* Cincinnati: Southwestern.

Kotler, P. (2000). *Marketing Management. The Millennium Edition*, New Jersey: Prentice Hall.

Kotler, P. Haider, D.H. & Rein, I. (1993). *Marketing Places*, New York: Free Press.

Kotler, P. (2003). *Principles of Marketing*, 2nd ed. Frenchs Forest, New South Wales: Prentice Hall.

Law, R., Qi, S. & Buhalis, D. (2010). Progress in tourism research management: a review of web site evaluation. *Tourism Management* 31, 297 – 313.

Merz, M.A., He, Y. & Vargo, S.L. (2009). The evolving brand logic: A service dominant logic perspective. *Journal of the Academy of Marketing Science* 37(3), 328–344.

Middleton, V.T.C. (2000) Marketing, Destination. In J. Jafari (Ed.), *Encyclopedia of Tourism*, pp. 378-379. London: Routledge.

Milano, R., Baggio, R. & Piattelli, R. (2011). The effects of online social media on tourism web sites. In R. Law, M. Fuchs & F. Ricci (Eds), *ICT in Tourism 2011*, pp. 471-483. New York: Springer.

Morgan, N. Pritchard, A. & Pride, R. (2004). *Destination Branding Creating the Unique Destination Proposition*, 2nd ed. Oxford: Elsevier.

Morgan, N., Pritchard, A. & Pride, R. (2011). *Destination Brands*, 3rd ed. London: Routledge.

Morrison, A.M. & Anderson, D.J. (2002). Destination Branding, Missouri Association of Convention and Visitor Bureaus Annual Meeting, Missouri.

Pan, B., Xiang, Z., Law, R. & Fessenmaier, D (2010). The dynamics of search engine marketing for tourist destinations. *Journal of Travel Research* 50, 365 – 377.

Park, Y.A. & Gretzel, U. (2007). Success factors for destination marketing web sites: a qualitative meta analysis. *Journal of Travel Research* 46, 46 – 63.

Pike, S. (2004). *Destination Marketing Organizations*, London: Routledge.

Pike, S. (2008). *Destination Marketing*, London: Routledge.

Ritchie, J.R.B. and Ritchie J.R.R. (1998). The Branding of Tourist Destinations, AIEST Conference, Morocco.

UNWTO (2001) E-Business for Tourism. Practical Guidelines for Destinations and Businesses, UNWTO, Madrid

UNWTO (2005). *Evaluating and Improving Destination Web Sites - the Destination Web Watch*. Madrid: UNWTO.

UNWTO (2006). *Destination Positioning, Branding and Image Management*, Addis Ababa.

UNWTO (2008). *Handbook on E-Marketing for Tourism Destinations*. Madrid: UNWTO.

UNWTO (2009). *Handbook on Destination Branding*. Madrid: UNWTO.

Wang, Y. & Pizam, A. (2011). *Destination Marketing and Management*. Oxford: CABI.

Ward, S.V. (1998). *Selling Places. The Marketing and Promotion of Towns and Cities 1850 – 2000*, London: E and F N Spon.

Zach, F. (2011). Partners and innovation in American destination marketing organizations. *Journal of Travel Research* 51, 412 – 425.

Section 4:
The Contemporary Tourism Industry

10 The Scope of the Contemporary Tourism Sector

Chapter objectives

After reading this chapter you will:

■ Be aware of the scale and scope of the contemporary tourism industry.

■ Understand the difficulties of defining the contemporary tourism industry.

■ Be aware of the various approaches to defining tourism from a supply-side perspective.

■ Recognise that tourism is a partially-industrialised system.

■ Recognise the issues involved in measuring the contemporary tourism industry.

■ Understand the status of tourism in standard industrial classifications.

■ Appreciate the tourism satellite account approach and its benefits.

■ Be familiar with the challenges of measuring the scale of tourism employment.

Introduction

Tourism is often described as one of the world's largest industries with huge figures quoted for the value of the tourism industry and the numbers it employs. This chapter provides a reality check for this 'boosterism' by demonstrating that we are far from reaching agreement as to just how to define the tourism industry. The chapter outlines the approaches to date in trying to define and measure tourism as an industry and the problems faced in doing so, not least the fact that many industries are involved in delivering the tourism product. It demonstrates that tourism is in fact only partially an industry, as governments, communities and others are involved in delivering the tourism product. We go on to show how tourism is not recognised as an industry in standard industrial classifications and national statistical systems. It then outlines the breakthrough in defining and measuring the tourism industry in the form of the tourism satellite account (TSA). The TSA has now been accepted by the United Nations as the industry standard for defining and measuring the tourism industry. It can be used to compare tourism with other economic sectors and to provide policy makers and planners with useful information. The chapter closes by considering how tourism employment is measured and some of the problems involved.

The size and scope of the tourism industry

The World Travel and Tourism Council (WTTC) is an industry lobby group comprising the major tourism corporations in the world. As part of their work they have estimated the size and scope of the tourism industry using sophisticated economic techniques. They state that travel and tourism is:

> 'one of the largest and most dynamic industries of today's global economy, travel and tourism …it accounts for US£6 trillion, or 9%,'of global gross domestic product (GDP) and it supports 260 million jobs worldwide, either directly or indirectly. That's almost 1 in 12 of all jobs on the planet' (WTTC 2012: 3).

The question posed by these numbers is just how did the WTTC come up with these estimates, and what do they include as being a part of the travel and tourism industry? This is a key issue that is occupying the minds of academics and politicians alike, as well as industry lobbyists such as the WTTC. The problem is simple – how to measure the scale and scope of tourism, because tourism is an industry that challenges conventional paradigms. Yet it is important to do so, as tourism is a complex industrial system, a major employer and generator of revenues. Debbage and Ioannides (1998) speak of the commodification of tourism that has created this machinery of production:

> 'Although changes in consumer demand and the evolution of increasingly more sophisticated consumer preferences can play substantive roles in shaping the tourism product, it is the actual 'machinery of production' that helps to manipulate and facilitate origin-destination tourist flows across the world' (Debbage & Ioannides 1998: 287).

Ioannides and Debbage (1998) vent their frustration at the fact that we have not yet satisfactorily got to grips with analysing the supply side of tourism. They point to a lack of quality analysis of tourism as a supply-side phenomenon, despite the fact that tourism is bought and sold as a commodity and the industry is organised along capitalist lines, albeit with some unique characteristics. These include:

- The tourism industry is highly diverse – from size of establishment (SMEs to corporations); business type (IT to service provision); sector (air transport to accommodation); organisation (public and private sector); and process. It is therefore more a collection of industries than a single industry.

- The fact that tourism is not a single product but a diverse range of products and services that interact.

- It comprises tangible and non-tangible elements.

- It is produced where it is consumed.

To exacerbate this, the tourism industry is both misunderstood and under-explored (Debbage & Daniels 1998). This is because it is amorphous and complex, shrouded in conceptual fuzziness and imprecise terminology (is it tourism or travel?). This chapter aims to dispel some of this mystique and provide a clear description of how to approach examining the scope and scale of the contemporary tourism industry.

A tourism system

Leiper (1979) has clearly located the tourism industry within the wider tourism system as we showed in Chapter 1. His well-known tourism system comprises three key elements – the generating region, the transit zone and the destination region. Cutting across these three elements are the resources and industries required to deliver the tourism product. However, Leiper (1979) agrees that there are problems delineating these resources due to:

1 The difficulty of identifying the tourism element of an industry.

2 The difficulty of separating industry and non-industry elements.

3 Difficulties in specifying the number of industries inherently connected with tourism.

Leiper goes on to define the tourism industry element of the system as:

> 'All those firms, organizations and facilities which are intended to serve the specific needs and wants of tourists' (Leiper 1979: 400).

He further splits the industry into six sectors, each linked and specialising in a particular function:

1 Tourism marketing

2 Tourist carriers

3 Tourist accommodation

4 Tourist attractions

5 Miscellaneous tourism services (e.g. taxis)

6 Tourism regulation (including government and education).

Definitions of the contemporary tourism industry

Smith (1988) is concerned that the continued lack of agreement over definitions of the tourism industry is both frustrating and embarrassing for the credibility of the sector. The debate continues partly because economists refuse to accept that tourism is in fact an industry. Indeed, in 2006 the Australian Productivity Commission decided that the whole definition needed to be revisited and came up with a range of yet more new definitions. So why do we need definitions of the contemporary tourism industry?

1 For measurement and producing accurate statistics of supply. This includes the size of the tourism industry, the number of jobs it generates and what is included for the range of data collection and legitimate comparison with other economic sectors (Davidson 1994).

2 For legislative purposes – to ensure that laws and policy applying to the tourism sector do actually apply to that sector.

3 For credibility – to define and understand the sector for credibility in government and other economic sectors, as well as a sense of self-identity.

Generic definitions of an industry are based upon the manufacturing paradigm. Here, the notion of an industry is a group of independent firms all turning out the same product, and competing over these substitutable products. Another way to approach the definition is to think of an industry as a group of sellers of close substitutes to a common group of buyers. In other words, definitions of an industry focus around the people and activities involved in one type of business, or a distinct group of productive or profit-making enterprises. This clearly is problematic for tourism as:

1 The definitions are dominantly rooted in the economics of manufacturing.

2 The growth of tourism, and services more generally, has not been taken into account in such definitions.

3 Tourism statistical data are poor and do not support the sophisticated measurement of the industry.

As a result, supply-side definitions of tourism have proven more difficult to resolve and it is only since 2000 that real agreement has been reached. The key issue with supply-side definitions is to decide which businesses and organisations should be included in the definition of the contemporary tourism industry. But it is more than simply coming up with a list; there are complex technical issues to be tackled here. Smith (1996) illustrates this with the very practical example of a hotel – initially you may think that the hotel is wholly a tourism business. However, most hotels have a significant proportion of local business in the restaurants and function rooms. How should we apportion the tourists' consumption and the locals' consumption of the hotel's products in order to gauge the size of tourism's contribution to the hotel's income and jobs?

Smith (1988) shows that early definitions of the tourism industry focussed on the supply of commodities:

> 'The tourist sector or tourism industry can be broadly conceived as representing the sum of those industrial and commercial activities producing goods and services wholly consumed by foreign visitors or domestic tourists' (UNCTAD 1971).

Smith revises this with his own definition:

> 'Tourism is the aggregate of all businesses that directly provide goods and services to facilitate business, pleasure and leisure activities away from the home environment' (Smith 1988: 183).

Smith's position here is that tourism is an industry that can be approached and measured as any other. However, the issue of apportioning tourism and non-tourism consumption is an important one, as few businesses serve only tourists. Smith (1996) argues that some businesses are almost pure tourism whilst others have a significant element of demand for their commodities from local residents. He quotes the Canadian way around this issue by classifying enterprises as:

1 Tier 1 firms – which would not exist in the absence of travel. They include hotels, tour operators and airlines.

2 Tier 2 firms – which would still exist in the absence of travel but in a diminished form. They include taxis, car hire firms and restaurants.

This approach is consistent with the way that other industries are defined from a supply-side perspective and also allows relatively easy measurement. This however, depends on the scale of analysis, and as noted above in the hotel example, the best approach is to take the analysis down to the smallest operating unit.

Leiper (1990) however disagrees with this approach and views the tourism sector as comprising a range of industries, rather than a single industry. He sees the tourism industry as a short-hand notation for activities involving tourism, which can be better described as a set of interactions between a set of related markets, characterised by different types of competitive structures. He notes that industry definitions often involve the idea of competition. In other words, when businesses compete they begin to become an industry. Some industries have competition between companies, brands, products and compete on a national and international level. Whilst there is clearly competition in tourism, it is more unusual to find it at the international level.

A partially industrialised system

There is no doubt that lobbyists for tourism would prefer to define it as a single industry, as this allows them to grow the scale and value of industry. However, Leiper disagrees with this approach. It is clear that the tourism industry is now part of a complex tourism system designed to deliver the tourism experience (see

Chapter 1). This is a huge system, attracting statements that suggest it approaches the largest industry in the world, as already noted. But there is a debate as to whether tourism is a totally industrialised system or only partially industrialised.

As noted above, Leiper (1979) states clearly that a range of resources and industries are required to deliver the tourism product within his tourism system. Some of these resources will lie outside the private sector and will include the community and government (e.g. through DMOs). Equally, there will be a range of industries involved in delivering the tourism product that do not see themselves as part of the tourism system – petrol retailers or caterers, for example. He therefore sees the tourism system as one characterised by *partial industrialisation in tourism* (PIIT) where a number of organization who supply tourists are not part of the tourism industry network and do not engage (Leiper et al. 2008). Leiper (1979) defines PIIT as the 'proportion of a) goods and services stemming from that industry to b) total goods and services used by tourists can be termed an index of industrialisation, theoretically ranging from 100% (wholly industrialised) to zero (tourists present and spending money but no tourism industry)' (Leiper 1989: 25).

This explains why policymaking for tourism is so complex, particularly for the less industrialised types of tourism, and also why industry representation for tourism by say, trade associations, is so mixed. Partial industrialisation in tourism also introduces two related ideas.

1 The notion of dependent and independent tourists. Dependent tourists depend heavily on the tourism industry structures of tour operators, travel agents and inbound operators – an example is the inbound Japanese industry to Australia (Leiper et al. 2008) as noted above. Independent tourists can complete their travel without significant engagement with the tourism sector.

2 The idea of differential levels of industry linkages. There is a range of organizations supplying tourists who develop business strategies for tourism and therefore engage with other like-minded businesses. Others, such as the petrol retailers example given above, do not develop tourism business strategies and therefore do not engage with those that do. This is shown on Figure 10.1 which is a diagrammatic representation of PIIT.

In Figure 10.1 the vertical axis represents business strategy whilst the horizontal axis represents industry strategy. We can then populate each of the four quadrants in Figure 10.1 with suppliers to tourists.

1 Quadrant 1 is populated by highly industrialised suppliers such as tour operators, travel agents, accommodation or theme parks.

2 Quadrant 2 is populated by newly established suppliers or 'lone wolf' entrepreneurs who have not yet developed close linkages with other organizations. In time they may move to Quadrant 1.

3 Quadrant 3 is populated by organizations that have no business strategy for tourism (such as a caterers). It is these organizations that often need policy inducements to engage with the tourism sector.

4 Quadrant 4 is populated by those who are not in tourism but benefit from say, the marketing of a DMO and so they will support the DMO by paying membership. This avoids the 'free rider' accusation which could be levelled at them.

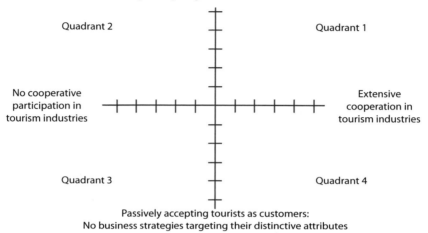

Figure 10.1: Partial industrialisation: possible positions of organisations directly supplying services and goods to tourists, in terms of their business strategies and degrees of industrial cooperation.

The notion of PIIT is an important and innovative concept and takes the same stance as this book; that tourism is about human behaviour rather than an industry. In summary, we can think of a complex tourism system, partially industrialised delivering the tourism product to the consumer. Bull (1995) summarises this with the following supply-side definition:

> *'The tourism industry, or industries, consists of any organizations supplying goods and services to those people now defined as tourists or excursionists, as part of their tourist requirements' (Bull 1995: 3).*

Measuring the scale and scope of the contemporary tourism industry

Given the difficulties of defining tourism from the supply side, it is remarkable that the WTTC is able to estimate the size and scope of the industry as quoted at the beginning of this chapter. Measuring the size and scope of the contemporary tourism industry faces two major challenges; first to develop a coherent and shared view of just what comprises the supply side of tourism and second, to credibly measure it. Until 2000, tourism was dependent upon the standard industrial classification of enterprises to define the industry. However, since then there have been significant breakthroughs in meeting the challenges of measurement, which have come from major advances led by UNWTO, WTTC and the Canadian Government in the development and implementation of 'tourism satellite accounts'. The most recent definitive statement came from UNIDO's recommendations on tourism statistics in 2008.

The Standard Industrial Classification approach

Before turning to tourism satellite accounts, it is important to understand how tourism maps onto standard industrial classification (SIC) systems and as a result, why a new approach was required. Tourism is not a recognised industry in the SIC and as a result the accommodation, restaurant and catering industry is often used as a proxy for tourism (Riley et al. 2002). This is a problem as it means that many parts of the tourism industry are missed from a statistical point of view in terms of employment and turnover.

The idea of a SIC is to classify establishments by their economic activity, where establishments are economic units that produce goods or services. This helps to understand the structure of the economy, the impact of policy changes, and the impact of competition and international events (Roehl 1998). There are a number of types of SICs but all use a similar basis for classification. The idea is to create categories that are externally heterogenous (e.g. transport and accommodation) but internally homogeneous. The challenge is in the level of aggregation used, as there is no sense in every establishment being in a separate category. As a result, accommodation would normally include camping as well as hotels, but exclude restaurants. The International Standard Industrial Classification (ISIC) has been developed by the UN to encourage consistency of SIC codes internationally. The UN agency responsible for producing global statistics of economic activity is the UN Industrial Development Organization (UNIDO) (www.unido.org) which works in collaboration with the OECD for data collection.

When grappling with the complexities of determining what comprises the tourism industry, an obvious approach is to allocate tourism consumption to different categories in the standard industrial classification (such as accommodation or restaurants). But again we have the problem that many enterprises earn a considerable income from tourism (such as shopping malls) but are not categorised as part of the tourism industry, whilst others (such as hotels) have a considerable proportion of local consumption. In an attempt to get around this problem, the WTO began a tourism version of the ISIC in 1990 – the 'standard industrial classification of tourism activity' (SICTA) whereby enterprises with substantial tourism revenues were assigned to particular codes. The following classification was used:

■ Tourism characteristic products – all tourism services.

■ Tourism characteristic activities – activities whose principal output is characteristic of tourism.

■ Tourism characteristics industries – a group of establishments whose principal activity is tourism characteristic activity.

Over the years, a number of attempts have been made to assign tourism consumption to establishments using variants of the SIC codes. The following case study shows that whilst there is a level of agreement in this, there are still differences according to different countries.

Case study 10.1: Mapping the contemporary tourism industry onto the SIC system

The SIC does not treat tourism as an industry. However, one approach to defining tourism using the SIC codes is to apportion tourism enterprises to SIC codes. In other words, a number of SIC codes are viewed as containing significant elements of tourism consumption and so tourism can be mapped onto the SIC system. However, getting agreement on just which SIC codes are significant from a tourism point of view is difficult. Table 10.1 in this case study shows a number of international approaches to mapping SIC codes to tourism, and three country approaches. The table demonstrates that whilst there is some general agreement as to what comprises the tourism industry, there is also variation around the edges, particularly in relation to transport, cultural attractions and sport. There is also variation by country, dependent upon the particular types of tourism that are important in the particular country.

Table 10.1: Mapping tourism enterprises onto various SIC and country approaches

Sectors	TS Accounts	ISIC	SICTA
Hotels, campsites and other short stay accommodation	Hotels, campsites and other short stay accommodation	Hotels, campsites and other short stay accommodation	Hotels, camping sites and other commercial accommodations
Restaurants and bars	Restaurants, bars, and canteens	Restaurants, bars, and canteens	Restaurants, bars and canteens
Travel agents and intermediaries	Travel agents and packagers	Included in transport	Travel agents, tour operators and guides
Cultural, attractions and entertainment	Cultural attractions and entertainment	Entertainment (museums etc., sporting and other recreational activities)	Operation of recreational fairs and shows
Passenger transport	Passenger transport	Land transport, water transport, air transport, activities of travel agencies and tour operators	Transport, storage and communications
Sports facilities	Sports facility operators	Included in cultural attractions	
Other			Exchange of currencies, real estate agencies, education, visitor and convention bureaus, gambling and betting operations, casinos

Sectors	UK	Canada	Israel
Hotels, campsites and other short stay accommodation	Hotels and other tourist accommodation	Traveller accommodation	Hotels, youth hostels, Christian hospices, field schools, rural tourism
Restaurants and bars	Restaurants, cafes and snack bars	Full service restaurants, limited service eating places, drinking places	Restaurants (listed for tourists)
Travel agents and intermediaries	Travel agents and tour operators	Travel arrangement and reservation services	Travels agencies, tour offices and tour guides
Cultural, attractions and entertainment	Libraries, museums and other cultural attractions	Recreation and entertainment, including spectator sports	
Passenger transport		Air transport, all other transportation industries	
Sports facilities	Sports and other recreational activities	Included in cultural attractions	
Other	Public houses, bars, night clubs/licensed clubs	Recreational vehicle parks and camp grounds	

Key sources

British Tourist Authority/English Tourist Board (1997). *Employment in Tourist Related industries in Great Britain*. London: BTA/ETB.

Israel Central Bureau of Statistics with Ministry of Tourism (quarterly) *Tourism and Hotel Statistics Quarterly*. Jerusalem: ICBS.

Statistics Canada (2006). *Human Resource Module of the Tourism Satellite Account 1997-2002*, Ottawa: Statistics Canada.

UNSTAT (1990). *International Standard Classification of all Economic Activities*. New York: UNSTAT.

WTO (1995). *Concepts, Definitions and Classifications of Tourism Statistics*. Madrid: WTO.

Discussion questions

1   Are you convinced that these classification systems have captured the totality of the tourism industry?

2   Devise your own classification of the enterprises that you would include in tourism, using variants of Table 10.1 and your own ideas.

3   Why do you think it is taking so long to get agreement of the sectors to be included as comprising the tourism industry?

Tourism satellite accounts

Partly as a result of the frustration about the failure to satisfactorily measure the tourism industry from a supply side point of view, and recognising that national statistical systems did not treat tourism as a single sector, the tourism satellite account (TSA) approach was developed from the mid-1990s. Politically, this was an important initiative as it allows tourism to be directly compared with other sectors and therefore creates economic credibility for tourism (UNWTO 2010).

As noted above, to be defined as an industry, tourism would need to have a single production process, a homogenous product and a locationally-confined market. In other words, by conventional definitions, tourism is not an industry. Tourism products are however functionally linked to deliver a single product in the eye of the consumer. This led to the idea of a satellite account which is effectively a sub-set of a nation's accounts that involves expenditures by individuals defined as tourists by the UNWTO. A satellite account is a term developed by the United Nations to measure the size of economic sectors that are not defined as industries in national accounts. As such the TSA is a statistical instrument – a satellite revolving around concepts, definitions and aggregates of national accounts.

Tourism satellite accounts represent a real breakthrough in defining tourism from the supply side. Indeed, tourism is the first activity to use worldwide satellite account standards to measure its impact on national economies. The United Nations Statistical Commission approved the methodology in March 2000.

The TSA, surprisingly, is more of a demand-side measure than a supply-side one as it measures the expenditure made for tourism commodities and non-tourism commodities. Visitors buy goods and services both tourism and non-tourism enterprises alike, so the key from a measurement standpoint is associating their purchases to the total supply of these goods and services within a country.

The commodities are defined as follows:

1 Tourism commodities – goods or services for which a considerable portion of demand comes from tourists – airlines for example.

2 Non-tourism commodities – commodities that experience no or little demand from tourists.

In practice, the TSA is an information system that combines, orders and manipulates statistics describing all significant and measurable aspects of tourism within a framework that organises tourism data according to the real world relationships from which they originate (Smith 1998). It is based upon the financial flows.

The TSA allows for valid comparisons of tourism with other industries and allows comparison from country to country and between groups of countries. Such measures are also comparable with other internationally-recognized economic statistics. The TSA measures:

- Tourism's contribution to GDP.
- Tourism's ranking compared to other economic sectors.
- The number of jobs created by tourism in an economy.
- The amount of tax revenues generated by tourism industries.
- Tourism consumption.
- Tourism's impact on a nation's balance of payments.

10

- Characteristics of tourism human resources.

The TSA can be used to:

- Provide credible data on the impact of tourism and the associated employment.
- Develop a standard framework for organizing statistical data on tourism.
- Set a new international standard endorsed by the UN Statistical Commission.
- Design economic policies related to tourism development.
- Provide data on tourism's impact on a nation's balance of payments.
- Provide information on tourism human resource characteristics.

More generally, the TSA can also be used to:

- Increase and improve knowledge of tourism's importance relative to overall economic activity in a given country.
- Provide an instrument for designing more efficient policies relating to tourism and its employment aspects.
- Create awareness among the various stakeholders, directly and indirectly involved with tourism, of the economic importance of this activity and by extension, its role in all the industries involved in the production of goods and services demanded by visitors.
- Develop predictive tourism indicators, industry outlooks and risk scenarios.

Case study 10.2: The way forward for TSAs

As the TSA has become accepted and the methodology refined, the UNWTO and other agencies have begun to examine the way forward for the TSA. In particular there is a need to understand the general impact of tourism on economies at both the national and regional scale. At the first T.20 Ministers meeting in South Africa in 2010 a key recommendation was to 'strengthen the analytical base that underpins the economic and development case for travel and tourism' (UNWTO 2010: 9). Here the UN is developing a new and robust System of Tourism Statistics (STS) which will provide early warning indicators, short-term performance indicators of turnover and employment and business cycle indicators. In addition, sophisticated methodologies allow the TSA to examine the impact of tourism on communities, the environment and employment.

There have been two important meetings assessing the way forward for TSAs.

- The first was in October 2005 in Iguazu, on the borders of Argentina, Brazil and Paraguay. This meeting assessed the actual level of development, analysis and application of the TSA worldwide. Titled 'The Tourism Satellite Account (TSA): Understanding Tourism and Designing Strategies', this meeting set the agenda for the development of TSAs (UNWTO 2005a).
- The second meeting was in October 2010 in Korea and dealt with the important issue of positioning tourism in economic policy.

The two meetings had a number of themes, reflecting the development of TSAs in the first decade of the twenty first century. The key themes were:

1   The TSA's relevance for policy makers – the role of TSAs in supporting knowledge-led policy. In particular there is a need to integrate tourism with other national policies and forge links with policy makers in other areas. Here the UNWTO are taking a leadership role in asking countries to weave tourism into their economic policy framework.

2   TSA implications for trade policies – the role of the TSA in developing credible statistics on tourism to ensure the integration of tourism development and trade – within the national system of developing countries in particular.

3   Adapting the TSA conceptual framework: The regional perspective – developing a regional level model of the TSA using the same framework and language as the national TSA. Here the sub-national framework is seen as a priority – tourism is not equally distributed across countries. The UNWTO has launched a network on regional economics, mobility and tourism which will share expertise at the sub national level – an expert knowledge driven project.

4   Sharing experiences in TSA implementation – the sharing of good practice and joint solutions to conceptual and measurement issues.

5   Monitoring labour markets in the tourism sector – to better inform manpower planning and disentangle the problems surrounding tourism employment statistics. Here the quantification of employment gaps is enabled by the TSA.

6   Measuring the meetings industry – to better measure a 'hidden' sector of tourism.

7   Market intelligence for action and forecasting – better using the TSA to develop tourism indicators, risk scenarios and forecasts.

8   Using the TSA framework to design tourism strategies.

9   Linking environmental accounting and the TSA to judge the performance of tourism in terms of sustainability.

The conference developed a range of conclusions and recommendations for the future direction of TSAs. These are:

- The integration of tourism statistics into the IMF's calculations on balance of payments.

- Using the TSA to deliver a broader base of tourism statistics instead of simply arrivals and expenditure.

- Working with the International Labour Organization (ILO) on measurement of tourism employment and quality of labour under the ILOs 'decent work' agenda.

- Working with the WTO on balance of payments, country capacity building and analysing the impact of globalisation on national tourism sectors.

- Using TSA to model total economic impact of tourism (UNWTO 2011).

- Ensuring the legitimacy and credibility of a TSA exercise by not over-promising the value of the TSA. This is particularly a problem if a national tourism

10

administration is given unreasonable expectations as to the value of tourism, which are then disproved by the TSA.

■ Protecting the TSA brand by policing the mis-use of terminology formally integrating the TSA into the United Nations statistical system.

■ Stressing the importance of the TSA concept to other agencies, both nationally and internationally, to create an 'inter-institutional platform' including tourism statistical and banking agencies. This will promote strategic alliances between tourism and statistical agencies.

■ Bringing economic analysis to the forefront. The TSA is a powerful tool of economic analysis and it is necessary to increase the understanding of the TSA amongst politicians and the business community through the use of correct concepts and language.

■ Fostering the use of TSAs to support policy and strategy. TSAs can be used to deliver knowledge-based public policy and business strategy for tourism.

Key sources

UNWTO (2005a). *The Iguazu Conference: UNWTO Findings and Evaluation*, Madrid: UNWTO.

UNWTO (2005b). *The Tourism Satellite Account (TSA): Understanding Tourism and Designing Strategies. Iguazu (Argentina/Brazil/Paraguay). Technical Note*. Madrid: UNWTO.

UNWTO (2010). *Positioning Tourism in Economic Policy: Evidence and Some Proposals*, Madrid: UNWTO.

UNWTO (2011). *Exploring the Full Economic Impact of Tourism for Policy Making*, Madrid: UNWTO.

Discussion questions

1   What type of indicators do you think the TSA could provide to aid policy makers in tourism to be more effective?

2   The International Labour Organization is keen to measure the quality of jobs in TSAs as well as just the numbers of jobs. What do you think a TSA could measure to help the ILO?

3   TSAs are now being developed at the regional level. What types of TSA indicators would help destination marketers to be more effective?

There is no doubt that TSAs have become the industry standard for defining and measuring tourism from the supply side. By 2012 over 60 countries had developed or were developing a TSA (UNWTO 2010). The next stage of the TSA development is now underway. A particularly useful adaptation is to implement the TSA methodology for regions and destinations. However, due to the technical complexities involved, only a small number of countries have experimented with the development of these sub-national TSAs. Statistics Canada has been a lead agency here, developing satellite accounts for its provinces and territories.

These regional tourism satellite accounts (RTSAs) are designed to meet a growing demand for regional data, particularly as many tourism administrations decentralise their operations. RTSAs are used to provide an economic portrait of tourism at the regional level in Canada and can be used as a policy-relevant tool to strengthen regional and local tourism organisations.

Whilst there are clear benefits from the development and implementation of TSAs, there remain a number of challenges to their use (Smith 1998). These include:

1 The fact that they really are a demand-side measure.
2 They are expensive to produce as they often need further data collection.
3 They are only updated infrequently and can be anything up to eight years old.
4 They are shaped by a nation's SIC system and so can be imprecise or a poor fit with the structure of the industry.
5 They demand powerful education of the industry to interpret them.
6 They are dependent upon the availability, quality and quantity of data.

Tourism employment

It is important to consider the issues related to the measurement and scope of tourism employment when considering the contemporary tourism industry. Basically, tourism employment can only be measured once decisions about what comprises the industry have been made and jobs can then be apportioned to the different industry sectors in the TSA. This is normally done using the notion of 'full time equivalent jobs' (FTEs) where part-time or non-standard work is then converted to a full-time equivalent on the basis of hours worked. The TSA allows estimates to be made of total tourism employment as well as by sector, such as accommodation, and by demographics and job type, seasonality and productivity.

However, as Riley et al. (2002) note, the statistical reporting of tourism employment is not as mature as other tourism reporting. A better system is needed to understand the functioning of the labour market, immigration, education and training. Specific problems of tourism employment statistics include the fact that:

- Tourism not seen as an industry for statistical purposes.
- Tourism has strong linkages with other economic sectors making it difficult to discern pure tourism jobs.
- Tourism is highly diverse (as noted in the first case study in this chapter).
- It remains difficult to separate the contribution of tourism jobs serving tourists and those serving locals.
- It is difficult to factor in the informal economy and family jobs, which are not counted.

Finally, whilst the TSA methodology is relatively good at estimating the number of jobs generated by tourism, it is less effective in discerning the type of work or the quality of the job. The ILO is now working on statistical indicators for their 'decent work' agenda – in other words the measurement of the quality of the job as well as its simple statistical unit. For tourism this is being done in cooperation with the UNWTO and priorities are to analyse the uneven geographic distribution of tourism employment, measure gaps in tourism related occupations and examine education/training provision (UNWTO 2010). This issue of tourism human resources and the quality of work will be covered in the next chapter.

Summary

This chapter has provided a comprehensive review of the approaches and technical issues involved in defining the scale and scope of the contemporary tourism industry. It began with a range of quotes from the WTTC as to the magnitude of the industry, often claimed as one of the largest in the world. The chapter then considered in detail the various supply-side definitions of tourism and the range of complexities involved in defining an industry made up of multiple sectors, some of which are community and public sector based. The chapter has outlined the issues involved in measuring the scale and scope of the contemporary tourism industry, a process handicapped by the fact that tourism is not recognised as an industry in standard industrial classifications, which are rooted in a manufacturing approach. A case study demonstrated just how difficult it is to map the tourism industry onto these standard industrial classifications. The tourism satellite account approach was described in detail, as it is now the industry standard for defining and measuring the contemporary tourism industry. The TSA was examined not only in terms of its development and approach, but also its uses to aid planners and policy makers and its future development, as outlined in a second case study. Finally the chapter considered the measurement of tourism employment and the challenges faced in developing a contemporary reporting system that is not only quantitative, but can also tease out indicators of the quality of tourism jobs.

Self review questions

1 Discuss Leiper's view that tourism is a group of businesses in search of an industry.

2 List the key characteristics of tourism that have created problems in coming up with a supply-side definition.

3 This chapter has provided a number of supply-side definitions of tourism – which do you think captures the nature of the contemporary tourism industry and why?

4 Map the tourism industry onto Leiper's tourism system (generating region, transit zone and destination region). How might you expect this mapping to vary for different types of tourism – for example nature-based tourism and business tourism?

5   Do you agree with Leiper's view that tourism is a partially industrialised system?

6   Find the TSA report for your own country. Which of the indicators provided will be of use to those marketing your country on the international stage?

7   Critics of the TSA say that it measures tourism demand, not tourism supply. Do you agree with this statement?

8   Which indicators developed in the TSA will be of most use to tourism planners?

9   The majority of tourism jobs are in the hospitality sector. How true is this statement?

10 Examine the ILO's 'decent work' agenda. As a lobbyist for the tourism industry, how would you present a case that tourism jobs are 'decent jobs'?

Recommended reading

Bull, A. (1995). *The Economics of Travel and Tourism*, Melbourne: Longman Australia.
Good coverage of the supply-side debate and measurement issues.

Ioannides, D. & Debbage, K.G. (eds) (1998). *The Economic Geography of the Tourist Industry. A Supply Side Analysis*. London: Routledge.
Excellent and comprehensive edited volume on the supply side of tourism.

Leiper, N. (1979). The framework of tourism. Toward a definition of tourism, tourist and the tourism industry. *Annals of Tourism Research*, 390-405.
Classic paper covering all elements of the tourism system

Leiper, N., Stear, L., Hing N. & Firth, T. (2008). Partial industrialisation in tourism. A new model. *Current Issues in Tourism* 11(3), 207 – 235.
Excellent paper outlining Leiper's partial industrialisation approach

Hall, C.M. & Page (2010). The contribution of Neil Leiper to tourism studies. *Current Issues in Tourism* 13(4), 299-309.
An account of Leiper's contributions to tourism including the understanding of tourism systems and partial-industrialisation.

Riley, M., Ladkin, A. & Szivas, E. (2002). *Tourism Employment. Analysis and Planning*. Clevedon: Channelview.
Comprehensive and readable volume on tourism employment issues and measurement

Smith, S.L.J. (1988). Defining tourism a supply-side view. *Annals of Tourism Research* 15, 179-190
A classic paper contrasting with Leiper's views

Smith, S.L.J. (1996). *Tourism Analysis. A Handbook*, Harlow: Longman.
Thorough text on supply side definitions and measurement

UNWTO (2008). *The Tourism Satellite Account*, Madrid: UNWTO.
Excellent summary of the development, concept and use of the TSA

10

WTTC (2012). *Progress and Priorities 2010 – 2011*, London: WTTC.
Comprehensive review of the supply side scale and scope of the tourism industry and WTTC initiatives

Frechtling, D. (2010). The TSA. A primer. *Annals of Tourism Research* 37, 136–153.
A clear explanation of the TSA and the issues surrounding their use

Hara, T. (2008). *Quantitative Tourism Industry Analysis*, Oxford: Elsevier Butterworth Heinemann.
A useful introduction to the scope of the industry and to Tourism Satellite Accounts

Dwyer, L., Forsyth, P. & Dwyer, W. (2010). *Tourism Economics and Policy*. Bristol: Channel View.
Excellent economic handbook covering all the issues raised in this chapter in an accessible format.

Recommended web sites

Tourism Industry Association of Canada: www.tiac-aitc.ca/

Aboriginal Tourism Canada: www.aboriginaltourism.ca/

Tourism Industry Association of New Zealand: www.tianz.org.nz/

World Travel and Tourism Council: www.wttc.org

Visit Britain UK Industry website: www.tourismtrade.org.uk/

UNWTO www.unwto.org

International Labour Organization www.ilo.org

References cited

British Tourist Authority/English Tourist Board (1997). *Employment in Tourist Related industries in Great Britain*. London: BTA/ETB.

Bull, A. (1995). *The Economics of Travel and Tourism*, Melbourne: Longman Australia.

Davidson, T.L. (1994). What are travel and tourism: Are they really an industry? In W. Theobald (ed.), *Global Tourism. The Next Decade*, pp. 20-26. Oxford: Butterworth Heinemann.

Debbage, K.G. & Daniels, P. (1998). The tourist industry and economic geography. Missed opportunities? In D. Ioannides and K.G. Debbage (eds), *The Economic Geography of the Tourist Industry. A Supply Side Analysis*, pp. 17-30. London: Routledge.

Debbage, K.G. & Ioannides, D. (1998). Conclusion. The commodification of tourism. In D. Ioannides and K.G. Debbage (eds), *The Economic Geography of the Tourist Industry. A Supply Side Analysis*, pp. 287-292. London: Routledge.

Ioannides, D. & Debbage, K.G. (eds) (1998). *The Economic Geography of the Tourist Industry. A Supply Side Analysis*. London: Routledge.

Israel Central Bureau of Statistics with Ministry of Tourism (quarterly) *Tourism and Hotel Statistics Quarterly*, Jerusalem: ICBS.

Leiper, N. (1979). The framework of tourism. Toward a definition of tourism, tourist and the tourism industry. *Annals of Tourism Research* 6(4), 390–407.

Leiper, N. (1989). *Tourism and Tourism Systems*, Department of Management Systems Occasional Paper No 1. Palmerston North: Massey University.

Leiper, N. (1990). Partial industrialisation of tourism systems. *Annals of Tourism Research* 7, 600-605.

Leiper, N. (2008). Why 'the tourism industry' is misleading as a generic expression: The case for the plural variation, 'tourism industries'. *Tourism Management* 29(2), 237–251.

Leiper, N., Stear, L., Hing N. & Firth, T. (2008). Partial industrialisation in tourism. A new model. *Current Issues in Tourism* 11(3), 207 – 235.

Riley, M., Ladkin, A. & Szivas, E. (2002). *Tourism Employment. Analysis and Planning.* Clevedon: Channelview.

Roehl, W. (1998). The tourism production system. The logic of standard industrial classification. In D. Ioannides and K.G. Debbage (eds), *The Economic Geography of the Tourist Industry. A Supply Side Analysis*, pp. 53-76. London: Routledge.

Smith, S.L.J. (1988). Defining tourism a supply-side view. *Annals of Tourism Research* 15, 179-190.

Smith, S.L.J. (1996). *Tourism Analysis. A Handbook.* Harlow: Longman.

Smith, S.L.J. (1998). Tourism as an industry. debates and concepts. In D. Ioannides and K.G. Debbage (eds), *The Economic Geography of the Tourist Industry. A Supply Side Analysis*, pp. 31-52. London: Routledge.

Statistics Canada (2006). *Human Resource Module of the Tourism Satellite Account 1997-2002*, Ottawa: Statistics Canada.

UNCTAD (1971). A note on the 'tourist sector'. In *Guidelines for Tourism Statistics* 30, New York: UNCTAD.

UNSTAT (1990). *International Standard Classification of all Economic Activities*, New York: UNSTST.

UNWTO (2005a). *The Tourism Satellite Account (TSA): Understanding Tourism and Designing Strategies. Iguazu (Argentina/Brazil/Paraguay). Technical Note.* Madrid: UNWTO

UNWTO (2005b). *The Iguazu Conference: UNWTO Findings and Evaluation.* Madrid: UNWTO.

UNWTO (2010). *Positioning Tourism in Economic Policy: Evidence and Some Proposals*, Madrid: UNWTO.

UNWTO (2011). *Exploring the Full Economic Impact of Tourism for Policy Making*, Madrid: UNWTO.

WTO (1995). *Concepts, Definitions and Classifications of Tourism Statistics.* Madrid: WTO.

WTTC (2012). *Progress and Priorities 2010 – 2011*, London: WTTC.

10

11 The Tourism Industry: Contemporary Issues

Chapter objectives

After reading this chapter you will:

- Understand that tourism businesses have a range of objectives.

- Be familiar with the causes of globalisation.

- Recognise the responses of tourism businesses to globalisation.

- Appreciate the benefits of knowledge management for tourism businesses.

- Realise the explanatory power of network analysis for understanding the tourism industry.

- Be aware of the importance of embedding within networks for tourism businesses.

- Recognise the distinction between small businesses and entrepreneurs.

- Understand the characteristics of tourism small businesses.

- Appreciate the critical importance of human resources to tourism businesses.

- Be aware of the challenges facing tourism human resources.

Introduction

In this chapter we turn to the contemporary tourism industry and identify and expand upon five key issues facing the industry. We begin with the challenges posed to the contemporary tourism industry by globalisation. This section identifies the key drivers of globalisation, particularly the lowered cost of travel and technology. Tourism businesses are responding to globalisation by internationalising and building alliances and partnerships, whilst the public sector is concerned to protect small businesses threatened by the shifting competitive landscape that globalisation delivers. We then consider the fact that the tourism industry has been slow to embrace the benefits of the knowledge economy, particularly in terms of adopting knowledge management practices and boosting competitiveness through utilising knowledge for innovation and new product development. Both globalisation and the knowledge economy demand that tourism businesses are well networked. Only in this way can they ensure that they benefit from both global trends and the flexible specialisation that characterises the industry. Network analysis can be used to examine networks of destination and tourism business and to diagnose problems and weak links. Embeddeddness within networks is identified as a key strategy for survival for the contemporary tourism business. The chapter then turns to small businesses, the lifeblood of tourism destinations, and makes the distinction between small businesses and entrepreneurs. A particular feature of the tourism industry – the lifestyle entrepreneur – is then examined. Finally, the chapter examines the crisis facing human resources in tourism, a crisis partly due to demographics and partly to the nature of tourism jobs and their working conditions.

Tourism businesses

The contemporary tourism industry comprises a range of businesses each with different objectives. Bull (1995) summarises these objectives as:

- *Profit maximisation*, requiring a long term view of revenue and cost, a perspective often absent in tourism.

- *Sales maximisation*, which is often the default option for service businesses and tourism due to capacity constraints.

- *Empire building or prestige*, here as businesses grow there may be a separation of ownership and control and non-monetary objectives emerge.

- *Output maximisation*, which is more relevant for product-oriented businesses where volume is more important than yield.

- *Satisficing*, where the goal is to set satisfactory level of revenue or profit.

- *A quiet life (profit minimisation)* where the business is small, often family owned and may be run for life style reasons.

Together these businesses form the contemporary tourism industry, an industry difficult to define as noted in the previous chapter. Debbage and Ioannides (1998) state that this machinery of tourism production manipulates and permits the tourist experience to happen, and in recent years has been restructured. This has been in response to technology, changing consumer demand, increasing concentration in the industry (albeit off a low base), and the demands of flexible specialisation creating networks of supply and destinations with vertical, horizontal and diagonal integration.

In this chapter, rather than examining the industry sector by sector we have adopted a thematic approach, drawing out and analysing five key issues which characterise the contemporary tourism industry.

11

These issues are:

1 Globalisation
2 The knowledge economy
3 Networks
4 Small businesses
5 Human resources.

The globalising contemporary tourism industry

Globalisation is a fundamental consideration for all tourism businesses. Globalisation can be thought of as *boundarylessness* and has various organisational responses to it (Parker 1998): responses that are characterised by speed, flexibility integration and innovation (Wahab & Cooper 2001). Globalisation not only reduces borders and barriers for trade between nations, but it also renders these boundaries permeable both within and between organizations. Globalisation therefore demands a different perspective and position to be taken on the management and operation of tourism businesses. It also demands a response from the public sector in terms of networked governance. This is because globalisation creates an interdependent world – think for example of the financial and economic crisis that began in 2008 and spread to become a global issue and problem. Of course, whilst tourism businesses themselves are affected by globalisation, so too they enhance and sustain the process of globalisation (Diamantis & El-Mourhabi 2004).

■ Contemporary drivers of globalization

There are a number of drivers of globalisation that impact upon the tourism industry, although these are often outside the control of individual businesses. We can identify six inter-related drivers of globalisation:

1 **Technological drivers** Globalisation has been facilitated by two technologies:

   ■ Transport technology has reduced both the monetary and the time-related costs of travel and acted as a 'space shrinking' technology, in turn breaking down geographical boundaries and constraints.

   ■ Communication technology with the synergy between the processing power of computers and the transmission capabilities of digital media has boosted both the speed and capacity of communication. Tourism has certainly been influenced by the revolution in global communications, allowing fast and cheap international communication, the development of global distribution systems and increasing the reach of small businesses.

2 **Economic drivers** Economic drivers of globalisation include the shifting patterns of production and consumption across the world, which are challenging traditional economic assumptions of world trade and markets.

3 **Political drivers** Political events have fuelled globalisation, creating a new world order. As the traditional core-periphery pattern no longer explains the location and success of businesses and nations, Dicken (1992) argues for a multi-polar economy with three economic regions dominant – North America, the European Union and the economies of Asia. A key issue here is the way that developing countries are being marginalised in the global trading environment. The resultant trade tensions in the global market place have prompted a response by the World Trade Organization to draw up the General Agreement on Trade in Services (GATS). The GATS has a range of impacts upon tourism businesses including:

■ Promoting free movement of labour globally.

■ Enabling the international development of, and access to, computer reservation systems.

■ Removing barriers to overseas investment.

Despite some success in encouraging developing country exports to the developed world as a result of the reduction in tariffs and quotas, there is still a long way to go. This is partly due to the technical problems that developing countries face in meeting the technical standards demanded of exports, and their lack of capacity to produce the goods. In response, the World Trade Organization has encouraged 'Mutual Recognition Arrangements (MRAs) which reduce the technical burden on exporters and have attempted to reduce the technical barriers to trade (TBT). MRAs have been applied in tourism, particularly in the areas of technical qualifications for cross-border workers.

4 **Cultural drivers** The rise of global culture impacts significantly upon tourism. Many resorts are criticised for their uniform landscape of fast food restaurants, international hotels and chain stores. This *coca-cola-isation* or *McDonalds-isation* of destinations is a consequence of the globalisation process, converging business practices and communication of both ideas and brands through the media.

5 **Environmental drivers** The natural environment is a global resource for tourism and non-sustainable practices in one destination impact upon others. Whilst globalisation does have positive consequences for the environment, there are also a number of problematic issues:

■ The reduced effectiveness of governments acting unilaterally weakens those who regulate and prevent pollution.

■ In an increasingly market-based economy, externalities will not be addressed.

■ Environmental problems do not respect traditional political boundaries, and there will be a blurring between economic and environmental boundaries.

■ Rapid tourism growth in Asia means that governments are grappling with the impacts upon both environments and cultures.

6 **Business drivers** Creation of a global society means that tourism businesses have the ability to operate globally and many have opted for a competitive strategy of internationalisation. Global businesses view the world as their operating environment and establish both global strategies and a global market presence. Changing business practices in response to the drivers of globalisation in turn sustain, extend and facilitate the process of globalisation, and reshape the very boundaries that previously constrained them. In tourism, these boundary-breaking processes include:

- Creating global brands, products and personalities.

- International tourism education and training transmitting global concepts and approaches.

- Reduced transport costs through innovations such as the low cost carrier business model.

- International communication mechanisms such as global distribution systems.

Tourism and the service sector

Many of the forces and consequences of globalisation are creating new forms of service company, not only the large trans-national companies such as Disney, but also the small niche specialist that can take advantage of the Internet, international communications, and market positioning and targeting. Whilst much of the writing on globalisation is focused on manufacturing, the service sector's response to the challenges of globalisation is quite different. Dicken (1992) argues that services internationalise through overseas market presence whilst also demanding the *right conditions* within which to deliver the service – in terms of labour, technology and government regulation. Campbell and Verbeke (1994) argue that there needs to be a clear recognition of the distinctive characteristics of services as they drive the strategy adopted for internationalisation. For example:

- Service businesses can use economies of scale in the marketing area, and in particular train personnel to market the product whilst it is being experienced.

- It is more difficult to separate the businesses delivery of the service from marketing as the service is 'produced where it is consumed'. This enhances the role of responsiveness at the national and local level, whilst ensuring strict quality control through head office marketing and quality management procedures.

- The intangibility of the service product underscores the importance of a business's reputation and thus creates a real pressure to choose credible and legitimate partners in any alliance. Also, the enhanced scope for the delivery of all elements of the service product through alliances is heightened. Networking flexibility is a typical service sector strategy, allowing the business to develop networks of relationships at different levels, as noted later in this chapter.

Campbell and Verbeke (1994) suggest that an international strategy for service sector businesses may be done in two stages:

1 Development of a strategic capability to allow national responsiveness or centralised innovation.

2 Development of an administrative structure to allow networking flexibility.

Poon (1993) terms this approach the new 'post-Fordist' tourism characterised by a more flexible delivery system of loosely-linked worldwide-acting businesses and purchased by the 'new' tourist who is experienced and discerning, seeking value-for-money, customised quality-controlled products, but not necessarily low prices. Here, delivery of the product is 'just in time', flexibly-produced, customer-designed and uses technology to extend the 'value chain'. By this stage, the labour force is functionally flexible and technically skilled. This post-Fordist 'new' tourism is characterised by a number of key features in direct response to the forces of globalisation. These include alliances, partnerships and internationalisation strategies:

■ Alliances and partnerships

One of the consequences of tourism in a boundaryless world is the opportunity to give competitive advantage by working with other organisations to pool resources. Dyer and Singh (1998) list four approaches to inter-organisational competitiveness:

■ Matching relation-specific assets – matching specific assets between organisations to gain competitive advantage.

■ Knowledge-sharing routines and inter-organisation communication such as those promoted by international agencies (e.g. The Pacific Asia Travel Association).

■ Integrating complementary resources and capabilities – a critical area in tourism where the product is an amalgam of resources created by differing organisations (including the public sector). The integration strategies of tourism businesses are clearly evident here in the structuring of global conglomerates of tourism businesses such as airlines. Equally, we see a synergy between tourism and the knowledge-based industries utilising know how, entertainment and information.

■ Developing effective governance – a final critical area in terms of the management of the relationship and the value chain, and one where tourism is lagging behind other sectors.

■ Internationalisation strategy

Globalisation is both a consequence of, and an influence upon, the internationalisation strategy of businesses. Internationalisation models are based on businesses slowly acquiring and using knowledge about overseas markets and competitors and increasingly committing to operating internationally. Dicken (1992) argues that the clearest view of internationalisation strategy is seen in trans-national corporations where strategies have three key components:

■ Cost leadership – lowest cost producer

■ Differentiation – differentiation from competitors

■ Focus – applying these two components to a market.

This section has shown that for tourism, the competitive landscape is changing and driving businesses to rethink their strategies and organisational structures to allow them to operate successfully in a boundaryless world. Globalisation therefore raises a number of key questions for tourism businesses:

■ How do businesses transfer their corporate practice, culture and operations internationally and maintain their quality standards, particularly given that the tourism product is delivered locally?

■ What should be the balance between local or national practices and the international approach?

■ How can the pubic sector develop policies to protect tourism SMEs and workers threatened by global competition, given that businesses can operate across national boundaries and so evade responsibility?

Globalisation also demands that tourism creates the ability to balance a global vision (including international standards) with local demands and needs, and can meet the material needs of a global community without increasing inequalities and without destroying the environment. In part, this will require a knowledge-based approach to managing businesses, an approach that we now turn to.

Managing knowledge in the contemporary tourism industry

The generation and use of new tourism knowledge for innovation and product development is critical for the competitiveness of tourism businesses. In fact, researchers, consultants, the industry and government are constantly generating new tourism knowledge. Yet the tourism industry has been slow to harness that knowledge and in particular, the effective *transfer* of knowledge to tourism businesses has been slow to develop. As a result, unlike many other economic sectors, tourism has not been subject to a knowledge management approach and businesses are less globally competitive as a result.

Knowledge management is a relatively new approach that addresses the critical issue of organizational adaptation, survival, and competitiveness in the face of increasingly discontinuous environmental change. For tourism, this environmental change is evident not only in the turbulence of the supply environment but also through the changing nature of tourism consumer behaviour. This pace of change underscores the fact that knowledge-based innovation is a core competency needed by all tourism businesses if they are to be competitive in a changing world.

■ The knowledge-based economy

In the late 1990s, the *knowledge-based economy* emerged from the previous *information age*. There was recognition that not only was knowledge more than information but also that it was a resource to be valued and managed. The knowledge economy can therefore be thought of as an economy directly based upon the production, distribution and use of knowledge. As the next stage of the post-industrial economy, the knowledge economy sees intellectual assets replace goods and services as the basis for growth and power. The knowledge-based economy has a number of important features that demand a rethinking of our approach to tourism business, for example:

- Structural economic change is driven by the development of new products and innovations that are brought about by technology. Technology, particularly the Internet, breaks down barriers to knowledge sharing. The knowledge-based economy is characterised by the development of interactive knowledge management systems that were only really possible once the Internet was available as a major facilitator.

- The employment and development of highly skilled labour is seen as a means of competitive advantage and long-run economic growth. This is an important issue for tourism where many of the sector's human resource practices militate against employment and retention of highly skilled employees – as outlined later in this chapter.

- The fact that the knowledge economy is characterised not by the scarcity of a resource, but by the abundance of information and knowledge.

- The creation of a new paradigm of *knowledge commerce* (k-commerce) where traditional competitive measures, such as location, are less important.

■ Types of knowledge

Knowledge can be thought of as the use of skills and experience to add intelligence to information in order to make decisions or provide reliable grounds for action. Knowledge management classifies knowledge according to its ability to be *codified* and therefore communicated. For tourism, this distinction is fundamental and goes a long way to explaining the failure of businesses to adequately capitalise on and manage knowledge. Polanyi (1966) provides possibly the most useful classification, distinguishing between two types of knowledge:

1 **Tacit knowledge** is difficult to codify, difficult to communicate to others as information, and it is difficult to digitise. A good example of tacit knowledge would be the knowledge that is passed from master to apprentice, or from sports coach to player. The majority of knowledge in the tourism sector is tacit (for example in tourism organizations and the entrepreneurial community) yet

11

is often ignored. Indeed, estimates suggest that over 90% of any organization's knowledge assets are tacit.

2 **Explicit knowledge,** in contrast, is transferable and easy to codify and communicate. It is therefore usually the focus of an organization's interest and is found in the form of documents, databases, files, customer directories and other media. Explicit knowledge can be relatively easily formulated by means of symbols and can be digitised. It can therefore be transferred and communicated to those that need it in the organization.

The conversion of tacit to explicit knowledge is critical for tourism, as there is so much tacit knowledge in the sector that could benefit other businesses – and destinations and governments. It is here that the knowledge management approach provides a significant benefit for tourism as it focuses upon the management of tacit and explicit knowledge to create organizational learning, innovation and sustainable competitive advantage.

■ Rethinking knowledge management for tourism businesses

If knowledge management is to be utilised by tourism businesses to cooperate at the destination level, then the micro-level focus on the organization, which dominates knowledge management thinking, needs to be expanded to embrace knowledge stocks and flows within networks of organizations at the destination. Here, Hislop et al. (1997) provide a solution by arguing that knowledge *articulation* occurs in networks of organizations attempting to innovate and build upon knowledge. They identify two types of network.

1 First, micro-level networks within organizations where knowledge is created and is dominantly tacit and 'in-house'. This can be thought of as *demand-side* knowledge creation satisfying the organizational needs of new knowledge.

2 A second macro-level, inter-organizational network where knowledge is transferred around a network of organizations – at the destination, say – and tends therefore to be explicit in nature. This can be viewed as a *supply-side* response to the need to distribute and transfer knowledge.

Hislop et al's (1997) notion of knowledge 'articulation' involves the gradual conversion of tacit knowledge at the individual organization level into explicit knowledge, which is transmitted through the wider network of organizations i.e. the destination. In this way, useful knowledge is widely dispersed across a network to boost competitiveness and the analogy with tourism destinations is clear.

In tourism, knowledge management embraces both levels of aggregation: i.e. both the individual business as well as networks of businesses. At the destination level, the networks of businesses can be either destination or sector specific and the knowledge management process will be facilitated by either:

■ *Traded interactions* where knowledge sharing is facilitated by members of the supply chain or by trade organizations for industry sectors.

- *Untraded interactions* where knowledge sharing is facilitated by destination management organizations to boost the competitiveness of businesses at the destination.

In both cases, knowledge sharing demands high degrees of trust and the often competitive environment of small businesses at destinations can work against this.

■ The benefits of knowledge management for contemporary tourism businesses

A knowledge management approach delivers a range of significant benefits to tourism businesses:

- Managed access to knowledge reduces search time and shortens learning curves, facilitating new product development and innovation.
- Within the organization, a knowledge management approach encourages and facilitates enhanced and smarter problem-solving techniques.
- Managed access to knowledge provides an organization with the ability to respond rapidly to customers, technology and markets.
- Across the organization, knowledge management systems contribute to more efficient business processes.
- Within the organization, knowledge management enhances staff performance by encouraging knowledge sharing, mutual trust and so reducing staff turnover.
- A knowledge management system allows an organization to leverage and use its intellectual assets; indeed there are exponential benefits from knowledge as more people use it within the organization.
- Knowledge management encourages partnering and the sharing of core competencies with suppliers, vendors, customers and other external stakeholders.

Clearly then, tourism businesses have to recognise that they are part of the knowledge economy as well as part of a globalising economy. Both globalisation and the knowledge economy demand that businesses are networked and can not only communicate with both their markets and their competitors, but also leverage from the flexible specialisation inherent in tourism.

We now turn to the central issue of networking and how it can be approached in the contemporary tourism industry.

Contemporary tourism industry networks

We argued above that we are now living in a global knowledge economy, whilst others suggest that the future lies in a networked society. In fact, both statements are true as the key resource traded in networks is knowledge, facilitated by technology. The contemporary tourism industry is characterised by flatter structures, globalization-driven alliances and partnerships, instant communication, flexible specialization and the imperative to collaborate and share resources such as knowledge. This equates to loosely articulated networks of organizations either configured as destinations, or as economic structures such as value chains.

One way to analyse this new configuration of businesses is through network analysis. In business and economics, network analysis draws upon the 'competencies-based theory' of business, where relationships create competitive advantage through shaping and enhancing organizational performance (Tremblay 1999). This theory argues that organizations evolve according to their internal capabilities and how they can leverage these in the external environment. Applied to tourism, business performance is not only dependent upon the resources of that business itself, but also upon that of other businesses and the nature of their relationships. This system of businesses can then be viewed as a network comprising architecture of nodes and interconnected relationships. This means that increasingly tourism businesses are competing with networks of businesses rather than with individual businesses. In other words, competitiveness depends upon how well an organization is networked and strategically embedded within its networks. It is this notion of 'embeddedness' that is the fundamental difference in the network approach, contrasting it with economic theories of organization.

Whilst, network analysis has a long pedigree in the social sciences and business disciplines, it has seldom been used in tourism despite the fact that tourism is ideally suited to the approach (Scott et al. 2008). Tourism lends itself to network analysis for a number of reasons.

- First, tourism, more than most economic sectors, through flexible specialisation, involves the development of formal and informal collaboration, partnerships and networks. In other words, the tourism industry and destinations can be viewed as loosely articulated groups of independent suppliers who link together to deliver the overall product. Network analysis can provide useful insights on the structure and behaviour of the industry and destinations and can be used to recommend strengthening of links and coordination between destination organizations.

- Second, network analysis delivers a flexible tool with which to analyse the dynamics of businesses and destinations as they operate within a turbulent and shifting system. Businesses and destinations represent networks of cooperative and competitive linkages and are fashioned by both their internal capabilities and those of the external environment (Tremblay 1999).

- Third, network analysis provides insights into the behaviour of businesses at destinations where we can think of the tourism sector as a complex adaptive socio-economic system (Baggio 2011). Networks themselves have loose governance systems, which, at the destination level, act as an alterative to the public sector. The behaviour of destination networks acts to encourage cooperative ventures and to avoid cutthroat competition, allowing businesses to find a balance between competition and innovation. For tourism destinations, an important notion is that of networks having their own embedded macro-culture, with the behaviour of suppliers reflecting the branding, symbols and images of the destination environment (Pavlovich 2001).

■ Fourth, network analysis provides insights as to how a network can be made more efficient in terms of linkage and coordination. For business and destination networks, policy can be effective in increasing the efficiency of the overall network through strengthening links, reducing barriers and encouraging members to share information.

Above all tourism is about relationships and network analysis provides an approach to examining the quantity and quality of those connections (Baggio 2011).

Tourism networks

There are three basic units of analysis in a tourism network: actors, relationships and resources:

1 *Actors* perform activities in relationship with other actors and control network resources. These actors can be of different sizes and are very diverse.

2 *Relationships* may be considered as transactions between actors. These relationships are the building blocks of network analysis.

3 *Resources* that are exchanged among actors represent the third element of a network. These resources may include knowledge or money.

Tremblay (1999) identifies three types of tourism network:

1 Innovative networks where businesses share complementary assets – such as airline alliances and hotel consortia.

2 Networks of businesses sharing in the marketing knowledge of specific customer segments. Here tourism examples include the vertical and horizontal integration strategies of larger companies.

3 Networks coordinating complementary assets at the destination level. This includes destination marketing alliances and promotion (a common approach in the past) and the more recent approach of jointly shaping new products and innovation. Tourism businesses then strategically position themselves within the network to leverage from innovation and future organizational configurations.

The nodes of any tourism network can be thought of as businesses and other organizations, of varying size, cooperating to compete, as a direct response to an externally turbulent environment. The strategy is for a business to 'embed' within a network to gain security as other members develop and maintain effective relationships with each other. A member's position within a destination network depends upon the number of its relationships and its role in the network. Members gain power from their position within a network, and the more centrally located they are, the stronger the power and influence of that organization within

11

the destination. In turn, weaker organizations can develop ties with central ones to leverage benefits.

For tourism businesses, membership of a network delivers a range of benefits including:

- Scale and scope economies (such as alliances).
- Coordination of complementary assets (such as marketing synergies).
- Higher strategic benefits where the members of the network share a common vision (such as destination branding).

Case study 11.1: Tourism destination and business networks in Australia

This case study shows the clear benefit of using network analysis to graphically show the structure of business networks. This can then be used to remedy any failures in communication and coordination across the network. A study of destination and business networks in Australia clearly shows how this can be used as an analytical tool to diagnose problems. In each of the examples below we present destination networks made up of nodes, which are the key stakeholders (businesses and the public sector), and the links, which are the contacts they make with each other for business, information etc. The networks were constructed from data collected in 2005.

Victoria

The first examples are drawn from the southern Australian state of Victoria. Examining Figure 11.1, we see an integrated network created from the Geelong-Otway regional tourism organization (RTO). This is the Great Ocean Road region of the state, a stunning ocean scenic drive linking three local authority areas. Here the network structure shows the implementation of a strong regional tourism marketing and management region, due to innovative organization across three separate local authority areas. This has developed from a regional initiative to market the region using the Great Ocean Road as the central coordinating feature.

This network contrasts with that for an inland valley based upon two local authority areas (Figure 11.2). Here the interaction between tourism stakeholders in the Bright and Wangaratta Shires demonstrates a more decentralized structure in which more than one organization assumes the role of coordination. These two local authority areas are geographically and politically dissimilar and there is little incentive for them to link together through the regional tourism organization. The network structure suggests that the more centralized network in the Great Ocean Road Region is associated with a more developed RTO structure and highlights the enhanced formal coordination provided in this region. From these Victorian examples it is clear that there are significant differences between local authorities in the organization of tourism.

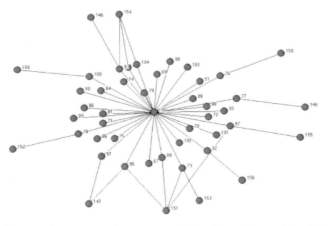

Figure 11. 1: The tourism network structure of the Great Ocean Road Region

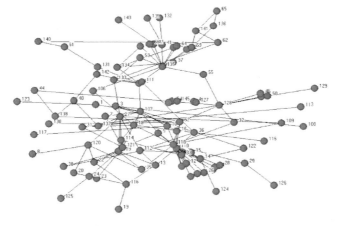

Figure 11.2: The tourism network structure of the Bright and Wangaratta Valley Region

Townsville, Queensland

The Townsville network demonstrates two distinct clusters of organizations. These two clusters are linked by Townsville Business (the RTO) and to a lesser extent Tourism Queensland (the state tourism organization) (Figure 11.3). The first cluster comprises commercial tourism operators in a tightly knit grouping due to their many relationships with each other, based upon mutual interest in terms of the value chain and marketing. These nodes are all major hotels or accommodation providers in the region. The second cluster lies below the RTO and is comprised primarily of public sector organizations. This cluster is more diffuse and is made up of organizations primarily involved in planning and projects, or organizations that provide access to other sectoral clusters (such as mining). The Townsville network shows the interconnections of the separate public and private sector networks.

11

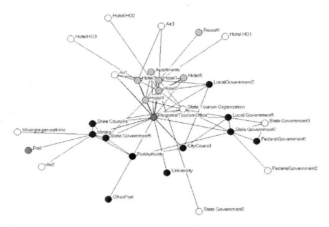

Figure 11.3: The tourism network structure for Townsville

The Gold Coast, Queensland

The network structure for the Gold Coast exposes a structural divide between the Gold Coast itself and its hinterland (Figure 11.4). This appears to relate to geography as well as to the main markets for these two sub-regions. The hinterland cluster is linked both to the nearby largest city RTO (Brisbane) as well as to the Gold Coast RTO as might be expected from the dual source markets for this area. Tourism Queensland, the state organization, is central to the whole Gold Coast cluster. Such structural divides are common in tourism due to political boundaries, geographical features or organizational conflict. The position of the Gold Coast Tourism Bureau in the network indicates that it is addressing this structural divide by performing a linking function.

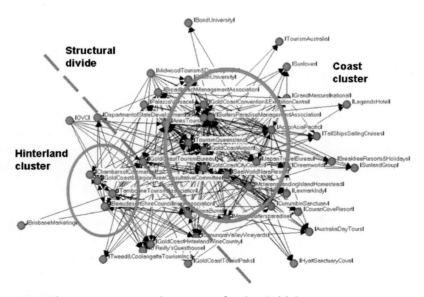

Figure 11.4: The tourism network structure for the Gold Coast

The Southern Downs, Queensland

In the rural Southern Downs region, the network demonstrates clear sectoral clusters (Figure 11.5). These are first, a wine tourism cluster, and second, a bed and breakfast cluster. It is interesting that the wine cluster overlaps more with the bed and breakfast cluster than the wider tourism sector. This is most likely explained by the need to forge alliances between the two types of complementary tourism businesses in order to deliver the wine tourism product. Instead the wine cluster is represented in the tourism cluster through a number of key industry organizations. Such representative organizations have a gatekeeper function, facilitating the flow of information between different clusters. As gatekeepers, these organizations acquire the ability to influence the issues and activities within the destination.

There is also a structural divide between organizations based on the political boundary of the two local authority areas of Stanthorpe and Warwick. This appears to relate to differences in the economies of these areas. The bed and breakfast and wine clusters are focused on the Stanthorpe area. This area is further from capital city markets and operates as a weekend break destination. In contrast, Warwick Shire is more focused on agricultural production. The RTO links these two areas through its planning and management role.

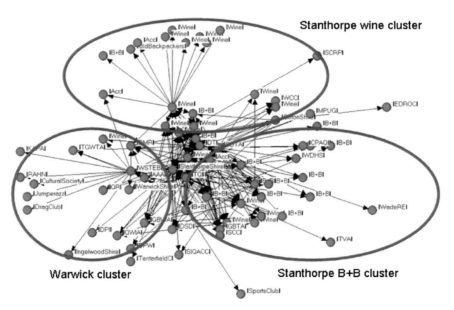

Figure 11.5: The tourism network structure for the Southern Downs

By using these four examples, this case study demonstrates how network analysis can provide insights into the structure and functioning of destination and business networks and can be used both to gain insights into their structure and to diagnose and remedy problems.

Acknowledgements

This case is derived from research funded by Tourism Queensland and The Sustainable Tourism Cooperative Research Centre, an Australian Government initiative. We are grateful to Dr Noel Scott for his work on this case study.

Discussion questions

1   Examining the five network diagrams, discuss the relative influence of the geographical situation of the destination upon the network structure.

2   What types of problems faced by tourism businesses can be diagnosed by network analysis?

3   Examining Figures 11.3, 11.4 and 11.5, tease out value chains and explain their structure.

Networked tourism businesses

There is no doubt that reconceptualizing the tourism industry using a network approach is very beneficial for tourism. Networked organizations are ideally suited to thrive in Poon's post-Fordist era of 'new' tourism, characterized by flexible specialisation, rapid communication and globalisation. Indeed, network analysis underscores the need for competitive destinations to be collaborative (Baggio 2011). Achrol and Kotler (1999) agree and state that the business of the future will be a networked organization characterised as:

> 'An interdependent coalition of task- or skill-specialised economic entities (independent firms or autonomous organisational units) that operates without hierarchical control but is embedded, by dense lateral connections, mutuality, and reciprocity, in a shared value system that defines 'membership', roles and responsibilities' (Achrol & Kotler 1999: 148).

They distinguish four categories of network organizations for the future, based upon theoretical and practical grounds:

1   *Internal networks* that are designed to reduce hierarchy and open businesses to their environments – in other words to enhance customer responsiveness and awareness of the external environment.

2   *Vertical networks* that maximise the productivity of serially-dependent functions by creating partnerships among independent, skill-specialised businesses – essential in the delivery of the tourism product and inherent in flexible specialisation.

3   *Inter-market networks* that seek to leverage horizontal synergies across industries – the rise of the technology companies in tourism distribution channels are a good example.

4   *Opportunity networks* that are organised around customer needs and market opportunities and designed to search for the best solutions to them – clusters

of businesses serving particular specialist tourism products such as adventure tourism are examples here.

Finally, network analysis links neatly with knowledge management to facilitate the flow of knowledge around business and destination systems, whilst it is also perfectly suited to the demands of globalisation, driven by technological networks and networked alliances of business. Of course, SMEs also benefit from this approach allowing them to embed securely within business and destination networks for enhanced competitiveness. We turn to SMEs and entrepreneurs in the next section of this chapter.

Small firms and entrepreneurship in the contemporary tourism industry

■ Small firms

The contemporary tourism industry is dominated by small firms and particularly micro-businesses (Ateljevic & Page 2009). In France for example, it is estimated that over 90% of all tourism firms employ fewer than ten people. Some authors suggest that this domination by small firms makes tourism in some way different to other economic sectors from a policy and management perspective, yet in fact, real estate, agriculture and forestry have a greater percentage of small firms. Whilst there is no agreed international definition of small firms, there are two fundamental approaches. The first uses size as a measure whilst the other takes a broader view (Table 11.1). The broader view is adopted by Thomas (1998) who characterises them as those firms which have a small market share, are managed in a personalised way, are independent of external control and do not influence market prices.

Table 11.1: Approaches to defining small tourism firms. Source: Morrison et al. (2010)

Quantifiable variables	A broader view
Number of employees and/or family members	Business orientation/motivation
Physical facilities and services provided	Management style and structure
Financial investment	Ownership configuration
Market share	Service orientation and commitment
Economic rewards	Social rewards

Goffee and Scase (1983) take the broader view, classifying small firms according to their source of capital and organisational structure. Their classification ranges from marginal self-employed companies to the owner director company (Table 11.2).

Table 11.2: Organisational structures and entrepreneurial characteristics. Source: Goffee and Scase (1983) and Shaw and Williams (1990)

Category	Entrepreneurial characteristics
Self employed	Use of family labour, little market stability, low levels of capital investment, weakly developed management skills
Small employer	Use of family and non-family labour, less economically marginalised but shares other characteristics of the self employed group
Owner controller	Use of non-family labour, higher levels of capital investment, often a formal level of management control, but no separation of ownership and control
Owner director	Segmentation of ownership and management functions, higher levels of capital investment

Small tourism firms have become a focus for policy by both governments and development agencies. On the one hand they have seen the development of policy to protect them from the forces of globalisation and the dominance of large multi-national companies with increasing concentration in the sector. On the other hand they are seen as a force for good in the economic development of more remote areas or regions that are converting to a market economy (such as the countries of the former Eastern European communist bloc). More specifically, small firms bring a number of advantages to a destination:

- They rapidly diffuse income into the economy through strong backward linkages into the economy of a destination.

- Similarly, they contribute to employment.

- They provide a localised welcome and character by acting as a point of direct contact between the host community and the visitor.

- In a market that increasingly demands tailored experiences, small firms play an important role in responding to tourists' demand and so facilitating 'flexible specialisation' (Ateljeic & Doorne 2001).

However, small firms also contribute to the 'under-management' of the tourism industry as they are often run and owned by those who are inexperienced in business skills and strategy. Indeed, many micro-tourism businesses are owned and run by one family. As most small firms are family owned and run, there tends to be an emotional attachment to the firm and rational business thinking is not applied. Nor is there a desire for firm expansion. Non-economic motives therefore are common in small tourism firms. This also means that small tourism firms may not think strategically in terms of developing their business nor engage in training their staff (Buhalis & Cooper 1998). In addition, many tourism entrepreneurs have little or no tourism training or experience themselves; Stallibrass (1980) in her study of the UK resort of Scarborough, for example, found only one third of small hotel owners had previous experience in tourism. And to compound these issues, small firms are often part of the 'informal economy' where family labour is assumed and not paid for. All of this means that there is considerable turnover or 'churn' at destinations, as new firms enter the market and others fail.

■ Entrepreneurs

There is a real conundrum over small firms and tourism – on the one hand they are seen as the lifeblood of a destination, whilst on the other hand they are often regarded as under-managed, failing to invest or innovate. This tends to go against the views of small firms as enterprising and entrepreneurial and begs the question – are all small firms run by entrepreneurs? The distinction here is important: a small firm is the organising unit of production, but it is the individual who is (or is not) the entrepreneur. In tourism it seems the answer to the question is that many small firms are run in an entrepreneurial fashion, but many are not – and there are specific tourism-related reasons for this.

The notion of an entrepreneur is a romantic one, individuals who are nimble, flexible, eager to spot an opportunity in the market place and to add value. Indeed this has led some to ask the question – is there a blueprint for entrepreneurship? (Rimmington 2010). Entrepreneurial firms are adaptive, flexible and tend to integrate their operations around customers. They underpin creativity and innovation and take risks. Their flexibility is essential as at each stage of the business life cycle – from launch to maturity – they face particular opportunities and challenges and require a certain level of resourcing. Indeed, small hospitality and tourism firms tend to be at the forefront of economic cycles and their fortunes can be used as a barometer of economic change (Getz *et al.* 2004).

Entrepreneurship therefore plays a key role in economic development, but in tourism there is a specific type of entrepreneur that seems to break all the rules – the lifestyle entrepreneur. Lifestyle entrepreneurs are common in tourism given the attraction of tourism to special locations, yet the concept is not clearly defined. They tend to blur the distinction between production and consumption as they are living in and enjoying the amenity values and products of the destination. Shaw and Williams (1990) identify three characteristics of entrepreneurs in tourism in their study of Cornwall:

- *Level of experience and expertise* – many entrepreneurs have little experience in tourism having come to the sector through employment elsewhere in the economy with no obvious access to capital or expertise. Tourism, particularly the accommodation sector, has low barriers to entry – which in turn explains their poverty of resources and expertise, and the ease of entry as a lifestyle entrepreneur.

- *Business motivation* – non-economic motives are important reasons for becoming an entrepreneur in tourism, particularly in terms of lifestyle and environment.

- *Source of capital* – informal sources of capital are common in small tourism firms, often using personal or family savings. This is symptomatic of a group who have little idea of the importance of firm plans and targets.

To answer the question posed above, Morrison et al. (1999) are clear that there is no entrepreneurial blueprint for success; rather it is the particular fit of an entrepreneurial approach that takes into account the various dynamic components present

11

in a destination or market. Indeed, because of their closeness to the destination and its products, entrepreneurial behaviour in tourism is strongly influenced by locale. Nonetheless there are a growing number of guides, menus and literature available to prospective entrepreneurs as our knowledge increases. These guides are often put out by economic development units and tourism agencies to assist potential entrepreneurs who may be relocating and investing in a region.

The development of strong networks and information sharing is key to the survival of both entrepreneurs and SMEs in tourism. Morrison et al. (1999) state that small firms operate within a context of formal and informal networks:

- Family – support and labour
- Financial institutes – source of capital
- Public sector – legislation and policy to foster an environment for success
- A destination network.

As with all tourism firms, it is the successful leveraging from these networks that distinguishes a successful SME in tourism. Future trends in entrepreneurship include the notion of the social entrepreneur working with a social enterprise where the aim is not to generate profit for the shareholder, but rather to reinvest in the business or cause (Rimmington 2010). Examples include The Eden Project in Cornwall (www.edenproject.com) and Jamie Oliver's Fifteen chain of restaurants (www.fifteen.net)

Contemporary tourism human resources

In the final section of this chapter we turn to one of the most important resources of the contemporary tourism industry, that of human resources. Tourism is a labour intensive industry, supporting a wide range of jobs in many different sectors. Of course, this is due to the importance of personal service in tourism and, whilst there are question marks over the quality of some of these jobs, there is no doubt that the tourism industry provides job opportunities for the young, women and the less advantaged groups in society (Ross & Pryce 2010). The World Travel and Tourism Council estimates that the travel and tourism sector supports up to 260 million jobs both directly and indirectly worldwide, representing 9% of all jobs in the world (WTTC 2012). As we would expect, these figures are higher for countries which have a large tourism industry such as Spain or Mauritius. By 2021, tourism is expected to generate a further 69 million jobs (WTTC 2012). As the WTTC go on to say however, this challenge is more than just one of numbers – the tourism sector will need to develop new skills, as well as high levels of cultural awareness and adaptability if it is to cope with the issues identified in this book – new consumers, new technologies and a focus on the green economy.

Human resources (HR) are an essential pre-requisite to delivering the contemporary tourism product. Yet, they remain the Cinderella of the tourism industry; the industry knows they are important, but they are not taken seriously. As a result, in the first two decades of the twenty first century the tourism industry worldwide is facing a human resources crisis. This final section of the chapter analyses the underlying reasons for this crisis and outlines some possible solutions. The reasons for the HR crisis in tourism are complex and interlinked. They are rooted in the type of work that tourism involves, the working conditions in the industry, the dominance of small businesses (SMEs) and the shifting demographics and social attitudes of the twenty first century.

■ Demographics and attitudes

In much of the developing world birth-rates are falling. Add to this the fact that many countries have ageing populations who have the income and time to travel and it is clear that whilst this travel is generating tourism jobs, the work force is not being sustained to deliver those jobs. This 'demographic squeeze' is exacerbated by the fact that the new generations of workers, such as generation Y, have very different attitudes to work and careers as we saw in the case study in Chapter 4. This partly explains why there is not only a labour shortage in tourism but also a skills shortage where catering for example is not seen as a desirable profession. Indeed, in some regions of the world – such as much of the Middle East – service positions are frowned upon and seen only as jobs of last resort (see for example, Saee 2008).

■ Tourism jobs and working conditions

Tourism jobs have a range of interesting and contradictory features which, when combined with many aspects of their associated working conditions go some way to explaining the crisis (see for example Riley et al. 2002). Tourism jobs can be characterised as follows:

- The bulk of service jobs tend to be temporary, held by people with no career aspirations in tourism and no commitment to the industry.

- They are dominated by younger people – the average age of hospitality workers in the Netherlands for example is 23 years.

- Females are in the majority in many tourism jobs.

- They are perceived as glamorous and attractive, often involving work in exotic settings and with opportunity for customer contact. Their attraction is also seen in the opportunities to be creatively engaged in, say, nature-based tourism or marketing.

- They provide great flexibility in terms of hours and working arrangements. This suits specific groups in society such as working mothers.

- They are accessible, with few or no barriers to entry in many jobs; indeed tourism is a highly 'underqualified' industry.

- They are highly diverse, ranging from hospitality-related jobs, which tend to be make up the bulk of employment in tourism but are also the lowest paid

11

and the most seasonal, to the smaller number of jobs in air transport, but also the highest paid.

- They are characterised by a rigid occupational structure with strong job traditions.

Of course, these characteristics are self-reinforcing – young people take temporary tourism jobs to tide them over student life because they are no barriers to entry and the jobs are flexible. This is made worse by the lack of a strong union presence in tourism in many (but not all) countries. As a result, working conditions in tourism are often problematic and can be summarised as:

1 *Low paid* – in many countries, tourism jobs pay up to 20% below the average.

2 *Demanding anti-social hours*, often involving work on holidays, weekends, and over meal times. This can impact on the balance between family and work life.

3 *Creating emotional pressures*, not only in terms of the pressure to deliver good service and always to be smiling, but also in terms of attitudes in working environments such as kitchens. Whilst this may be common to other service sector jobs, it may be that the pressures in the tourism environment are particularly acute and demand coping strategies by employees.

4 *Having health and safety issues* – for example there are many accidents in kitchens, and workers face safety issues on the way home after late shifts.

■ Managing contemporary tourism human resources

As noted earlier, we must recognise that the majority of tourism jobs are supported by tourism SMEs. Estimates suggest that worldwide, SMEs (with less than 10 employees) employ at least half of the tourism labour force. This creates a problem of under-management in the sector and under-utilisation of the workforce, as many small entrepreneurs do not have grounding in good HR practice. Add to this the problem of creating career pathways in SMEs, and it becomes clear why there is a crisis in the sector. However, this is not the only reason that there is an HR crisis. The tourism industry is innately conservative and resistant to change. Many companies retain HR management styles from previous decades and have failed to move into the knowledge economy where it is a company's human capital, knowledge and skills which deliver competitiveness, as we saw earlier.

However, it must also be recognised that tourism HR planning is complex. The key is to match the scheduling of employees to the throughput of tourists. This throughput is unpredictable and highly seasonal – on a daily, weekly and monthly basis. As a result, companies find it difficult to plan and manage their HR function and resort to short-term tactics of non-standard employment (such as temporary, seasonal or part-time workers, perhaps keeping a group of employees on call in case of unforeseen demand).

Combine all of these factors together, and the industry finds itself with a shortage of employees, and high turnover of people in many job functions. Turnover is expensive for the industry and yet it runs at over 100% in many city centre hotels.

■ Contemporary tourism HR management

Whilst the issues raised above are severe, there are a range of things that can be done. Solutions to the HR crisis in tourism include:

1   Greater understanding of the operation of the tourism labour market – how for example do school leavers view the tourism sector against other opportunities (Riley et al. 2002) and what are the views of generation Y to the job market? This also requires intervention by government and industry to promote jobs in tourism and to polish the image of working in the sector.

2   Recognition that tourism is in the knowledge economy and needs to invest in and develop its workforce rather than exploiting it. This will involve a shift in attitude and operation by the industry, particularly in terms of investing in training and education. However, the industry can also be more innovative in its HR management. For example:

   ■ In seasonal destinations, smart companies use the off-peak for training rather than letting staff go.

   ■ Companies can invest in multi-skilling by identifying the core skills needed for job functions.

   ■ Recognising that for some groups of employees (students, parents, retirees) part time or seasonal work is actually a benefit (UNWTO 2010).

   ■ The industry needs to develop future leaders.

3   At the destination level, DMOs can encourage SMEs to work together to create career paths across companies and begin to think beyond *managing people in organizations* and make the jump to *managing people in destinations*.

4   In 2009, the OECD recognised the need for education and training to support a more attractive labour market and business environment in tourism, to maintain a skilled workforce and improve productivity (OECD 2011). This was required because education for tourism is often mired in the final quarter of the 20th century and for businesses and destinations to be competitive, they need to embrace the new tourism environment and educate the workforce to deal with change and to be competent in areas demanded by 'post-tourists' (Cooper 2012). These include fields such as guiding and special interest tourism, with a thorough grounding in business and people skills, and technology.

5   Finally, there is a need for government and the international agencies to encourage quality jobs in tourism and to move away from simply treating tourism as a means to generate jobs with no eye for quality. The International Labour Organization's 'decent work' agenda is an important initiative here, with the mission of enhancing the quality of jobs and the working environment. Governments will also be increasingly called upon to facilitate international labour movement in tourism to solve the workforce shortage in certain countries. This will demand harmonising qualifications and educating for the acceptance of foreign workers, an issue we now turn to.

11

■ Tourism human resources: the impact of globalisation

Globalisation renders national borders permeable and is encouraging international labour migration and a global market for tourism human resources. Indeed, some countries are well known as net exporters of tourism labour – Portugal and the Philippines for example. Globalisation is having a major impact upon the way that human resources are viewed and managed in tourism (Becherel & Cooper 2002). Whilst, globalisation boosts economic growth, it also jeopardises social equality and threatens vulnerable groups of employees. The impact of globalisation on the tourism labour market has three key dimensions:

1 *The informal labour market* – at the tourism destination, the growth of international companies, such as chain hotels, creates a demand for flexible labour that can adjust to fluctuating levels of tourism demand. Managers therefore come to rely upon informal labour markets at the destination, operating through networking, recommendations and word of mouth, and so avoid expensive and continual hiring of staff (Baldacchino 1997).

2 *Productivity* – globalisation is tending to drive companies towards countries that demonstrate higher productivity. It is also enhancing the role of technology and, in contrast to manufacturing where technology replaces jobs, tourism employees work alongside technology in, say, hotel reception. Here however, the impact of technology is mixed – it tends to be greater in back-of-house jobs and less evident in face-to-face customer service roles.

3 *Non-standard employment* – non-standard jobs are perfectly suited to tourism as they allow flexibility through part-time, contracting, temping or self employment. Whilst this is beneficial from the employers' point of view, these types of jobs tend to attract vulnerable classes of workers – such as women, the disabled and in some countries, children.

Different stakeholders are developing responses to the impact of a globalising tourism workforce. Businesses for example have to decide how to handle an international workforce, from global hiring, to language and cultural training and location of the HR function in the company. Governments are developing policies to protect vulnerable workers and SMEs, as well as dealing with the impact of international policies such as GATS. Unions are aware that their penetration is very patchy internationally – in Scandinavia for example their influence in tourism is strong, whilst in the UK and Australia it is much weaker. The unions are therefore grappling to come to terms with a labour market that does not respect national boundaries and national union membership.

For the future, the tourism sector will need to engage in the notion of 'green' jobs. As the world transitions from a fossil fuel economy to one of low carbon and renewable energy, tourism will need to play its part (UNIDO 2011). Sustainable tourism will generate green jobs, which will aim to reduce the environmental impact of tourism and its enterprises, promote biodiversity and reduce both energy and water use, whilst avoiding waste and pollution (ILO 2008). Tourism will need to manage this transition to a green economy by transforming the labour market in a just way that does not exploit workers. The drivers of this change will be the innovation of enterprises and government policies leading to the greening of destinations, green tourism activities, innovation in both the air transport and automobile sectors and the development of (and adherence to) green industry standards for both products and services (Law et al. 2012).

Summary

This chapter has examined five key issues facing the contemporary tourism industry. A range of factors, including technology and lower travel costs, have driven globalisation. Tourism businesses have responded by internationalising and building alliances and partnerships. We also identified that there are losers in the globalisation equation, particularly SMEs who are faced with competition from large companies, and vulnerable workers who can be exploited. Not only are we living in a global society, but also we are part of the knowledge economy. Tourism businesses have been slow to embrace the benefits of the knowledge economy, especially in terms of adopting knowledge management practices and boosting competitiveness through utilising knowledge for innovation and new product development. Both globalisation and the knowledge economy demand that tourism businesses are well networked. Only in this way can they ensure that they benefit from global trends and the flexible specialisation inherent in delivering the total tourism product. The chapter identified the benefits of using network analysis can to examine networks of destination and tourism businesses and to diagnose problems and weak links. A case study of five different network structures then outlined how networks can illuminate particular structures and issues in tourism. New networked organizations were recommended as future organisational structures, and embeddedness within networks was identified as a key strategy for survival for the contemporary tourism business. There is no doubt that these first three issues – globalisation, the knowledge economy and networking are all linked and combine to create the new paradigm for understanding the contemporary tourism industry in the twenty first century.

The chapter outlined the characteristics of small businesses, the lifeblood of tourism destinations, and made the distinction between small businesses and entrepreneurs, whilst focussing on a particular feature of the tourism industry – the lifestyle entrepreneur. Finally, the chapter examined the crisis facing human resources in tourism, a crisis partly due to demographics and partly to the nature of tourism jobs and their conditions. A range of recommendations was made as to how this conundrum can be solved. Whilst the chapter has dissected and separated these issues for explanatory purposes, it must be remembered that all five issues are linked and combine to characterise the contemporary tourism industry.

11

Self review questions

1   Considering the main drivers of globalisation, rank them in order of importance from a tourism point of view and explain your reasoning.

2   Identify possible strategies that tourism SMEs may adopt to survive in the face of globalisation.

3   Explain the significance of different types of knowledge from the point of view of tourism businesses.

4   How can tourism businesses take advantage of knowledge management?

5   From a tourism business point of view, what are the benefits of embedding within a network?

6   How does network analysis help understand the functioning of tourism business networks?

7   Is the term 'life style entrepreneur' a contradiction in terms?

8   Construct a definition of an entrepreneur and then test it against the example of Richard Branson.

9   What do you understand by the term *demographic squeeze* in terms of tourism human resources?

10 How should tourism businesses respond to the tourism HR crisis?

Recommended reading

Baggio, R. (2011). *Tourism and Network Analysis, Contemporary Tourism Reviews.* Oxford: Goodfellow Publishing.
A comprehensive review of the field focussing on tourism applications

Cooper, C. (2006). Knowledge management and tourism. *Annals of Tourism Research* 33(1), 47-64.
A review paper covering all aspects of knowledge management and its use in tourism.

Dicken, P. (1992). *Global Shift,* 2nd ed. London: Paul Chapman.
An excellent generic review of globalisation.

Morrison, A., Rimmington, M. & Williams, C. (1999). *Entrepreneurship in the Hospitality, Tourism and Leisure Industries,* Oxford: Butterworth Heinemann.
A comprehensive review of entrepreneurs in tourism.

Rimmington, M. (2010). *Tourism and Entrepreneurship, Contemporary, Tourism Reviews.* Oxford: Goodfellow Publishing.
Contemporary and comprehensive review of tourism and entrepreneurship with an excellent set of reference materials

Ross, D.L. & Pryce, J. (2010). *Human Resources and Tourism. Skills, Culture and Industry.* Bristol: Channel View.
Excellent text on the issues of HR and tourism

Riley, M., Ladkin, A. & Szivas, E. (2002). *Tourism Employment. Analysis and Planning*. Clevedon: Channelview.
Thorough coverage of tourism jobs and HR planning and management.

Thomas, R. (1998). *The Management of Small Tourism and Hospitality Businesses*. London: Cassell.
Excellent volume covering all aspects of tourism small businesses

Tremblay, P. (1998). The economic organization of tourism. *Annals of Tourism Research* 24(4): 837-859.
Review paper with a good section on networks.

Wahab, S. & Cooper, C. (Eds) (2001). *Tourism in the Age of Globalisation*, London: Routledge.
Edited volume examining the impact of globalisation on tourism and the response of various sectors.

Thomas, R., Shaw, G. & Page, S.J. (2011). Understanding small firms in tourism. A perspective on research trends and challenges. *Tourism Management* 32, 963-976.
Excellent contemporary review of the key issues relating to tourism small firms.

Ateljevic, J. & Page, S. (Eds) (2009). Tourism and Entrepreneurship, London: Routledge.
Excellent edited text covering entrepreneurship and its application in tourism

Scott, N., Baggio, R. & Cooper, C. (Eds) (2008). *Network Analysis and Tourism: From Theory to Practice*. Clevedon: Channelview.
Comprehensive coverage of the application of network analysis to tourism

Recommended web sites

World Travel and Tourism Council: www.wttc.org

Belize Tourism Industry Association: www.btia.org/

Travel Industry Association of America: www.tia.org/

Queensland Tourism Industry Council: www.qtic.com.au/

Utah Tourism Industry Coalition: www.utahtourism.org/

References cited

11

Achrol, R.S. & Kotler, P. (1999). Marketing in the network economy. *Journal of Marketing* 63(Special Issue), 146-163.

Ateljevic, J. & Doorne, S. (2001). Staying within the fence: lifestyle entrepreneurship in tourism. *Journal of Sustainable Tourism* 8(5), 378-392.

Ateljevic, J. & Page, S. (Eds) (2009). *Tourism and Entrepreneurship*, London: Routledge.

Baggio, R. (2011). *Tourism and Network Analysis, Contemporary Tourism Reviews*. Oxford: Goodfellow Publishing.

Baldacchino, G. (1997). *Global Tourism and Informal Labour Relations*. London: Mansell.

Becherel, L. & Cooper, C.P. (2002). The impact of globalisation on human resource management in the tourism sector. *Tourism Recreation Research* 27(1), 1-12.

Buhalis, D. & Cooper, C. (1998). Competition and cooperation? Small and medium sized tourism businesses at the destination. In E. Laws, B. Faulkner and G. Moscardo (eds), *Embracing and Managing Change in Tourism*, pp. 324-346. London: Routledge.

Campbell, A.J. & Verbeke, A. (1994). The globalisation of service sector multinationals. *Long Range Planning* 27(2), 95-102.

Cooper, C.P. (2012). Contemporary tourism education: Notes from the front line. In T.V. Singh (ed.), *Critical Debates in Tourism*, pp. 199-209. Bristol: Channel View.

Debbage, K.G. & Ioannides, D (1998). Conclusion. The commodification of tourism. In D. Ioannides and K.G. Debbage (eds), *The Economic Geography of the Tourist Industry. A Supply Side Analysis*, pp. 287-292. London: Routledge.

Diamantis, D. & El-Mourhabi, J.B. (2004). *The Globalisation of Tourism and Hospitality*. London: Thomson.

Dicken, P. (1992). *Global Shift*, 2nd ed. London: Paul Chapman.

Dyer, J.H. & Singh, H. (1988). The relational view: Co-operative strategy and sources of inter-organisational competitive advantage. *Academy of Management Review* 23(4), 660-679.

Getz, D., Carlsen, J. & Morrison, A. (2004). *The Family Business in Tourism and Hospitality*, Oxford: CABI.

Goffee, R. & Scase, R. (1983). Class entrepreneurship and the service sector: towards a conceptual clarification. *Service Industries Journal* 3, 146-160.

Hislop, D., Newell, S., Scarborough, H. & Swan, J. (1997). Innovation and networks: Linking diffusion and implementation. *International Journal of Innovation Management* 1(4), 427- 448.

International Labour Organization (2008). *Green Jobs. Facts and Figures*. Geneva: ILO.

Law, A., De Lacy, T., McGrath, M.G., Whitelaw, P.A., Lipman, G. & Buckley, G. (2012). Towards a green economy support system for tourism destinations. *Journal of Sustainable Tourism* 20(6), 823-843.

Morrison, A., Carlsen, J. & Weber, P. (2010). Small tourism business research change and evolution. *International Journal of Tourism Research* 12, 739–749.

Morrison, A., Rimmington, M. & Williams, C. (1999). *Entrepreneurship in the Hospitality, Tourism and Leisure Industries*, Oxford: Butterworth Heinemann.

OECD (2011). *Education and Training for Competitiveness and Growth in Tourism: Final Report*. Paris: OECD.

Parker, B. (1998). *Globalisation and Business Practice. Managing Across Boundaries*. London: Sage.

Pavlovich, K. (2001). The twin landscapes of Waitomo: Tourism network and sustainability through the Landcare Group. *Journal of Sustainable Tourism* 9, 491-504.

Polanyi, M. (1966). *The Tacit Dimension*. New York: Doubleday.

Poon, A. (1993). *Tourism, Technology and Competitive Strategies*. Wallingford: CABI.

Riley, M., Ladkin, A. & Szivas, E. (2002). *Tourism Employment. Analysis and Planning*. Clevedon: Channelview.

Rimmington, M. (2010). *Tourism and Entrepreneurship, Contemporary Tourism Reviews*. Oxford: Goodfellow Publishing.

Ross, D.L. & Pryce, J. (2010). *Human Resources and Tourism. Skills, Culture and Industry*. Bristol: Channel View.

Saee, J. (Ed.) (2008). *Managerial Competence Within the Tourism and Hospitality Service Industries*. London: Routledge.

Scott, N., Baggio, R. & Cooper, C. (2008). *Network Analysis and Tourism: From Theory to Practice*. Clevedon: Channel View.

Shaw, G. & William, A. (1990). Tourism, economic development and the role of entrepreneurial activity. In C.P. Cooper (ed.), *Progress in Tourism, Recreation and Hospitality Management*, Vol 2, pp. 67-81. London: Belhaven.

Stallibrass, C. (1980). Seaside resorts and the hotel accommodation industry. *Progress in Planning* 13, 103-174,

Thomas, R. (1998). *The Management of Small Tourism and Hospitality Businesses*, London: Cassell.

Tremblay, P. (1998). The economic organization of tourism. *Annals of Tourism Research* 24(4), 837-859.

UNIDO (2011). *UNIDO Green Industry. Policies for Supporting Green Industry*. Vienna: UNIDO.

UNWTO (2010). *Positioning Tourism in Economic Policy: Evidence and Some Proposals*, Madrid: UNWTO.

Wahab, S. & Cooper, C. (2001). *Tourism in the Age of Globalisation*. London: Routledge.

WTTC (2012). *Progress and Priorities 2010 – 2011*, London: WTTC.

11

12 Supporting the Contemporary Tourism Product – Tourism Service Management

Chapter objectives

After reading this chapter, you will:

- Further appreciate the linkages and relationships between the various elements that combine to make up the destination product and experience.

- Understand the service management perspective.

- Recognise the difference between a product and customer orientation.

- Be aware of current issues related to visitor/customer/tourist satisfaction, and whether satisfaction is an ambitious enough aim.

- Be familiar with the concept of, and challenges with, managing and measuring service quality.

- Understand the conceptual frameworks which link employees, customers and organisational performance.

- View human resource management as a strategic function.

- Understand innovative practices designed to measure and therefore manage service industry performance.

Introduction

Tourism is a complex system – an assemblage or interrelated combination of things or elements forming a unitary whole. As Chapter 1 explained, this system includes various forms of individual products including the trip product, the destination product, the tourism business product and the service product. Underlying this tourism system is a need to understand how to best manage the experience in order to reach satisfying outcomes for tourists, individual organizations and destinations. The total tourist experience encompasses many aspects, but the primary aim of tourism businesses – customer, or tourist 'satisfaction' – is ultimately determined as an emotional experiential evaluation by the tourist. This is done as part of a tourist's overall appraisal of the destination experience through the co-creation and co-production of experience between tourists and formal (tourism and other businesses) and informal (communities) producers. As a result, the management of each component of the tourism system by tourism businesses, either individually or as part of organisational networks, is particularly important. This chapter provides the foundation for understanding the key issues related to managing tourism service organizations in contemporary tourism.

The chapter first explains the importance of individual business performance within the context of a tourism system, then outlines the ways in which a service-oriented strategy facilitates heightened tourist satisfaction. An overview of the evolution of thought from a manufacturing to a services paradigm is then explained, before a series of service management principles are defined and discussed. Understanding the links between tourism business inter-organizational practices, organisational performance and enhanced destination perceptions are outlined in a tourism context, as is the importance of a strategic approach to human resources management. The creation of a service-oriented culture and climate is then discussed. The final section overviews an innovative approach to measuring organisational performance in service organizations, linking business strategy to performance measures and the remuneration of staff and management.

Context

How do tourists evaluate their tourism experiences? The answer is rather complicated! The following are some examples:

- Think about a tourist's first encounter with a tourism destination. It might be an advertisement for that destination on television or in a newspaper, or it could be on a website (see for example www.Australia.com or www.France.com). Destination websites often contain many links to travel packages, accommodation choices, car rental business, places to visit and things to do within that destination. Nested within these destination-marketing activities is a reliance on the individual performance of each organization promoted through such a marketing offer.

12

- Do you think that impressions of Singapore as a satisfying tourism destination can be influenced by a trip to Singapore on Singapore Airlines? Or a first visit to Australia on Qantas? (Even experiences on non national airlines, such as United in the USA or budget airlines, such as Ryanair, can potentially influence satisfaction perceptions).

- What if the person you speak to on the phone regarding destination services on a toll-free number is less than friendly or enthusiastic?

- How would a tourist react upon stopping at a Visitor Information Centre and finding that the employees (often volunteers) are indifferent or apathetic about the region's tourism activities?

- What if the reservation in the hotel, where you plan on spending your first night at the destination, has no sign of your reservation – and they have no rooms available?

As you can see, the experience of the tourist is dependent on many component parts, many of which exist before someone ever becomes a tourist at a destination, and destination marketers hope that none of these links will lead to dissatisfaction with the overall tourist experience.

Given the challenges and importance of ensuring that the links in the tourism system are strong, it is important to understand some of the factors which define individual organisational management and performance. The study of management has traditionally been viewed from a manufacturing or industrial perspective. However, in tourism, a different perspective is necessary, since tourism is about managing not only products and assets, but also, and most importantly, about managing service, experience and customer expectations (see Chapter 1).

Evolution toward a service mindset

Tourism systems are comprised of many individual businesses, organizations and servicescapes (Chapter 5), all interrelated and in many cases reliant on each other (think of a ferry service when staying on an island resort, or restaurants which might accompany a cottage rental). Most of these businesses provide aspects of the tourist experience, from flight reservations, rental car arrangements, accommodation, tours, dining and the like. The predominance of these tourist purchases are in fact services, rather than goods or products. This is an important consideration because of the distinct differences in managing goods versus managing services (Bowen & Ford 2002).

There has been a gradual shift in management thinking away from the predominant manufacturing paradigm, towards recognition of the role played by services in the economy (Fisk et al. 1993). Grönroos (2007: 4) emphasises:

Customers do not buy goods or services, they buy the benefits goods and services provide them with. They buy offerings consisting of goods, services, information, personal attention and other components. Such offerings render services to them, and it is this customer-perceived service of an offering that creates value for them. In the final analysis, firms always offer a service to customers, regardless of what they produce.

Yet, despite the extraordinary growth, and recognition of the importance that services play in modern economies, many tourism firms still rely predominantly on the management paradigm drawn from managing in the context of manufacturing. This approach has been challenged, with ongoing acknowledgment that there are many differences involved in managing service businesses, such as the relative intangibility of services and the heavy reliance on person-to-person interactions. In fact, it is the service aspect of an offering that often provides the means of gaining competitive advantage. To return to Grönroos (2007: 4):

...whatever customers buy should function as a service for them. Sometimes this service requirement can be offset by a low price. Sometimes it can be offset by imaginary factors surrounding the physical product or service... Sometimes a technologically advanced core solution is preferred, although it may be difficult or expensive to use. When firms choose a strategic perspective they should carefully analyse their customers' everyday activities and value-generating processes and know what their customers are doing. Generally speaking, customers always benefit from firms that consider a service perspective.

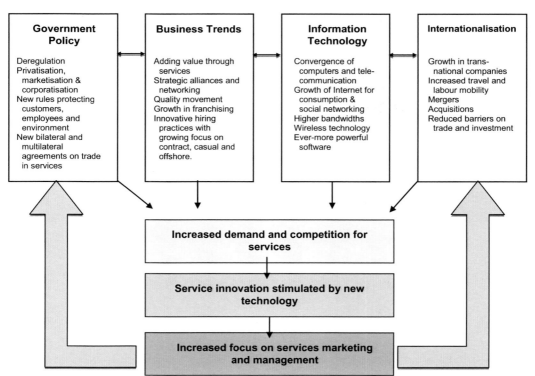

Figure 12.1: Contributing factors to the transformation of the service economy (after Lovelock & Wirtz 2004; Hall & Coles 2008)

It is essential to understand that providing customers with additional services (and service!) over and above the core product in order to add value for the consumer, is a clear strategy toward outperforming competitors. It is rare today to find long term competitive advantage from a core product offering alone (e.g., a room at a hotel), unless the firm has a sustainable competitive advantage based on some core technology or cost structure which allows for continually lower costs for customers (e.g., a favourable lease agreement which negates or significantly reduces fixed overhead costs). However, neither technology nor price can ever be seen as permanent sustainable advantages, because before long somebody will have copied the technology or found further ways to reduce prices (even if only temporarily).

Every tourism firm, therefore, has the option of taking a *service* perspective, which enables management to see service and the role of service components in customer relationships from a *strategic* perspective (Grönroos 2007). The driving force behind taking a service perspective is that a core product/offering is a prerequisite for success, but the creation of an entire service offering, with an unending focus on customer needs, satisfaction and loyalty, enhances long term sustainable competitive advantage. The central requirement of managing a tourism business is therefore to:

- Appreciate that a service perspective is a strategic approach – *managing* service versus just *doing* service.

- Understand that the service management approach is an alternative approach to the old manufacturing management paradigm, and to price- and image-based approaches, and is geared toward customers, service and value.

Service management has been described as 'the new paradigm' in hospitality (Kandampully 2002). The central tenet of this new paradigm was defined by Albrecht (1988: 20) as, 'a total organizational approach that makes quality of service, as perceived by the customer, the number one driving force for the operations of the business'. According to Grönroos (2007) the development of every element of the customer relationship into one overall package can create a sustainable competitive advantage for firms:

> 'The driving force is the service perspective, according to which customers are served with goods and services of a core solution, additional separately billable services and other non-billable services, such as invoicing, complaints handling, advice and personal attention, information and other value-enhancing components' (Grönroos 2007: 6).

Essentially, from a commercial service management perspective, all areas of a tourism firm must be managed with a focus squarely on the tourist, with tourist *perceived value* being the driving force for all decisions. Because a true service orientation requires the integration of all the activities of the firm (e.g., marketing, human resources, finance, operations) towards the customer, the term *service management* is therefore usually seen as a more appropriate and holistically accurate term than the more limiting *service marketing*. As noted in Chapter 5, the development of service perspective strategies for tourism is much easier within the context of a firm than of the destination, because firms, like destination management organisations, clearly do not control all areas of the tourist experience. Effective destination involvement in service management therefore requires firms and other tourism stakeholders to be actively engaged in persuading members of the community of the overall value of tourism and its contribution to enhancing place, so as to enhance the tourist experience within the destination (Hall 2008).

Customer and service orientation

At the centre of the service management paradigm is the idea that all decisions made by the firm must be made with the customer (or tourist) as the focal point. This might seem a logical idea, but businesses for many years often made decisions based on internal motivations – such as cost savings, ease of distribution or convenience for employees. Customer (or in this case, tourist) obsession is at the centre of the service management paradigm.

The idea of customer centricity is not a new one. For example, Peter Drucker wrote in his 1954 book *The Practice of Management* that it is a customer that ultimately defines what a business is, what it actually produces and whether or not it will prosper (Drucker 1954). Five trends have been identified in today's marketplace which reinforce the need for tourism firms to make a transformation from a product to a customer-centric focus (Sheth et al. 2000). These trends are:

1 Intensifying pressures to improve marketing productivity
2 Intensifying competition
3 Increasing market diversity
4 Demanding and more well-informed consumers
5 Advances in technology.

Clearly, tourism operates within an environment where all of these trends exist, and tourism firms have realised that the best means to develop long-term customer relationships, is the one which is the most difficult to emulate, and has the customer squarely in the middle of all efforts. However, many companies today across all industries struggle with this as an underlying concept, despite its logic and seeming simplicity (for a thorough explanation, see Shah et al. 2006).

Product-centric versus customer-centric

Table 12.1 summarizes some of the key differences and distinguishing features of product and customer centricity. Although it should also be noted that some firms take a price perspective, whereby firms believe that price is the dominating purchasing criterion of its customers, and that being able to offer a low price is necessary for survival. From this perspective, price is regarded as the main contribution to the customer's value-creating processes. Other businesses may take an

12

image perspective whereby firms differentiate their offerings by creating a brand image around their core product. Such firms believe that the development of the brand image is central to the customer's value-creating processes (Grönroos 2007).

The product-centric approach is drawn from the early years of marketing, where scholars and industry directed their attention toward the exchange of goods, and where the prime function of marketing was to find ways to bring products to the market (Vargo & Lusch 2004a). From the core product perspective, 'the firm concentrates on the development of the core solution, whether this is a physical product or a service, as the main provider of value for the customer's value-creating processes (the customer's use of solutions to create value for himself or for an organizational user)' (Grönroos 2007: 7). The ramifications of Table 12.1 are numerous, but at its heart lies the essence of a customer-centred management paradigm which proposes not *how to sell things* but rather *how to create value* for the customer and in so doing, enhance the value of the firm or destination. Customer-centricity should be at the heart of the strategy of any tourism business, and because of the high customer contact nature of most tourism businesses, must predominate in the culture of a tourism business (service culture is discussed later in this chapter). Case study 12.1 provides examples of the customer-centric approach in tourism firms and how they communicate their strategy.

Table 12.1: Comparison of the product-centric and customer-centric approaches

	Product-centric approach	**Customer-centric approach**
Basic philosophy	Sell things to whoever will buy	All decisions start with the customer and are focused on present and future customer needs
Business orientation	Transaction-oriented	Relationship-oriented
Product positioning	Highlight features and advantages of product	Highlight benefits and value to customer
Organizational focus	Internally focused on ways to increase sales; development of new products; marketing a separate function	Externally focused, based on making profits as the result of customer loyalty; sees employees as strategic resources; marketing orientation integrated into all departments
Performance metrics	Numbers of products; profit per product; market share by brand	Share of customer, customer satisfaction, customer loyalty, customer lifetime value, service climate
Selling philosophy	How many customers can we sell to? How many tourists can we attract?	How can we most appropriately satisfy each customer by providing as many products and services as are required to meet their individual needs?
Customer knowledge	Customer data a control mechanism	Customer knowledge a valuable asset

Source: After Shah et al. 2006

The focus on customer-centricity has also influenced the development of a service-dominant (S-D) logic of marketing. S-D Logic argues that service provision rather than goods is fundamental to economic exchange and is based on ten premises (Vargo & Lusch 2004b, 2008a, 2008b, 2008c; Lusch & Vargo 2006):

1 Service is the fundamental basis of exchange.

2 Indirect exchange masks the fundamental basis of exchange.

3 Goods are a distribution mechanism for service provision.

4 Operant resources are the fundamental source of competitive advantage.

5 All economies are service economies.

6 The customer is always a co-creator of value. Value creation is therefore interactional.

7 The enterprise cannot deliver value, but only offer value propositions. This means that firms cannot create and/or deliver value independently of the interaction with the customer. Instead, enterprises can offer their applied resources for value creation, with value creation then occurring collaboratively following acceptance of value propositions.

8 A service-centered view is inherently customer oriented and relational.

9 All social and economic actors are resource integrators.

10 Value is always phenomenologically and uniquely determined by the beneficiary. Value is therefore experiential, contextual, and laden with meaning.

Achrol and Kotler (2006) argued that, rather than representing a radical break with marketing philosophies, S-D Logic continues previous understandings of the nature of market exchange, with the notion of exchanging value for value and concern for what customers require already being embedded in the philosophy of marketing. Instead, they argue that S-D Logic provides 'a great impetus to look more closely at how and how much value creation is done by customer in the consumption process, and how this is shifting among service deliverers, support services, and post-consumption services' (Achrol & Kotler 2006: 327). Grönroos provides a more fundamental critique by suggesting:

> 'that some of the 10 foundational premises of the so-called service-dominant logic do not fully support an understanding of value creation and co-creation in a way that is meaningful for theoretical development and decision making in business and marketing practice'. (Grönroos 2011: 279)

Instead, Grönroos (2011) argues that the unique contribution of a service perspective on business is not that customers are always co-creators of value, but rather that under certain circumstances the service provider gets opportunities to co-create value together with its customers. Such an observation is significant given the seeming implicit assumptions in S-D Logic with respect to there being an equal allocation of power between customers and firms. With Hall (2011) arguing in the context of tourism that much consumer research in tourism has not noted the political dimensions of consumption.

'The assumption of agency has emphasized the creative role of the consumer, which has only been reinforced by the current marketing fashion of reference to co-creation, while simultaneously turning away from the political and oppressive potential of the symbolic' (Hall 2011: 300).

Case study 12.1: Customer-centric firms

This case study outlines two examples of how customer-centric firms communicate their strategies both internally (to employees) and externally (to the marketplace). The examples below are drawn from two tourism-related businesses – a restaurant company, and a theme park. Both are industry leaders and respected for the ways in which they are able to engender a customer-oriented culture into their businesses, despite being large organizations employing thousands of people.

Disney is so committed to customers that they coined a term – *guestology* – for the science of knowing and understanding customers. Guestology challenges traditional management thinking (Disney Institute 2001). Instead of focusing on organizational design, managerial hierarchy, and production systems to maximize organizational efficiency, it forces the organization to look systematically at the customer experience from the customer or guest's point of view. This concept reflects the importance placed on understanding precisely how Disney guests behave, what they want, need, value and expect from the Disney experience. Disney places the customer at the centre of what they call the Disney Service Cycle, which consists of four main elements: the service theme, service standards, delivery systems and integration.

Everything Disney does is based on customer wants, needs and behaviours. For example, hotel room doors at Disney have two peepholes – one at the usual height, and one at a child's level. Rubbish bins are placed at 27-foot intervals around the parks, the calculated distance a person would walk before dropping garbage on the ground. Disney also studies behaviour, such as how long a person would be willing to queue before becoming unhappy. The company then intervenes with entertainment designed to keep people occupied in queues. They have also studied how many drops the elevator in the Tower of Terror must have to satisfy customer quality standards. Disney seeks to measure everything that is important to customers and to manage each of these key elements continuously.

The Olive Garden is a casual dining American restaurant chain specializing in Italian food. It bills itself as a traditional family restaurant with 'old world' inspired dishes. Founded in 1982 in Orlando, Florida, there are presently about 600 Olive Garden locations throughout the United States and Canada. In order to engender the importance of customers to their business, managers at The Olive Garden often use stories to illustrate how the company focuses on their needs. One such story is about a customer named

Larry, who after dining at an Olive Garden, wrote a letter to the company, praising the food but complaining about the chairs. Larry is a rather large man, and the armchairs did not allow Larry to sit comfortably in his chair. The company then ordered two 'Larry's Chairs' for *every* Olive Garden Restaurant. These chairs are discreetly substituted for more normal chairs when a particularly large person is taken to their table. This story, when explained to new employees, conveys the message of how far the company is willing to go to meet and respond to customer's needs (Ford & Heaton 2001).

These examples of customer-centric firms demonstrate how some companies can gain significant competitive advantage by being particularly customer focused.

Key sources

Disney Institute (2001). *Be Our Guest: Perfecting the Art of Customer Service*. New York: The Disney Institute.

Ford, R.C. & Heaton, C.P. (2001). Lessons from hospitality that can serve anyone. *Organizational Dynamics*, 30(1), 30-47.

Discussion questions

1   Explain in your own words how each of these three companies use a customer focus as part of their firm strategy.

2   In relation to the above examples, reflect on similar companies with whom you are familiar. Do you believe that they are truly customer centric? What could they do differently to improve their customer focus?

3   Identify three tourism firms who you believe would benefit from a customer focus, and list some strategies they might use to achieve this.

Important concepts in service management

As discussed above, the emphasis on the service management mindset is a relatively new one. This section identifies key concepts which encompass the service management perspective, and ones that are useful in understanding service-related issues in a tourism context.

Service encounter

A service encounter can be defined as an interaction between a tourist and a tourism firm through its frontline employees. The outcomes of service encounters thus depend on the skills, knowledge, personality, behaviour, and performance of these employees. If successful, effective service encounters can lead to many favourable outcomes, including satisfaction, loyalty, and positive word-of-mouth recommendation. It is therefore imperative that tourism firms understand how to manage these critical service encounters.

12

At the heart of service management is the unavoidable fact that a significant proportion of tourism experiences are delivered by people (tourism employees, managers, owners). The unfortunate irony about this fact is that many customer contact employees are the youngest and least trained of employees (more on that later). Although many services have become more reliant on technology (vending machines, airline self- or e-check in), person-to-person interactions still predominate in most tourism businesses. The employees who deliver the service obviously have a direct influence on the tourist experience, as of course do owners, managers, and other stakeholders who indirectly contribute to the service. Moreover, other people in the service environment at the time of service delivery, including other tourists, also play a part. The personal appearance, attitudes, and behaviour of all involved, directly or indirectly, have an influence on a tourist's perception of a service.

From the tourist's perspective, the most immediate evidence of service quality is the service encounter itself. Interactions with service employees are the experiences that tourists remember best, and employees who are uncomfortable in dealing with tourists or who lack the training and expertise to meet expectations can cause tourists to retain unpleasant memories of a service experience. Service employees are thus the primary resource through which service businesses can gain a competitive advantage (Lovelock & Wirtz 2004; Homburg et al. 2009).

A number of management approaches have been suggested which can help tourism businesses manage or control service encounters. Examples of these include:

- *Scripts* – where service providers follow pre-determined statements, such as, "would you like fries with that?"

- *Role play training* – putting employees into mock service situations to assist them in correctly dealing with a range of circumstances.

- *Clearly defined service processes* – a more general approach than scripts, but with clear expectations of steps of service.

- *Engrained service culture* – embedding the importance of customers into the fabric of the organization.

- *Effective recruitment and human resource management* – ensuring that the right people are employed and that individual development continues throughout the term of employment.

■ Customer contact employees

Customer contact, or front line, employees have been given many labels, including 'boundary spanners', 'gatekeepers' and 'image makers' (Bowen & Schneider 1985). They are a tourism organization's primary interface with customers and, as such, are often perceived by the customer as *the* product. Bowen and Schneider (1985) insist that employees not only create and deliver the service, but also are the entire image of the organization. Within tourism businesses, service is performed for a customer by a service person (e.g., a waiter, front desk receptionist, a tour guide). From the customer's point of view, service is essentially presented by the performance of the staff who serve as the public face of the organization or destination. It should be noted that most services do have a tangible aspect which must also be acceptable to the customer, yet it is this package of tangible and intangible aspects that define a tourist's experience .

Many challenges exist in relation to the multidimensional role of service workers. For example, the same person must attend to operational (serving the customer), emotional (establishing rapport with the customer), and marketing (up-selling) tasks simultaneously. This multiplicity of roles in such jobs often leads to role conflict and stress. Lovelock (2004) suggests this conflict is caused by three underlying relationship paradoxes:

1 Person-role conflict (conflict between what the job requires and the person's own personality).

2 Organisational-client conflict (the dilemma of whether an employee should act to please the client or adhere to company rules).

3 Inter-client conflict (conflict between customers such as smoking in a non smoking section, jumping queues or talking during a movie).

There is a problematic paradox in the tourism industry, in that the skills needed to provide service quality are sometimes not in alignment with the skills often found in tourism businesses front-line positions. This disconnect presents an array of challenges for industry as, in many situations such as in restaurants and hotels, the lesser-skilled, lesser-experienced and lesser-paid employees are the ones who contribute most to the tourist experience!

Bowen and Ford (2002) argue that managing the service employee is different to managing employees located in positions with little or no customer contact. There are six basic differences:

1 Service employees must be both task and interactive capable, because customers are present in the service 'factory' (producing and engaging simultaneously).

2 Attitudes and behaviours are more critical than technical skills for service employees (and skills can be taught more easily than attitude).

3 Formal mechanisms for employee control cannot be used with service employees. Instead, a service culture and climate must be in evidence to fill the gaps which form as the result of unexpected or unplanned customer-interactions or circumstances.

4 Emotions play a role with service employees, as observable facial and body displays create impressions, and emotional displays by service providers can have positive/negative effects on customers. Therefore, service employees, to be most effective, must understand which emotions are appropriate in different circumstances (empathy when something has gone wrong, excited when a customer is, etc.).

12

5 Service employees must be trained to deal with role-related conflict. For example, if a customer is unhappy with a service standard, he might become angry with the service provider, even though the employee was doing their job as expected by the organization.

6 Service employees are expected to be 'part-time marketers'. This implies that service employees are expected to fully understand their firm's offerings and demonstrate enthusiasm for them. This can be enhanced through the concept known as 'internal marketing'. Here, a firm's products and service should first be marketed to its employees so that they are in the best position to 'sell' when interacting with customers.

Customer (tourist) satisfaction

The term *customer satisfaction* is used often as an ideal to which tourism businesses and destinations strive. But what *exactly* is meant by the term? How is it measured? And is mere 'satisfaction' sufficient? Customer satisfaction is difficult to define. Oliver (1997) concluded that everyone knows what customer satisfaction is, until they are asked to define it. Oliver did, however, define customer satisfaction as, 'a judgement that a product or service feature, or the product or service itself, provided (or is providing) a pleasurable level of consumption-related fulfilment' (Oliver 1997: 13). This section seeks to provide a brief overview of the construct, its importance and its implications (for a good source of information about customer satisfaction definitions, see Giese and Cote 2000).

Figure 12.2 illustrates some of the drivers of tourist satisfaction, highlighting the challenges in:

- Determining specific drivers of satisfaction depending on the nature of the destination and the individual tourists.
- Incorporating the right systems and training in order to maximise satisfaction levels to the greatest number of tourists possible.

Regardless of its definition or conceptualisation, there is general agreement that when tourists are satisfied, a range of actions and behaviours follow. Tourists who are satisfied with a destination or tourism business:

1 Are likely to become loyal and visit repeatedly.

2 Will deepen their relationships with the destination and its individual service providers.

3 Are more likely to recommend the destination to others.

4 Demonstrate less price sensitivity.

It is therefore important for destination marketers, as well as individual organizations within a destination, to understand the importance of customer perceptions of their experiences and to work hard to measure and continually improve ways to satisfy tourists.

Figure 12.2: Factors that influence tourist satisfaction

■ More than 'satisfaction'

Just when it seems safe to assume that customer 'satisfaction' is the ultimate aim for businesses, we find that merely *satisfied* customers may not be enough! An interesting study suggests a non-linear relationship between customer satisfaction and loyalty (Sasser Jr. & Jones 1995). These authors illustrate that customer loyalty does not increase proportionally as satisfaction levels increase (as logic would suggest it would). Their research concluded:

1 Moderate levels of satisfaction (say a 4 on a 5-point scale) equates to significant likelihood that customers will *defect* to a competitor, but ...

2 ...on the other hand, those who responded with at or near to <u>totally satisfied</u> were *six times* more likely to *repurchase* within 18 months.

In other words, any customer who is less than *fully* satisfied is likely to defect to another business or another destination!

Rather than satisfaction, some suggest 'delight' as the more appropriate ambition (Rust & Oliver 2000). Customer delight has been defined as a higher emotional state than satisfaction, more of a pleasant or unexpected surprise. This type of provision, however, does not come without extra effort on the part of the tourism firm. Therefore, some suggest that a policy of customer delight is not sustainable, as the expectations of customers will continue to rise, making it more and more difficult to delight customers on subsequent visits. Nonetheless, the lesson is an interesting one, and one which tourism industry practitioners can learn from: We must do more than aim to merely satisfy our visitors!

Service quality

One of the more prominent themes in service management thinking centres on the idea of service quality. Service quality has been defined as a cognitive evaluation of a performance by a service provider (Parasuraman et al. 1988). There is broad agreement that in terms of conceptualising and measuring service quality, its dimensions include some degrees (depending on the type of service) of reliability, responsiveness, tangibles, empathy and assurance.

Until the mid-1980s little work had been done to define service quality and identify those elements which determine how service quality could be delivered or measured. Before management can realistically call for improved service quality – it is vital to first:

1   Clarify the strategic position and objectives of the organization (quality ambitions would be very different for a fast food restaurant versus a 5-star hotel).

2   Identify the relevant dimensions which comprise the delivery of service quality.

There is general agreement in the literature that quality judgments cause satisfaction, or that perceived service quality is an antecedent to satisfaction (Heskett et al. 1997). Both constructs are obviously closely related, as each is concerned with how consumers experience a firm's offering and, although the terms are conceptually distinct, in practice they are often used interchangeably (Schneider & White 2004). Perhaps the most important points fundamental to understanding the two constructs are that:

1   Satisfaction tends to be an emotional response ('that was a great experience, and I feel really good as a result').

2   Quality is more of a descriptive evaluation ('the staff there are very caring and the service excellent').

However, whilst it is clear that the two constructs are highly correlated, researchers disagree on the causal direction of the relationships between them. Regardless of any debate as to distinctiveness or overlap in these two constructs, few doubt the importance of both, yet the ways to measure them remain controversial and unresolved. It is also clear that many aspects of satisfaction can be out of the control of a business (think of a crying baby on an overnight flight, loud customers in a quiet restaurant).

It is clear from this discussion that measuring service quality is particularly difficult, because different people rate individual dimensions of service in different ways and with different weightings of importance. One of the earliest models for service quality identified three dimensions of service quality (Sasser et al. 1978):

1   Materials

2   Facilities

3   Personnel.

This early study highlights the importance of people in delivering service as well as highlighting the fact that service quality is not only about an *outcome*, but also about a *process*.

While these approaches differ, most agree that service quality is both elusive and multidimensional. In addition, agreement exists that services are more or less subjectively experienced and perceptions of quality should be as it is *perceived* by the customer, or by the person receiving the service. In his summary of the service quality research, Brady (2001) suggests that scholars have advanced various forms of two distinct models of service quality: SERVQUAL and the Nordic Model.

■ SERVQUAL

The first of these models is known as SERVQUAL and has five dimensions (Parasuraman et al. 1988: 8):

1 *Reliability* – accurate and dependable service
2 *Responsiveness* – prompt and helpful service
3 *Empathy* – caring and personalised attention
4 *Assurance* – Knowledgeable and trustworthy
5 *Tangibles* – appearance of physical facilities.

These dimensions are used in a pre- and post-evaluation of a service in order to compare the variance between expectation and actual performance.

The SERVQUAL model is known as a 'gaps' model because of its measurement of the variance between expectations and performance. It has been used extensively in the services literature including in tourism and hospitality (Kandampully et al. 2001; Bhat 2012), although it is not without significant criticism (Coulthard 2004). Some of the primary criticisms of SERVQUAL include:

1 Concerns with the disconfirmation paradigm (asking a person to compare a service against their expectations for that service).
2 The lack of evidence as to the validity of the 'gaps' type model.
3 The lack of consistent dimensionality with the five-factor scale.
4 Its failure to work as an effective measure across different type of service industries.

■ The Nordic Model

The second model, developed by Gronroos and Gummesson in the early 1980s, is known as the Nordic model (Grönroos & Gummesson 1985). This model has two dimensions, a *technical* or *outcome* dimension, which might be referred to as the 'what'; and a *functional* or *process-related* dimension, which might be referred to as the 'how.'

As an example, a hotel guest will be provided with a hotel room, an airline passenger will be provided with transport, or a tourist with a bus tour of a city.

12

All of these 'outcomes' of the service process are part of the perceived quality experience. However, a tourist's overall determination of quality is not based solely on the room, the arrival to the destination or the ride in the tour bus. There will be many interactions, or service encounters, between a service provider and a customer, which will influence the tourist's overall impressions of quality. The friendliness and professionalism of the front desk employee, the airline cabin crew and the tour bus operator, for example, will all influence the tourist's perceptions of quality. In other words, a tourist is influence by the actual service (the 'what') and the way in which the service was performed (the 'how').

The Nordic model also proposes other influences in total perceived service quality. For example, customer expectations can influence their final perceptions of quality, as can company image, which is thought to play a central role in customer perceptions of service quality. It is therefore important for tourism operators to manage their image in the proper manner, as the perceived image might affect quality perceptions. If, for example, a firm has a favourable image, minor mistakes are more likely to be forgiven. Conversely, if the image is negative, the impact of any mistake will often be considerably greater (Gronroos 2000).

Links between tourists, tourism employees and tourism business performance

Although we have been addressing the concept of service from the perspective of how to improve tourist satisfaction within a tourism firm or destination, individual organizations are generally motivated to initiate quality programs which can be directly tied to financial performance. In other words, business owners are most interested in profitability – hence any motivation to improve service must have direct implications for profitability.

Two related conceptual frameworks link internal organisational function to customers and firm performance outcome measures. These are:

- The service-profit chain
- Employee-customer linkage research.

■ Service-profit chain

The service-profit chain conceptual framework proposes a hypothetical chain of events which link the internal functioning of an organization to employee loyalty and productivity, service value, customer satisfaction and finally to revenue growth and profitability (Figure 12.3) (Heskett et al. 1997).

Figure 12.3 highlights the fact that tourism firms would benefit from focusing on the left side of the chain, including investment in the various elements that make up the chain, rather than directly focusing on revenues and profits. The internal functioning of the organization is defined as what goes on within an organization in terms of workplace design, and those functions which facilitate employees' ability to service customers. The key aspects of the service-profit chain are:

1 Customer satisfaction drives customer loyalty, which drives revenues and profits.

2 Customer perceived value drives customer satisfaction.

3 Employee satisfaction drives employee productivity which enhances customer value.

4 Solid internal organizational practices drive employee satisfaction.

5 Top-management leadership in the chain underlies the chain's success.

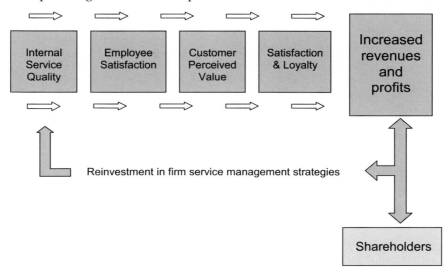

Figure 12.3: The service-profit chain (after Heskett et al. 1997).

■ Employee-customer linkage research

The boundaries between employees and customers in most tourism organizations are fairly permeable – a condition termed 'psychological closeness' between employee and customer (Schneider & Bowen 1993). Because of the closeness between employees and customers in services, further interest in better understanding these links has become known as *linkage* research (Pugh et al. 2002). Linkage research is similar to the service-profit chain, in that it suggests a relationship between employees, customers and firm performance. However, linkage research focuses *explicitly* on employee perceptions of various inter-organizational practices and the corresponding relationships to customer perceptions. In other words, linkage research is interested in a more detailed picture of the left-hand side of the service-profit chain (Figure 12.4).

12

Figure 12.4: Employee-customer linkage model (after Wiley 1996)

The specific dimensions of internal organisational function mirror measures of organisational climate (discussed below). Linkage research finds the specific levers, or drivers, which *link* employee perceptions to customer perceptions. By doing so, management can become acutely aware of these areas which have the greatest influence on customers, and can therefore focus on improving those areas. Figure 12.4 illustrates the fundamental relationships evident in the linkage research stream, drawing assumptions that improved customer satisfaction will lead to corresponding improvements in organisational performance.

The main differences between linkage research and the service-profit chain approaches are:

1. The service-profit chain purports employee satisfaction to be an important part of the chain, whereas linkage research suggests it is more about employee perceptions of service-climate factors which link to customer outcomes.

2. Linkage research focuses on the direct links between employee perceptions and customer perceptions, whereas the service-profit chain conceptualises links directly to organizational performance criteria.

Given the importance that front line service workers have in the effective provision of tourism services, it is logical to infer the corresponding importance of human resource management practices. The next section examines human resource management from a service perspective, suggesting that the task should be seen as a strategic role, central to the success of any service or tourism enterprise.

Strategic human resource management (SHRM)

Today's tourism businesses and destinations must always seek ways to obtain competitive advantage over other destinations and other businesses within a particular destination. There are many means available to try to achieve competitive advantage, including innovation, quality, price and location.

Another strategic approach aimed at competitive advantage involves focusing on the creation of particular strengths inside the firm. According to the resource-based view of a firm (RBV), competitive advantage can be achieved by capabilities that are internal to a firm – including expertise, systems, and knowledge (Voola et al. 2004). Using the RBV approach, it has been found that firm-specific strategic variables explain more than twice as much profit variance as external (or industry-related) effects (Spanos et al. 2004). Apart from the relatively rare scenario of a natural-resource monopoly, the intangible resources of a firm (especially its human resources) are more likely to produce a real competitive advantage – because it is committed people who render the services that are difficult for competitors to emulate .

A gradual shift in the focus of human resource management has occurred since the early 1980s, mirrored by the gradually diminishing use of the term *personnel management*. The old human resource function in organizations was often been seen as a passive, administrative function (e.g. payroll, benefits, files). In fact, in a more traditional (non-service) management approach, employees are usually considered as *costs* rather than as revenue generating resources. However, a *strategic* view (rather than an *administrative* view) places great importance on people as a means to gain competitive advantage, particularly in service businesses with high frequency of employee-customer interaction. Of course, this does not necessarily mean that tourism and hospitality businesses will retain staff should they come under financial pressure or change the nature of labour contracts so as to reduce costs. Nevertheless, according to Huselid (1995: 636):

> The belief that individual employee performance has implications for firm-level outcomes has been prevalent among academics and practitioners for many years. Interest in this area has recently intensified, however, as scholars have begun to argue that, collectively, a firm's employees can also provide a unique source of competitive advantage that is difficult for competitors to replicate.

So a strategic human resources management (SHRM) approach is largely about integrating the human resource function into the strategic planning and operations of a business, particularly in circumstances where customers and employee interaction occurs frequently. Wright and McMahon (1992: 298) defined SHRM as 'the pattern of planned human resource deployments and activities intended to enable the firm to achieve its goals' and suggested its application implies four components:

1 A focus on a firm's 'human resources' (i.e., people) as the primary resource to be strategically leveraged as a source of competitive advantage.

2 The concept of 'activities' highlight HR programs, policies and practices as the means to gain competitive advantage.

3 Both 'pattern' and 'plan' describe the goal and process of strategy; a consistent alignment or design which could also be described as 'fit'. ... vertical fit with the firm's strategy and horizontal fit with all HR activities aligned).

4 All planned HR activities are purposeful and focused on goal achievement.

It is therefore suggested that tourism industry practitioners should provide greater emphasis on the human resource function in their organization in order to enhance tourist experiences and organizational performance. The following case study provides an example of a large international hotel company that made this strategic shift in HR thinking.

Case study 12.2: Intercontinental Hotels Group – an evolution to a strategic approach to HRM

Intercontinental Hotels Group (IHG) has the greatest global coverage and is the largest by number of rooms of all the world's hotel companies. The Group has over 4,500 owned, leased, managed and franchised hotels and 666,873 guest rooms across nearly 100 countries and territories. IHG owns a portfolio of well-recognised and respected brands – including Intercontinental Hotels, Crowne Plaza and Holiday Inn. IHG had over 153 million room nights booked in 2011 with gross revenues of $20.2 billion (IHG 2012).

Its current stated corporate strategy emphasises building brand performance through delivery of a more consistent brand experience for its customers. The company recognizes that people – the ongoing development of vibrant individuals to lead the growth strategy – are of paramount importance to the goal of building brand performance. According to the IHG Strategy 'IHG believes talented and passionate people at all levels of the business are a key competitive advantage to delivering Great Hotels Guests Love and enhanced shareholder returns' (IHG 2012).

Our talented people create our culture, and IHG is aligned around great values which are consistently brought to life through a suite of five IHG behaviours, the 'Winning Ways':

- do the right thing;
- show we care;
- aim higher;
- celebrate difference; and
- work better together.

Across the company, the HR function has changed over the past three decades along the following general pattern:

1   1980s –A 'personnel management' approach, driven by policy creation, procedures, and industry relations, dealing with unions and administrative issues.

2   1990s – Evolution to a 'human resource management' approach, where training and development and Employee Champion activities were added to the personal and administration issues of the 1980s.

3   2000s – A total rethink took place, challenging the ways in which the HR function was integrated into the business. The HR function now works in partnership with operations and strategic planners and partners and has been completely restructured to accommodate the changed focus.

In trying to break free from the old HR model, the company undertook the following steps:

1   A thorough assessment of all HR functions and how and by whom they were being accomplished.

2   A series of meetings took place with senior executives (inside and outside of the company) to find out exactly what senior managers wanted from HR. The message was clear. Senior managers made clear the need for:

■   Business-knowledgeable people in HR roles – who understand key performance metrics and important success drivers for the company.

■   HR managers to work as integrated partners in the business, providing relevant HR advice, guidance, systems and strategies.

■   Mature dialogue between HR and other senior management functions.

■   Less focus on administrative/bureaucratic functions and a greater emphasis on change management and strategic partnerships.

3   A new HR structure was formed which included a separation of the recruitment function (currently called 'talent resourcing') and the developmental function (now called 'talent development'). This was coupled with the need to have high calibre specialists delivering improved outcomes in these areas of the business.

4   Specialisations became centralised across geographical regions, thus reducing or eliminating duplication in activity and process. For example, one highly trained professional could oversee the 'talent resourcing' function across 5-6 hotels in one geographical area.

5   Administration functions were localised, and in many cases outsourced or re-allocated to other functional or operating departments who readily accommodate this work. For example, payroll functions were distributed to payroll departments and line-level recruitment handed back to departments, thus eliminating the unnecessary delays and bureaucracy of line-level recruitment becoming bogged down in administration.

These strategies created a more strategic and singular long term future focus, allowing the right type of people to undertake important roles, where traditionally, HR 'generalists' were asked to recruit, train, develop staff and administer which was merely delivering a day to day operational focus.

12

These strategies have created a whole new way of operating, where the HRM function is fully integrated into the hotel operation, where the senior HR managers are part of the senior management group at hotel, regional, national and international levels, and where the right focus is placed on the tasks which HR can help to provide in order for the company to most effectively manage the people part of its business.

The journey to ensure that HR creates value, drives performance and delivers measurable results to the business continues in IHG as part of the company's overall strategy to provide the best service and results that it can to its people, customers, owners and shareholders.

Acknowledgements

This case is partly derived from collaborative work undertaken between The University of Queensland and IHG Australia. We are grateful to Chris Bulmer, Regional Director of Human Resources for IHG (Queensland and Northern Territory and PNG) and David Solnet from the University of Queensland for their assistance in preparing this case study.

Key sources

Intercontinental Hotels Group: http://www.ihgplc.com/

(The site include details of IHG strategy, annual reports, investor information among other useful information on the group)

Discussion questions

1   What is meant by strategic HRM? How is it different from traditional HRM?
2   How might the new approach taken by IHG improve the company's service focus?
3   What challenges do you believe face HR managers in today's employment markets?

Service culture and climate

Every organization, whether intended or not, has a culture of some kind. Culture, from an organisational point of view, is often defined as the values and norms embedded into an organization. An organisational culture, particularly in a service business, has the ability to fill the gaps between:

1   What the organization can anticipate and train its people do deal with.
2   The opportunities and problems that arise in daily encounters with customers (Ford & Heaton 2001).

Since managers cannot supervise every interaction which takes place between employees and tourists it is important for tourism service organizations to develop a predominating norm of behaviour which is focused on customers and service quality. Such an approach minimises the gaps which unforeseen circumstances might cause in services and also work to motivate unsupervised employees. One such strategy is to create a *service climate*.

The study of climate is drawn from organisational psychology, a field that seeks to better understand how individuals behave, or are likely to behave, in an organization or business setting. This focus is particularly important when studying tourism service businesses because of the aforementioned 'psychological closeness' between employees and tourists in tourism-related businesses. Knowledge gleaned from the study of individuals in organisational settings can be applied in order to assist organizations to function more effectively – a generally accepted precursor to hard performance measures, such as profits.

Organisational climate is defined as employee perceptions of the practices and procedures in the organization (Denison 1996). It differs from culture in that it represents an assessment of how employees perceive various aspects of an organization, whereas culture represents the values and norms, often the aspirations of management. Climate represents how well these aspirations are actually perceived by employees and those who come into contact with an organization (Schneider et al. 2006). These aspirations are often communicated through artefacts, stories and myths, like the 'Larry's Chair' story mentioned earlier.

Climate is normally obtained by measuring respondent perceptions of what goes on around them, in terms of organisational events, policies, practices, expectations, and so on. Tagiuri (1968: 25) defined climate as, 'a relatively enduring quality of the total environment that (a) is experienced by the occupants; (b) influences their behaviour; and (c) can be described in terms of the values of a particular set of characteristics (or attributes) of the environment'.

A service climate represents the degree to which all of a firm's activities, policies and practices are focused on service quality and customer satisfaction. Schneider and White (2004: 100) summarise it:

So, when employees perceive that they are rewarded for delivering quality service *and* when employees perceive that management devotes time, energy, and resources to service quality *and* when employees receive the training they require to effectively deal with diverse customers, *then* a positive service climate is more likely to be the theme or meaning attached to these experiences.

When all of the aggregate conditions are present for excellent service to be provided to customers, a positive climate for service is said to exist.

Climate is usually measured by using a survey methodology. Many best practice tourism organizations employ climate measures as a part of their organisational learning process. With regular measures of an organisational climate, progressive-thinking companies use the results to improve employee perceptions, and then base improvement outcomes as a part of performance measurement (see the final section on Balanced Scorecards for ways in which service climate can be

12

used strategically). A recent study of the Spanish hospitality industry (Potočnika et al. 2011) reported that their cross-sectional empirical results confirmed that high climate strength in managerial practices fosters a positive impact of managerial practices on customer service quality evaluations. However, other results related to customer orientation of services questioned the idea that service climate strength is always a precursor of service quality. They found that high climate strength in customer orientation enhanced the negative relationship between customer orientation and functional service quality in a cross-sectional study, and between customer orientation and relational service quality in a lagged study. In addition, an examination of curvilinear effects of climate strength revealed an inverted U-shaped relationship between climate strength in customer orientation and relational service quality over time. Such findings raise important questions as to the contribution of climate strength to customer service quality perceptions over time as well as demonstrating the practical value of empirical research on service climate in tourism and hospitality.

Measuring performance – the Balanced Scorecard

Sound management practices align the strategy of tourism firms with operations, human resources and performance measures. Tourism businesses must be tourist-centric, and understand that their employees are paramount to success. Traditionally, however, organisational performance has been based only on a range of financial metrics. Kaplan and Norton (1992), devised a new way to link firm strategy (value drivers) with measuring performance. They named this system the '*Balanced Scorecard*'. Recognizing some of the weaknesses and vagueness of previous management approaches, the Balanced Scorecard approach provides a clear prescription as to what companies should measure in order to 'balance' the financial perspective.

The Balanced Scorecard is a management and measurement system that enables organizations to clarify their vision and strategy and translate them into action. It provides feedback around both the internal business processes and external outcomes in order to continuously improve strategic performance and results. When fully deployed, the Balanced Scorecard transforms strategic planning from an academic exercise into the nerve centre of an enterprise.

The Balanced Scorecard allows managers to look at the business from many different perspectives, based on the strategic objectives of the particular organization. Its application provides answers to four basic questions:

1 How do customers see us?
2 What must we be good at in order to satisfy our customers (internal processes)?
3 How can we continue to improve and grow (learning and training)?
4 How do we look to our owners/shareholders (financial picture)?

When used effectively, the Balanced Scorecard forces managers and employees to focus on key drivers of organisational success. In many ways, the Balanced Scorecard becomes a quantitative yardstick which measures various aspects of the service-profit chain or the linkage research model discussed earlier in the chapter. Whilst there are challenges in its implementation, such as costs, time, expertise and references, the Balanced Scorecard can be an effective conceptual tool or program by which service organizations can be managed and measured.

Summary

This chapter has introduced 'service' as a vital aspect to understanding contemporary tourism. The context is that tourism is an assemblage of interrelated elements, each of which contributes to a tourist's overall experience. By understanding some of the key drivers for managing service, a more holistic understanding for managing tourism destination and organizational performance can occur. The principle of placing tourist perceptions as the predominant and central tenet for all tourism management and planning activities was introduced. This was explained as a contrasting view to conventional management thinking, which places a more industrial or manufacturing paradigm to management, focused on organisational systems, efficiencies, waste minimisation, cost controls, distribution (and the like) as the core of management activities. A number of examples were provided by way of a case study which illustrated some specific customer- (tourist) centric strategies currently employed by various tourism businesses.

A number of key concepts were identified as important for understanding service management in tourism. These concepts include the service encounter – and the important role which front-line tourism employees play in tourist experiences; a review of customer satisfaction in the context of tourism; issues of service quality – conceptualisation and measurement; and the important links which connect tourists, tourism employees, and tourism organisational performance. A more appropriate human resource management approach for the tourism industry was introduced, suggesting that HRM should adopt a 'strategic' focus, thus allowing tourism organizations to turn their people into an important resource for competitive advantage. Strategic HRM was further explained by way of a case study of a major international hotel company. Creating a service-oriented culture and climate was introduced, as was a modern approach to linking tourism strategy with performance measurement, called the Balanced Scorecard.

Whilst the chapter has offered a range of concepts and frameworks for understanding why service is such an important aspect of managing tourist destinations, it must be remembered that tourism is complex and that there is no 'off the shelf' approach to tourism management or to managing the service aspect of tourism. However, this introduction is meant to provide a conceptual starting point for better understanding of tourism from a service perspective.

Self review questions

1 Why is it important to understand service management principles in the context of tourism?

2 Why are service encounters such an important concept in tourism?

3 What is meant by the terms 'boundary spanners'? What is the significance of this term to tourism managers?

4 What is meant by the 'problematic paradox' referred to in relation to tourism employees and required skills?

5 Explain the differences between 'tourist satisfaction' and 'service quality'.

6 Why might 'satisfaction' not be an ambitious enough aim for tourism managers?

7 What is SERVQUAL? How might this concept (and the component parts) be useful to understanding the management of tourism organizations and destinations?

8 What is the service-profit chain? How can this principle be used to facilitate improved tourism business performance?

9 How can tourism businesses utilise strategic human resource management as a path toward competitive advantage?

10 What is the Balanced Scorecard? Why is this type of approach sensible in tourism?

Recommended reading

Carú, A. & Cova, B. (2003). Revisiting consumption experience: a more humble but complete view of the concept. *Marketing Theory* 3(2), 267-286.
A valuable account of contemporary thinking over the nature of the consumption experience.

Heinonen, K., Strandvik, T., Mickelsson, K-J., Edvardsson, B., Sundström, B. & Andersson, P. (2010). A customer-dominant logic of service. *Journal of Service Management* 21(4), 531-548.
Paper that reinforces the importance of customer focus in service management.

Grönroos, C. (2006). Adopting a service logic for marketing. *Marketing Theory* 6(3), 317-333.
Focuses on the significance of service logic for marketing practice and theory.

Grönroos, C. (2007). *Service Management and Marketing: Customer Management in Service Competition*, Chichester: John Wiley.
A text that focuses on service dominant logic in all aspects of firm behaviour.

Heskett, J.L., Sasser, W.E. & Schlesinger, L.A. (1997). *The Service-Profit Chain*. New York: Free Press.
The book which followed a series of oft-cited journal articles.

Lovelock, C. & Wirtz, J. (2004). *Services Marketing: People, Technology, Strategy*, 5th ed. Upper Saddle River, NJ: Pearson / Prentice Hall.
An excellent text.

Parasuraman, A., Berry, L. & Zeithaml, V. (1988). SERVQUAL: A multiple-item scale for measuring consumer perceptions of service quality. *Journal of Retailing* 64(1), 12-40.
The seminal article on SERVQUAL service quality measures.

Pugh, S.D., Dietz, J., Wiley, J.W. & Brooks, S.M. (2002). Driving service effectiveness through employee-customer linkages. *Academy of Management Executive,* 16(4), 73-84.
Explains the employee-customer linkage model.

Vargo, S.L. & Lusch, R.F. (Eds.) (2006). *The Service-dominant Logic of Marketing. Dialog, Debate, and Directions.* Armonk, NY: M.E.Sharpe.
Significant book on notion of service-dominant logic which includes some critique.

Schneider, B. & White, S. (2004). *Service Quality Research Perspectives.* Thousand Oaks, CA: Sage.
A very good summary outlining the history of service quality research.

References cited

Achrol, R.S. & Kotler, P. (2006). The service-dominant logic for marketing: A critique. In R.F. Lusch and S.L. Vargo (Eds.) *The Service-dominant Logic of Marketing: Dialog, Debate, and Directions*, pp. 320-333. New York: M.E. Sharpe.

Albrecht, K. (1988). *At America's Service: How your company can join the customer service revolution.* New York: Warner Books.

Bhat, M.A. (2012). Tourism service quality: A dimension-specific assessment of SERVQUAL. *Global Business Review* 13(2), 327-337.

Bowen, D.E. & Schneider, B. (1985). Boundary-spanning role employees and the service encounter: Some guidelines for management and research. In J. Czepiel, M. Solomon and C. Suprenant (Eds.), *The Service Encounter*, pp. 127-147. Lexington: Lexington Books.

Bowen, J. & Ford, R.C. (2002). Managing service organizations: Does having a "thing" make a difference? *Journal of Management* 28(3), 447-469.

Brady, M. (2001). Some new thoughts on conceptualizing perceived service quality: A hierarchical approach. *Journal of Marketing* 65(3).

Coulthard, L. (2004). Measuring service quality: A review and critique of research using SERVQUAL. *International Journal of Marketing Research* 46(4), 479-497.

Denison, D. (1996). What is the difference between organizational culture and organizational climate? A native's point of view on a decade of paradigm wars. *Academy of Management Review* 21(3), 619-654.

12

Disney Institute (2001). *Be Our Guest: Perfecting the Art of Customer Service*. New York: The Disney Institute.

Drucker, P.F. (1954). *The Practice of Management*. New York: Harper Collins.

Fisk, R., Brown, S. & Bitner, M.J. (1993). Tracking the evolution of the services marketing literature. *Journal of Retailing* 60(1), 61-100.

Ford, R.C. & Heaton, C.P. (2001). Lessons from hospitality that can serve anyone. *Organizational Dynamics* 30(1), 30-47.

Giese, J.L. & Cote, J.A. (2000). Defining customer satisfaction. *Academy of Marketing Science Review* 2000(1), 1-24.

Gronroos, C. (2000). *Service Management and Marketing: A Customer Relationship Management Approach* (2nd ed.). Chichester: John Wiley & Sons.

Grönroos, C. (2007). *Service Management and Marketing: Customer Management in Service Competition*, Chichester: John Wiley.

Grönroos, C. (2011). Value co-creation in service logic: A critical analysis. *Marketing Theory* 11(3), 279-301.

Grönroos, C. & Gummesson, E. (Eds) (1985). *Service Marketing – Nordic School Perspectives*. Stockholm: Stockholm University.

Hall, C.M. (2008). *Tourism Planning* (2nd ed.). Harlow: Pearson.

Hall, C.M. (2011). Consumerism, tourism and voluntary simplicity: We all have to consume, but do we really have to travel so much to be happy? *Tourism Recreation Research* 36(3), 298-303.

Hall, C.M. & Coles, T. (2008). Introduction: tourism and international business – tourism as international business. In T. Coles & C.M. Hall (Eds) *International Business and Tourism: Global Issues, Contemporary Interactions* (pp. 1-25). London: Routledge.

Heskett, J.L., Sasser, W.E. & Schlesinger, L.A. (1997). *The Service-Profit Chain*. New York: Free Press.

Homburg, C., Wieseke, J. & Bornemann, T. (2009). Implementing the marketing concept at employee-customer interface. *Journal of Marketing* 73(4), 64-81.

Huselid, M.A. (1995). The impact of human reason management practices on turnover, productivity, and corporate financial program. *Academy of Management Journal* 38, 635-672.

Intercontinental Hotels Group (IHG) (2012) Online. Available at: http://www.ihgplc.com

Kandampully, J., Mok, C. & Sparks, B. (Eds.) (2001) *Service Quality Management in Hospitality, Tourism, and Leisure*. Binghampton: Haworth Hospitality Press.

Kandampully, J. (2002). *Services Management: The New Paradigm in Hospitality*. Frenchs Forest, NSW: Pearson Education Australia.

Kaplan, R.S. & Norton, D.P. (1992). The balanced scorecard - measures that drive performance. *Harvard Business Review* 70(1), 71-79.

Lovelock, C. & Wirtz, J. (2004). *Services Marketing: People, Technology, Strategy* (5th ed.). Upper Saddle River, NJ: Pearson / Prentice Hall.

Lusch, R.F. & Vargo, S.L. (2006). Service dominant logic: reactions, reflections, and refinements. *Marketing Theory* 6(3), 281-288.

Oliver, R. (1997). *Satisfaction: A behavioral perspective on the consumer*. New York: McGraw-Hill.

Parasuraman, A., Berry, L. & Zeithaml, V. (1988). SERVQUAL: A multiple-item scale for measuring consumer perceptions of service quality. *Journal of Retailing* 64(1), 12-40.

Potočnika, K., Torderaa, N., Martínez-Tura, V., Peiró, J.M. & Ramos, J. (2011). Service climate strength beneficial or detrimental for service quality delivery? *European Journal of Work and Organizational Psychology* 20(5), 681-699.

Pugh, S.D., Dietz, J., Wiley, J.W. & Brooks, S.M. (2002). Driving service effectiveness through employee-customer linkages. *Academy of Management Executive* 16(4), 73-84.

Rust, R., & Oliver, R. (2000). Should we delight the customer? *Journal of Academy of Marketing Science* 28(1), 86-94.

Sasser Jr., E. & Jones, T.O. (1995). Why satisfied customers defect. *Harvard Business Review,* 73(Nov-Dec), 88-99.

Sasser, W., Olsen, R. & Wyckoff, D. (1978). *Management of service operations: Text and cases*. Boston: Allyn and Bacon.

Schneider, B. & Bowen, D. (1993). The service organization: Human resources management is crucial. *Organizational Dynamics* 21(4), 39-43.

Schneider, B., Macey, W.H. & Young, S.A. (2006). The climate for service: A review of the construct with implications for achieving CLV goals. *Journal of Relationship Marketing* 5(2-3), 111-132.

Schneider, B. & White, S. (2004). *Service Quality Research Perspectives*. Thousand Oaks, CA: Sage.

Shah, D., Rust, R., Parasuraman, A., Staelin, R. & Day, G.S. (2006). The path to customer centricity. *Journal of Service Research* 9(2), 113-124.

Sheth, J.N., Sisodia, R.S. & Sharma, A. (2000). The antecedents and consequences of customer-centric marketing. *Academy of Marketing Science Journal* 28(1), 55-66.

Spanos, Y., Zaralis, G. & Lioukas, S. (2004). Strategy and industry effects on profitability: Evidence from Greece. *Strategic Management Journal* 25, 139-165.

Tagiuri, R. (1968). *The Concept of Organizational Climate*. Boston: Harvard University Press.

Voola, R., Carlson, J. & West, M. (2004). Emotional intelligence and competitive advantage: Examining the relationship from a resource-based view. *Strategic Change* 13(2), 83-93.

Vargo, S.L. & Lusch, R.F. (2004a). The four service marketing myths: remnants of a goods-based manufacturing model. *Journal of Service Research* 6(4): 324-335.

12

Vargo, S.L. & Lusch, R.F. (2004b). Evolving to a new dominant logic for marketing. *Journal of Marketing*, 68, 1-17.

Vargo, S.L. & Lusch, R.F. (2008a). From goods to service(s): divergences and convergences of logics. *Industrial Marketing Management* 37, 254-259.

Vargo, S.L. & Lusch, R.F. (2008b). Service-dominant logic: continuing the evolution. *Journal of the Academy of Marketing Science* 36(1), 1-10.

Vargo, S.L. & Lusch, R.F. (2008c). Why service. *Journal of the Academy of Marketing Science* 36(1), 25-38.

Wiley, J.W. (1996). Linking survey data to the bottom line. In A.I. Kraut (Ed.), *Organizational Surveys: Tools for Assessment and Change*, pp. 330-359. San Francisco: Jossey-Bass.

Wright, P. & McMahan, G. (1992). Theoretical perspectives for strategic human resource management. *Journal of Management* 18, 295-320.

13 Tourism in the 21st Century – Contemporary Tourism in an Uncertain World

Chapter objectives

After reading this chapter you will:

- Be able to appreciate some of the key factors influencing tourism in this century.

- Understand why the condition of the physical environment is directly and indirectly significant for the future of tourism.

- Understand the potential significance of climate change for tourism environments and destinations.

- Be able to identify some of the difficulties associated with predicting tourist flows and patterns.

- Understand the implications for tourism of the end of easily accessible oil supplies.

- Be able to appreciate the role that aviation plays with respect to both climate change and energy supply issues in tourism.

- Appreciate the value of scenarios as a decision-making tool.

Introduction

The future, by definition, is unknown. Trying to predict what the future will bring has become an important element in tourism management because of the need to try to bring a degree of control and certainty to business management processes, as well as providing desired returns for destinations. Yet such processes are extremely difficult because of the possibilities of 'wildcard' – high impact, low probability, system-destabilising – events occurring that affect the consumption and production of tourism. Since the start of this century there have been a large number of wildcard events that have affected tourism patterns and flows at a global scale (see also Hall 2010d). These include:

- Terrorist attacks, such as 911 or the bombings in Bali.
- Disease outbreaks, such as SARS, foot and mouth disease in the UK or avian flu.
- Natural disasters, such as tsunamis in the Indian Ocean and Japan, massive earthquakes in China, Japan and New Zealand, and hurricanes in the East Asia and the United States.
- Economic events, such as a rapid increase in the price of fuel and the global economic and financial crisis from 2008 on.
- Political events, such as the 'Arab Spring' in North Africa and the Middle East, or regulatory changes in boarding and passport requirements for travelers as a result of increased concerns over security. This also includes sudden changes in terms of what you can take onto aircraft as hand luggage.

To wildcard events there are also a number of other trends that contribute to an increasingly complex business environment for tourism. These include:

- Demographic changes in developed countries, such as an aging population and increase in the number of single-parent families.
- Rapid population growth in the developing world.
- Increased urbanization on a global scale.
- Global environmental change, including climate change, biodiversity loss and changes in water availability.
- Increasing costs of energy, particularly with respect to the costs of conventional oil, with flow on affects on energy and food security.

All of these trends affect the production and consumption of tourism. Production is affected because the resource base of tourism is changed. Consumption is impacted both directly and indirectly. An example of a direct impact is the higher cost of getting to destinations as a result of increases in the price of fuel. Such an example also highlights that the accessibility of a destination is not just determined by the relative travel distance between a generating area and the destination in terms of kilometers or miles, but also in terms of cost. Indirect impacts of the above trends on consumption relate to the overall contribution of these trends to the state of the economy, as economic downturns tend to correspond with slow-downs in outbound travel. Ultimately underlying the health of the economy is the health of the environment, therefore increasingly issues of global environmental change are influencing consideration of trends in tourism (Figure 13.1).

Figure 13.1: Trends and influences affecting contemporary tourism

Trying to anticipate the future of tourism may be a particularly fraught task, especially as there is a very large body of research that suggests that experts in various areas seldom generate better predictions than non-experts who have received some training, and that the predictions of experts are completely out-performed by those made by simple statistical models (Hall 2005b). Furthermore, most experts overestimate their ability to perform accurately in comparison with non-experts, meaning that experts are overconfident in their knowledge and forecasting capacities. In his review of the work of futurists, Sherden (1998) concluded that meteorologists were not always correct, but had by far the best accuracy compared to economists, stock-market analysts, population researchers, management prophets, and social-trend spotters. All of this does not mean that trying to predict or anticipate the future is not without value. From a business perspective examining the future enables firms to anticipate new business conditions and develop new strategies. From a destination perspective, reflections on the future enable consideration of how to maintain or improve the qualities of a destination and work towards desired futures (Yeoman 2012). Importantly, such exercises should always highlight that, in terms of wildcards and trends, there are opportunities as well as challenges. What may be damaging for one destination or firm may be an opportunity for another (Gössling & Hall 2006a). Similarly, wildcard events in one location will only affect so much of the tourism system, and other parts of the system will be unaffected or may even benefit from events elsewhere. Furthermore, as humans make their own futures, the future is not set in stone.

Growth in international tourism vs global environmental change?

In examining the future of tourism, there is a great contrast between different scenarios of the directions tourism may take over the next twenty years. In the 1990s the UNWTO's (1997) *Tourism 2020 Vision* forecast that international arrivals were expected to reach nearly 1.6 billion by the year 2020. The enthusiasm of the tourism industry for such expansion was well illustrated in the World Tourism Organization's (WTO) 2020 vision:

> By the year 2020, tourists will have conquered every part of the globe as well as engaging in low orbit space tours, and maybe moon tours. The Tourism 2020 Vision study forecasts that the number of international arrivals worldwide will increase to almost 1.6 billion in 2020. This is 2.5 times the volume recorded in the late 1990s… Although the pace of growth will slow down to a forecast average 4 per cent a year – which signifies a doubling in 18 years, there are no signs at all of an end to the rapid expansion of tourism… Despite the great volumes of tourism forecast for 2020, it is important to recognise that international tourism still has much potential to exploit… the proportion of the world's population engaged in international tourism is calculated at just 3.5 per cent (WTO 2001: 9, 10)

As noted in Chapter 3, the UNWTO revised its long-term forecasts for international tourism in 2011. According to the UNWTO (2011, 2012), the number of international tourist arrivals worldwide is now expected to reach 1.36 billion by 2020 and 1.809 billion by the year 2030, after exceeding one billion for the first time in 2012. Nevertheless, international tourism is still expected to increase by an average 3.3% a year from 2010 to 2030. Over time, the rate of growth is forecast to gradually slow down, from 3.8% between 2010 and 2020 to 2.9% from 2020 to 2030. In absolute numbers, international tourist arrivals are forecast to increase by some 43 million a year, compared to an average increase of 28 million a year during the period 1995 to 2010. It is also important to bear in mind, as also noted in Chapter 3, that international tourism only accounts for about 16% of all tourist trips. Therefore this means that in 2030 there is expected to be over nine billion domestic arrivals (see Table 3.6), with the total number of visitor arrivals by international and domestic overnight visitors exceeding the world's population for the first time sometime between 2013-2015.

At one level, of course, all this growth in human mobility is good for the travel and tourism industry providing for the development and construction of new infrastructure as well as creating employment. Yet at the same time that there are predictions of massive growth in international tourism as well as positive comments from the UNWTO with respect to tourism's potential to contribute to poverty alleviation, there are simultaneously increased concerns over the impacts of political insecurity, cost and availability of energy, and global environmental change on tourism (Gössling 2002). Indeed, even though the WTO (2003) recognised the interaction of tourism and climate change as a 'two-way relationship', one of the implications of the growth of the global aviation fleet is that there will be longer operation times of aircraft and concomitant high fuel use of the older models that will still be in use (Gössling & Hall 2006b; Peeters et al. 2007; Scott et al. 2012). Therefore, it seems almost inevitable that if global tourism can grow at the forecast rate then it will only do so at great cost to the environment.

Notwithstanding the conceptual fuzziness of what comprises sustainable tourism (Lane 2009; Weaver 2009; Hall 2011), there is considerable evidence that tourism is becoming less sustainable, primarily as a result of the sector's rapid growth and limited progress towards implementing more environmentally friendly operations on a global scale (e.g. Gössling et al. 2008; Hall 2010a, b, c; 2011). With respect to several key dimensions of sustainability dimensions, including parks (biodiversity, conservation), pollution (climate change), prosperity (poverty alleviation), peace (security and safety) and population (stabilization and reduction), Buckley (2012) argued that global tourism is not sustainable, and does not make a positive net contribution to sustainability. Similarly, Hall (2011: 650) states:

> *'Despite the success of the concept of sustainable tourism in academic and policy discourse, tourism's contribution to environmental change, one of the benchmarks of sustainability in terms of the maintenance of "natural" or "ecological" capital... is greater than ever'.*

Gössling (2002) provided the first comprehensive overview of the global environmental consequences of tourism and argued that, from a global perspective, tourism contributed to: changes in land cover and land use; energy use; biotic exchange and extinction of wild species; and the exchange and dispersion of diseases as well as, in cultural terms, changes in the perception and understanding of the environment. His study concluded:

13

> *...the environmental consequences of travel are substantial, particularly if looked at from a per capita perspective: there is strong evidence that a minority of the world population causes the majority of the negative effects associated with tourism and travel. Simultaneously, it seems as if humans in developing countries may suffer most from the negative consequences, often those with the least financial resources. In the future, leisure-related tourism will experience further rapid growth. It thus seems necessary to deepen the debate on sustainability in tourism, and address the existing problems from a social, ecological and economic perspective. ... Tourism can thus be said to be a major agent in global environmental change, and it will in itself be affected by this change. The restructuring of the tourist industry towards sustainability should thus lie in its own interest (Gössling 2002: 299).*

Gössling's (2002) estimates with respect to tourism's contribution to global environmental change, and updated in Gössling and Hall (2006), have been more recently examined in Hall and Lew (2009) and Hall (2011) (Table 13.1). They suggest that the contribution of tourism to global change is continuing to grow as a result of increasing numbers of domestic and international tourist trips as well as increases in distance travelled (see also Chapter 3).

Although some figures are difficult to determine, it is apparent that tourism is a major contributor to rates of biotic exchange. For example, in a study of the socio-economic parameters influencing plant invasions in Europe and North Africa, Vilà and Pujadas (2001) found that the number of naturalised species was positively correlated to the number of tourists that visit a country (r = 0.49). Similarly, Mozumder et al. (2006) also found a strong association of tourism with increasing biodiversity risk when examining the regression results between the log of tourist arrivals and the log of an upgraded national biodiversity risk index for 61 countries (see also Hall et al. 2010). Given the relationship observed by Ehrlich (1994) between energy and emissions as well as energy use and biodiversity loss, Hall (2010a) provided a conservative estimate that tourism was responsible for approximately 3.5-5.5% of species loss with a future higher figure being likely if climate change scenarios are considered (Hall 2011).

With respect to tourism related CO_2 emissions, the United Nations World Tourism Organization, United Nations Environmental Programme & World Meteorological Organization (UNWTO, UNEP & WMO) (2008) estimated that approximately 40% come from air transport, 32% from car transport and 21% from accommodation, with growth continuing to occur in all areas (Gössling et al. 2010; Scott et al. 2012). The UNWTO et al. (2008) report suggested that tourism was responsible for approximately 5% of all emissions. However, more recently Scott et al. (2010) estimated that tourism contributed 5.2–12.5% of all anthropogenic forcing in 2005 and provide a better estimate of the impact of tourism on climate than an estimate based on CO_2 alone. Scenarios suggest that the amount of greenhouse gas emissions (GHG) from tourism will continue to grow.

Table 13.1: Tourism's contribution to global environmental change

Dimension	2001 estimates	2007 estimates
Number of international tourist arrivals	682 million[1]	898 million[1]
Number of domestic tourist arrivals	3 580.5 million[2]	4 714.5 million[2]
Total number of tourist arrivals	4 262.5 million[2]	5 612.5 million[2]
Change of land cover – alteration of biologically productive lands	0.5% contribution[3]	0.6-0.66% contribution[4]
Energy consumption	14,080 PJ[3]	18,585.6 PJ[4]
Emissions	1400 Mt of CO_2-e[3]	1848 Mt of CO_2-e[4] (1461.6 Mt of CO_2)[5]
Biotic exchange	Difficult to assess[3]	Difficult to assess, but rate of exchange is increasing[4]
Extinction of wild species	Difficult to assess[3]	Difficult to assess[6]
Health	Difficult to assess[3]	Difficult to assess[7]
World Population[8]	6 169.8 million	6 632.2 million
Total number of tourist arrivals as % of world population	69.1%	84.6%
Number of international tourist arrivals as % of world population	11.1%	13.5%

1. UNWTO figures

2. Hall and Lew (2009) estimates based on UNWTO data in UNWTO, UNEP and WMO (2008)

3. Gössling (2002) estimate

4. Hall and Lew (2009) extrapolation based on Gössling's estimates and other research

5. UNWTO and UNEP (2008) estimate for 2005 that excludes cruise ships and does not account for radiative forcing (see Scott et al. 2012 for a fuller discussion and analysis)

6. In Hall (2010a), difficult to assess, particularly because of time between initial tourism effects and extinction events but increasing. One estimate of 3.5-5.5% of species loss with a future higher figure being likely if climate change factors are considered

7. World Health Organisation (2003), difficult to assess in host populations, but sickness in tourists in tropical destinations assessed at 50% by WHO

8. Mid-year world population estimate by US Census Bureau International Data Base (http://www.census.gov/ipc/www/idb/worldpop.html)

Based on a business-as-usual scenario for 2035, which considers changes in travel frequency, length of stay, travel distance and technological efficiency gains, UNWTO et al. (2008) suggest that CO_2 emissions will increase by about 135% compared with 2005, reaching 3059 Mt CO_2 by 2035. These estimates are reasonably similar to World Economic Forum (WEF 2009) projections that estimate that CO_2 emissions from tourism (excluding aviation) will grow at 2.5% per year until 2035, and emissions from aviation at 2.7%, which suggests emissions of 3164 Mt CO_2 by 2035 (Scott et al. 2012). As Scott et al. (2012: 101) suggest,

> 'Even if the per capita per trip contribution of tourists to GHG emissions continues to fall as a result of increased efficiencies from technological and management

innovations, along the lines suggested by the UNWTO, WEF, WTTC and IATA, the absolute contribution will continue to grow as a result of increasing tourism mobility'.

These issues are a concern because, with respect to climate change alone, global warming is destined to have a far more destructive and earlier impact than previously estimated. For example, the Global Humanitarian Forum (GHF) (2009: 1) indicate that every year climate change already leaves over 300,000 people dead, 325 million people seriously affected, and economic losses of US$125 billion (more than the all present world aid) primarily in the less developed countries. According to the GHF (2009), in all, four billion people are regarded as vulnerable to climate change, and 500 million people are at extreme risk, with approximately half a million lives expected to be lost per annum to climate change by 2029. To which Hall (2010a) responded, this means that in proportional terms, tourism as a generator of greenhouse emissions is already responsible in 2009 for about 15,000 deaths, seriously affecting 8.25 million people, and producing economic losses of US$6.25 billion – a figure greater than the amount of tourism expenditure in the least developed countries.

The Fourth Assessment Report of the Intergovernmental Panel on Climate Change (IPCC) indicated that:

- The frequency of hurricanes and storms will increase dramatically.
- Sea levels will rise over the century by around half a metre.
- Snow will disappear from all but the highest mountains.
- Deserts will spread.
- Oceans will become acidic, leading to the destruction of coral reefs and atolls.
- Deadly heatwaves will become more prevalent.

(Parry et al. 2007; Solomon et al. 2007)

Such changes will undoubtedly have substantial affects on the relative attractiveness of many destinations (Scott et al. 2012) - an issue which is already being taken seriously by the business community. For example, UK travel insurer Churchill commissioned two reports on the future of travel. One report (Churchill 2006a) indicated that because of climate change and too many visitors, some sites and attractions 'could be in danger of disappearing by 2020'. The destinations and the reasons why they are regarded as threatened are listed below:

- *Puerto de Mazarron* (South-East Spain) Outbreaks of malaria as well as increased threats of flash floods, heat stress and forest fires
- *Everglades* (USA) Increasing hurricane danger.
- *Athens* (Greece) Increase in summer temperatures
- *Crete* (Greece) Increase in high temperatures, increased desertification and water scarcity
- *Cologne Cathedral* (Germany) Environmental pollution

- *Dalmatian coast* (Croatia) Increase in visitation
- *Kathmandu Valley* (Nepal) Increase in visitation
- *Great Barrier Reef* (Australia) Increase in visitation
- *Amalfi Coast and Tuscany* (Italy) Increase in heat waves
- *Goa* (India) Increase in beach erosion and likelihood of greater hurricane danger
- *Taj Coral Reef* (Maldives) increased coastal erosion and damage to coral reefs.

Perhaps understandably not all destinations reacted well to being identified in the Churchill research. For example, the author of the research suggested that there is a conflict between environmental concerns and commercial interests with respect to the conservation of the Great Barrier Reef (Gupta 2006). Given that the reef attracts 1.8 million people a year and generates A\$5 billion per annum, it is not surprising that the Queensland Tourism Industry Council rejected the suggestion that parts of the Great Barrier Reef should be closed off to tourism. The then Australian Federal Tourism Minister Fran Bailey said tourism operators were ferocious defenders of the Reef's pristine environment. 'They rely on the health of the Reef and so have become intimately involved in protecting that environment' (in Gupta 2006). Yet the operators themselves realize that there is a problem, with their biggest fear being that there will be significant coral bleaching as a result of global warming which may result in:

- Coral loss
- World wide bad publicity
- Development of an algae reef
- Loss of tourists

(Association of Marine Park Operators [AMPO] 2006)

In response, marine operators have identified a number of adaption and mitigation strategies that they can undertake themselves, but more particularly they have also identified a series of needs (Table 13.2). However, while a marketing and public relations strategy may assist with maintaining visitor numbers or satisfaction, it does not solve the underlying problem of climate change.

In October 2012 it was reported that coral cover in the Great Barrier Reef has dropped by more than half over the previous 27 years as a result of increased storms, bleaching and predation by population explosions of the crown-of-thorns starfish (Jha 2012). At the present rates of decline, the coral cover will halve again by 2022, though the reef could recover if the crown-of-thorns starfish can be brought under control and, longer term, if global carbon dioxide emissions are reduced. According to John Gunn, chief executive of the Australian Institute of Marine Science:

> We can achieve better water quality, we can tackle the challenge of crown-of-thorns, and we can continue to work to ensure the resilience of the reef to climate change is enhanced. However, its future also lies with the global response to reducing carbon

13

dioxide emissions. The coral decline revealed by this study – shocking as it is – has happened before the most severe impacts of ocean warming and acidification associated with climate change have kicked in, so we undoubtedly have more challenges ahead (in Jha 2012).

Table 13.2: Operator actions and needs with respect to climate change events on the Great Barrier Reef. *Source*: AMPO 2006

What operators are doing	What is needed
Planning to handle bad public relations on coral bleaching through media and marketing campaigns	Research into coral bleaching
Looking at better/stronger vessel and pontoon designs to cope with stronger/cyclonic weather	Development of heat resistant coral
Working with researchers and government to find answers to water quality, COTS and bleaching	An active transplantation/site restoration policy
Hoping that we will still be able to get insurance	Factual information
Lobbying to get bio-diesel and government action	Government recognition of the problem, the costs and the economic and moral need for all Australians to positively contribute to the world's climate
	If all else fails – a world wide campaign to 'See it now when you can!'

Winter tourism

The problems facing reef and coastal destinations with respect to their long-term viability are also to be found at other natural resource based destinations. For example, alpine and high latitude destinations are particularly vulnerable (Benniston 2003; Gossling & Hall 2006a; Scott et al. 2012) (see also Case Study 13.1). The European Alps are regarded as being particularly sensitive to climate change, with recent warming being approximately three times the global average. Climate model projections show even greater changes in the coming decades, predicting less snow at low altitudes and receding glaciers and melting permafrost higher up. From 1850 to 1980, glaciers in the region lost 30% to 40% of their area. Since 1980 a further 20% of the ice has been lost. The summer of 2003 led to the loss of a further 10%. By 2050 about 75% of the glaciers in the Swiss Alps are likely to have disappeared, rising to 100% in 2100 (Agrawala 2006). Such a scenario led Smith (2007) to observe, 'The grandchildren of today's skiers are likely to know the white peaks of Switzerland only from the wrappers of chocolate bars'. This situation is clearly very serious for the tourism industry as the Alps attract 60-80 million tourists and approximately 160 million skier days in Austria, France, Germany and Switzerland each year (Agrawala 2006).

As of the end of 2006, 91% (609 out of 666) medium to large Alpine ski areas normally have adequate snow cover for at least 100 days per year. The remaining 9% are already operating under marginal conditions. According to Agrawala (2006), future climate change could mean a drop in the number of 'snow-reliable' ski areas with a 1°C increase in temperature dropping the number to 500, to 404 under 2°C, and to 202 under a 4 °C warming of climate. Germany is the most at risk, with a 1°C warming scenario leading to a 60% decrease in the number of naturally snow-reliable ski areas from the present-day. Practically, none of the ski-areas in Germany will be left naturally snow reliable under a 4 °C warming scenario. Switzerland would suffer the least from climate change though even a 1°C increase would reduce natural snow by 10% and 4°C warming would halve the number of snow-reliable slopes (Agrawala 2006).

Winter tourism operators are already adapting to rising snow lines and shorter winter seasons, though most are using technology rather than changing behaviour patterns. Artificial snow-making, which is the dominant adaption strategy, may be cost effective for ski operators but increases demand for water and energy and affects the ecology and landscape (Scott et al. 2012). The costs of snow-making will increase non-linearly as temperatures warm and making snow will no longer be a viable option if temperatures increase above a certain threshold. Grooming of snow slopes can reduce the mini depth of snow required for skiing by 10-20 cm. However, as Agrawala (2006: 2) states, 'no amount of grooming can overcome significant declines or the total absence of snow cover'.

Andermatt, a popular ski resort in central Switzerland has decided to act on the threat to winter sports tourism that climate change represents, and have started to experiment with a high-technology protective blanket in order to stop the Gurschen Glacier from melting away. Yet the amount of area that can be covered remains limited. Changing the terrain by grading the slopes and rerouting natural streams also carries risks to the natural environment and increases chances of natural hazards such as flash floods and rockfalls. 'Insurance, meanwhile, can reduce the financial losses from occasional instances of snow-deficient winters, but cannot protect against systematic long-term trends towards warmer winters' (Agrawala 2006: 2). Overall Agrawala (2006) concludes that market forces are driving adaptation with more emphasis on preserving the status quo than transitions that might be economically and politically expensive in the short term. Nevertheless, such is the potential for changes in patterns of demand that Churchill Insurance (2006b) claim that the effects of climate change will lead to very different ski travel patterns by British skiers in the future as they seek snow-assured holidays with the ski destinations of 2050 potentially being:

- Valle Nevado, Chile
- Mt. Xiling, China
- Mt. Hutt, New Zealand
- Mt. Hermon, Israel

13

- Manali, India
- Oukaimeden, Morocco
- Tiffindell, South Africa

An online survey of 578 UK skiers by Churchill Insurance (2006b) indicated that British skiers currently look to traditional Alpine destinations when they want to ski with nearly half of all skiers (48%) having been to France, followed by Austria (29%), Switzerland (18%) and Italy (18%). Furthermore, 96% of British skiers are unaware of Israel and Morocco as skiing destinations. However, 48% would consider visiting such countries for skiing in the future.

Responding to change

From a global point of view, transport is the most relevant sector in terms of the long-term environmental sustainability of tourism, with approximately 40% of emissions coming from air transport and 32% from car transport (UNWTO et al. 2008). However, the contribution of GHG emissions from aviation is obviously not spread evenly across the world and instead is concentrated in the wealthier countries from whence the vast majority of tourists actually come, although even here there is a small minority that account for most emissions (Gössling et al. 2009). According to Richard Dyer of Friends of the Earth (FOE) 'Airlines do not pay for their environmental impact... The industry screams every time there is a chance the government will do something about fuel exemption [Airlines] don't have to pay the taxes the other industries have to pay'. FOE argue that the introduction of a fuel duty which increase the cost of air travel which would then have a corresponding impact on demand thereby reducing the number of flights and the amount of emissions. In addition, they argue that many current air routes in Europe could be reached by high-speed rail links. According to FOE on a typical rail journey from London to Edinburgh, carbon dioxide emissions per passenger are 11.9kg, by contrast carbon dioxide emissions per passenger by air travel rise to 96.4kg. However, industry groups, such as the International Air Transport Association argue that it is wrong to single out the aviation industry for its fuel emissions. According to Anthony Concil of IATA

> Are we saying we are going to try and stop people visiting their grandmothers... We have to look at the economic value that air transport brings to the world. Air transport employs directly 4m people. It creates $400bn of direct economic output – and if you add in the indirect employment it takes it to about 4.5 per cent of global gross domestic product. We are not against paying our fair share. We are taxed in a lot of cases as if we were 'sin' industries like alcohol and tobacco. But at some point we need to bring some sense to this argument and understand we are not a cash cow that can be milked at every opportunity (in Garrahan 2005: 1).

Shortly after the G8 Summit in Scotland in July 2005 a group of travel industry associations jointly declared their opposition to any proposed aviation tax to fund development in poor countries. Airports Council International, the Asia

Pacific Travel Retail Association, the Association of Asia Pacific Airlines, the Duty Free World Council, the International Air Transport Association, the Pacific Asia Travel Association, and the Tax Free World Association jointly denounce the taxation proposal. Instead suggesting that any additional tax would decrease airline efficiencies and reduce demand for travel and tourism, which they argued is a major driver of economic development in many poor countries.

The Pacific Asia Travel Association (PATA) Chairman Nobutaka Ishikure (who is also Japan Airlines Chief industry Affairs Officer), stated: 'We must remind governments that airlines are not under-taxed, but are over-charged. Airlines play a critical role as a catalyst for economic development. Development is a serious issue in need of a serious solution. More tax on air travel is not the way forward' (Travelpress 2005). IATA Director General and CEO Giovanni Bisignani 'slammed the proposal', saying: 'We are not an industry of millionaire customers able to travel at any price. Air transport is an essential part of the fabric of modern life. If governments are truly serious about development, there are glaring opportunities to generate billions for aid simply by removing trade barriers' (Travelpress 2005). Similarly, ACI Director Robert J Aaronson argued that targeted training of a skilled aviation workforce in developing markets was 'far more meaningful than a new tax', claiming, 'Airports are catalysts for economic development by creating jobs, encouraging new business development and building capacity to underpin travel, trade and tourism. Airports have demonstrated their long-term commitment to relevant assistance for developing nations' (Travelpress 2005).

The response of airlines to a pilot project, led by France and Germany, for a 'contribution of air travel tickets to support specific development projects' as part of the G8's funding of extra money for poor African countries as well as contributing to fighting climate change was similarly negative. According to a spokeswoman for British Airways the notion of a tax was 'illogical... There is no justification for singling out air passengers for an additional tax to fund development in the Third World'. According to Thornton (2005: 2), 'she said it was hard to see why aid for a small business in Mozambique should be funded in part by a family traveling from Glasgow to Malaga for a holiday'. Similarly, a spokeman for EasyJet described the proposal as 'confused... Why only target airline passengers – why not bus passengers? ...If you want to go after a particular industry why not go after the oil industry, where companies such as BP and Shell make record profits'. Nevertheless, there was some support for the proposal. John Stewart, the chairman of Transport 2000, commented, 'Aviation is a great contributor to global warming and it is African countries which will be the greatest sufferers from it... It seems there is a logic about a tax on aviation, which is a great polluter, to help those will be the top victims. It could be a Live Aid of the air' (in Thornton 2005: 2). Indeed, the Global Humanitarian Forum (2009) highlighted the extent to which the impacts of climate change are vastly disproportionately felt in developing countries, suggesting that they suffer 99% of the casualties attributable to climate change.

Case Study 13.1: Tourism entrepreneur attitudes to climate change

Despite some notable niche initiatives in areas such as ecotourism, voluntary action by businesses with respect to sustainability is considered unlikely on a global scale (Gössling et al. 2012). Buckley (2012) asserts that pressures arising from rising oil prices and/or climate change will make voluntary improvements in sustainable business practices even less probable. Despite enthusiasm from business associations and neoliberal political parties, self-regulation, as evident by its lack of success in global initiatives, does not appear to be a viable option for achieving significant change towards greater sustainability (Lane 2009). As Buckley (2012) noted:

> Currently, there are few individual commercial tourism enterprises with positive triple bottom lines… There are rather more which take voluntary measures to reduce environmental impacts, and make voluntary contributions to community wellbeing. The vast majority take such measures only for legal compliance or cost cutting. Tourism industry advocates lobby against government environmental regulation, proposing self-regulation as an alternative (Buckley 2012).

This case study presents the results of research undertaken between 2002 to 2005 of 43 rural tourism businesses and entrepreneurs in the Bay of Plenty (North Island) (32) and Otago/Southland (South Island) (11) regions of New Zealand. This was a part of a broader study of attitudes and behaviours in relation to global environmental change (GEC) (Hall 2007). Respondents participated in an annual interview regarding business and environment issues that was conducted either face to face or by phone. Interviews were conducted because of participant preference for interviews over written surveys. All businesses had an accommodation dimension although other tourism activities were also available including hunting, fishing, garden tours, wine and food; all were rural land properties some of which were also diversified commercial farms with others being best described as 'lifestyle' properties. Respondents were selected through a convenience snowball sampling developed through personal contact, with some respondents having participated in previous provider research and having indicated an interest in being involved in future projects.

In terms of the profile of the businesses, the accommodation component tended to be quite seasonal and was managed by respondents, usually with the help of other family members. This meant that there was a relatively low level of employment of non-family staff. There was substantial variation in length of time of family ownership, ranging from one to 90 years, with a median of eight years and a mean of 14 years. Respondents tended to have a low level of formal engagement in the tourism industry, e.g. through association memberships at a regional or national level, although otherwise they did tend to hold a high degree of social capital in their communities through membership of a range of national and local organizations such as chambers of commerce and service clubs. The profile of respondents is consistent with that identified in a previous survey of small accommodation providers in New Zealand (Hall & Rusher 2004).

The majority of interviewees did identify climate change as a potential issue that may affect their business and personal well-being, but importantly climate change ranked well below other more immediate business concerns in terms of changes to business behaviour. Many respondents noted that although they were interested in climate change concerns it was not an immediate or even main priority as they have more day-to-day concerns with running a business. The five most important issues being:

- Costs of operating a business.
- Regulation by government – in terms of costs and time taken by small businesses to meet regulatory requirements.
- Competition – in terms of too many operators which may then lead to a loss of market share as well as price-cutting.
- Quality – concern over the entrance of other operators that provided a poor standard of service which could then be seen as affecting their own business viability.
- Inappropriate rural development and pollution and its impact on the landscape and personal and visitor amenity

Climate change was seen by some respondents as a potentially significant business and even personal issue. But in comparison with more immediate issues that were identified as more important in terms of business survival (see above), climate change was recognised as a possible medium to long-term issue (5+ years). Importantly, such comments were consistent over the research period, meaning that climate change was constantly being seen as a problem in the longer-term. The comments of one respondent, 'Look, if it doesn't affect my daily business operations then I can't afford to think about it, let alone spend money on it' representing a widespread sentiment among interviewees. The only exception to this attitude being when a storm, flood or other high-impact event had occurred that respondents potentially associated with climate change, and which was perceived as potentially damaging to the environment on which the business partly relied, and/or to the property of the respondent.

Familiarity with climate change issues was gained through general media, although interestingly other GEC issues (biosecurity, water security) were understood through more technical media, such as that available through government agencies at the national and regional level, as well as through agricultural field days operated in part through agricultural and farming associations. The extent to which information regarding different dimensions of environmental change was gained through various media appeared to have substantial influence on the extent such information was seen as

13

trustworthy and reliable. A clear hierarchy existed with respect to trustworthiness of information source across all respondents with Ministry of Agriculture and Fisheries information and agricultural field days being regarded as highly trustworthy; Ministry of the Environment, Regional and Local Council sources and other operators and business people were held as moderately trustworthy; and the general media (radio, television and newspapers) and politicians were perceived to have a low level of trust with respect to statements regarding climate change and other aspects of GEC.

Innovation and adaption measures were developed by some respondents in relation to environmental change issues with respect to biosecurity and water security concerns but were not necessarily overtly directly to climate change. A number of respondents whose businesses had horticultural or agricultural components, in addition to accommodation or other tourism offerings, had started to restrict visitor access to parts of their property as a result of biosecurity concerns. However, such restrictions were primarily connected to concerns over visitor health and safety and any breach of law in relation to safety.

Water conservation was emerging as a major focus of respondents in terms of making existing use more efficient as well as developing new storage strategies. For many larger properties that also had farm operations, concern over water security was also leading to consideration of new management strategies including irrigation or developing an economic base, i.e. through new crops such as olives or almonds, which require less water. Nevertheless, even small accommodation operations were looking at installing dual-flush toilets or other mechanisms to restrict water use. Interestingly, such innovations were often seen as being acceptable to the market as well as having water security and environmental benefits. Several respondents commented that because they had stayed in hotels and motels in the larger New Zealand cities as well as internationally that had dual flush toilets and statements regarding towel use in bathrooms they felt that they could also adopt such initiatives without affecting the attractiveness of their operation. One respondent stated that they made changes shortly after they commenced their farm accommodation business as a result of feedback from German visitors who told them that they felt that water saving measures would 'fit in' better with the image of such rural tourism operations in a country promoting itself as being environmentally friendly as well as being welcomed by environmentally-conscious customers.

Even though many respondents commented that the felt that weather patterns were changing and that these may be related to climate change, they generally did not associate climate change with new potential new seasonal visitor patterns. Many commented that New Zealand always will have 'Four seasons in one day' and that this was just a part of the visitor experience. Overall, if discussed further, respondents felt that seasonal change was 'usually, something they hadn't thought about' but if prompted respondents suggested that official public holidays and institutionalised periods of holiday-taking, such as school holidays, were the most important determinants of seasonality, although some interviewees did also state that they did not believe that climate change would be so substantial as to, according to one respondent, 'completely change tourist patterns'. Again, these types of statements were consistently held over the research period with many interviewees consistently stating that seasonal change was not an issue for them.

Where changes to operator behaviour were expressed as occurring as a result of climate change it was often associated with perceived immediate weather impacts on business operations, for example severe storm and flooding events or extended dry periods in relation to farms which are also used for homestays or other guest accommodation. The greatest expressions of concern over climate change and its potential affects, at both a personal and national level, were from those respondents who had been directly affected by extreme weather events or has seen the effects of such events. Significantly, those respondents who had directly experienced extreme weather events were also those whose responses to questions of climate change were more likely to have shifted over the study period, although certainly not in all cases.

Despite the recognition of a number of respondents of the potential longer-term effects of climate change and the need for 'government to do something', increased regulation or 'green' taxes on carbon or greenhouse gas emissions were opposed if they added to business costs. This reflected the prime focus on respondents on managing day-to-day immediate business risk rather than what was seen as a potential future hazard, even if it was regarded as one that was likely to occur. Responses of businesses whether at the personal (what would they do?) or a national level (what should New Zealand do?) therefore focussed on adaption to climate change rather than mitigation. Indeed, concerns were expressed over the potential of 'green' or 'carbon taxes' to increase the cost of aviation or car travel, and therefore affect the travel market to the regions in which respondents were located, which are away from the main tourist flows in New Zealand, as well as any direct cost to the business.

The results of the New Zealand study were reasonably similar to a survey of winter tourism entrepreneurs in Finland undertaken at the same time (Saarinen & Tervo 2006). The Finnish entrepreneurs were aware of the issue of global climate change. However, half of the interviewees did not believe that the phenomenon actually exists and will influence tourism in their destinations in the future. Their main source of information on climate change was the general media. However, more than three-quarters of the Finnish respondents criticised the information provided by the media, and it was very common for personal observations of climatic phenomena to be used to not only critically evaluate but also reinforce such information. Half of the interviewees had observed events that had strengthened their image of climate change. These included both events that support the climate change thesis, but also events that seem to have run counter to it. Few entrepreneurs gained information from academic or scientific studies on the subject.

13

As in New Zealand the issue of climate change was seen only as a minor threat by Finnish tourism operators, if a threat at all, particularly relative to other factors that might have an effect on the industry or their businesses. The Finnish operators were able to rationalise why they had not considered, or why they were not even considering, plans for adaptation strategies and measures to face projected climate change. According to respondents, the most important reason was the slow pace of change. As Saarinen and Tevo (2007) comment,

> 'A tourism entrepreneur hardly ever plans his future more than five years in advance; in some cases, one year's forethought is sufficient… Although the tourism business is often based on taking risks, entrepreneurs were not willing to rush into implementing uncertain actions if they do not know if the climate in the future is going to be warmer, colder, or more unstable in their region, and how it will actually affect their operations'.

The scepticism towards the climate change may also help explain why there were almost no adaptation strategies. Interestingly, more recent research has shown a change in the attitudes and behaviour of northern Finnish tourism entrepreneurs as they have had to respond to a series of poor winters that have affected their businesses (Saarinen & Tervo 2010).

Both abnormal weather and climate conditions (e.g. the occurrence of the warmest December for 100 years) and media attention to climate change have influenced tourism stakeholder perceptions of winter tourism in the Nordic countries (Hall et al. 2009; Saarinen & Tervo 2010). Because of more snow-free days in the Christmas period and the predicted shortening of the snow season, tourism businesses in Rovaniemi are concerned over their adaptive capacity (Saarinen & Tervo 2006), and the future reactions of tourists and distant markets (Tervo et al. 2012). However, if the number of subzero days in northern Finland decrease as suggested and prevent the use of snow cannons in the early Christmas season, this may restrict 'traditional' winter tourism activities even more. Indeed, the relocation of operations by tourism entrepreneurs and travel agencies has already started to occur (Saarinen & Tervo 2006) with tourist groups being directed to more northern locations such as Levi (Kittilä) and Enontekiö by some British Christmas season package tour operators in order to avoid any snow deficiency in Rovaniemi (Hall 2008).

Nevertheless, despite the threat of climate change, including to Christmas tourism, it is likely that traditional winter tourism activities in northern Finland will continue in one guise or another for at least another 50 years and potentially longer. As many of the Finnish operators argued, they have been working and also struggling with climatic variability and extreme weather events with moderate or good success during the existence of their business career. Furthermore, as they as well as some of the destination marketing organisations also point out, things are likely to be much worse elsewhere.

Key sources

Hall, C.M. (2006). New Zealand tourism entrepreneur attitudes and behaviours with respect to climate change adaption and mitigation. *International Journal of Innovation and Sustainable Development* 1, 229 – 237. (This article provides a more detailed account of the New Zealand case study).

Hall, C.M. (2008). Santa Claus, place branding and competition, *Fennia*, 186(1), 59–67.

Hall, C.M., Müller, D. & Saarinen, J. (2009). *Nordic Tourism: Issues and Cases*. Bristol: Channel View Publications.

Hall, C.M. & Rusher, K. (2004). 'Risky lifestyles? Entrepreneurial characteristics of the New Zealand bed and breakfast sector. In R. Thomas (Ed.) *Small Firms in Tourism: International Perspectives* (pp.83-97). Oxford: Elsevier.

Saarinen, J. & Tervo, K. (2006). 'Perceptions and adaptation strategies of the tourism industry to climate change: The Case of Finnish nature-based tourism entrepreneurs', *International Journal of Innovation and Sustainable Development*, 1, 214 – 228.

Saarinen, J. & Tervo, K. (2010). Sustainability and emerging awareness of a changing climate. The tourism industry's knowledge and perceptions of the future of nature-based winter tourism in Finland. In C.M. Hall and J. Saarinen (Eds), *Polar Tourism and Change: Climate, environments and experience*, pp.147–164. London: Routledge.

Tervo-Kankare, K., Hall, C.M. & Saarinen, J. (2012). Christmas tourists' perceptions of climate change in Rovaniemi, Finnish Lapland. *Tourism Geographies*. Online. DOI: 10.1080/14616688.2012.726265

Discussion questions

1   To what extent might the scepticism of tourism entrepreneurs towards climate change effects on their business be warranted?

2   What sort of communication and information strategies should be developed so as to improve operator knowledge of climate change?

3   Would operator initiatives to lessen their environmental impact improve their attractiveness to consumers?

Predicting change

Despite substantial concerns over the impacts of climate change there are enormous difficulties in predicting the effects of such change as it is extremely unrealistic to assume linearity in tourist behaviour change, i.e. that there will be direct causality in the relationship between changes in temperature and destination choice and behaviour. Such linearity is dangerous because, in addition to temperature, the relationship between tourism and climate also includes factors

13

such as 'rain', 'storms', 'humidity', 'hours of sunshine', 'wind strength' and 'air pollution'; and the role of weather information in decision making (Gössling & Hall 2006). In addition, destination choice is also predicated on a number of non-climate related factors such as cost, accessibility, perception and image of destinations, security and other impacting variables, including the travel budget (in time and money) of the consumer (Gössling, Scott et al. 2012).

Even if some climate change does change tourist behaviour, this does not necessarily mean that the overall number of visitors to a destination will necessarily decline (Scott et al. 2012). For example, rather than travel elsewhere tourists may select a different time of travel. In addition, much will depend on the relative elasticity of demand associated with different types of travel. Leisure travel is probably the most flexible in terms of destination and time of travel, but business travel and VFR are far more inelastic. Some destinations will also benefit from climate change. For example, in the case of the ski industry those resorts that are snow-assured will likely increase their market share, while new markets will emerge for other alpine resorts such as year round hiking and mountain biking opportunities. Similarly, even in the case of the predicted dramatic loss of permanent sea ice in the Arctic, with the subsequent threats to iconic wildlife such as polar bears, it has nevertheless been concluded that there is a likelihood of further expansion of tourism in the Arctic because there will be greater accessibility to the region (Arctic Climate Impact Assessment 2004; Hall & Saarinen 2010a, b).

Tourism and oil

As serious as climate change and other aspects of global environmental change are, one of the most significant issues facing tourism is the increased costs of energy and issues of availability. (Scott et al. 2012). According to the Energy Committee at the Royal Swedish Academy of Sciences (2005: 1):

> 'It is very likely that the world is now entering a challenging period for energy supply, due to the limited resources and production problems now facing conventional (easily accessible) oil. Nearly 40% of the world's energy is provided by oil, and over 50% of the latter is used in the transport sector'.

According to the Committee, mitigation measures must be initiated in the next few years in order to secure a continued adequate supply of liquid fuels, especially for the transport sector. Aviation will be more fuel efficient in the future as a result of technological innovations but possibilities are limited and although energy use per person per km will fall, the predicted increase in the number and distance of people flying will mean that overall fuel use and amount of emissions will continue to grow (Gössling et al. 2010; Hall 2010, 2011). However, over the longer term, completely new energy solutions are required, given the decline of cheap conventional oil (Scot et al 2012). Key issues with respect to oil supply are detailed in Table 13.3.

Table 13.3: Key issues associated with oil supply

1. Shortage of oil

The global demand for oil is presently growing by almost 2% per year with consumption at the end of 2005 set at 84 million barrels per day (1 barrel = 159 litres) or 30 billion barrels per year. Finding additional supplies is increasingly problematical since most major oil fields are well matured. Already 54 of the 65 most important oil-producing countries have declining production and the rate of discoveries of new reserves is less than a third of the rate of consumption as of the end of 2005.

2. Reserves of conventional oil

In the last 10-15 years, two-thirds of the increases in reserves of conventional oil have been based on increased estimates of recovery from existing fields and only one-third on discovery of new fields. A conservative estimate of discovered oil reserves and undiscovered recoverable oil resources is about 1200 billion barrels, according to the US Geological Survey; this includes 300 billion barrels in the world's, as yet unexplored, sedimentary basins.

3. The key role of the Middle East

Only in the Middle East and possibly the countries of the former Soviet Union is there potential (proven reserves of 130 billion barrels) to significantly increase production rates to compensate for decreasing rates in other countries. As of the end of 2005 Saudi Arabia provided 9.5 million barrels per day (11% of the current global production).

4. Unconventional oil resources

There are very large hydrocarbon resources, so-called unconventional oil, including gas (c. 1,000 billion barrels of oil equivalent, much of which could be converted to liquid fuels), heavy oil and tar sands (c. 800 billion barrels), oil shales (c. 2,700 billion barrels); and coal. Problems with unconventional resources include long lead times in development, environmental impacts, and the availability of water and natural gas for the production process.

5. Immediate action on supplies

Improvements in the search for and recovery of conventional oil as well as the production rate of unconventional oil are required to avoid price spikes, which would lead to instability of the world economy over the next few decades.

6. Liquid fuels and the transport system

Oil supply is a severe liquid fuels problem and less of a general energy supply problem; 57% of the world's oil is consumed in the transport sector. Alternatives need to be developed to oil in the transport sector, otherwise not only will there be increased oil prices but also increased competition between transport and other oil users.

7. Economic considerations

In the long run, the price of crude oil will be determined by the price of substitutes. Continued high oil prices are anticipated as long as the pressure from the expanding Asian economies is maintained.

8. Environmental concerns

Unconventional oil will significantly extend the length of the hydrocarbon era and its subsequent contributions to greenhouse gas emissions. Constraints similar to those imposed on other fossil fuels (for example emission controls and CO_2 sequestration) will be necessary and provide major challenges for industry.

Source: Adapted from Energy Committee at the Royal Swedish Academy of Sciences 2005.

13

In the immediate term, the impacts of increased oil prices on tourism seem relatively small. According to the WTO (2006) the impact of rising oil prices on international tourism has so far been limited because the effect of price increases, as reflected in constant currency rates, has been mainly to catch up with inflation, and the direct impact of oil prices in 2005 was within a range of less than 5%, which was regarded as insufficient to alter consumer behaviour. Although the WTO did not make any comment with respect to the impact of increased real oil prices, they did note that 'uncertainty as to price levels is already affecting behaviour, as tour operators find it increasingly difficult to anticipate short-term demand. Tourism enterprises unable to make the necessary adjustments in time could therefore find their profitability at risk' (WTO 2006: 36). When domestic and international travel markets are combined, the impacts of increased oil prices are more significant. An Australian study by O'Mahony et al. (2006) found that approximately 25-35% of those that had taken a holiday or were planning one did suggest changes to their plans to negotiate the impact of fuel. As may be expected given consideration of the role of budgets in determining travel patterns (Hall 2005a), in the O'Mahony et al. (2006) survey, money was the biggest constraint on travel, with the price of fuel having most affect on those on the lowest income (under $50k), some influence at middle income level ($50-$100k) and least influence among those on the highest income ($100k plus).

In examining the impacts of climate change, or increases in the cost of conventional oil, a key finding is that people will continue to travel but that the relative attractiveness and accessibility of some destinations will likely change in relation to other destinations (Scott et al. 2012). Such a situation does not mean the end of tourism but instead will provide for new opportunities for destinations and businesses. In such a dynamic environment the provision of positive service and visitor experiences and improved marketing will become even more important. In addition, there will be an even greater onus on destinations and firms to understand key elements of the business environment, such as changing consumer lifestyles and the new regulatory frameworks that are implemented by government to manage human mobility at a time of increased concerns over energy and environmental security.

Case study 13.2: Transition management and tourism in Norway

The perceived long-term unsustainability of contemporary tourism means that there is a search for new instruments that may help policy makers, industry and destination communities become sustainable. One approach is that of transition management, in which transitions are processes in which society changes fundamentally within a relatively short period of time, such as a generation (Rotmans et al. 2001). Transitions, also known as regime change, refer to the change in the dynamic equilibrium of a system from one state to another (Smith et al. 2005).

Transition management involves integrative and multi-level governance being used to shape and foster development processes, and the choice of policy instruments and actions by individuals and private and public organizations, based on common visions (Figure 13.2). Its main objective is to empower stakeholders to develop their knowledge base and to implement new practices and technology change (Kemp et al. 2007). According to Rotmans et al. (2001: 22) the main characteristics of transition management are:

1   Long-term thinking (at least 25 years) as a framework for shaping short-term policy.

2   Thinking in terms of more than one domain (multi-domain) and different actors (multi-actor) at different scale levels (multi-level).

3   A focus on learning and a special learning philosophy (learning-by-doing and doing-by-learning).

4   To bring about system innovation alongside system improvement.

5   Keeping a large number of options open (wide playing field).

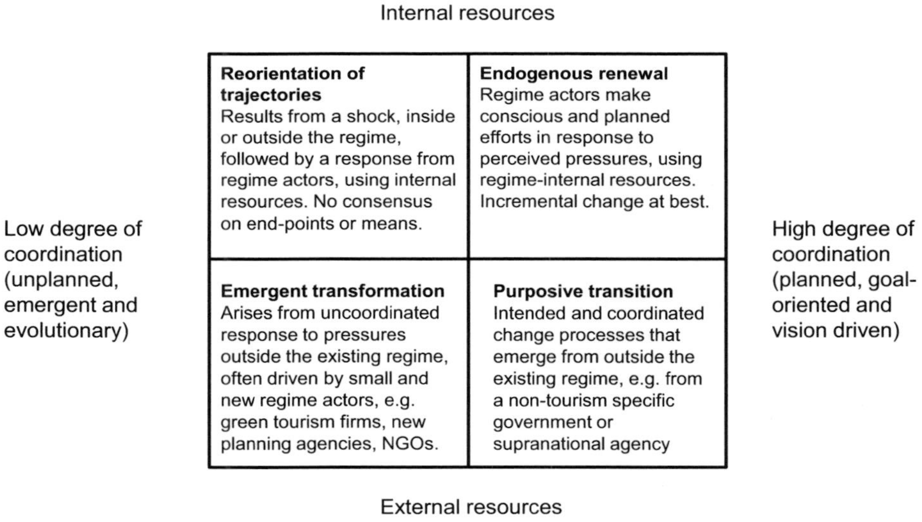

Internal resources

Reorientation of trajectories Results from a shock, inside or outside the regime, followed by a response from regime actors, using internal resources. No consensus on end-points or means.	**Endogenous renewal** Regime actors make conscious and planned efforts in response to perceived pressures, using regime-internal resources. Incremental change at best.
Emergent transformation Arises from uncoordinated response to pressures outside the existing regime, often driven by small and new regime actors, e.g. green tourism firms, new planning agencies, NGOs.	**Purposive transition** Intended and coordinated change processes that emerge from outside the existing regime, e.g. from a non-tourism specific government or supranational agency

Low degree of coordination (unplanned, emergent and evolutionary)

High degree of coordination (planned, goal-oriented and vision driven)

External resources

Figure 13.2: A typology of transitions. Source: After Berkhout et al. 2004; Kemp & Rotman 2004; Smith et al. 2005; Gössling et al. 2012.

Gössling et al. (2012) used a transition management framework to examine initiatives by the Norwegian Government to involve tourism stakeholders in tourism planning and development for sustainability. Observation of the process of stakeholder-driven policy formulation suggests that the high-level invitation by the government to participate led to significant interest among stakeholders. Although they also noted that this may not be due to an interest in sustainability per se, and also appeared related to an opportunity to influence policy development – or, vice versa, as they might have been afraid of having to accept policy arising out of the process that might be less desirable to them.

13

Innovation Norway summarized the outcome of the process as:

> Through this process, branch groups have developed suggestions for specific measures. This includes a more systematic focus on environmental certification of businesses, competence programmes, development funds for sustainable tourism, national and sub-sector specific indicators to monitor developments… (Innovation Norway 2011: 26).

Tangible outcomes of the process include agreement on:

1   The most critical issues in the development of sustainable tourism in Norway, including:

- The difficulty in finding common ground in the definition of sustainable tourism
- The role of motorized road traffic in developing tourism in Norway
- 'Critical' tourism products such as helicopter flights
- The cruise ship sector and its development
- International marketing and relevant markets
- The respective roles of incentives and regulation.

2   Specific goals and sub-goals to work towards in each of the six groups.

3   Measures to achieve goals, including a certification system.

4   Incentives and regulation to be introduced by government (Innovation Norway 2011).

The Innovation Norway stakeholder involvement process led to a clear definition of responsibilities, a vision for future tourism, and, significantly, agreement on the specific instruments to achieve change. However, as Gössling et al. (2012) note, none of the Norwegian airlines, which account for the bulk of energy consumption in tourism, supported the process, while at the time of survey after the process had concluded only four stakeholders had reported that they had actually changed their operations to become more sustainable. Nevertheless, given that regulatory and institutional frameworks had changed as a result of the process, this means that a reorientation of the transition trajectory has begun. Furthermore, a key dimension of the transition management process is to change transition pathways via steps that are doable and not immediately disruptive. As Gössling et al. (2012: 914) conclude: 'the success of the process is now being dependent on the government to actually change policy and maintain transition management processes over time'.

Key readings

Gössling, S., Hall, C.M., Ekström, F., Brudvik Engeset, A. & Aall, C. (2012). Transition management: a tool for implementing sustainable tourism scenarios? *Journal of Sustainable Tourism* 20(6), 899-916.

Innovation Norway: http://www.innovasjonnorge.no/Reiseliv/ (mainly in Norwegian but some information in English, including link to Visit Norway site).

What future for tourism? Scenarios and alternative paradigms

People make their own history. They also make their own future. A number of different possible futures for tourism exist that will perhaps be more dependent on factors outside of the industry, such as environmental change, economic conditions and lifestyles, than things within the control of tourism destinations and firms. Therefore, the future of tourism, and arguably the study of tourism, are embedded as much within concerns over *how* people get there, i.e. issues of human mobility, as over more traditional concerns such as what they *do* when they get there, i.e. a destination and activity focus. Indeed, issues over *how* and *do* are also at the heart of determining the type of transition (see Figure 13.2) that tourism may have to a post-carbon world, and whether we have a reorientation of trajectory based upon a shock or crisis, incremental endogenous renewal, or a more inclusive purposive transition (Gössling et al. 2012).

Much of today's tourism infrastructure is shaped by almost half a century's assumptions that we would have cheap oil and energy, that it was possible to respond to market demand by building more capacity, and that 'predict and provide' assumptions of infrastructure supply would meet transport needs. Not only has infrastructure been shaped by such assumptions, but also successive generations of people in developed countries, who take long-distance mobility as a norm and lead the high-consumption lifestyles, to which the people of the rapidly emerging economic of Asia seem to aspire (Scott et al. 2010, 2012; Gössling, Scott et al. 2012). As the UK Foresight Directorate (2006a) report on Intelligent Infrastructure Systems observed:

> *Energy is not cheap, and is most unlikely to be cheaper 50 years hence. Indeed, most people would anticipate significantly higher prices. The idea that the UK could build new roads at the same pace as it did during the past half-century is simply untenable – 'road protests' did not exist 50 years ago. As to market forces, the new presumptions of future circumstances – that we have to anticipate and ameliorate the likely impacts of climate change, and that sustainability now deserves as much attention as economic growth – make it hard to see how the private sector alone can make the difficult choices.*

The Foresight Directorate outline four scenarios set in a post-oil world of personal transport for the future of human mobility, including tourism (2006b). The main uncertainties which drove the scenarios were: whether or not we will develop low environmental-impact transport systems; and whether or not people will accept intelligent infrastructure. Four scenarios were developed which were labeled perpetual motion, urban colonies, tribal trading and good intentions (Table 13.4). Each of the scenarios provides a different picture of mobility in the developed world in the year 2055. These scenarios allow people to see how certain combinations of events, innovations and social changes could change the future. As the Directorate noted, the real world 50 years from now will likely contain elements of all scenarios. 'The scenarios allow us to see what we might need to prepare for and the opportunities that await us if we set the right path ahead' (Foresight Directorate 2006a: 43).

Table 13.4: Foresight scenarios

Good intentions
The need to reduce carbon emissions constrains personal mobility. Traffic volumes have fallen and mass transportation is used more widely. Businesses have adopted energy-efficient practices: they use wireless identification and tracking systems to optimise logistics and distribution. Some rural areas pool community carbon credits for local transport provision, but many are struggling. Airlines continue to exploit loopholes in the carbon enforcement framework.
Perpetual motion
Society is driven by constant information, consumption and competition. In this world, instant communication and continuing globalisation has fuelled growth: demand for travel remains strong. New, cleaner, fuel technologies are increasingly popular. Road use is causing less environmental damage, although the volume and speed of traffic remains high. Aviation still relies on carbon fuels – it remains expensive and is increasingly replaced by 'telepresencing' for business, and rapid trains for travel.
Tribal trading
The world has been through a sharp and savage energy shock. The global economic system is severely damaged and infrastructure is falling into disrepair. Long-distance travel is a luxury that few can afford and for most people, the world has shrunk to their own community. Cities have declined and local food production and services have increased. There are still some cars, but local transport is typically by bike and by horse. There are local conflicts over resources: lawlessness and mistrust are high.
Urban colonies
Investment in technology primarily focuses on minimising environmental impact. Good environmental practice is at the heart of the UK's economic and social policies: sustainable buildings, distributed power generation and new urban planning policies have created compact, dense cities. Transport is permitted only if green and clean – car use is energy-expensive and restricted. Public transport – electric and low energy – is efficient and widely used.

Source: Foresight Directorate 2006: 44.

The different scenarios raise fundamental questions about the future of tourism and the world we will be living in. People are more mobile than ever before, particularly in terms of long-distance travel. Many believe that they have a right to mobility, even though nowhere is that principle to be found in international law, including with respect to human rights (Hall & Coles 2008). But at the same time the opportunities for mobility are likely to become increasingly constrained.

In some respects, the most fundamental question for the future of tourism is the extent to which it might be possible to have continued tourism growth, as well as tourism's contribution to economic growth, without further running down the stock of natural capital (Hall 2009, 2010a, 2011; Gössling et al. 2010; Scott et al. 2010, 2012). Given the clear failure of tourism to reduce its absolute impact on the global environment (see above), it is appropriate to reconsider how sustainable tourism should be conceptualised. Fundamental to this must be the issue of whether its 'balance' or a 'business as usual' approach is compatible with the need to conserve natural capital, given that constancy of total natural capital is the key idea in sustainable development (Constanza & Daly 1992).

Many institutions, such as the UNWTO, the WTTC and the UNEP, as well as tourism academics and consultants, champion the notion of green economic growth in which sustainable tourism is regarded as compatible with economic growth (Hall 2011). For example, Edgell (2006: 24) states that, 'For sustainable tourism to be successful, long-term policies that balance environmental, social, and economic issues must be fashioned' while Edgell's book on sustainable tourism:

> stresses that positive sustainable tourism development is dependent on forward-looking policies and new management philosophies that seek harmonious relations between local communities, the private sector, not-for-profit organizations, academic institutions, and governments at all levels to develop practices that protect natural, built, and cultural environments in a way compatible with economic growth (2006: xiii) (our emphasis).

There is already considerable evidence that suggests that much tourism growth, as with much economic growth in general, is already uneconomic at the present margin as we currently measure it, given that it is leading to a clear running down of natural capital (Hall 2009, 2010a, 2011; Scott et al. 2010, 2012; Buckley 2012). As Daly (2008: 2) commented in a report to the UK Sustainable Development Commission:

> The growth economy is failing. In other words, the quantitative expansion of the economic subsystem increases environmental and social costs faster than production benefits, making us poorer not richer, at least in high-consumption countries. Given the laws of diminishing marginal utility and increasing marginal costs, this should not have been unexpected... It is hard to know for sure that growth now increases costs faster than benefits since we do not bother to separate costs from benefits in our national accounts. Instead we lump them together as 'activity' in the calculation of GDP.

Daly (2008) also stressed the distinction between growth and development. Growth refers to the quantitative increase in economic output, whereas development refers to an increase in the quality of output without an increase in material and energy use (Hall 2010). Hall (2009) argues that sustainable tourism needs to be understood from a steady-state economic perspective that explicitly recognizes the extent to which economic development, including tourism, is dependent on

13

the stock of natural capital. According to Hall (2009), steady state tourism is a tourism system that encourages qualitative development but not aggregate quantitative growth to the detriment of natural capital. A steady state economy, including at the destination level, can therefore be defined in terms of 'a constant flow of throughput at a sustainable (low) level, with population and capital stock free to adjust to whatever size can be maintained by the constant throughput beginning with depletion and ending with pollution' (Daly 2008: 3). According to Hall (2010), under such an approach sustainable tourism policies should be therefore designed to stop tourism growing when marginal costs equal marginal benefits, although the willingness of destination authorities to do this, except in the most ecologically sensitive areas, appears minimal.

One means of reducing resource demands is via what is referred to as sustainable consumption (Jackson 2005). From a tourism perspective this means both consuming less tourism with respect to reducing energy demands and therefore emissions, by not travelling so far, as well as becoming part of a circular economy rather than a linear one, so that resource inputs and outputs, in the form of emissions and waste requiring disposal, are reduced (Hall 2010a, 2011). The reduction of the overall level or rate of demand can be described as a *sufficiency* based approach to sustainability, while making more productive use of materials and energy is *efficiency* based (Figure 13.3).

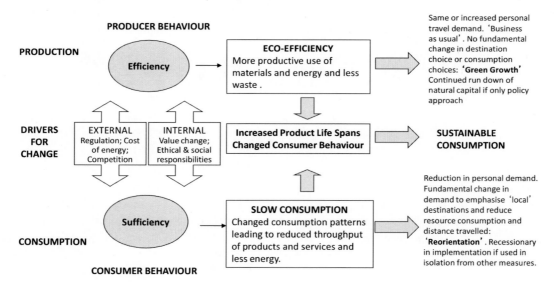

Figure 13.3: Sustainable consumption. *Source:* After Hall 2007

The *efficiency* approach is dominant in current industry approaches towards sustainable tourism, especially with respect to reducing emissions. For example, the WEF (2009b) focus on technological and regulatory innovation as a way of developing 'low carbon' travel and tourism, rather than shifting consumer demand or regulatory strategies (Table 13.5). Yet, the technological solution is extremely questionable as 'technological progress does not reconcile the conflict between economic growth and biodiversity conservation because it arises only in tandem with the conflict' (Czech 2003: 1456). As Hall (2010) noted, the problem in tourism with respect to efficiency, as with many sectors, is that the focus is on the maximisation of maintenance efficiency, rather than production efficiency. 'As a mature scale is reached, production is seen more and more as a cost of maintaining what already exists rather than as the source of additional services from added stock. The larger something has grown, the greater, all other things being equal, are its maintenance costs. More new production, more throughput, is required just to keep the larger stock constant' (Daly 1996: 68).

Table 13.5: Most promising travel and tourism emissions mitigation measures identified by the WEF. Source: WEF (2009b)

Travel and tourism specific

1	Encourage modal-shift from cars to mass-transit systems (bus and rails)
2	Acceleration of fleet renewal with more fuel efficient planes
3	Removal of infrastructure inefficiencies in the airspace and air-traffic management
4	Integration of international aviation in the post-Kyoto climate change agreement at a global sector level
5	Acceleration of hotel refurbishment to support the highest degree of energy efficiency

Cross-sector

1	Accelerated development and deployment of low carbon sustainable fuels in the aviation sector
2	Accelerated deployment of renewable energy in the accommodation sector
3	Improvements in cruise ship fuel efficiency
4	Removal of mass-transit inefficiencies
5	Generate consensus on global and regional sustainability standards and metrics
6	Pro-active leverage of various funding mechanisms

The *sufficiency* approach aims to slow the rate of consumption and therefore reduce the cost nature of throughput via changing consumption behaviours and patterns, including the amount of consumption. The focus on time in much of the sufficiency literature has meant the approach is often related to the notion of 'slow' consumption (Dickinson & Lumsdon 2010; Nilsson et al. 2010; Hall & Gössling 2013; Nilsson 2013) as well as the concept of 'degrowth' (Hall 2009). Elements of the approach include (Hall 2007):

■ The *development of environmental standards* at the community, regional, national and international scales, e.g. such as the Nordic Swan label, that aim to reduce throughput and the decline of environmental qualities (also utilised under the efficiency approach).

13

- The *adoption of lifecycle thinking and analysis (cradle-to-cradle)* in determining tourism infrastructure and product life spans (also under the efficiency approach). This means that research on tourism and its impacts broadens attention to consumption beyond the points of purchase to all phases in the life of the tourism product and experience, from start to finish and from conception to final disposal.

- *Relocalisation* schemes such as farmers markets and 'local diets' that reinforce the potential economic, social and environmental benefits of purchasing, consuming and producing locally, as well as travelling locally.

- *Ethical consumption*, through ethical and responsible tourism. This can include such items as fair-trade, local and organic purchasing, Slow Food, low carbon travel, staycations, slow travel and local tourism.

- The so-called *'new politics of consumption'* such as anti-consumerism, consumer boycotts and culture jamming, and which may include 'downsizing', voluntary simplicity, and even commitments to have less children, that focus on living better by consuming less and the satisfaction of non-material needs.

Although initially based in consumer activism, it is potentially significant in terms of transitions that the sufficiency approach includes industry and public policy initiatives that are also applied in the efficiency approach. Nevertheless, as Hall (2010) notes, the sufficiency approach and its connection to the broader politics of consumption also provides the basis for an even more radical critique of tourism policy, with respect to the central role of economic growth in some interpretations of sustainable tourism and tourism and the green economy. For example, degrowth is not a theory of contraction equivalent to theories of growth, but is instead a term that seeks to provide a conceptual alternative to the dominant doctrines of 'economism' in which growth is the ultimate good by positing the formulation of an ecologically bounded form of economics (Hall 2009). According to Hall (2010: 140):

> … the achievement of more sustainable forms of tourism is concerned not so much with more technological change but is instead grounded in paradigm change. At first glance, the notion that sustainable tourism policies should be geared to stop tourism growing where marginal costs equal marginal benefits, does not appear too radical. Unfortunately, much of the thinking about tourism, even if it does acknowledge economic costs, does not fully consider the extent to which the marginal benefits of economic growth relate to those costs. In particular, for all the talk about the importance of 'the environment' to tourism, tourism as an industry and, to a lesser extent as a subject of study, does not adequately deal with how tourism impacts on natural capital and instead focuses on economic growth, without fully considering the maintenance of the natural resources that allow such growth.

Yet steady-state tourism does not mean the end of tourism or even people holidaying or travelling less. Instead, it means that the current internalisation of external diseconomies – those costs incurred by the activity of one actor but borne by the community at large, i.e. emissions and the loss of natural capital – needs to stop.

A changing tourism?

The various alternative visions and scenarios for tourism, along with challenges posed by climate change, biodiversity loss and maintenance of quality of life mean that it is therefore highly probable that tourism itself will have undergone significant change in 50 years time. This will be not only with respect to the products and services that destinations and firms offer but also in terms of how it is conceptualized and perceived. To an extent such processes are already taking place, as the borders between leisure, tourism, and migration become increasingly hazy. These changes will be seen in the working lives of the people who read this text. Yet in all of this, the service dimension at the heart of tourism will stay a constant.

We cannot understand the consumption of tourism without also understanding its production, and vice versa. In this book we have sought to emphasise the relational dimension of consumption and production through an examination of the key elements of tourism. People will continue to travel from their permanent home to visit other places, some of which are even so close that they can be visited in a day, and people will continue to provide services that enable such movement and the opportunity to visit elsewhere. Much of the attention to such provision is on the physical infrastructure yet just as significant, if not more so, is the intellectual capital of tourism. A contemporary perspective on tourism understands the complex supply and value chains that affects how services are produced and acknowledges that the consumer and the supplier of tourism are interdependent. And it is this intellectual capital that allows not only for a better understanding of tourism as an area of study, but also how the future of tourism may be improved for those who work in the industry, those who are affected by the industry, the places that become destinations, and those tourists who make the industry.

Self-review questions

1 What is a *wildcard* event?
2 How accurate is *expert knowledge* with respect to forecasting?
3 What are the main *values* of undertaking forecasting exercises?
4 What are the forecast key effects of *climate change* and their likely affect on destination environments?
5 Why is it difficult to predict the impacts of climate change on *travel flows and patterns*?
6 What are the key issues for tourism in relation to *oil supply*? How have these understandings changed since the 2005 Reports of the Energy Committee at the Royal Swedish Academy of Sciences (Table 13.3).

13

7 What might be the effects of continued high *energy prices* on tourism? Are the effects of high oil prices different from other sources of energy?

8 What values may *scenarios* have when considering the future of tourism?

9 To what extent do people believe they have *rights of mobility* and how might this affect future transport planning?

10 Should we go see the world's major attractions now if we believe they are going to otherwise disappear?

Recommended reading

Gössling, S. & Hall, C.M. (2006) Uncertainties in predicting tourist flows under scenarios of climate change. *Climatic Change* 79(3-4), 163-73.
This article outlines some of the key difficulties in determining the influences of climate change and leads a debate on the topic in the same issue of the journal.

Foresight Directorate (2006) *Intelligent Infrastructure Futures: The Scenarios – Towards 2055*. London: Foresight Directorate.
The four different scenarios provide fascinating accounts of potential trends in human mobility.

Hall, C.M. (2005). *Tourism: Rethinking the Social Science of Mobility*. Harlow: Prentice-Hall.
The last four chapters deal with the future of tourism and of tourism studies.

Gössling, S. & Hall, C.M. (eds) (2006). *Tourism and Global Environmental Change*, Routledge, London.
The most comprehensive account of the relationships between tourism and global environmental change.

Hall, C.M. (2011). Policy learning and policy failure in sustainable tourism governance: From first and second to third order change? *Journal of Sustainable Tourism* 19(3&4), 649–671.
Paper questions as to whether it is even possible for 'official' concepts of sustainable tourism to be changed from ones that focus on growth.

Scott, D., Gössling, S. & Hall, C.M. (2012). *Tourism and Climate Change: Impacts, Adaptation and Mitigation*, London: Routledge.
Provides a detailed discussion of the science of climate change, the interrelationships between tourism and climate change, and their implications. It is also interesting to compare this book with the first book on the topic (Hall & Higham 2005) with respect to how the debate has advanced on tourism and climate change.

Agrawala, S. (2007). *Climate Change in the European Alps: Adapting Winter Tourism and Natural Hazard Management*. Paris: OECD.
An important study on the environmental, economic, and social impacts of climate change on winter destinations in Europe that is also significant as it comes from a conservative economic organisation.

Lemelin, H., Dawson, J. and Stewart, E.J. (Eds.) (2012). *Last Chance Tourism: Adapting Tourism Opportunities in a Changing World.* London: Routledge.
Discusses how concerns over the disappearance of destinations may impact tourist and destination behaviours.

Sharpley, R., Hall, C.M. & Henderson, J.C. (2012). Consumerism and tourism: are they cousins? In T.V. Singh (Ed.), *Critical Debates in Tourism*, pp.53-79. Bristol: Channelview.
Questions the role of consumerism in tourism including whether we have to travel so much (or so far) to be happy.

Hall, D. and Brown, F. (2006) *Tourism and Welfare: Ethics, Responsibility and Sustained Well-Being,* Wallingford: CABI.
Provides an excellent account of the issues of participation and non-participation in tourism and how this relates to ethical, quality of life and sustainability concerns.

Gössling, S. (2010). *Carbon Management in Tourism.* London: Routledge.
Book provides one of the first comprehensive accounts of ways in which the various sectors of the tourism industry can reduce emissions.

Hall, C.M. & Saarinen, J. (eds) (2010). *Polar Tourism and Change: Climate, environments and experiences,* London: Routledge.
Provides a detailed overview of tourism and change in the regions that are arguably most affected by climate change. The book includes chapters on the future of such icons of climate change as polar bears.

Hall, C.M. (2010). Crisis events in tourism: Subjects of crisis in tourism. *Current Issues in Tourism* 13(5), 401–417.
Introduction to a special issue on crisis in tourism that highlights the way in which international tourism has always rebound from crisis as well as the interconnectedness of crises. Also provides an overview of the tourism and crisis literature.

Recommended web sites

Convention on Biological Diversity (CBD): http://www.cbd.int/

Intergovernmental Panel on Climate Change (IPPC): http://www.ipcc.ch/

United Nations Environment Programme (UNEP Geneva): http://www.unep.ch/

United Nations Framework Convention on Climate Change (UNFCCC): http://unfccc.int/2860.php

References cited

13

Agrawala, S. (2007). *Climate Change in the European Alps: Adapting Winter Tourism and Natural Hazard Management.* Paris: OECD.

Arctic Climate Impact Assessment (2004). *Impacts of a Warming Arctic.* Cambridge: Cambridge University Press.

Association of Marine Park Operators [AMPO] (2006). *A Time of Uncertainty. Presentation at Ecotourism & Climate Change: Challenges for the Future, A Workshop at Ecotourism Australia's 14th International Conference*, October 31, Townsville.

Beniston, M. (2003). Climate change in mountain regions: A review of possible impacts. *Climatic Change* 59, 5–31.

Buckley, R. (2012). Sustainable tourism: Research and reality. *Annals of Tourism Research* 39(2), 528–546.

Churchill Insurance (2006a). *The Future of Travel: The 'Disappearing Destinations' of 2020*. Press Release September 9, Churchill Insurance.

Churchill Insurance (2006b). *The Future of Skiing: France and Austria make way for Morocco and Israel*. Press Release September 9, Churchill Insurance.

Costanza, R. & Daly, H. (1992). Natural capital and sustainable development. *Conservation Biology* 6(1), 37-46.

Czech, B. (2003). Technological progress and biodiversity conservation: A dollar spent, a dollar burned. *Conservation Biology* 17(5): 1455-1457.

Daly, H.E. (1996). *Beyond Growth*. Boston. Beacon Press.

Daly, H.E. (2008). *A Steady-State Economy*. London. Sustainable Development Commission.

Dickinson, J. & Lumsdon, L. (2010). *Slow Travel and Tourism*. London: Earthscan.

Ehrlich, P.R. (1994). Energy use and biodiversity loss. *Philosophical Transactions: Biological Sciences,* 344(1307), 99-104.

Edgell Sr., D.L. (2006). *Managing Sustainable Tourism – A Legacy for the Future*. Binghamption: Haworth Press.

Energy Committee at the Royal Swedish Academy of Sciences (2005) *Statements on Oil*, October 14, Stockholm: Energy Committee at the Royal Swedish Academy of Sciences.

Garrahan, M. (2005). Balancing act on fuel emissions. *Financial Times* [Europe], FT Business Travel 13 June: 1.

Foresight Directorate (2006a) *Intelligent Infrastructure Futures: Project Overview*. London: Foresight Directorate.

Foresight Directorate (2006b) *Intelligent Infrastructure Futures: The Scenarios – Towards 2055*. London: Foresight Directorate.

Global Humanitarian Forum (2009). *The Anatomy of a Silent Crisis*. London. Global Humanitarian Forum.

Gössling, S. (2002). Global environmental consequences of tourism. *Global Environmental Change* 12: 283-302.

Gössling, S., Ceron, J.-P., Dubois , G. & Hall, C.M. (2009) 'Hypermobile travellers. In S, Gössling and P. Upham (eds), *Climate Change and Aviation*. London: Earthscan .

Gössling, S. & Hall, C.M. (eds) (2006a). *Tourism and Global Environmental Change*, London: Routledge.

Gössling, S. & Hall, C.M. (2006b) Uncertainties in predicting tourist flows under scenarios of climate change. *Climatic Change* 79(3-4), 163-73.

Gössling, S., Hall, C.M., Ekström, F., Brudvik Engeset, A. & Aall, C. (2012). Transition management: a tool for implementing sustainable tourism scenarios? *Journal of Sustainable Tourism* 20(6), 899-916.

Gössling, S., Scott, D., Hall, C.M., Ceron, J-P. & Dubois, G. (2012). Consumer behaviour and demand response of tourists to climate change. *Annals of Tourism Research*, 39(1), 36-58

Gössling, S., Hall, C.M., Lane, B., & Weaver, D. (2008). The Helsingborg statement on sustainable tourism. *Journal of Sustainable Tourism* 16(1), 122–124.

Gössling, S., Hall, C.M., Peeters, P. & Scott, D. (2010). The future of tourism: Can tourism growth and climate policy be reconciled? A climate change mitigation perspective. *Tourism Recreation Research* 35(2), 119-130.

Gupta, S. (2006). Queensland vehemently quashes concerns pertaining to the Great Barrier Reef. *ETurboNews* October 12, http://www.travelwirenews.com/cgi-script/csArticles/articles/000097/009786.htm

Hall, C.M. (2005a). *Tourism: Rethinking the Social Science of Mobility*. Harlow: Prentice-Hall.

Hall, C.M. (2005b). The future of tourism research. In P. Burns, C. Palmer, & B. Ritchie (Eds) *Tourism Research Methods: Integrating Theory with Practice*, pp.221-229. Wallingford: CABI.

Hall, C.M. (2006). New Zealand tourism entrepreneur attitudes and behaviours with respect to climate change adaption and mitigation. *International Journal of Innovation and Sustainable Development* 1, 229 – 237.

Hall, C.M. (2007). The Possibilities of Slow Tourism: Can the Slow Movement Help Develop Sustainable Forms of Tourism Consumption? Paper presented at Achieving Sustainable Tourism, Helsingborg, Sweden, 11-14 September.

Hall, C.M. (2008). Santa Claus, place branding and competition, *Fennia*, 186(1), 59–67.

Hall, C.M. (2009). Degrowing tourism: Décroissance, sustainable consumption and steady-state tourism. *Anatolia: An International Journal of Tourism and Hospitality Research* 20(1), 46-61.

Hall, C.M. (2010a). Changing paradigms and global change: From sustainable to steady-state tourism. *Tourism Recreation Research* 35(2), 131–145.

Hall, C.M. (2010b). Tourism and the implementation of the convention on biological diversity. *Journal of Heritage Tourism* 5(4), 267–284.

Hall, C.M. (2010c). Tourism and biodiversity: More significant than climate change? *Journal of Heritage Tourism* 5(4), 253–266.

Hall, C.M. (2010d). Crisis events in tourism: Subjects of crisis in tourism. *Current Issues in Tourism* 13(5), 401–417.

13

Hall, C.M. (2011). Policy learning and policy failure in sustainable tourism governance: From first and second to third order change? *Journal of Sustainable Tourism* 19(3&4), 649–671.

Hall, C.M. & Coles, T. (2008). Introduction: tourism and international business – tourism as international business. In T. Coles & C.M. Hall (Eds), *International Business and Tourism: Global Issues, Contemporary Interactions*, pp.1-25. London: Routledge.

Hall, C.M. & Gössling, S. (eds) (2013). *Sustainable Culinary Systems: Local Foods, Innovation, and Tourism & Hospitality*, London: Routledge.

Hall, C.M. & Higham, J. (Eds) (2005). *Tourism, Recreation and Climate Change*, Clevedon: Channelview Publications.

Hall, C.M., James, M. & Wilson, S. (2010). Biodiversity, biosecurity, and cruising in the Arctic and sub-Arctic. *Journal of Heritage Tourism* 5(4), 351-364.

Hall, C.M., Müller, D. & Saarinen, J. (2009). *Nordic Tourism: Issues and Cases*. Bristol: Channel View Publications.

Hall, C.M. & Rusher, K. (2004). 'Risky lifestyles? Entrepreneurial characteristics of the New Zealand bed and breakfast sector. In R. Thomas (Ed.) *Small Firms in Tourism: International Perspectives* (pp.83-97). Oxford: Elsevier.

Hall, C.M. & Saarinen, J. (2010a). Polar tourism: Definitions and dimensions, *Scandinavian Journal of Hospitality and Tourism*, 10(4), 448-467.

Hall, C.M. & Saarinen, J. (eds) (2010b). *Polar Tourism and Change: Climate, environments and experiences*, London: Routledge.

Innovation Norway (2011). Prinsipper for et bærekraftig reiseliv. Retrieved from http://www.innovasjonnorge.no/Satsinger/Reiseliv/Barekraftig-reiseliv/Barekraftig-Reiseliv-2015/

Jackson, T. (2005). Live better by consuming less? Is there a "double dividend" in sustainable consumption. *Journal of Industrial Ecology* 9(1-2), 19-36.

Jha, A. (2012). Great Barrier Reef loses more than half its coral cover. The Guardian, 1 October. Online. Available at: http://www.guardian.co.uk/environment/2012/oct/01/great-barrier-reef-coral-cover

Kemp, R., Loorbach, D. & Rotmans, J. (2007). Transition management as a model for manageming processes of co-evolution towards sustainable development. *International Journal of Sustainable Development and World Ecology* 14(1), 78–91.

Kemp, R. & Rotmans, J. (2004). Managing the transition to sustainable mobility. In B. Elzen, F.W. Geels and K. Green (Eds.), *System Innovation and the Transition to Sustainability: Theory, evidence and policy*, pp. 137-167. Cheltenham: Edward Elgar.

Lane, B. (2009). Thirty years of sustainable tourism. In S. Gössling, C.M. Hall and D. Weaver (Eds.), *Sustainable tourism futures*, pp. 19–32. New York: Routledge.

Mozumder, P., Berrens, R.P. & Bohara, A.K. (2006). Is there an environmental Kuznets curve for the risk of biodiversity loss? *The Journal of Developing Areas*, 39(2), 175-190.

Nilsson, J.H. (2013). Slow Baltic: the Slow Food concept in relation to Baltic gastronomy. In C.M. Hall and S. Gössling (eds), *Sustainable Culinary Systems: Local Foods, Innovation, and Tourism & Hospitality*, pp. 189-204. London: Routledge.

Nilsson, J.H., Svärd, A-C., Widarsson, Å. & Wirell, T. (2010). "Cittáslow" Sustainable destination management through the pleasures of food and ecological concern. *Current Issues in Tourism* 14(4): 373–386.

O'Mahony, B., Whitelaw, P. & Ritchie, B.W. (2006). The effect of fuel price rises on tourism behaviour: An exploratory Australian study. *Tourism and the End of Oil ATLAS Asia-Pacific Conference*, December. Dunedin: University of Otago.

Parry, M.L., Canziani, O.F., Palutikof, J.P., van der Linden, P.J. & Hanson, C.E. (eds) (2007) *Climate Change 2007: Impacts, Adaptation and Vulnerability. Contribution of Working Group II to the Fourth Assessment Report of the Intergovernmental Panel on Climate Change*. Cambridge: Cambridge University Press.

Peeters, P., Gössling, S. & Becken, S. (2007) Innovation towards tourism sustainability: climate change and aviation. *International Journal of Innovation and Sustainable Development*, Vol.2.

Rotmans, J., Van Asselt, M. & Kemp, R. (2001). More evolution than revolution: transition management in public policy. *Foresight* 3(1), 15–31.

Saarinen, J. & Tervo, K. (2006) 'Perceptions and adaptation strategies of the tourism industry to climate change: The Case of Finnish nature-based tourism entrepreneurs', *International Journal of Innovation and Sustainable Development*, 1, 214 – 228.

Saarinen, J. & Tervo, K. (2010). Sustainability and emerging awareness of a changing climate. The tourism industry's knowledge and perceptions of the future of nature-based winter tourism in Finland. In C.M. Hall and J. Saarinen (eds), *Polar Tourism and Change: Climate, environments and experience*, pp.147–164. London: Routledge.

Scott, D., Peeters, P. & Gössling, S. (2010). Can tourism deliver on its aspirational green-house gas emission reduction targets? *Journal of Sustainable Tourism* 18(3), 393–408.

Scott, D., Gössling, S. & Hall, C.M. (2012). *Tourism and Climate Change: Impacts, Adaptation and Mitigation*, London: Routledge.

Sherden, W.A. (1998). *The Fortune Sellers: The Big Business of Buying and Selling Predictions*, New York: Wiley.

Simonian, H. (2005) Blanket coverage could save Europe's famed Alps. *Financial Times* [Europe] 14 June: 14.

Smith, A., Stirling, A. & Berkhout, F. (2005). The governance of sustainable socio-technical transitions. *Research Policy* 34(10), 1491–1510.

Smith, A.D. (2007). Melting glaciers will destroy Alpine resorts within 45 years, says report. *The Observer* January 14.

Solomon, S., Qin, D., Manning, M., Chen, Z., Marquis, M., Avery, K.B., Tignor, M. & Miller, H.L. (eds) (2007). *Climate Change 2007: The Physical Science Basis. Contribution of Working Group I to the Fourth Assessment Report of the Intergovernmental Panel on Climate Change*. Cambridge: Cambridge University Press.

13

Tervo-Kankare, K., Hall, C.M. & Saarinen, J. (2012). Christmas tourists' perceptions of climate change in Rovaniemi, Finnish Lapland. *Tourism Geographies*. Online. DOI: 10.1080/14616688.2012.726265

Thornton, P. (2005) G8 wants tax on airline tickets to help world poor. *The Independent* 13 June: 2.

Travellpress (2005) Travel Industry Unites Against Proposed Aviation Tax. Press release Bangkok, Thailand, July 15, http://www.travelwirenews.com/news/19JUL2005.htm

United Nations World Tourism Organization (2011). *Tourism Towards 2030 Global Overview, UNWTO General Assembly 19th Session, Gyeongju, Republic of Korea, 10 October 2011*. Madrid: United Nations World Tourism Organization.

United Nations World Tourism Organization (2012). *UNWTO Tourism Highlights, 2012 Edition – Annex*. Madrid: United Nations World Tourism Organization.

United Nations World Tourism Organization, United Nations Environmental Programme, & World Meteorological Organization (2008). *Climate Change and Tourism: Responding to global challenges*. Madrid: UNWTO, UNEP, WMO.

Vilà, M. & Pujadas, J. (2001). Socio-economic parameters influencing plant invasions in Europe and North Africa. In J.A. McNeely (Ed.), *The Great Reshuffling: Human dimensions of invasive alien species*, pp. 75-79. Gland: IUCN Biodiversity Policy Coordination Division.

Weaver, D. (2009). Reflections on sustainable tourism and paradigm change. In S. Gössling, C.M. Hall and D. Weaver (Eds.), *Sustainable tourism futures*, pp. 33–40. New York: Routledge.

World Economic Forum (2009a). *Towards a Low Carbon Travel & Tourism Sector*. Davos: World Economic Forum.

World Economic Forum (WEF) (2009b). *Towards a Low Carbon Travel & Tourism Sector*. Davros: World Economic Forum.

World Health Organization (WHO) (2003). *International Travel and Health*. Geneva: Information Resource Centre Communicable Diseases.

World Tourism Organization (1997). *Tourism 2020 Vision*. Madrid: World Tourism Organization.

World Tourism Organization (WTO) (2001). *Tourism 2020 Vision – Global Forecasts and Profiles of Market Segments*, Madrid: World Tourism Organization.

World Tourism Organization (WTO) (2003). *Climate Change and Tourism. Proceedings of the 1st International Conference on Climate Change and Tourism*. 9-11 April, Djerba, Tunisia. Madrid: World Tourism Organization.

World Tourism Organization (2006). *The Impact of Rising Oil Prices on International Tourism*, Special Report no.26, Madrid: World Tourism Organization.

Yeoman, I. with Tan, L.Y.R., Mars, M. & Wouters, M. (Ed.) (2012). *2050 - Tomorrow's Tourism*. Bristol: Channel View Publications.

Index